The book of origins

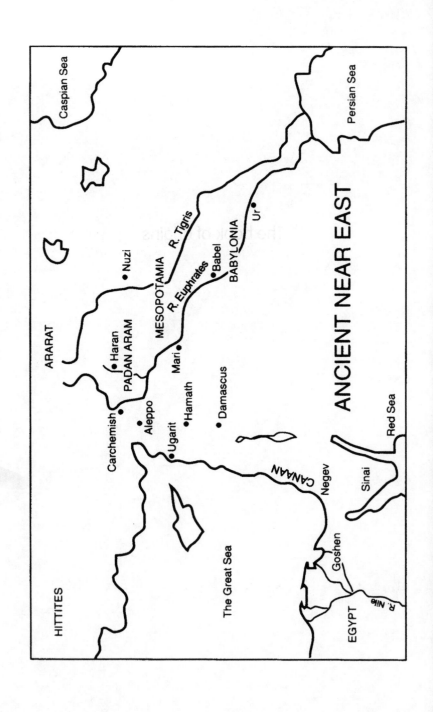

ANCIENT NEAR EAST

The book of origins

Genesis simply explained

Philip H. Eveson

 **EVANGELICAL PRESS**

EVANGELICAL PRESS
Faverdale North Industrial Estate, Darlington, DL3 0PH, England

Evangelical Press USA
P. O. Box 84, Auburn, MA 01501, USA

e-mail: sales@evangelicalpress.org

web: http://www.evangelicalpress.org

First published 2001

British Library Cataloguing in Publication Data available

ISBN 0 85234 484 8

Printed and bound in Great Britain by Creative Print and Design Wales, Ebbw Vale

To Kensit Evangelical Church,
Finchley, London

Contents

Maps

Preface

It is one thing to lecture and preach on Genesis; it is quite another to write a commentary on the text of this crucially important part of God's Word. David Clark of Evangelical Press encouraged me to undertake this daunting task, and ministerial colleagues and former students of the London Theological Seminary have been enthusiastic in their support. I trust that something of the power of the Genesis message will grip us and cause us to worship the great Creator and Saviour of the world and to witness to his wonderful works and ways.

I dedicate this book to the church where I have had the privilege of serving as minister for twenty-five years and where my wife and I continue to worship. The fellowship of God's people at Finchley has been a great blessing over the years.

Philip H. Eveson
The London Theological Seminary
October 2001

Introduction

A question of origins

'We find ourselves in a bewildering world. We want to make sense of what we see around us and to ask: What is the nature of the universe? What is our place in it? Where did it and we come from? Why is it the way it is?' This is how Stephen Hawking begins the concluding chapter of his book *A Brief History of Time*. As he proceeds, he expresses the hope that human beings will answer these questions without recourse to God.

We can be immensely grateful that the answers to our deepest questions are not left to the uncertain hope that one day a scientist somewhere will come up with the right answers. In addition, we can be thankful that the true God is not 'a god of the gaps', someone to turn to when human reason fails to explain a mystery. Such a god is not worthy of the name. The God of the Bible is the God of those things we humans can reason out for ourselves as well as of the matters which our finite minds are incapable of comprehending.

The book of Genesis introduces us to this great God who is Lord of all, the Creator and Sustainer of everything. As its name implies, Genesis is a book of origins. We are told of the origin of the universe, the beginnings of the human race and the birth of the Israelite nation. But it is more than an early record of origins. Genesis is the first of sixty-six books which make up the Bible. It is part of God's Word to us, what the apostle Paul calls 'God-breathed' Scripture (2 Tim. 3:16). Consequently, it tells us what is true and straightens out our thinking. Here we are given infallible instruction concerning where we all came from and why things are the way they are. As Calvin puts it, 'However fitting it may be for man seriously to turn his eyes to contemplate God's works, since he has been placed in this most glorious theatre to be a spectator of them, it is fitting that he pricks up his ears to the Word, the better to profit.'[1]

Genesis was not written to be a science textbook. But when it does touch upon matters dealt with by scientists it is accurate. M. F. Maury, the founder of the science of oceanography (1806–1873), laid down the rule that we must not forget that the Author of nature is also the Author of Scripture and that these records, though different, 'are equally true, and when they bear upon the same point ... it is as impossible that they should contradict each other as it is that either should contradict itself. If the two cannot be reconciled the fault is ours, and it is because, in our blindness and weakness, we have not been able to interpret aright either the one or the other or both.'

E. J. Young observes that if the Church Fathers had insisted that Genesis 'conform to the "science" of their day, how tragic the result would have been. Had Luther done the same thing, the result would have been no better. And we must be cautious not to reject Scripture merely because at some points it may appear not to harmonize with what some modern scientists teach. Of one thing we may be sure: the statements of Genesis and the facts of nature are in perfect harmony.'[2]

Importance

Genesis is foundational for all that is to follow in God's Word. In the first place, it must be remembered that Genesis is part of a larger work which early Greek-speaking Christians called the Pentateuch (the five-part book). The Jews speak of it as the 'Torah' ('Law'), which is the term used in the New Testament (Matt. 5:17; 7:12; Luke 24:44). The Hebrew word for 'law' has a much wider meaning than our understanding of it. The Law of Moses is more than a list of dos and don'ts. 'Law' means 'instruction' or 'teaching', and such instruction is given through narrative as well as commandment. In the book of Genesis we have one narrative after another, all interlinked, each one having its own message and all of them together instructing us concerning God and his purposes for the human race.

Each part of the Law, from Genesis to Deuteronomy, is distinct and complete in itself, and yet each is intimately related to the other parts to form one whole work. There is one story-line from the creation of the world to the death of Moses. Genesis acts as the introduction to the rest of the Pentateuch. It sets the scene for the momentous happenings described in the book of Exodus. The rescuing of Israel from Egyptian slavery, the forming of them into a nation set apart for God and the establishing of God's covenant with them at Mt Sinai are the fulfilment of promises recorded in Genesis. These events are not seen as ends in themselves, however, but pointers to something greater and more wonderful to come.

In order to appreciate this wider dimension the book of Genesis is again crucially important. It provides the basis for understanding the rest of Scripture. Genesis introduces us to the true and living God, to the beginnings of sin, its consequences and how it has affected the whole created order. This first book of the Bible also tells of God's grace and of his promises to bless a world of lost sinners under God's curse. We are introduced to God's covenant with Abraham and to the great plan of salvation for all nations. The book is a signpost to the fulfilment of these promises in the coming of the Messiah, Jesus Christ, the redemption he achieved and the new covenant he established through his atoning death. The last book of the Bible uses the language of Genesis to show how all God's plans come to fruition. It depicts God's victory over the serpent through the Seed of the woman, the Lion King of Judah, who is the Lamb slain from before the foundation of the world. Those redeemed by the Lamb from every nation are found in a new creation enjoying a paradise where all that is evil is excluded and God lives with his people.

Contents

The need for a new creation and a new paradise is the theme of the first eleven chapters. They concern the human race over a large period of time, whereas the following thirty-nine chapters cover just a few centuries and concentrate on the lives of only four individuals. This would suggest that the opening chapters provide an introduction and preparation for the rest of Genesis. They give the background to the call of Abraham, who is clearly the central figure, and all that follows arises out of the record of his life. One man's sin brought about universal catastrophe, whereas the calling and setting apart of one man, and the promised blessing made to him and through him to all humanity, counteracts the curses that human sin merited.

Author

Like many other biblical books, Genesis does not state the name of the human author. Since it is part of the Pentateuch, we may safely assume that it is the work of Moses, the servant of the Lord. Both Old and New Testaments confirm that Moses is the author of the whole. When 2 Chronicles 35:12 and Nehemiah 13:1 mention passages in Exodus and Deuteronomy they refer to them as taken from 'the Book of Moses'. Our Lord said that Moses 'wrote about me' (John 5:46) and on the Emmaus road he expounded the Scriptures 'beginning at Moses' (Luke 24:27,44). Paul speaks of a veil covering the hearts of the Jews when 'Moses is read' (2 Cor. 3:15; see also Rom. 10:5,19; 1 Cor. 9:9).

Title

The English title comes to us via the Latin from the title in the Greek translation of the Old Testament, called the Septuagint. 'Genesis' is actually derived from the Septuagint rendering of a word used in 2:4 and numerous other places throughout the book, variously translated into English as 'generations', 'history', 'account' or 'genealogy'. The Greek word *genesis* actually means 'origin' or 'source'. The name of the book in Hebrew is taken from the opening, 'In the beginning'. Both names are good titles as the book does deal with origins or beginnings.

Structure

The Greek title 'Genesis' taken from 2:4 also draws our attention to the structure of the book. 'This is the history of...' or 'This is the genealogy of...' (NIV, 'This is the account of..'; AV, 'These are the generations of...') is an oft-repeated formula in Genesis. It occurs eleven times and in each case (apart from 36:9) it introduces a new section of material (2:4; 5:1; 6:9; 10:1; 11:10; 11:27; 25:12; 25:19; 36:1,9; 37:2). After the prologue (1:1 – 2:3) describing the formation of the universe, and particularly the earth, there are ten main sections introduced by this formula:

1.	2:4 – 4:26	The offspring of heaven and earth
2.	5:1 – 6:8	The offspring of Adam
3.	6:9 – 9:29	The offspring of Noah
4.	10:1 – 11:9	The offspring of Noah's sons
5.	11:10-26	The offspring of Shem
6.	11:27 – 25:11	The offspring of Terah
7.	25:12-18	The offspring of Ishmael
8.	25:19 – 35:29	The offspring of Isaac
9.	36:1 – 37:1	The offspring of Esau (in two parts: 36:1-8; 36:9 – 37:1)
10.	37:2 – 50:26	The offspring of Jacob

It is interesting to notice that there are five sections dealing with the pre-patriarchal times and five concerning the patriarchal period. These are the natural divisions of the book which we shall follow in the commentary.

Part 1:
The prologue (1:1 – 2:3)

Part 1
The prologue (1.1 - 2.3)

1.
The origin of the universe and of life

Please read Genesis 1:1-25

The Prologue to Genesis (1:1 – 2:3) is a most sublime and stately section. It is not poetry, neither is it a hymn of praise. Rather, it is a moving and powerful statement of God's creative activity which should stir us to worship and adore the great King of creation.[1]

God

On Christmas Eve 1968 the crew of the spaceship Apollo 8 became the first humans to orbit the moon. In their Christmas greetings to earth, the astronauts quoted these words: **'In the beginning God created the heavens and the earth.'**

This opening sentence, so simple yet so profound, sets the tone for the whole prologue. It makes us sit up and prepare for what follows. Appropriately, the subject of the first sentence of the Bible and of Genesis is God. He is the subject of nearly every sentence in this first section: 'God said...', 'God saw...', 'God divided...', 'God called...', 'God made...', 'God created...', 'God set...', 'God blessed...' The Bible is first and foremost revelation concerning God. From the very first verse God discloses truth about himself. The term used for 'God' is *Elohim*, the most common word in the Old Testament when referring to the deity. Like our English word 'God', it can be used of pagan gods, but here it is used for the one true and living God, the God who communicates and does things.

The Bible does not set out to prove God. God is bigger than any mathematical calculation or philosophical argument. The very fact of creation bears testimony to the reality of God: 'The heavens declare the glory of God; and the firmament shows his handiwork' (Ps. 19:1). When Paul took the gospel to the pagan cities of the Roman empire he taught the people to turn from their worthless idols to the living God who made heaven and earth, the sea and everything in them (cf. Acts 14:15; 17:24-31; 1 Thess. 1:8-9).

No human being is qualified to speak with certainty on the subject of origins. 'Where were you when I laid the foundations of the earth? Tell me, if you have understanding' (Job 38:4). Only God can give authoritative information. This book of Genesis is not the result of some thoughtful person's trying to grapple with the origin of all things and coming up with the great idea that behind everything there is a first cause, or a being above whom no greater can be conceived. Moses could have tossed such ideas around in the Egyptian court with the wise men of his day. But the first chapter of Genesis is not Moses' thoughts on God. Far from it! Here is God speaking through Moses. Moses is a prophet, God's spokesman, declaring God's Word. The verse tells us that there was a commencement to everything — to time and space and the whole universe. Matter is not eternal, as the ancient Babylonians and Greeks thought, and as some scientists of today postulate. Everything that is in the universe had a beginning, and the universe itself had a beginning.

Before the commencement of all things God was already there. God was there when time began, when the universe began. John, in the opening words of his Gospel, has this verse of Genesis in mind when he writes concerning Jesus Christ:

'In the beginning was the Word... He was in the beginning with God' (John 1:1-2). By implication, we are being told about God's eternity.

> Before the mountains were brought forth,
> Or ever you had formed the earth and the world,
> Even from everlasting to everlasting, you are God
>   (Ps. 90:2).

We bow in wonder and amazement at the greatness of God.

The creator God

We are also informed that God is the Creator. This whole chapter is about God's creative power. Verse 1 is an introductory, comprehensive statement. It informs us of the origin of all things, as well as summarizing the whole creative process described in the following verses. Before the beginning only God existed.

The phrase **'the heavens and the earth'** is often used in the Bible to mean the whole universe and all that is in it. God is the origin of the universe. It teaches us that God is the Creator of the heavenly realm as well as the earthly; of the unseen, spirit world of angelic beings as well as the physical things which we can see. Psalm 148:1-5 includes angels as well as sun, moon and stars under the heading of 'heavens' and calls out: 'Let them praise the name of the LORD, for he commanded and they were created.' What is true of God the Father is also true of the Son, Jesus Christ (see John 1:3; Col. 1:16).

A common belief among 'New Agers' is the ancient idea that God is another term for everything. This belief is known as pantheism. The opening verse of Genesis is contrary to such a notion. The universe is not God. God is quite distinct from what he has made. Though all things have their being in God, God is above all. He remains transcendent and the only self-existent being in the whole universe. Everything that exists depends ultimately on God.

The word translated **'created'** is used very sparingly in the Old Testament, and every time it is used, God is the subject. Though the term is not always used for 'creation out of nothing', it is significant that no materials are ever mentioned when it is employed. It is never said that God created *out of* something. The word always refers to what is new, unusual or wonderful. No human, no other so-called god, can create in this sense. Creation is God's work and in this first verse of the Bible the ultimate wonder is clearly implied that the raw material out of which everything exists in the universe was made from nothing. It appeared because God willed it into being. All the other creative acts described in this chapter follow from this initial act.

Our universe, therefore, is not the result of an accident. There was nothing there to have an accident! Human beings in rebellion against God hate the thought that before anything existed there was nothing but God. Does anyone really believe that nothing evolved into something? Our universe did not evolve through chance happenings. Sinful humanity would sooner believe a lie than face up to the reality of God. The Bible's estimate of the human mind is so accurate: 'Although they knew God, they did not glorify him as God, nor were thankful, but became futile in their thoughts, and their foolish hearts were darkened. Professing to be wise, they became fools...' (Rom. 1:21-22).

Because the universe is the result of God's creative activity people can be assured that there is meaning and purpose to life. Creation is a purposeful act. It is not like an unexpected or unwanted pregnancy. God ordered it and planned it. He created all things for his glory. There is no higher purpose, no greater reason for living. God himself is the highest end, the chief and ultimate goal.

> You are worthy, O Lord,
> To receive glory and honour and power;
> For you created all things,
> And by your will they exist and were created
>   (Rev. 4:11).

Earth

A more accurate translation of the opening words of verse 2 would be **'Now the earth...'**[2] Attention is drawn to the earth. The rest of the chapter deals with items that are in one way or another related to this world. Nothing is said about the creation of spirit beings who belong to the heavenly, invisible realm. There is a very good reason why the text so quickly focuses on the earth. This is where human beings were placed, where they rebelled against God and where God eventually came in the person of his Son, Jesus Christ. It was on this earth that the Son of God shed his precious blood to bring us to God. It was here in our world that his body was placed in a tomb and on the third day was resurrected. From earth he ascended bodily into heaven, and it will be to this earth that he will return a second time in great power to judge the living and the dead and to bring in a new creation. Then the earth will be populated with redeemed humanity and God will be as much at home here as he is in heaven.

After the general declaration concerning the creation of the entire universe, we zoom in on the earth and we are told what it looked like before its transformation into the lovely ordered world that we read of later. The earth **'was without form, and void; and darkness was on the face of the deep'**. It was a mass of fluid, dark and totally incapable of sustaining life. It was a trackless waste, a great void. Imagine yourself standing on a raft in the middle of the Pacific Ocean on a dark, misty night. That was the kind of state the whole earth was in at first. 'Chaos', when used as the opposite of 'cosmos', is the term to describe the state of the earth at that time. 'Chaos', in this context, is not to be taken in its more popular sense of an absolute mess, or a totally confused, out-of-control state as if a bomb had hit it. 'Cosmos' is the world as a habitable, well-formed place to live. 'Chaos', therefore, in this technical sense, stands for the original unformed state of the earth, unfit for human and animal habitation.

Some have argued that verse 2 is describing the results of a great catastrophe that occurred between the original creation of verse 1 and the situation presented in verse 2. They suggest that it was the result of Satan's fall causing complete devastation on the earth. To further support this idea the beginning of verse 2 is rendered: 'And the earth *became* without form and void.' The 'gap theory', as it is called, uses Jeremiah 4:23, which speaks of the coming judgement in terms of the earth's being 'without form, and void' and the heavens having 'no light' because of the wickedness of the people. This idea was first suggested in the nineteenth century to take account of the evidence of the fossils and the length of time needed for the rock formations. It is a clear case of allowing a particular theory to influence the interpretation and translation of the Scriptures. The passage gives no hint of any satanic rebellion or divine judgement and the Hebrew text does not allow for the force of the verb to be changed from 'was' to 'become'.

The Spirit of God

That things were not out of control or under judgement is confirmed by the phrase: **'And the Spirit of God was**

hovering over the face of the waters.' 'Hovering' is found elsewhere in the Old Testament only in Deuteronomy 32:11, where it is used to describe an eagle hovering over her young to keep watch over them, ready to swoop into action if necessary. Here in Genesis, the Spirit of God was present to protect and control, and was ready to act. Some scholars have tried to translate 'Spirit of God' as 'mighty wind'. While it is true that the word for God *(Elohim)* can occasionally be used as a superlative,[3] this is unlikely in a chapter where all the other references to *Elohim* refer to God. Furthermore, in every other case where the phrase occurs in the Old Testament, it means 'Spirit of God'. For instance, God says of Bezalel, the master craftsman, 'I have filled him with the Spirit of God' (Exod. 31:3). Not only is the Son of God associated with creation, but also the Spirit of God (Ps. 104:29-30). The Son and the Spirit are also involved in the new creation (John 3:5-8; Rom. 7:6; 8:9-11,23; 2 Cor. 5:17; Gal. 6:15).

Notice the parallel between the last two lines. **'On the face of the deep'** parallels **'over the face of the waters'** and **'darkness'** parallels **'Spirit of God'**. Darkness is primarily a reference to the lack of light and prepares for the commanding word of verse 3. In some contexts darkness can include a more sinister idea associated with evil or judgement. In view of the parallel with 'Spirit of God', darkness certainly has no such connotations here. When God spoke from Sinai he appeared with darkness, cloud and thick darkness (Deut. 4:11; 5:23). 'God can veil himself in darkness at moments of great revelation,' and the phrase could be hinting 'at the hidden presence of God waiting to reveal himself'.[4] In other words, God was powerfully present by his Spirit in that darkness (Ps. 18:11), watching over what had already been brought into being by his creative action and poised to continue the good work.

The situation in verse 2 prepares us for the revelatory words of command that follow. What God commences he finishes. There is a principle here that holds good in connection with

the new creation as it applies to the church and individual believers. Paul reminds us in Philippians 1:6 'that he who has
begun a good work in you will complete it until the day of
Jesus Christ'. God does not leave jobs half done.

The days of creation

The way in which God transformed the earth from an inhospitable, unformed mass into the beautiful, well-ordered world
teeming with various forms of life and fit for human habitation
is now described. God took time to do it. He could have produced the final product the moment he first created the universe from nothing. This was not God's way of doing things
then, nor is it God's general way of working in our created
world.

In the matter of salvation, the right moment in God's plan
for sending his Son to redeem us was thousands of years after
the initial promise in the Garden of Eden and nearly two thousand years after God's promise to Abraham. Even preparing
believers for glory takes time. Though we are created anew in
Christ Jesus in a moment and are positionally complete in him,
in practice our conformity to what we are in Christ takes time.
Only when Christ appears at the end of the age will we be
completely transformed into his likeness, physically as well as
spiritually. The final act, however, will be as quick as the initial act for we read, 'We shall not all sleep, but we shall all be
changed — in a moment, in the twinkling of an eye, at the last
trumpet. For the trumpet will sound, and the dead will be raised
incorruptible, and we shall be changed' (1 Cor. 15:51-52). We
often like things done in a hurry and we live in an age where
the word 'instant' is the order of the day. God does things in
his own time and way, and we are called to wait on him patiently with an obedient, submissive spirit.

The time it took to make the earth a habitable place and to produce the various life forms, including humans, is given as six days. The question that often arises at this point is whether these days are literal or a literary figure of speech. There is no warrant in this first chapter, or in the rest of Scripture, to indicate that the days are merely an artistic device. There is art and literary style, but this does not mean that the text must be read in a non-literal, non-chronological way. In Exodus 20:11 God through Moses reminds us that 'In six days the LORD made the heavens and the earth, the sea, and all that is in them.'[5]

Each of these days is spoken of as having an evening and morning. This should not lead us to think that the first day started with the evening and that the morning was the second half of the day. Evening is mentioned first because the first period of light had come to an end. When morning came it meant that the first day had been brought to an end and the second day had begun. This again would suggest that the days are at least similar to our twenty-four-hour days.

Immediately the cry goes up: 'You can't be serious! Science has proved that the earth with its life forms took millions of years to develop.' This kind of reaction is like saying, 'We know that dead men don't come back to life again; therefore the resurrection of Jesus can't be literally true; it must be symbolic.' But Jesus did literally rise from the dead, contrary to the normal rules of science. It is equally possible, then, for God to have brought our world to its present ordered position in six literal days of twenty-four hours. God is capable of doing such things.

Before we dismiss Christians who take a different view of these 'days', we do need to bear in mind a number of other pointers in the text. It is possible for all of us to jump to wrong conclusions. If scientists can misinterpret the evidence in nature, we must reckon with the fact that Christians are fallible and can misinterpret Scripture. We can be in danger of imposing our present knowledge of things on to the text of Scripture. Can we be sure that in this first week the earth was revolving on its axis at the same speed that it does today, or that it was revolving around the sun in the way it does today?

As we go through this chapter we find that although light was created on day one, the setting of the sun, moon and stars in relation to the earth did not take place until day four. Today we cannot conceive of a morning or evening without the sun. As we look at the text it suggests that for the first three days the sun and moon were not the deciding factors in measuring time. Again, though the impression we gain from this section is of an instantaneous creation, the next chapter implies a process with time gaps. On day six, for instance, after the land animals were made, we are told that humans, male and female, were created. However, in chapter 2, it is only after the man had named the animals that the woman was formed and we see that it involved a process. It is also interesting that in connection with the seventh day there is no mention of evening and morning. There is something never-ending about God's rest day.

Having said this, we are certainly given the impression that the days of Genesis 1 are like our twenty-four-hour days. In so far as those six days do have some unique features about them, some biblical scholars who want to be true to Scripture think of them as special divine days, the actual length of which is known only to God. Nevertheless, God created over a period of six successive days similar to our own with an added day of rest, and in this way set a pattern for our seven-day week.[6]

Divine power and goodness

'**And God said**' occurs ten times in this chapter (1:3,6,9,11,14, 20,24,26,28,29) and is used to emphasize his commanding word, which is introduced by the word **'Let...'** This same God spoke the Ten Commandments (Exod. 20:1-19). In these last days God has spoken through his Son, who is the Word of God seen in the flesh (Heb. 1:1-3; John 1:14). We are reminded of God's creative word in Psalm 33:6-9: 'By the word of the LORD the heavens were made...' God's authoritative word expresses his will. The sovereign will of God always comes to fulfilment and this is emphasized by the repeated formula, **'and it was so'** (1:7,9,11,15,24,30). We all ought to 'stand in awe of him' as the psalmist reminds us (Ps. 33:8). From the outset it is made clear that God's will was being done on earth. Because of the great rebellion against God's rule described in chapter 3, human beings have been opposed to God's will. The rest of the Bible shows how God has acted to bring that rebellion to an end. Christians are taught to pray for the coming of God's kingdom and for his will to be done on earth as it is in heaven.

Another recurring phrase is the statement concerning God's approval: **'God saw that it was good'** (1:4,10,12,18, 21,25,31). We often step back to view what we have made or to examine whether it comes up to our expectations. After each creative action, apart from that on day two, God was able to declare that it came up to his standard. God is good and all the works of God can only be good and beautiful. The 'Preacher' draws our attention to this point when he says that God 'has made everything beautiful in its time' (Eccles. 3:11). The reason why no such approval was mentioned on day two is because the great expanse was not yet as God intended it. More needed to be done. Only when the heavenly bodies had been set in their appointed places in the sky could it be pronounced good. At the end of the whole process God was absolutely satisfied with everything that he had made, and it was not just good, but **'very good'** (1:31). The stuff of physical life is not evil. Any dualistic idea that some parts of the original creation were evil is completely ruled out by these words. There was no evil, nothing unpleasant, distasteful, or out of harmony, in what God had made. This makes any evolutionary theory about the way in which our world and its life forms came into being a complete non-starter.

Light

The God whose thunderous voice Israel heard on Mount Sinai out of the thick darkness (Deut. 5:22-23) is the one who called for light to shine in the darkness (1:3). God first created the darkness, but now he created the light. 'I form the light and create darkness' (Isa. 45:7). The Latin translation of **'Let there be light'**, *fiat lux*, has given rise to the phrase 'creation by *fiat*'. It was creation by God's commanding word and it was immediately effective. This created light was from a God who is described as 'light' in whom there is 'no darkness at all' (1 John 1:5), and who dwells 'in unapproachable light' (1 Tim. 6:16). God was able to dispel the darkness without reference to the sun, moon and stars. Scientists tell us that light existed long before our sun did. When the Egyptians were struck by the plague of thick darkness, a darkness which could be felt, Israel had light (Exod. 10:21-23). In John's vision of the holy city there was no need of sun or moon, 'for the glory of God illuminated it', and 'The Lamb is its light' (Rev. 21:23; 22:5).

What is true in the physical realm also applies in the spiritual. Those once dead in trespasses and sins but now made alive in Christ are described in these terms: 'You were once darkness, but now you are light in the Lord' (Eph. 5:8). Paul explains this as a new creation (Gal. 6:15; 2 Cor. 5:17). He uses the language of Genesis to describe the change: 'For it is the God who commanded light to shine out of darkness who has shone in our hearts to give the light of the knowledge of the glory of God in the face of Jesus Christ' (2 Cor. 4:6). Do you know God's creative light in your own life?

The work of separation and naming

In order to make our world habitable (see Isa. 45:18) a series of separations took place. On the first day, **'God divided the light from the darkness'** (1:4). By placing God's evaluation ('God saw the light, that it was good') before the dividing, and not after it, as is the case from day three onwards, the passage teaches us, not only God's preference for light, but that there is more to come in connection with dividing the light from the darkness. How God divided the two at the beginning is not revealed, but this was not to be the final means. Only after the creation and setting in place of the light-giving heavenly bodies did God pronounce it good (cf. 1:14-18).

On the second day, **'God made the firmament, and divided the waters...'** (1:7). At first it would appear that there was no atmosphere in which to live and breathe properly. There was not only water on the surface of the earth but water, perhaps heavy mist or dense fog, swirling above the surface of the earth. The firmament, or expanse, provided the space between the earth's watery surface and the waters above it — i.e., the clouds. Again, there is no evaluation because more dividing was necessary before dry land emerged (1:10).

Though the word 'divide' is not used, a further separation took place on day three: **'Let the waters under the heavens be gathered together into one place, and let the dry land appear'** (1:9). A shoreless ocean was transformed so that there was dry land and seas. God set the boundaries (Jer. 5:22). At the time of the flood God allowed those boundaries to be overstepped so that there was a partial return to the unformed and inhospitable place of Genesis 1:2.

It was God who called the darkness **'Night'** and light **'Day'**, the firmament **'Heaven'**, or 'sky', the dry land **'Earth'** and the gathered waters **'Seas'**. By naming them God showed his authority and control over them (2 Kings 23:34). Pagans think in terms of a sky god, a sea god and an earth god. Genesis shows that they are all creations of the one true God and are subject to him. With these fundamental separations in place God could then pronounce that **'it was good'** (1:10). From a transitional state without form, where everything was mixed, there was now form and there were clear demarcations.

Not all division or separation is wrong, but God is not a God of confusion. That is why things must be done decently and in order in church life (1 Cor. 14:33,40). This same verb for 'divide' or 'separate' is used for the separation of the holy from the common and the clean from the unclean (Lev. 10:10). The reason for all the separation laws in the old covenant legislation was to remind Israel, and to show to the world, in every aspect of their lives, that Israel was called by God to be his holy people, separate from all the other nations (Lev. 20:25-26). Under the new covenant, while the old rules separating Jew from Gentile no longer apply in Christ, the principle behind those laws is the same. God's holy people have been separated from the world to be the Lord's. 'Do not be unequally yoked together with unbelievers. For what fellowship has righteousness with lawlessness? And what communion has light with darkness? ... Therefore "Come out from among them and be separate, says the Lord"' (2 Cor. 6:14-17). There is a moral order expressed in the Old Testament and underlined in the New by Jesus' life and teaching which points to the character of God as the absolute standard and which should characterize the people of God in all ages: 'You shall be perfect, even as your Father in heaven is perfect' (Matt. 5:48). God is the judge of what is good. He establishes what is right and everything must conform to his standard.

Plant life and the heavenly bodies

More creative activity takes place on day three: **'Let the earth bring forth grass'** (1:11). In this context 'grass' is most probably being used as an all-inclusive term for vegetation. Two basic categories of plant life are then given: the seed-bearing herbs and the fruit-bearing trees. Having had a supernatural creation, the plants go on to propagate naturally: the herb **'yields seed'** and the tree produces fruit **'whose seed is in itself'**. Fertility and vegetation are the result, not of depraved pagan rituals, but of God's sovereign decree. The phrase **'according to its kind'** (1:12) is broad enough to include 'species' as well as 'class' or 'group'. It is used not only of plant life, but of the creatures in the sea and air and on the land (1:21,24).

This introduces us to another type of separation and order in creation. Gordon Wenham comments: 'The different species of plant and animal life again bear testimony to God's creative plan. The implication, though not stated, is clear: what God has distinguished and created distinct, man ought not to confuse... Things are the way they are because God made it so, and men and women should accept his decree' (Lev. 19:19; Deut. 22:9-11).[7] In the light of this, public opinion is right to be concerned about genetically modified plants and animals.

The separation laws of the old covenant were built on this creation law and acted as reminders to the Israelites of their own distinctiveness and the importance of not mixing with pagans in their religious practices. Christians are reminded of Paul's words: 'You cannot drink the cup of the Lord and the cup of demons'; 'What part has a believer with an unbeliever? And what agreement has the temple of God with idols?' (1 Cor. 10:21; 2 Cor. 6:15-16).

The anti-pagan message of the chapter is again strong in the account of God's creative activity on the fourth and fifth days. In the ancient world the heavenly bodies held a very important place in people's lives. The sun and moon were among their chief gods, and stars were thought to control human affairs. Such beliefs are not uncommon today and the reading of horoscopes has increased in popularity. To counter this, the biblical record gives much space to spelling out the place that these God-given lights have in our world. **'God made two great lights: the greater light to rule the day, and the lesser light to rule the night.'** In the rest of Moses' writings the word for 'light' or 'light-bearer' is used to denote the lamp in the tabernacle (Exod. 35:14,28). **'He made the stars also'** (1:16). The stars are mentioned at the end almost as an afterthought. Things which come to be feared by humans are all creations of God. They are not eternal, they do not have any independent existence and they are not to be worshipped (Deut. 4:19). The account does not even mention the sun *(shemesh)* and moon *(yariah)* by name lest people associate them with Shamash the sun god and Yarih the moon god. It is their function that is emphasized: **'to give light on the earth, and to rule over the day and over the night'**, not as powers but as light-bearers, **'and to divide the light from the darkness'** (1:17-18), thus completing what God had started on the first day. From this day onward daylight was to be determined by the sun. The luminaries were also given **'for signs and seasons, and for days and years'** (1:14). In other words, they would enable people to measure and keep time and to determine the festive seasons mentioned in the law.

'God set them in the firmament of the heavens' (1:17). Kidner remarks that 'The description is unashamedly geocentric.'[8] From the perspective of a human observer on the earth they appear to be in the sky's atmosphere. In the same way the Bible speaks, as do all of us today (including scientists!), of the sun rising and setting.

Living creatures

Days four to six present the second phase of God's creative work. The first three days brought about form and order to an earth 'without form' through a series of 'separations'. In the days that follow the earth is no longer 'void' but filled with an abundance of living creatures. The second set of three days corresponds to the first set. Thus we find the creation of lights on the fourth day matches the creation of light on the first day. On the fifth day God created the creatures that occupy the waters of the seas and that fly in the sky, and this corresponds to some extent to the creation of the waters and the formation of the expanse on the second day. The creation of land animals and humans on the sixth day accords with that of the dry land and its productivity on the third day.

Notice the emphasis on the profusion of life: **'Let the waters abound with an abundance of living creatures'** (1:20). This is the first reference to conscious life. The expression 'living creatures' (also 1:24) is translated 'life' (1:30) and 'living being' (2:7). Such life did not appear by accident, but was the direct result of God's command. Special attention is drawn to the creation of the **'great sea creatures'** (1:21). For the first time since the opening sentence the word 'create' is used. In Near-Eastern mythology such powerful creatures were worshipped and associated with all that was evil and rebellious. Later biblical writers used these pagan allusions, such as Leviathan the sea serpent and Rahab the sea dragon, to symbolize God's enemies and to show God's power and control over all that seemed threatening and fearful (Ps. 74:13-14; Isa. 27:1; 51:9). Here the point is made that these so-called monsters are not rival deities needing to be defeated, but awe-inspiring creatures subject to God (see Job 41; Ps. 104:26). When they were created they too could be pronounced good (1:21-22).

God not only inspected what he had created, but for the first time he pronounced a blessing: **'And God blessed them, saying, "Be fruitful and multiply, and fill..."'** (1:22). The same words occur again in verses 27 and 28 after the creation of human beings. It seems clear that God's blessing is associated with the ability to be fertile and procreate. Infertility, on the other hand, is often associated with divine judgement. The blessing of God is one of the great themes of Genesis. God not only blessed animals, humans and the Sabbath, but went on to bless Adam, Noah and the patriarchs in particular. The divine blessing involved filling the earth with animals and human beings. On the other hand, the curse of God brought about depopulation and the extinction of life, as we see most solemnly at the time of the Flood and in the destruction of Sodom.

The unusual expression, **'Let the earth bring forth the living creature'** (1:24), reminds us of what was said earlier concerning the earth producing vegetation (1:12). It highlights the parallel between days three and six. As the dry land 'brought forth' vegetation on the third day, so every animal that inhabited the dry land was brought into being on the sixth day. The use of the expression 'bring forth' does not mean that the animals sprouted like plants, but that God made them from the ground (see 2:19).

'The living creature' (see 1:21) is classified into three main categories: **'cattle'**, which includes domesticated animals; **'creeping thing'** refers to reptiles and other creatures and insects that have such short legs that they crawl, or appear to slide along the ground; and **'beast of the earth'** covers the non-domesticated animals that remain in the wild. Before the Fall all these animals would have lived together safely, as they will do in the redeemed creation (Hosea 2:18; Isa. 11:6-9). Again, **'God saw that it was good'** (1:25). This is the God from whom every good and perfect gift comes (James 1:17).

2.
The origin of human beings

Please read Genesis 1:26-31

David wrote:

> When I consider your heavens, the work of your fingers,
> The moon and stars, which you have ordained,
> What is man that you are mindful of him,
> And the son of man that you visit him?
>
> (Ps. 8:3-4).

These Bible verses were written out and left on the moon by
Buzz Aldrin in July 1969 when he and Neil Armstrong became the first humans to walk on the lunar surface.

Who are we? Where have we come from? As we look at
the vast heavens made larger by all that astronomers tell us,
what is our place in the universe? The only true and satisfying
answer is found in this revelation from God.

God's image-bearers

We come to the climax of God's creative activity: **'Then God
said, "Let us make man"'** (1:26). The significance of this
act is brought to our attention in a number of ways.

In the first place, this is *the final activity of the week*. When the jewel in the crown had been formed and put in place God finished his creative work.

Secondly, *more space* is given over to describing the creation of human beings than anything else in the chapter (1:26-30).

Thirdly, the word **'create'** has been used sparingly in this chapter (1:1,21). In relation to human beings it appears three times in one verse (1:27). Here is something unique and special.

Fourthly, this is such a momentous step that *God deliberates with himself*: **'Let us make man.'** In all previous cases the divine word expressed the divine will: 'God said, "Let there be..."', followed by the words of accomplishment: '... and it was so.' This is not the case here. It is as if we are being allowed to peep into God's secret council-chamber and to listen to him making decisions. John Calvin comments: 'Hitherto God has been introduced simply as *commanding*; now, when he approaches the most excellent of all his works, he enters into *consultation*.' In this way our attention is drawn to 'the dignity of our nature'.[1] There is also reason behind our existence on this earth. That he was consulting with himself and not angels is suggested by the words of the prophet:

> Who has directed the Spirit of the LORD,
> Or as his counsellor has taught him?
> With whom did he take counsel, and who instructed him...?
>
> (Isa. 40:13-14).

The significance of this creative act is also highlighted in the way God refers to himself: **'Let us make man in our image, according to our likeness.'** The credal statement in Deuteronomy 6:4 that God is one LORD affirms that there is only one absolute Being, but it does not mean that God is solitary, or a single person. In the plural word for God *(Elohim)* and the use of the first person plural forms 'us' and 'our', we have the first hint that God's being is much more profound than we imagined and that there is in God a plurality of persons. Other parts of Genesis will confirm this and point us forward to the New Testament's revelation of a Trinity within the unity of the Godhead. Notice how the text moves from the plural, 'in our image, according to our likeness', in verse 26 to the singular in the following verse: **'So God created man in his own image; in the image of God he created him'** (1:27).

Not only does God give us truth about himself when referring to the creation of humans, but this verse teaches that we are, in certain respects, like God. We are not gods, but there is something about us which makes us godlike. No distinction can be made in this passage between 'image' and 'likeness' (see 5:1; 9:6). The two words reinforce one another and convey the truth that, unlike any other earthly creature, man's whole make-up is a reminder of God. 'To be human is to bear the image of God.'[2] While all creation bears witness to the being and glory of God (Ps. 19:1), humanity above everything else expresses God and represents God. We are living proof that God exists (see 5:1 for further information). The New Testament tells us that the incarnate Son of God, Jesus Christ, is the image of God (Col. 1:15; Heb. 1:3) and some suggest that human beings were created like Christ, a copy of the true image. We find Ephesians 4:24 and Colossians 3:10 referring to God's image in moral and mental terms — righteousness, holiness and knowledge — items lost as a result of the Fall but belonging to the Christian's new nature. Nevertheless, all human beings, even in their fallen, unregenerate state, are still human and bear some resemblance to God, as is shown from Genesis 9:6 and James 3:9.

We also see that human kind, male and female, is according to God's likeness: **'God created man in his own image ...**

male and female he created them.' Political correctness pre-
vents us these days from using the word 'man' as a general
term for humanity. The Hebrew word *adam* is used in precisely the ways we have traditionally used the word 'man'.
The primary meaning of *adam*, or 'man', is 'human being' or
'human race', without differentiating between the sexes. Such
usage has nothing to do with sexist language or male domin-
ation, as some would have us believe. That God's Word does
not encourage male superiority or female inferiority is made
clear here. It was not considered necessary to mention gender
in the case of the other living creatures, but it is an important
element in reference to human beings. 'The man and the woman
are images of God separately, and they are also the image of
God together.'[3]

The difference between human beings and the rest of the
living creatures is emphasized by the phrases **'according to
our likeness'** and **'in his own image'** (1:26-27) which replace 'according to its kind' (see 1:11-12,21,24-25). There
are various types and species of vegetation, of birds, of sea
creatures and of land animals. Man is not broken down into
types. The only breakdown, as we have seen, is in terms of
sexuality. Human beings may have many bodily features and
functions similar to other creatures, but there is this fundamental distinction in that they share a likeness to God.

Something of what it means for human beings to be in the
image of God is indicated in the words that introduce the command to be fruitful. Though they are similar to the words of
verse 22 ('God blessed them, saying…'), there is this significant addition: **'and God said to them…'** (1:28). God addresses them personally. A personal relationship existed between God and these creatures. The God who already had
personal relationships within his own being made humans in
such a way that this fellowship might be extended to them.

Another element in what it means for humans to be in God's likeness is spelled out in the blessing: **'Be fruitful and multiply; fill the earth and subdue it'** (1:28). Humans share part of the blessing with the other animals (1:22). Human kind is male and female and, along with the rest of the living creatures, is able to reproduce. Man, however, being in the image of God, has this amazing privilege of bringing into the world other beings who are in the image of God (see 5:3; 9:6; James 3:9). The old English word 'replenish' found in the Authorized, or King James, Version simply means 'fill'. There is no indication in the Hebrew original of a refilling of the earth after a supposed destruction of a pre-Adamic race (see verse 22 where the same word appears). **'Subdue'** goes with the previous word, 'fill', and suggests taking over and controlling the whole earth. Later in the Pentateuch, 'subdue' is used to describe the subjugation of the land of Canaan (see Num. 32:22). Some in the past have taken these words as 'the colonist's charter'. Such language is frowned on today but it was God's original intention that people should reproduce, spread out and settle in the uninhabited places of the earth instead of remaining overcrowded in one area.

The additional element in the blessing, **'have dominion over...'**, raises human beings, male and female, to the position of kings. They are supreme over the created order. The command to rule is given twice (1:26,28), which emphasizes its importance. Human beings are called to be like the heavenly Ruler. They are God's representatives on earth. Such dominion does not mean selfishly exploiting the earth, but it does include caring for, and looking after, it (see 2:15). It was a common view in the ancient Near East that the king represented his god on earth and the king was described as bearing the god's image. Here we are taught that not only monarchs but all human beings have kingly functions in that they bear the image of the true God and are his viceroys on earth. Psalm 8 expresses the same truth in poetical language:

> You have made him a little lower than the angels [or
>   'God'; the Hebrew is *elohim*],
> And you have crowned him with glory and honour.
> You have made him to have dominion over the works of
>   your hands...
>
>   (vv. 5-6).

Though sin, Satan and death have endeavoured to frustrate this purpose, Psalm 8 is fulfilled through the coming of the Son of God into our world. He has stooped to undo the effects of sin and Satan by his atoning death, so that all who belong to Jesus Christ can reign in and with him (Heb. 2:9-10; Rev. 5:10).

Again, in verses 29 and 30 God addresses human beings directly concerning the food they and the other animals are to eat. In the ancient Near-Eastern myths man was made to provide food for the gods. The biblical record shows God looking after the bodily needs of both man and animals. It will be noticed that for both there was a vegetarian diet. This is no idealistic dream but the situation that existed before the Fall, and it is a state that Isaiah predicts will prevail in the new creation when 'The lion will eat straw like the ox' (see Isa. 11:6-9; 65:25). These verses of Genesis are an embarrassment to those who believe that God used evolution to make creatures (the theistic evolutionary view). Nature red in tooth and claw is not the original picture. Also, it is only after the Fall that we hear of man's use of animals for clothing, sacrifice and food (3:21; 4:2-4; 9:3).

It is when man has been created that we are told of God's profound satisfaction with all that he had made: **'Then God saw everything that he had made, and indeed it was very**

good' (1:31). This is the seventh occurrence of the word 'good', to which the adverb 'very' is now added. The word translated **'indeed'** (AV, 'behold') suggests a degree of excitement and enthusiasm, which Wenham catches by using the phrase: 'It was really very good.'

In the original Hebrew, the final phrase, **'the sixth day'**, also draws our attention to the significance of this day. In the case of days two to five the same formula is used on each occasion — 'a second day', a 'third day', etc. For the day when human beings were created the Hebrew uses the definite article, '*the* sixth day'. We have now reached the high point of God's creative activity. This slight change also prepares for the final day, which also uses the same phraseology — '*the* seventh day'.

Implications

The fact that we are created in God's image has a number of important implications for us.

Firstly, *human beings are without excuse* concerning God. They hold down the truth about God in unbelief (see Rom. 1:18-25).

Secondly, *only in God*, as Augustine of Hippo indicated, *can human beings find true rest* (see Isa. 57:19-21; Matt. 11:29).

Thirdly, people are not puppets or robots, but *moral beings* with the liberty to act according to their own wills and responsible to God for their actions.

Fourthly, though man (male and female) is a creature, he is *a special creature*. He is different from the other animals because he is like God. Man's whole being — body, mind and spirit — is a reminder of God. There are some philosophers and scientists who suggest that humans have no more right to special status than any other creature. This is the logic of naturalistic evolution. It is not uncommon for some extremists to put 'animal rights' above the worth of human life. Most people are aware that this is not right. It is the Bible which gives the only satisfactory explanation why we are different to animals.

We also see that *every human being is of inestimable value.* Loss of personal self-esteem results from a failure to reckon with who we really are. Worthlessness must be clearly distinguished from unworthiness. Before God we acknowledge how inferior and undeserving we are, but as God's image-bearers we are never rubbish and we are never without significance. Every human being deserves to be treated with respect.

It follows that *it is an affront to God to murder a human being* created in God's image, and this crime deserves the ultimate penalty (Gen. 9:6). James reminds us of the utter hypocrisy of praising God with one breath and in the very next cursing the one made in God's image (James 3:9).

The fact that we humans are created in God's image also highlights *the gravity of our rebellion against God.* The punishment we deserve fits the crime. Nowhere does it suggest that God's image-bearers are reduced to the position of animals who cease to exist. They are not annihilated. Rather, they experience in body, mind and spirit the torment of an eternity in hell (Mark 9:42-48; Rev. 20:10-15; 21:8).

God so loved his rebellious image-bearers that he went to infinite lengths to redeem them. He gave himself in his own unique Son, Jesus Christ, who took human nature and in body, mind and spirit suffered the torments of hell on the cross at Calvary. Because we are of such immense value, the ultimate price was paid by God himself in Christ, in order that whoever 'believes in him should not perish but have eternal life' (John 3:16; see Ps. 49:5-15; 1 Peter 1:18-19).

Finally, *we were created,* not *to worship and serve* the creature, but *the Creator.* He is to be praised for ever (Rom. 1:25).

Above the rest of creation we human beings express something of God's stunning importance. We are not God, but because we are like God we can appreciate, and rejoice in, the
created order and respond to God's love with understanding
and devoted service.

> O LORD, how manifold are your works!
> In wisdom you have made them all...
> I will sing to the LORD as long as I live;
> I will sing praise to my God while I have my being
> (Ps. 104:24,33).

3.
The origin of the holy day

Please read Genesis 2:1-3

We all like holidays. Most of us first learned about the benefit of them at school, looking forward eagerly to the Christmas, Easter and Summer holidays. Who first thought of holidays? God did! He arranged for us to have fifty-two days off a year — not that we should take them all at once, but one at a time after every six days. We probably do not think of a weekly rest day as a holiday, but that is what it is. A holiday means a change from the usual routine, a break from work, a time to relax. In the opening verses of Genesis 2 we have the origins of the holiday, or holy day.

These three verses bring the account of creation to an impressive conclusion. The introduction to Genesis has two peaks: the creation of human beings and the creation of the day of rest. If humanity is the jewel in the crown of God's creative activity, the supreme goal or end of creation is the day of rest. God delighted in his finished work, and human beings in fellowship with their Maker are encouraged to worship the God of all creation.

Verse 1 is a summary statement informing us that the entire work of creation recounted in chapter 1 was brought to completion by the end of the sixth day. **'Host'** can refer to stars (Deut. 4:19), angels (1 Kings 22:19), or a human army (Gen. 21:22). Here it is used to express everything created, the total made up of every single item in the universe. In the statement, **'And on the seventh day God ended his work which he had done'** (2:2), there is no suggestion that God did some work on that day before he stopped. If the phrase is read in the light of 1:31 – 2:1 it means that when the seventh day had arrived the work had already been completed.

The seven-day week

Scholars who dismiss the Bible's evidence are at a complete loss to understand how our seven-day week came into being. Learned articles are written on the subject, but it remains a mystery. Those clever people called Sumerians from the Babylonian region, before the days of Abraham, seem to have been the first to divide time into sixty seconds to one minute, sixty minutes to one hour and twenty-four hours to one day. But a seven-day week does not fit exactly into the solar year of 365¼ days, nor into the lunar month of twenty-nine days. The ancient world bears testimony to experiments in weeks of less or more than seven days. During the French Revolution the seven-day week was abolished, only to be reinstated later. There have been brave attempts in the twentieth century to make the week longer or shorter, but without success. Where did the idea come from?

The seven-day week is modelled on that initial week when God made the world a habitable place for humans and animals and **'rested on the seventh day from all his work which he had done'** (2:2). God added another day in order to make it a seven-day week. It is interesting that the Hebrew word for 'week' means 'that which is divided into seven'. The seven-day cycle was known by Noah when he tested conditions outside the ark after the Flood began to subside (Gen. 8:10,12; cf. 7:4). In the patriarchal period marriage celebrations lasted a week (Gen. 29:27). The seven-day week was later enshrined in the Ten Commandments and specific reference is made there to the initial divine week: 'For in six days the LORD made the heavens and the earth, the sea, and all that is in them, and rested the seventh day' (Exod. 20:11). The divine week of six days plus one thus became the pattern set by God for human beings to follow.

A rest day

Why does it say that God rested? Surely God does not need to rest as if he were weary, or in need of a change. The word translated 'rest' means 'to cease' or 'to abstain from work'. What the text is emphasizing is that God ceased from the work in which he had been engaged. It stresses that God had finished the work of creating the world and all things in it, which is what verse 1 has expressed. After the six divine days of creation there is now this seventh day which celebrates a work finished. God's day of rest stands in close relation to the work of creation. God rested from the creative activity of those six special days. It is the rest of accomplishment. You will notice that there is no mention of an evening or morning to end this rest day. For us a day of rest is always followed by another weekly round. This is not so with God's week. The six days of creation give way to the seventh day of rest, in recognition of the fact that he had completed the specific work of creation. God's week is special and is not followed by another round of creation work.

When it says that God rested it does not mean that from then on God was inactive. God has been active from that time to this in many other ways. There is therefore no conflict between Genesis 2:2 and what Jesus says in John 5:17. This divine rest at the end of the creative process announces that there is a big difference between creating, on the one hand, and sustaining and providing, on the other. The biblical revelation is again on a collision course with evolutionary theories which assume that the evolving process has been going on since the first signs of life. The work of creation came to an end at the close of the divine sixth day. God produced a finished work (2:1). What God is now doing is sustaining and upholding what he completed on the sixth day. The seventh day makes this point very clearly.

The divine seventh day also suggests an eternal rest. We have noticed that no mention is made of the closing of this day. The refrain, 'the evening and the morning', which completes the other six days, is absent from the final day. This divine day of rest is perhaps the first hint of the eternal rest. Hebrews 4:4 quotes Genesis 2:2 in reference to the ultimate rest of the people of God from all their labours (see also Heb. 4:10). The number seven later becomes the symbol of wholeness or completeness and is used in the book of Revelation to bring us to the grand finale, to the perfect state of the new creation.

A special day

Though God's week is in many ways unique it does provide the pattern for our weeks, as we have seen. What is more, this final day, which points to the eternal rest, is to have its place in our week. That is why we read that **'God blessed the seventh day and sanctified it, because in it he rested from all his work which God had created and made'** (2:3). For us the weeks keep on coming round one after the other and seem to go quicker as we get older. God has decreed, however, that one day in seven will be different. The daily round is to be broken up and after every sixth day there is to be this holiday.

Moses draws attention to the special nature of this day in several ways.

Firstly, though 2:1-3 belongs together with 1:1-31 there is, nevertheless, a break. *The form and style of writing have changed.* There are no phrases to remind us of the other days. The introduction immediately sets this day apart from the other six days and it has its own unique ending.

Secondly, *the day is emphasized* in a way that the other days are not. With all the other days there is only one reference to each day (see 1:5,8,13,19,23,31). When we come to this day, the phrase **'the seventh day'** is repeated three times (2:2-3). What is more, in the original Hebrew, the phrase occurs in three separate sentences, each composed of seven words. Clearly, the attention of the reader is being drawn to the special character of the seventh day.

Thirdly, the word for **'rest'**, which, as already indicated, means 'to cease from work', is used frequently in the Old Testament for 'to keep the Sabbath'. There are those who wish to deny that the Fourth Commandment, 'Remember the Sabbath day, to keep it holy...' (Exod. 20:8-11), is a creation ordinance. They argue that it was first revealed at Sinai, that it was for the Israelites only and was part of the ceremonial law. It is argued that there is no mention of the Sabbath in Genesis 2:1-3. While it is true that the noun 'Sabbath' is missing, the associations of the verbal form with the Sabbath day would not have been lost on the Israelites, and later the Jews. In fact, most Old Testament scholars spend time pondering why the actual term 'Sabbath' is missing. One reason suggested is that it was to avoid confusion with the Babylonian term for the day of the full moon which sounded very similar. By not mentioning the name 'Sabbath', Moses was showing that the weekly Sabbath was not regulated by the moon and had no links with paganism.[1] Not to see any connection with the Sabbath is special pleading. There is a perfectly good word for 'rest' in

Hebrew that has no thought of Sabbath attached to it. Moses, however, did not use that word. Instead, he chose a word associated with the Sabbath.

Fourthly, it is a very striking and unusual thing to do for *God to bless a day*. In chapter 1 we have seen God blessing sea creatures, birds and human beings (1:22,28). The blessing includes the ability to reproduce and expand, and in the case of people it also involves rule over the rest of the created world. How can a day be blessed? Among the ancient Babylonians every seventh day of the lunar month was regarded as unlucky. Does the blessing of this day mean that it is a lucky day? Far from it! The Sabbath day operates quite independently of the phases of the moon, neither is it subject to impersonal fatalistic forces. There is nothing sinister about the seventh day. God from the beginning made it the special object of his favour. Implied is the thought that those who observe the day as a Sabbath, as a ceasing from the work of the week, will enjoy divine favour. To keep the day which God blesses is to experience the special presence and help of God. By keeping it ourselves, we are not only constantly reminding ourselves of the eternal Sabbath, but entering into something of its glories here and now.

Part of what was involved in God's blessing the day was the act of sanctifying it or *declaring it holy*. Holiness derives from God. God is holy. This is what makes God so unlike anything and everybody else. Anything described as holy in the Bible is precisely that because God has chosen it to be so. Usually people, places and religious objects are made, or declared, holy in the writings of Moses. This is the only place in the law of Moses where a day is pronounced holy.[2] It is also of interest to note that this day is the first thing to be sanctified in the Bible. The day has a special status. It is sacred, which means it is set apart from the other six days. What God pronounces holy we are to treat as holy. There are those who say that every day should be set apart for God. That sounds very pious and, of course, it is true that we should count every day as a day lived to the glory of God. The setting aside of one special day is not, however, a human idea. God set aside this day as a pattern for us to follow. To treat every day the same when God has said otherwise is the height of impiety and to imply that we are wiser than God.

By ceasing from the work carried out during the six days as God did from his, we observe a cessation from the working week. This does not mean idleness. While God ceased from the work of the six days, it did not mean that he was inactive. Jesus made this clear to his enemies who accused him of breaking the Sabbath: 'My Father has been working until now, and I have been working' (John 5:16-17).

The Christian Sabbath

It is often assumed that with the coming of Christ this creation commandment enshrined in the Ten Commandments is no longer applicable. Christ is said to have fulfilled this command, which it is claimed is part of the ceremonial law. But there is nothing ceremonial about the purpose of the Sabbath either in Genesis 2, Exodus 20:8-11 or Deuteronomy 5:12-15. Hebrews 3 and 4 are used to argue that the Sabbath command has been fulfilled in Christ. While it is true that we have rest in Christ from our own works (Matt. 11:28-29), Hebrews looks to the ultimate rest in the heavenly Canaan (Heb. 4:10; Rev. 14:12-13).

By his teaching and example Jesus showed that the Sabbath, the stopping of the daily work, was for gathering together to worship, for doing acts of kindness and engaging in works of necessity. The amount of space in each of the Gospels given over to questions concerning the Sabbath in Jesus' ministry is significant. Unlike the Old Testament ceremonial and religious rules, which he saw as coming to an end with his death and resurrection, nowhere does Jesus suggest the same with regard to the Sabbath. He kept it himself, expounded it in the light of the tradition of the elders, freed it from its Old Covenant associations and encouraged others to keep it. While other special feast days and sabbaths associated with the ceremonial law become outmoded with the coming of Christ (Col. 2:16-17), or matters of indifference (Rom. 14:5), this is not the case with the weekly Sabbath. The Sabbath is a creation ordinance and forms part of the ten basic principles of life known as the Ten Commandments.

Jesus made a very significant divine claim in connection with the Sabbath. He said that he was Lord of the Sabbath (Mark 2:28). By his atoning death and resurrection, and his ascension to the right hand of the Father, the lordship of Jesus is demonstrated. Jesus has been given the name which is above every name. He is LORD (Jehovah). It is because he is Lord of the Sabbath that we examine his teaching concerning the observance of the holy day. He did not tell us to stop keeping it special. As with the law concerning adultery, the day is freed from its setting within the Old Covenant, with its punishments for non-compliance. Commenting on Mark 2:27-28, Brian Edwards makes this important observation: 'If he [Jesus] had been intending to take out the Fourth Commandment from its place in the Decalogue this was a remarkably strange way of achieving it, since he did nothing more than reaffirm his Father's plan for the Sabbath day.'[3]

As Lord of the Sabbath he encouraged the first Christians to meet together on the first day of the week rather than the last. Even before his death his followers sang praises extolling Jesus as king (Messiah) on the first day of the week prior to his crucifixion when he rode into Jerusalem on a donkey. They sang from Psalm 118, which includes the words: 'This is the

day which the LORD has made; let us rejoice and be glad in it.'
He rose from the dead on the first day of the week and met
with his disciples both in the morning and in the evening. The
following week he met them again when Thomas was with
them. The Spirit came at Pentecost to those gathered together
on this day. In Acts 20:7 Paul met with the church at Troas
'on the first day of the week' to preach and partake of the
Lord's Supper. 1 Corinthians 16:2 also speaks of 'the first day
of the week' in reference to Christian giving. No other day of
the week is singled out for special mention in the New Testament, which suggests that it held special significance for the
early believers in Jesus. Revelation 1:10 speaks of 'the Lord's
Day', using an unusual word for 'Lord's' which only appears
on one other occasion in the New Testament, in 1 Corinthians
11:20. This is the day belonging to Jehovah Jesus, the day set
apart for the Lord. It is on this day Christians celebrate not
only God's initial creating work, but his gracious work in Christ,
salvation accomplished, resurrection life and new creation. This
creation ordinance will find its complete realization in the glory
of the new creation.

Part 2:
What heaven and earth produced (2:4 – 4:26)

4.
The original garden

Please read Genesis 2:4-17

Many suppose that these verses introduce a second and contradictory account of creation from that given in Genesis 1. This is to misunderstand completely their significance and purpose.

The heading (2:4a)

'**This is the history of...**' alerts us to the first of the section headings.[1] These headings are the original divisions of the book. Our present arrangement into chapters is an invention dating from the Middle Ages. The first part of this new section (2:4-25) concerns Adam's relationship to his Maker (2:4-7), to his natural surroundings (2:8-17), to the animal kingdom (2:18-20) and to someone like himself (2:21-25). It provides the introduction to, and setting for, the great tragedy recorded in chapter 3.

The word translated 'history' (or 'genealogy') means 'that which has been fathered by, produced by'. In this instance it is applied metaphorically to '**the heavens and the earth**'. After the account of creation in chapter 1 we are taken on to consider what happened afterwards. No longer are we dealing with the origins of heaven and earth, but with what has proceeded from them. Human beings are now the centre of attention. They are of both heavenly and earthly origin. Their bodies are from the earth but they were created for communion with God.

The introductory headings not only serve to divide up the book of Genesis; they have the effect of underlining the historicity of the whole. It will not do for scholars to think of Genesis 1-11 as unhistorical. Adam and Eve, Cain and Abel were as real as Abraham, Isaac, Jacob and the pharaohs of Egypt. 'This is the history of...', or 'this is the genealogy of...', means we are dealing with what happened in our world. The New Testament takes it for granted that the people and events mentioned in these early chapters of Genesis actually existed. For Paul, Adam is as real a historical person as Jesus Christ. Luke traces the line of the Messiah back through David and Abraham to Adam. This part of Genesis is not a parable or myth, but a record of what took place at the very beginnings of human history. As with all historical incidents recorded in the Bible, important theological and moral lessons are taught in the process.

From the stately, moving presentation of the prologue we move to a simple narrative style. God *(Elohim)* is still the prime mover, but there is an addition to his name. The combination **'Lord God'** is found only sixteen times elsewhere in the Old Testament but twenty times in Genesis 2 and 3. 'Lord' in capitals stands for Jehovah (or Yahweh) who revealed himself to Moses and redeemed Israel from slavery (Exod. 3:14-15; 6:1-8). He is no local god but the Ruler over all. The creator God of chapter 1 is also the loving, caring heavenly Father who is interested in the needs and welfare of human beings. This is also the God and Father of our Lord Jesus Christ. 'Blessed be the Lord God, the God of Israel, who only does wondrous things!' (Ps. 72:18).

Genesis 2:4-7 is not an easy passage to interpret and translate. Consulting various Bible versions will reveal this. The heading probably stops halfway through verse 4: **'This is the history of the heavens and the earth when they were created.'** A new sentence would then begin: 'In the day that the LORD God made the earth and the heavens...' As in the previous chapter, the emphasis falls on the earth, with the provision of a garden and human beings to care for it. Notice that 'the earth' is mentioned first, then the heavens, or sky. In verse 5 'before' would be better translated 'not yet'. The whole sentence begun in verse 4 would then read: 'In the day that the LORD God made the earth and the heavens, no plant of the field was yet in the earth and no herb of the field had yet grown.'

God's garden (2:4b-17)

Perhaps we have taken a pleasant stroll through some botanical garden and been impressed by its beauty and tranquillity. When we take a look at the original garden we see how well the Lord provided for Adam and Eve's every comfort and need. We shall consider some of its features.

A real place

The garden was **'in Eden'** (2:8). No one can work out for sure where this area was. Certainly it was on this earth. It was not a mythical place, or some utopian dream in the mind of the author. We must take into account the great Flood which would have altered the area from what it was originally. Nevertheless, Moses expresses the location in terms with which he and his people were familiar. We are told that it was 'eastward' (2:8), which, from a biblical perspective, means east of the land of Israel. Only the last two rivers mentioned in 2:14 are

known to us, namely, **'Hiddekel'** (the Tigris; see Dan. 10:4)
and **'the Euphrates'**. All the rivers apart from the Euphrates
are associated with particular lands. **'Pishon'** flows through
'the ... land of Havilah' (2:11), a name linked with Cush in
Genesis 10:7. This is of interest because the river **'Gihon en-
compasses the whole land of Cush'** (2:13). Although 'Cush'
usually means Ethiopia, the area of the Upper Nile, the name
is also associated with people of the Babylonian area (10:6-12).
As for the Tigris, we are informed that it **'goes towards the
east of Assyria'** (2:14). 'Assyria' (Hebrew *Ashur*) is probably a reference to the old capital of Assyria and not, as the
name normally means, the whole territorial empire. On the
basis of the information given, it would appear that Eden is to
be located somewhere in the Mesopotamian region.

   The future hope is no 'pie in the sky' either. Though it
sometimes uses symbolic language, the New Testament speaks
of an Eden associated with the new earth (2 Peter 3:13; Rev.
21-22; see Isa. 65:17-19; 66:22). We cannot find the original
Eden, but it should be the concern of us all to find the way into
the new Eden, which is through the last Adam, Jesus Christ.

A prepared place

God is pictured as a gardener setting out and preparing a large
area of land as a place of refreshment and enjoyment: **'The
Lord God planted a garden'** (2:8). It is called the 'garden of
the Lord' (13:10; Isa. 51:3; see also Ezek. 28:13). He used
this well-watered spot to produce a garden of plenty as well
as purposeful occupation for human beings. The God who
prepared a place for the first human couple to live has also
prepared a place for all his redeemed people. Jesus said, 'I go
to prepare a place for you' (John 14:2). Preparing this garden
was nothing compared with the cost involved in making ready
our heavenly home.

An exceptional place

The way in which verses 5-7 are written suggests a contrast between the land in general and the specially prepared garden. **'Plant'** refers to shrubs or bushes, particularly those found in arid areas that grow spontaneously in the rainy season, including thorns and thistles (21:15; Job 30:4,7). **'Herb'** includes cultivated plants that may be eaten, such as wheat and barley (Exod. 9:22,25,31-32). **'Field'** describes the uncultivated open spaces where the non-domestic animals live (cf. 'the beast of the field' — 2:19-20; 3:1). Such plains can look very barren and uninviting, but a downpour of rain can suddenly bring life and growth. Likewise, when people move in and irrigate such areas they begin to blossom. The garden of God was in a part of the world where there was plenty of water and where the first man was placed to look after it. What was lacking — no rain and no man (2:5) — was made good by **'a mist'** which **'went up from the earth and watered the whole face of the ground'** (2:6) and by God's forming **'man of the dust of the ground'** (2:7). While the whole earth was good and exactly as God wanted it, only a part of it was allotted special treatment. Compared with the rest of the earth, here was a garden with a proliferation of plant life all for the good of the first humans.

On the other hand, the passage may be preparing us for the situation that existed after the Fall. Both **'plant of the field'** and **'herb of the field'** call to mind life outside the garden after the ground had been cursed (see 3:18). **'For the LORD God had not caused it to rain on the earth'** may be pointing to the time of the Flood, where God states, 'I will cause it to rain on the earth' (7:4). The final phrase of the verse, **'There was no man to till the ground'**, could be looking to the time when Adam was thrown out of the garden 'to till the ground' (3:23).

Whichever view is taken, and the two could be combined, the garden was clearly a very exceptional place. The future state of God's people will be even more wonderful than anything experienced on earth previously. 'Eye has not seen, nor ear heard ... the things which God has prepared for those who love him' (1 Cor. 2:9).

A delightful place

There was plenty of water and plenty to eat. It is possible that the word **'mist'** (2:6) should be translated 'flood' or 'spring' and that this was originally responsible for the **'river'** which **'went out of Eden to water the garden'** and which divided into the four rivers (2:10-14). On the other hand, it could mean 'rain cloud' (see Job 36:27-28, the only other place where the word is found). Psalm 135:7 speaks of clouds arising from the earth — not literally, of course, but in terms of appearance, like the rising of the sun. The river would then have been fed by the rain cloud. With such an abundance of water, **'every tree'** grew which was **'pleasant to the sight and good for food'** (2:9). It was made very clear to Adam that there was no shortage of food: **'From every tree in the garden you may freely eat...'** (2:16). God is not miserly; he 'gives us richly all things to enjoy' (1 Tim. 6:17). He is not a drab God either. He created what was pleasant and beautiful to look at, a variety of colour and form. The 'Preacher' commented, 'He has made everything beautiful in its time' (Eccles. 3:11). The Garden of Eden was certainly a delightful place to live. This is what the name 'Eden' suggests — 'pleasure', 'delight'.[2] Whenever Eden is mentioned in the Bible it stands for a very lovely environment, especially so to anyone used to arid, desert areas. In comforting his people, the Lord promises to 'make her wilderness like Eden, and her desert like the garden of the LORD' (Isa. 51:3; see also Ezek. 36:35; Joel 2:3).

An active place

There is no suggestion that life in Eden was to be one long summer holiday, lounging about all day doing nothing and getting bored. The man was put in the garden to work (2:15). Some have the idea that work is a result of the Fall. This is not so. God is a worker and human beings were created to work. Genesis 1:28 has already suggested work in the form of sub-duing and having dominion. Something of that authority is seen when Adam named the animals (2:19-20). On that oc-casion he was using his mind. People today recognize that to be unemployed is a social evil, that it is degrading and soul-destroying. The Bible shows us why work is important to our well-being. God made us to work, and not to be idle. We are to use our bodies and mental powers in activity that is honour-ing to him. Adam was put in the garden **'to tend and keep it'** (2:15). The verb for 'tend' is the word most often translated 'serve' in the Bible. In these early chapters of Genesis it is used for cultivating the soil (2:5; 3:23; 4:2,12). It is also em-ployed by Moses in a religious sense for worshipping God (Exod. 3:12; Deut. 4:19). In addition, it is often used of the Levites' duties in the tabernacle (Num. 3:7-8).[3]

Adam was also to **'keep'**, or 'guard', the garden. Perhaps this means to keep it in order and to watch where the animals fed. On the other hand, it may be introducing a sinister note. It was the duty of the Levites to keep or guard the tabernacle from intruders (Num. 1:53; 3:38). The same word is used of the cherubim who guarded the way to the tree of life (Gen. 3:24). Was the man to guard against invaders? That such un-welcome visitors existed is evident in chapter 3 when the worst of all gatecrashers appeared on the scene.

A place of life

The garden vibrated with life. There was the life-giving running water and an abundance of vegetation. In addition, **'The
tree of life was also in the midst of the garden'** (2:9). When
the phrase 'tree of life' occurs in the Bible it conveys the thought
of abundance of life, of God's life sustaining his people. That
idea is not absent here. But, whereas in other parts of the Old
Testament the phrase is used metaphorically, in this context it
relates to a real tree. This tree stood in the centre of a garden
of trees (2:8-9,16-17). It was literally a tree, but we do not
need to assume that it contained some substance which prevented ageing or death. God appointed this tree to symbolize
life. In the Bible trees often do symbolize life. They lend themselves to this idea, especially to people living in areas where
there are long summer droughts. To see the green leaves of a
tree amid the parched, scorched ground is an outstanding image
of life (Ps. 1:3; Jer. 17:8). Here in the garden of God there was
one tree in particular that spoke of life — fulness of life, the
life of God. The garden was full of God's life, for God was
pleased to be present there. Eating the fruit of this tree was an
expression of Adam and Eve's fellowship with God, the Author
of life. It is commonly assumed, on the basis of Genesis 3:22,24
that the couple did not eat from the tree of life. There is no
word in chapter 2, however, prohibiting them from eating. In
fact, Adam is encouraged to eat of its fruit (2:16-17). Again,
there is no textual support for the view that God set Adam a
test associated with the tree of knowledge, which, if he passed,
would have led him to that higher, eternal life associated with
the tree of life. The man and the woman enjoyed God and
lived in communion with God. The eating of the tree of life
was a physical expression of this spiritual reality. Eating the
bread and drinking the wine at the Lord's Supper does not
give us spiritual life, but it is symbolic of our feeding on the
benefits of Christ's death by faith for life and salvation.

A God-fearing place

It was a place where God's will was to be respected and done, a place where people would live in dependence on God. Besides the tree of life, there was another named tree closely associated with it. Again, it was as real as all the other trees but, like the tree of life, this too had special significance — **'the tree of the knowledge of good and evil'** (2:9,17). This did not mean that the fruit possessed some special tonic to increase a person's knowledge. In view of the warning that those who ate from it would die, we might have expected the tree to be called the tree of death. But there was nothing contrary to life in that garden and there was certainly no poison in the fruit. What did the tree symbolize? In the only other passage in the books of Moses where the phrase 'knowledge of good and evil' is found, it is used of children who cannot be held accountable for their actions. They are dependent on their parents (Deut. 1:39). In like manner, Adam and Eve were to see themselves as children totally dependent on the creator God, their heavenly Father, for wisdom and understanding. He is the all-wise and righteous God who alone has the right to determine what is good and evil. The tree represented the ability to be morally autonomous. By refusing them the right to eat of this tree God was indicating that he alone is autonomous. Human beings are not to live independently of him. He is the lawgiver, and all moral choices are to be made with reference to God. By not taking of its fruit the couple would be expressing their faith in God and his right to order their lives. The prohibition is as strong as anything we find in the Ten Commandments: **'You shall not eat'** (2:17).

A warning is attached to the command: **'for in the day that you eat the fruit of it you shall surely die'** (2:17). Obeying God is life; disobeying means death. Adam was made aware that fellowship with God and partaking of God's life involve obeying God. The tree became the focus of God's law. The people of God would later learn that the beginning of wisdom means fearing God and keeping his commandments (Prov. 1:7; Eccles. 12:13). Moses, in urging the people to observe God's commandments, adds, 'For this is your wisdom and your understanding' (Deut. 4:6). In the garden Adam was taught to fear and obey God and at the same time to know that true wisdom is not a matter of 'going it alone' and acting independently of God. Proverbs 3:5-7 is a superb summary of what is taught in Genesis:

> Trust in the LORD with all your heart;
> And lean not to your own understanding...
> Do not be wise in your own eyes;
> Fear the LORD and depart from evil.

A holy place

This garden was heaven on earth. It was like a sanctuary. As we read on in the Law of Moses we cannot but be impressed by the similarities between the Garden of Eden and the tabernacle. It is almost as if the garden was a prototype of the later tabernacle and temple. The two verbs 'to tend' (serve) and 'to keep' (2:15) are only found together elsewhere in the books of Moses in the context of the Levites who served and kept the tabernacle (Num. 3:6-7).[4] The tree of life is represented in the tabernacle by the golden lampstand, spread out like a stylized tree. God's revealed will, associated in the garden with the tree of knowledge, has a central place in the tabernacle by being stored in the ark of the covenant. Are the gold and jewels of Eden (see 2:11-12) specially mentioned to draw attention to the gold and the onyx stone that later adorned the high priest and decorated the tabernacle and its furniture? (see Exod. 25:7,11,17,31). The cherubim that were placed at the east of the garden (3:24) are reminiscent of the ones embroidered on the veil of the sanctuary and the ones of pure gold that were at each end of the mercy seat (Exod. 25:18-22; 26:31). In the garden, as later in the tabernacle, God deigned to commune with human beings (3:8; Lev. 26:11-12). There was one big difference in the tabernacle, however: direct access to God was limited to the high priest once a year. In Eden, however, Adam and Eve were able to meet God face to face without fear or shame. The Lord's garden was God's earthly temple. All this was lost through disobedience.

Individually, each Christian's body is a sanctuary where God by his Spirit is pleased to live (1 Cor. 6:19; Rev. 3:20). Corporately, the church of Jesus Christ, as it meets together locally, is a temple of the Holy Spirit (1 Cor. 3:16; 2 Cor. 6:16). We look forward to the day when God will live among his redeemed people on a new earth and we shall see his face (Rev. 21:3; 22:4).

A prophetic place

Revelation ends where Genesis begins, with the garden of God in a new creation. In order to make the connection complete John even introduces the unusual combination 'Lord God' in Revelation 21:22 and 22:5,6. The Israelites were reminded of the lost paradise in the descriptions that are given of the land of promise (Deut. 8:7-10). Canaan had the prospects of becoming the new Eden where God promised to live among his people (Deut. 23:14). But as Adam rebelled and experienced God's curse and removal from the garden, so Israel disobeyed and experienced the covenant curses which included removal from the land. The prophets bring together these two thoughts of God's paradise and promised land in their view of the future (Isa. 51:3; cf. Ezek. 36:35).

The New Testament takes up the theme. It first speaks of a present state where believers in Christ are members of a heavenly kingdom (Phil. 3:20), 'the Jerusalem above' (Gal. 4:26) and 'the heavenly Jerusalem' (Heb. 12:22). When they die, though absent from the body, they are immediately in the presence of Christ (2 Cor. 5:8; Phil. 1:21-23). This intermediate resting-place is spoken of as a heavenly paradise. Jesus assured the penitent thief, 'Today you will be with me in paradise' (Luke 23:43; see also 2 Cor. 12:4). There is, however, a future paradise. The final state of believers is not a disembodied spirit condition. It has a physical and earthly aspect which involves living on a new earth with resurrected, glorified bodies (1 Cor. 15:51-53; Phil. 3:21). John, in his vision of the new creation, sees the new Jerusalem which is above 'coming down out of heaven from God' (Rev. 21:1-2). Jesus himself encourages his tempted and persecuted people with these words: 'To him who overcomes I will give to eat from the tree of life, which is in the midst of the paradise of God' (Rev. 2:7).

In the final chapters of Revelation, John describes the garden city in more detail. 'The tabernacle of God is with men,' and he himself lives among his people (21:3). The river of Genesis 2:10 becomes a river of life-giving water flowing from the throne of God and of the Lamb, and the tree of life becomes a line of trees on either side of the river (22:1-2). All this expresses superabundance and life in its fulness that excels anything found in the original garden of God or the old land of Canaan. Outside are all the evildoers (21:27; 22:15). There is no possibility of this paradise ever being invaded by deceivers or spoiled by sin. All opposition has been for ever removed to the lake of fire (20:10-15; 21:8). God's people will still 'serve' and live in obedience to him (22:3), but there will be no need to keep watch. Unlike the original Eden and Canaan, where the threat of curses hung ominously over people like dark storm clouds, we read that 'There shall be no more curse' (22:3). Every curse will be gone for ever (see 21:4). This is so because of Jesus, the Lamb of God. In this connection, it is interesting that John does not use the usual Greek word for tree in the phrase 'tree of life' (2:7; 22:2,14). Instead, he employs the word often translated 'wood'. We find it used of the cross of Jesus in Acts 10:39, Galatians 3:13 and 1 Peter 2:24. The background to its use is the 'curse' of Deuteronomy 21:23.[5] On a tree the Prince of Life was hung to redeem us 'from the curse of the law, having become a curse for us (for it is written, "Cursed is everyone who hangs on a tree").' The tree on which Jesus died has become for us the tree of life. Abundant life flows to us through that atoning death.

5.
The original couple

Please read Genesis 2:7,18-25

These verses give us more detail concerning the first man and woman, and they prepare us for what happens in chapter 3.

The first man

It is stressed again that God, not chance, is the reason for human existence: **'And the LORD God formed man of the dust of the ground ... a living being'** (2:7). The picture we have is of a talented potter shaping the material with his own hands to form a beautiful artefact. Other creatures have also been formed in a similar way by the same God and bear witness to his wonderful skill and planning (2:19). Humans are not out of place in God's creation. They fit in comfortably with their environment, having similar body parts and functions to the animals. Unlike animals, however, humans can appreciate their amazing bodies and express praise to God for them: 'I will praise you, for I am fearfully and wonderfully made; marvellous are your works' (Ps. 139:14).

It is clear that a human being is body as well as soul or spirit. Neither here nor in the rest of the Bible is it suggested that souls are created first and put into bodies. In fact, Genesis 2:7 would suggest otherwise. As for the notion that the soul is imprisoned in the body, this is of pagan origin. The separation of body and spirit in death is unnatural and the result of sin. The physical body is not something to be treated with disdain, or to be regarded as unimportant. For Christians, the body is a temple of the Holy Spirit and we are called to glorify God in our bodies (1 Cor. 6:19-20). What we do with our bodies matters to God and we shall be judged for the work done in the body (2 Cor. 5:10). The final state is not a disembodied existence. The Christian's body is to be transformed on the day of resurrection to become like our Lord's resurrected body in order to live and reign on the new earth, while the unrighteous will be raised to suffer the agonies of hell (Phil. 3:21; John 5:28-29; Rev. 20:11-15; 1 Cor. 15:51-52).

Emphasis is placed on the fact that man's body comes from **'the dust of the ground'**. In the original there is a play on words. 'Man' and 'ground' are similar-sounding words in Hebrew. It is as if we were to say, 'humans from humus'. He is taken from the ground to look after the ground. All this prepares us for the judgement statement in chapter 3 where we are told that man's body will return to the ground (3:19). In 1 Corinthians 15:47 Paul presses home this truth: 'The first man was of the earth, made of dust.' This should humble us to the dust. Abraham knew his place when he pleaded for Sodom: 'I who am but dust and ashes...' (Gen. 18:27).

We are also told that man is **'a living being'** (see 1 Cor. 15:45). Contrary to what we might have thought, this does not describe man's uniqueness when compared with the animals. In fact, the phrase is used more often of the animals than of humans (1:20-21,24; 2:19). This must not lead us to think that animals have 'souls' like humans and that they live on after death. This is not the case; nevertheless, humans and animals are living beings because **'the breath of life'** is in them all. That mysterious thing called 'life', which is associated with breathing, is from God. In Genesis 7:21-23 people and animals are lumped together in the judgement of the Flood: 'All flesh died... All in whose nostrils was the breath of the spirit of life, all that was on the dry land, died.' It is in this sense that the 'Preacher' uses 'spirit' in Ecclesiastes 3:21 for both people and animals.

But we do not have to wait until verses 18-20 to be reminded of the truth that humans are different from animals. What we have learnt from chapter 1 concerning man's likeness to God is suggested here in verse 7. The way the narrative describes the giving of life to man shows something of his unique place in creation. Only in the case of man is it stated that God **'breathed into his nostrils'**. This is something very special and intimate. The God who knew Moses 'face to face' (Deut. 34:10) and spoke to him 'mouth to mouth' (Num. 12:8, AV) gave Adam the first kiss of life. All life is a gift from God, and Adam was alive and breathing like the other animals, but there was more. The breath which animated him was given to him personally by God. It was person-to-person contact. This direct, personal involvement of God in giving life to Adam raised him above the rest of creation. Here was a person created to live in close fellowship with God. We catch something of what it means to be made in God's image. There is this spiritual aspect to us. Ecclesiastes 3:11 may have this verse in mind when it states that God 'has put eternity in their hearts'. All this could suggest that the 'breath of life' in this context is distinguishing man from the animals. It is not the usual Hebrew word for 'breath'. To 'have breath' frequently means to be human (see Josh. 11:11,14; Isa. 2:22; 42:5; Job 27:3). The life of God that was breathed into the man enabled him to have communion with 'the fountain of life'.

Genesis 2:7 makes clear that there was no 'pre-Adamic man', no human-like creature into which God breathed in order for it to become a human being bearing the divine image. There was no life at all before God breathed into his nostrils. 'Man did not appear in two stages of animate development, and we may not think of man as possessing an animate life common to him and other beings, and then in addition an animate life distinct from other beings.'[1] Human beings are a special creation.

The word used for **'breathed'** is more often translated 'blew' elsewhere (see Isa. 54:16) and we think of Ezekiel 37:9 where God directed the prophet to 'blow' on the re-created bodies to give them life. We are also reminded of an incident recorded in John's Gospel in connection with God's new creation in Christ. Face to face with his disciples, the risen Lord Jesus breathed and said to them, 'Receive the Holy Spirit' (John 20:22).

> Breathe on me, breath of God;
> Fill me with life anew.
>
> (Edwin Hatch)

Human companionship

It comes as a surprise to be told: **'And the LORD God said, "It is not good..."'** (2:18). All through chapter 1 we have had the refrain: 'And God saw that it was good.' We must remember, however, that extra information is being given here concerning the events of the sixth day of creation. In chapter 1 the stark facts have been presented that God created human beings, male and female, in his image. Now we are told that the man was created first and that there was a significant gap before the creation of the woman. Until the woman is formed God cannot pronounce the creation of humans as good. The work is incomplete. As we saw in chapter 1, God only regards his work as good when it is properly finished.

Two general principles arise out of the text.

1. Human beings are not meant to live in solitude

'It is not good that man should be alone; I will make him a helper comparable to him' (2:18). This is an interesting thing for God to say. The super-spiritual might comment, 'Surely the man should not feel lonely if he has fellowship with God!' God overrules this pious remark. Though human beings are created for fellowship with God, they are also meant to have relationships with fellow human beings. God, in whose image we are made, is not a lonely God. There is only one true God, but this God is not a unitary, solitary person. The first chapter has indicated that God deliberated within the Persons of the Godhead (1:26). The most perfect unity and fellowship of love exists within the being of God. Human beings are not like God in being tri-personal, but they are like God in being created to have personal communion with other persons. We are constituted in the divine image for a community, not a secluded life. How sad it is when families fall apart and individuals live detached and separated lives, even under the same roof! It is less than ideal for human beings to be living in isolation. Members of the new creation in Christ are not meant to exist on their own either, but are to belong to the family of God which assembles locally (Heb. 10:25). Those who claim to be Christians but desire their own company and want to worship in solitude betray a warped view of themselves and a disregard for God's will. The local church is to be a family where the married and the single find true friendship and fellowship in the gospel.

2. Animals are no substitute for humans

Francis of Assisi might tell us that the birds and the animals are our brothers but, whatever physical and mental features we have in common, humans alone are created in God's image.

The animals were brought to the man and we see him exercising his authority over them: **'Out of the ground the LORD God formed every beast of the field and every bird of the air, and brought them to Adam to see what he would call them. And whatever Adam called each living creature, that was its name'** (2:19). This verse is not contradicting chapter 1, but merely reminding us of what God had done and that the animals were now being brought for Adam to name. Naming the various creatures indicated his right over them, just as Pharaoh Necho later showed his sovereignty over the King of Judah by changing his name from Eliakim to Jehoiakim (2 Kings 23:34). Adam, however, looked in vain for someone who corresponded to him. The dog has been termed man's best friend and yet it cannot make up for the lack of humans. The monkey can perform impressive acts and a parrot can mimic words, but they do not bear God's image. However lovable or helpful an animal might be as a pet, it cannot replace human friendship. Loneliness is one of the awful results of the Fall. Adam, the first zoologist, distinguished and named the different species, but he found no one like himself. The experience only intensified Adam's lack of companionship and, by the way the account is written, we can sense how alone the man must have felt.

The first woman

Some have the idea that it is only in the light of modern science that questions have been raised concerning this description of the woman's creation. But in the sixteenth century John Calvin could write, 'Although to profane persons this method of forming woman may seem ridiculous, and some of these may say that Moses is dealing in fables, yet to us the wonderful providence of God here shines forth.'[2]

The long introduction to the creation of the woman suggests how important her position is. She may be the last on the
scene, but she is certainly not the least. The passage brings to
our attention the similarities and differences between the man
and the woman. She is as special and unique as the man. When
the Lord brought the animals to Adam, the man recognized
his own uniqueness and difference, and it stirred within him
the need of a fellow companion. It is against this background
that the woman was formed and brought to the man. The man
and the woman are set over against the rest of creation. The
words of verse 18 are repeated here for emphasis: **'But for
Adam there was not found a helper comparable to him'**
(2:20). 'Helper' is not a demeaning term. It is often used to
describe God (e.g., Exod. 18:4). The helper provides what is
lacking. 'Comparable to him' means not so much identical to
him as a counterpart to him. She shared the man's nature but
she did more: she complemented him. What he lacked she supplied, and what she lacked he supplied. They provided mutual
support. She was in no sense inferior or second-rate.

We are told that **'The LORD God caused a deep sleep to
fall on Adam, and he slept'** (2:21). Human beings, created
on day six, did not see God's creative activity on the previous
days. Adam and Eve were as dependent on divine revelation
as we are for their knowledge of how everything began. It is
by faith in God's revealed Word that 'we understand that the
worlds were framed by the word of God, so that things which
are seen were not made of things which are visible' (Heb. 11:3).
Here the man is put to sleep and not allowed to witness the
creation of the woman. Just because the man was first on the
scene, that did not give him any advantage over the woman in
this matter.

The similarity between the man and woman is also brought
out in the description of how God formed the woman: **'She
was taken out of Man'** (2:23). While the man was not taken

from some manlike creature, it is said of the woman that she was taken from the man. There is a radical difference between humans and animals, but there is a fundamental similarity between the man and the woman. She is of the same 'stuff' as the man. Woman is no less human than man. The fact that woman is made from man does not mean that woman is lower than man. She is taken from his side (2:21-22). 'Side' is a better translation than **'rib'**. The same word is used of the side of the ark of the covenant and the side of a building or mountain. Nowhere else is it translated 'rib'. The verb **'made'** is the common word for 'build'. It is used here of God's creative activity as in Amos 9:6.

What God did is not without significance. He teaches by the way he does things. Woman is a special creation, just like the man. God is as personally involved in her creation as he was in the creation of man. He created her from man's side. She is not his master; she is not his slave. She is his equal, one corresponding to him, a companion suitable for him. The differences between the sexes and the different roles they perform must not be so emphasized as to suggest that the male is essentially different from the female. They are both human beings. Neither must we so emphasize the similarities that we fail to appreciate the differences. There is no biblical or scientific warrant for the unisex mentality. The man and the woman are not the same in their physical, mental and psychological make-up. Woman was created the 'weaker vessel' both physically and emotionally (1 Peter 3:7). Of course, the results of the Fall have led to exceptions due to hormone deficiencies and faulty genes so that there are manly women and effeminate men and other more extreme anomalies. But the differences between man and woman as God originally created them are to be respected, without forgetting their common humanity. Instead of their differences resulting in rivalry, they are to be seen as perfectly matching and complementing one another.

There is, nevertheless, an order in creation. The woman came after and from the man, and the man named her 'Woman' (2:23). God could have created the woman at the same time as the man from the dust of the ground. But he did not do so. God teaches by the way he does things and the New Testament draws our attention to this order. The head of the woman is the man and he is to take the leadership position (1 Cor. 11:3,8-9; 1 Tim. 2:13). This headship is worked out in the New Testament in the context of the home as well as the church (Eph. 5:22-33; Col. 3:18-19; 1 Peter 3:1-7).

Headship does not necessarily imply inequality. The God who created human beings, male and female, in his own image has an order within his own being. There is the Father, the Son and the Holy Spirit — three Persons, one God. Though each is co-equal and co-eternal, the Father has the position of authority and headship so that the Son is sent by the Father and always does the will of the Father. The Spirit is sent by the Father and the Son and glorifies the Son, who in turn glorifies the Father. Man and woman together, two distinct persons yet one in nature, reflect something of the relationship that exists between the persons of the Godhead.

Marriage

Old values are being challenged today. What former generations took for granted is being questioned. Is marriage an outmoded institution? The passage describes the origins of marriage and it supplies us with fundamental principles for a healthy society and home life.

1. Marriage has been designed by God

It is not a human invention or social custom. There are, of course, special customs and ceremonies associated with marriage in different cultures, but the idea itself is not of human origin. We have already applied the statement, **'It is not good that man should be alone'** (2:18), to the need for human companionship in a general sense. However, the words refer specifically to the circumstances surrounding the marriage ordinance. Marriage is a good thing. God saw the need, fulfilled it and organized the first wedding. God himself was present to witness the ceremony. Like a father giving away his daughter to the bridegroom, so **'The LORD God ... brought her to the man'** (2:22). What God did on that occasion set a precedent for all time. The inspired author of Genesis comments: **'Therefore a man shall leave his father and mother and be joined to his wife, and they shall become one flesh'** (2:24). Our Lord quotes the verse as the words of God in Matthew 19:4-6 (see also Eph. 5:31). Jesus uses this verse to establish the point that marriage has been ordained by God. Human beings do not have the right to do as they like with it. If it were merely of human origin then they might legitimately decide to dispense with it in favour of something else. Premarital sex, or living together in an unmarried state, goes against God's revealed will, is fraught with personal and social problems and comes under God's judgement (Heb. 13:4).

2. Marriage is more than the legalizing of sexual relations and the mating instinct

It is true that Paul states that marriage is necessary to avoid sexual immorality (1 Cor. 7:2-3). Marriage does make sexual relations legal and above board and does not leave one with a guilty conscience. But marriage is more than that. Likewise, marriage is more than an institution designed to propagate the human race. One of the duties within the marriage bond is to be fruitful and multiply and fill the earth, but that is not the first and only reason. Some married couples find they cannot have children. Does that mean the marriage is finished? Or what about the time when the woman has passed the age of child-bearing and the children have grown up and left the home? There must be more to marriage than the producing and rearing of children. We are only too aware these days, when people act like animals, that it does not need marriage to propagate the human race. Marriage is more than legalizing mating.

3. Marriage is a binding commitment

Verse 24 applies the principles of that first marriage described in verses 22 and 23 to every subsequent marriage. In Malachi 2:14 it is spoken of as a covenant. It is a solemn commitment and agreement to live together.

4. Marriage is a loving commitment

Love is not mentioned in this chapter, but something of the romance of love is evident in the poetic outburst from Adam's lips when he first set eyes on his bride. It was love at first sight! His words present us with the very earliest love poem:

This is now bone of my bones
And flesh of my flesh;
She shall be called Woman,
Because she was taken out of Man

(2: 23).

5. Marriage is for companionship

To relieve the aloneness which he felt and which God saw, Adam was given a partner who perfectly matched his need. The marriage union is the closest and most intimate of all human relationships (see Eph. 5:28-29). **'They shall become one flesh'** (2:24) refers to that oneness of life of which sexual union is the consummation. Husbands and wives are to care and share and be perfectly at home with one another.

6. Marriage is to be a permanent union

They are **'joined'**, or glued, together to **'become one flesh'**. The bond is to be lifelong. 'Therefore what God has joined together, let not man separate,' said Jesus (Mark 10:9). As a result of sin, death separates (Rom. 7:2-3). Divorce, another result of sin and one which God hates, also separates (Mal. 2:16). Marriage is a commitment for life and only in extreme cases is separation allowed. The extreme has become the norm in our society. Christians are not to follow worldly thinking but to be examples of a better way.

7. Marriage is to be monogamous

God gave Adam one wife. Though many polygamous marriages were tolerated in the Old Testament, from the beginning it was not so. God's plan is that the man should have just one wife and the woman should have one husband. The New Testament encourages this by stipulating that church leaders should set a good example by having no more than one wife (1 Tim. 3:2,12; Titus 1:6).

8. Marriage is to be heterosexual

In the beginning God provided for Adam, not another male, but a female. At a time when homosexual marriages are being recognized in society and being blessed in some professing Christian churches, it is necessary to mention this subject. Those who attempt to mount a case for homosexual practices of whatever kind twist the Scriptures to suit their vile practices and to deaden their consciences. The strongest possible language is used in the Bible to describe unnatural unions. Male and female bodies are made perfect only for each other. Men are not meant to have sexual relationships with men, nor women with women. Neither are human beings of either sex to have such relationships with animals (Lev. 18:22-23; 1 Cor. 6:9-10).

9. Marriage involves a new family unit

The passage speaks of the man leaving father and mother and being joined to his wife. In-laws need to remember this as much as the couple themselves. It does not mean forgetting parents and family, but there has to be a measure of distancing from the old home in order for the new family unit to emerge. **'Bone of my bones and flesh of my flesh'** is used to express family ties. Laban said to Jacob, 'Surely you are my bone and my flesh' (Gen. 29:14). The husband and wife form a new family relationship. It is into this settled relationship that children are to be born and reared.

10. Marriage implies openness and frankness

We are told that **'They were both naked, the man and his wife, and were not ashamed'** (2:25). This verse immediately prepares us for the next chapter and reminds us that shame has to do with sin. Their lack of shame was not a moral weakness but an indication of their sinless perfection. Premarital sex often results in feelings of disgust, distrust and betrayal. Marriage alone proves the right setting for such openness and bodily union.

The Song of Songs takes up the theme of the first love song and celebrates this aspect of creation. Despite the Fall it is still a wonderful blessing and we are to make the most of it during this fleeting life, as Ecclesiastes 9:9 reminds us. Marital love is beautiful. Such passages of Scripture provide positive answers to the exploitation of sex for selfish ends and at the same time serve as a corrective to asceticism. They show that sexual union in marriage is not an inferior state. It is not a concession to human weakness. That was the teaching of the Middle Ages and it has persisted ever since in some circles. Physical love within the marriage bond is not something unclean. It is good and wholesome (see Heb. 13:4).

The apostle Paul quotes Genesis 2:24 in his teaching on husband-and-wife relationships. As he does so he immediately adds, 'This is a great mystery; but I speak concerning Christ and the church' (Eph. 5:31-32). The mystery is the special marriage relationship between Christ and his church revealed in the gospel. The spiritual union between the Lord and his people is the model for human marriage. The earthly type leads the believer to consider the heavenly antitype. There are many passages in the Old Testament suggesting the same idea, especially Psalm 45 and the Song of Solomon.

6.
The origin of human sin

Please read Genesis 3:1-24

After reading about the wonderful creation, we might well ask, 'Why are things not like that now? Where has all the evil come from?' Such questions would not arise if there was no God and everything that exists came about by chance happenings. The philosophical problem of the origin of evil belongs to the mystery of God and is left unanswered. What we *are* told is that the reason for all the trouble in the world is rebellion against God.

This is one of the most important chapters in the whole Bible. We are not studying these words for antiquarian interest or general knowledge. What we are considering has profound implications for our life today and presents us with the reason for God's gracious intervention on our behalf. Here we read of the need of a Saviour and why a new creation is necessary.

The great rebellion on earth (3:1-6)

Our attention is drawn to four subjects.

1. The tempter

The chapter opens with a statement concerning a snake: **'Now the serpent was more cunning than any beast of the field which the LORD God had made'** (3:1). The snake is one of those non-domestic creatures that lived in the uncultivated area outside God's garden. Adam had seen these animals and had given names to them all, including the snake. God made the snake and, like the rest of his creatures, it was under human authority. Psalm 8 reminds us, 'You have put all things under his feet ... even the beasts of the field' (vv. 6-7).

When Moses came to write up this account, the snake was among the unclean creatures that could not be eaten or offered in sacrifice (Lev. 11:42). It was also, by then, well known in the ancient world as a symbol of evil and magic.[1] The mythical serpent Leviathan becomes a type of all that is in opposition to God and which will be destroyed by God (Isa. 27:1; Job 26:13). We might well ask how did the snake come to have these negative associations in the ancient world-cultures? The answer is given in this chapter.

But how is it possible for a snake to tempt anybody? It seems too unbelievable for words. It is biologically impossible for snakes to talk. It is not in the nature of any animal to hold a rational conversation using human speech. The previous chapter has emphasized the point that Adam found no animal that corresponded to him. For these and other reasons many reject the story, believing it to have no historical basis. Some would say it is like one of Aesop's fables; others, that it is a myth that has spiritual and theological significance. A further group of scholars suggests that the snake is not a literal snake but is employed for a figurative purpose. However, the snake is presented as a real, live snake, like the rest of the animals mentioned in 1:24-25 and 2:19-20, as real as the first man and woman and the incidents recorded in this chapter. We must submit ourselves to the Word of God that a real snake spoke to the woman. If this is so, then it is right to ask, how could this snake talk?

The very way in which we are introduced to the snake suggests that there was something special about it.[2] Emphasis is put on the snake and the creature's special characteristic. The word translated **'cunning'** is used in the Bible in both a good and a bad sense (see Prov. 12:23, where it is translated 'prudent', and Job 5:12, where it is rendered 'crafty'). As all the animals were created good, the word need not suggest anything evil. We could translate it as 'clever' or 'astute'. Nevertheless, to call special attention to this creature's chief characteristic suggests that there is more to this serpent than meets the eye. When we come to God's judgement on the snake later in the story, we are made very aware that something bigger and more sinister lies behind this creature (3:14-15). What is hinted at in Genesis is fully explained in the New Testament. The snake is described as 'the great dragon..., that serpent of old, called the Devil and Satan' (Rev. 12:9; 20:2). Our Lord refers to the devil as a liar and a murderer from the beginning (John 8:44).

Does this mean that the snake is, after all, a figure of speech for the devil? This is what some evangelicals suggest. But why could the devil not have appeared as a literal snake and used it to speak to the woman? The God who enabled Balaam's donkey to speak (Num. 22:28-30) allowed the devil to use a snake to tempt human beings. In the New Testament we read of evil spirits possessing not only people but pigs (Mark 5:11-16). What we have here is a real snake, but one used by the devil.

Through the medium of the snake, the devil held a rational conversation with a human being. This suggests that what is at work here is more than an evil influence or power but an objective personal embodiment of evil. The temptation to go against God's will is part of the evil work of the devil. This means that sin existed in God's creation prior to the sin of Adam and Eve. The mystery surrounding the origin of sin goes back to the devil and the evil spirits associated with him. Between the absolute beginning and the situation in chapter 3, there must have been a rebellion in the angelic realm, a matter only hinted at in the Bible. The important thing for us to know is that Satan was not originally evil, that he is not some evil power who has always existed in opposition to God. God alone is uncreated and all that exists has been created by him. Satan and his angels are creatures of God, answerable to God and judged by him (Rev. 20:10).

Satan, nevertheless, has amazing powers given to him (Job 1-2), and we need to take account of this invisible, spiritual dimension to sin and evil (Eph. 6:12). We shall not fully appreciate the meaning of Christ's incarnation and atoning death if we do not accept the reality of a personal devil. The tempter who came to Adam and Eve in that lovely garden of God also came to Jesus, the last Adam, in the barren wilderness of Judea where the wild beasts roamed (Mark 1:13). Our Lord triumphed over the devil in his life and in his death on the cross (Matt. 4:1-11; John 12:31; Col. 2:15; Rev. 12:7-11). The Son of God came into our world 'that he might destroy the works of the devil' (1 John 3:8). Before his final end, the devil now comes to make war with the people of God as they journey through this earthly wilderness to the city of God (Rev. 12:17). We must not underestimate or dismiss the power of the Evil One. Thank God for the gospel armour! (Eph. 6:10-18).

> And let the prince of ill
> Look grim as e'er he will,
> He harms us not a whit:
> For why? His doom is writ;
> A word shall quickly slay him.
>
> (Martin Luther)

2. The tempted

As we look at the people being tempted we remember their situation. It was worlds away from what we find ourselves in today. They were in a perfect environment. Everything they needed was to hand. Life was pleasant. The couple were at peace with God, at peace with each other, at peace within themselves and at peace with the world. Genesis 2:25 summarizes their position. Their lives were transparent. They had nothing to hide. There was no distrust, no dishonour, no greed, no lust. Their human nature had no flaw or moral weakness. They had left the divine Potter's hand in perfect condition. Though they had minds and wills of their own, these minds and wills were also perfect in every way. They thought no evil and did no evil. Out of their innermost beings flowed only what was pleasing to God. It is worth stopping to consider the pleasant state our first parents enjoyed. We today find it almost impossible to conceive, and yet we long for such a situation. It is also hard to believe that anyone would want to spoil all this goodness, harmony and beauty. Yet this is what happened. The devil tempted the divine image-bearers and they rebelled against God.

Why did God permit Adam and Eve to be tempted? It was not because the devil was as powerful as God. Neither was it because God was unaware of what would happen. The answer lies in the mystery of God. What we can say is that God used the whole sorry event to display to angels and humans his stunning greatness.

3. The temptation

An intruder invaded the paradise of God. The seducer, in the form of a snake, slunk into the garden to carry out his sinister scheme. For the snake to rise above its station in life and speak to the woman was quite improper. This should have alerted the couple to the fact that something was wrong. As the man had the task of keeping, or guarding, this special garden, this snake should have been immediately stopped and sent out of the garden. As it was, the snake was allowed to stay and seduce.

Everything about the temptation reveals the devil's devious nature.

1. How he appeared

The devil came, not as a roaring lion, but as a beautiful, enchanting snake. There is a possible connection between the word for snake *(nahash)* and the word translated 'bronze' *(nehosheth)*. (See also the 'bronze serpent' later called *Nehushtan* — Num. 21:9; 2 Kings 18:4). This may suggest that the snake's appearance was quite striking, metallically bright and shiny like bronze. It was attractive. Paul warns that Satan can transform himself into an angel of light (2 Cor. 11:14).

2. To whom he spoke

Instead of going to the head of the household, he accosted the woman. Paul highlights this point in 1 Timothy 2:11-14. The woman was created to have a naturally receptive attitude and quality. This is not to be thought of as a physical, mental or spiritual failing, but a perfectly acceptable aspect of her makeup. The devil used it to his own advantage. Of the two people in the garden, he figured that the woman was more likely to give him a hearing, to welcome him and receive what he had to say. It has been one of the devil's devices ever since to attack where he considers there might be an apparent weakness. Think of the way he tempted Jesus in the wilderness when he was hungry and alone.

3. The subtlety of the temptation

There are at least three interesting features.

He asked innocent-sounding questions. The devil's first words
to the woman distorted God's original generous declaration
in 2:16-17. He suggested that they were not being allowed to
eat from any of the trees. But he covered up his tracks by
framing what he said into an innocent-sounding question which
had a touch of surprise to it: **'Has God indeed said, "You
shall not eat from every tree of the garden"?'** (3:1). There
is a hint in these words that God is being rather mean and that
the couple are somewhat restricted. In similar subtle ways Satan
will tempt us to drive a wedge between us and our loving
heavenly Father. A direct massive attack on God's fatherly
care would have no effect. It would probably make us more
eager to love and serve him. But those clever, carefully worded
innuendoes can take us off guard.

He spoke no outright lie. The devil's words sound like a head-
on rejection of God's word: **'You will not surely die...'**
(3:4-5). The rest of the chapter reads like a vindication of the
devil. Their eyes were opened, they did acquire knowledge
independently of God and they did not die — at any rate, not
for a long time. Adam remained on earth for what would seem
to us like an eternity. The devil is a master at making God out
to be a liar by presenting very plausible half-truths. He will do
anything to bring God's name into disrepute and make God's
Word look ridiculous. The devil will try to deceive the very
elect. He is always laying traps (see 2 Cor. 2:9-11).

He made no call to disobey. There was no directive to take
the forbidden fruit. The devil did not force the couple to rebel

against God's command. This is where the art of the tempter is so great. The seeds which he had sown in the mind made the disobedience appear to be the most natural thing in all the world to do. Do not underestimate the tempter's power. 'Let him who thinks he stands take heed lest he fall' (1 Cor. 10:12).

The temptation involved doubt concerning God's goodness (3:1) and concerning God's justice and the truth of his Word (3:4).

4. The transgression

It is important to make a clear distinction between temptation and sin. To be subject to temptation is not sin. Our Lord was tempted by the devil, but he did not sin (Heb. 4:14-15). The temptation to sin did not arise from within his nature but from outside. This was also the case with Eve. The evil thought came from the devil. To be subject to temptation is not sin. We, of course, are not in that pure and sinless state and we know that sinful thoughts can arise from within us. But the Christian is also aware of blasphemous and wicked thoughts which come from outside.

A temptation only becomes sin when the sinful suggestion or thought is taken on board and accepted. The hymn urges us:

> Yield not to temptation,
> For yielding is sin.

Jesus Christ refused to accept Satan's proposals. He threw them out immediately. Eve, on the other hand, entertained the ideas that had been so subtly placed in her mind and she decided of her own free will to take the forbidden fruit, and Adam also joined her. The snake was responsible for the evil suggestions, but the couple were responsible for succumbing to the temptation and eating what God had prohibited. They could have refused, but they did not.

Before the outward rebellious act was committed a change of attitude had taken place in Eve's innermost being. She began looking at the tree in a way she had never looked at it before. The fruit of this tree was just like the fruit of the other trees. It was good to eat and pleasing to look at (3:6). Previously, she had been content to accept God's word and to keep away from it. Now, through listening to the tempter, she had doubts concerning God's word, she received the serpent's half-truths and, as she saw the fruit, a desire welled up within her for gaining knowledge independently of God. She considered the good of the fruit and ignored the evil of disobeying God. She wanted to be wise and forgot the first principle of wisdom, which is the fear of the Lord.

Then came the act: **'She took its fruit and ate.'** We must be careful not to think of the rebellious act of taking and eating as a second sin after the initial sin of desire. Sin is a complex thing. The outward act of taking the fruit and eating was part and parcel of the inner covetous spirit. James reminds us that 'When desire has conceived, it gives birth to sin' (James 1:15). The man followed the woman in this deliberate and wilful act of rebellion. **'She also gave to her husband with her, and he ate'** (3:6). Adam tamely followed his wife. He went into sin with his eyes wide open.

Sin is transgression of God's law. Adam and Eve went beyond the bounds set by God. They disobeyed God. This is sin. It is rebellion against the revealed will of God. God's sovereignty as absolute ruler is rejected, his authority is called into question, the truth of his Word is denied and his goodness despised.

In the case of both the man and the woman, their rebellion against God was foolish and illogical. It is a great mystery why these two sinless people, having every advantage and comfort, should have transgressed God's express command. Nothing can excuse their rebellion. There are those who say that to be human is to sin. This is only true of those who are already sinners. When human beings were first created they were without sin. This did not mean that they were at that time less than human. They were truly human. The man Christ Jesus, the Son of God, was also without sin and yet he was a real human being. Through the virgin conception, his human nature was in a sinless state like Adam's before he rebelled. Unlike Adam, Jesus remained sinless. He resisted the devil and through his death and resurrection has become the head of a new humanity.

Christians are called not to sin (1 John 2:1), nor to give way to the devil. 'Submit to God. Resist the devil and he will flee from you' (James 4:7). When evil thoughts molest us, we must recognize where they come from and not allow them to take over. Let us beware of covetousness and sinful desires. This is the spirit of the ungodly world under the influence of the Evil One. It is seductive and we are warned: 'Do not love the world... For all that is in the world — the lust of the flesh, the lust of the eyes, and the pride of life — is not of the Father but is of the world' (1 John 2:15-16). Paul also warns us to beware of false teachers who will seek to corrupt our minds and lead us away 'from the simplicity that is in Christ', just as the serpent deceived Eve (2 Cor. 11:3-15).

The results of the rebellion (3:7-24)

Examples of what this rebellion led to are presented in the following chapters. Its immediate consequences, however, are detailed here. The rebellion affected all their relationships.

1. Relations with God (3:7-10)

They wanted to hide from God (3:8). There was a complete change of attitude. The surprising feature was not the fact of God's walking in the garden, but the couple's reaction. God's presence is often spoken of in terms of 'walking about' (Lev. 26:11-12; Deut. 23:14; 2 Cor. 6:16; Rev. 2:1). Adam and his wife were no longer comfortable in God's presence. Instead of enjoying fellowship with God during the late afternoon breeze (**'the cool of the day'** — 3:8), they were afraid and ashamed to face God (3:10) and tried to hide among the trees that God had given them.

It is impossible, of course, to hide from God (Ps. 139:7-12). Isaiah describes those who will try to hide from God on the Day of Judgement (Isa. 2:19; see Rev. 6:15-17). 'There is no creature hidden from his sight, but all things are naked and open to the eyes of him to whom we must give account' (Heb. 4:13).

2. Relations with others (3:7,12)

It brought division. The couple who had been living in perfect harmony with each other now found relationships strained. This is seen in the following ways.

Firstly, the devil had said their eyes would be opened, but what a let-down it proved to be! The knowledge they acquired was the sudden realization that they were naked (3:7). They began to feel uncomfortable and vulnerable in each other's company. Having broken free of their dependence on God, the God who had united them, they began to face each other as independent of one another. Their physical differences were now highlighted and they felt the need to hide and protect themselves from each other. We now live in a world where people's sexual differences are exploited for selfish ends.

Secondly, Adam blamed his wife and God: **'The woman whom you gave to be with me, she gave me the fruit of the tree, and I ate'** (3:12). Sin brings alienation between humans as well as between humans and God. When we are in a tight corner we do not mind who gets hurt, including those closest to us. All the divisions, fightings and wars in the world go back to this original sin in the garden.

Thirdly, God's sentence on the woman only added to the tensions already felt: **'Your desire shall be for your husband and he shall rule over you'** (3:16).

3. Their own personal selves (3:7-8,10,16,19)

Spiritually

Their relationship with God and with each other had changed because a fundamental change had taken place in their innermost being. A profound psychological, moral and spiritual revolution had occurred.

A guilty conscience. The fact that they were naked had not troubled them before their disobedience. Now they felt a sense of shame in God's presence. Just as children, and grown-ups, who have wronged someone will often seek to avoid the person concerned, so our first parents tried to lie low while God's special presence was in the garden. Their action betrayed their feelings, and their feelings witnessed to their true moral guilt. They were guilty before God. Not only were they aware that they had committed wrong, but they knew that they deserved to be punished.

A sinful nature. It was much more than physical nakedness that was worrying them. The couple realized that they had something to hide from God. They were ashamed and embarrassed because they were now guilty sinners. Sin had polluted their whole beings. They were now in an unclean condition.

Physically

They would know pain, sorrow, ageing and death. The separation of the inseparable would take place. What they had been threatened with, they would experience. They would be separated from the bodies in which they expressed themselves as persons.

4. God's relations with them (3:9-19)

The rebellious couple experienced that aspect of God's character that reacts to all opposition to his revealed will. For the first time they became aware of God's anger. In addition, instead of the relationship being that of Father/child it became one of Judge/criminal. From enjoying God's fatherly goodness they now cowered before the heavenly Judge as he examined them and passed sentence.

5. Their relations with God's enemy (3:13,15)

The couple had sided with the snake against God. They had tried to gain wisdom in independence of God, but they found themselves slaves of the devil. Satan's lies were believed in preference to God's truth. In God's judgement of the snake, reference is made to the 'seed' of the snake. From this time onward there would not only be fallen angels, but fallen men and women under the devil's authority, furthering his evil interests in this world against God.

6. Their relationship with the whole cosmos (3:17-18)

The ground was cursed, a sure sign that the whole cosmos was disrupted (Isa. 24:5-6). Paul confirms this. We are taught that the creation itself was subjected against its will to God's curse and is groaning right up to the present time (Rom. 8:20-22). Ecclesiastes emphasizes the sad state of a world affected by the curse. Life is frustrating, fleeting and failing.

7. Their relationship with the land (3:17-18,22-24)

Because of the curse, human beings would find the ground difficult and hard to manage. The ground would be working against them. They would find themselves at odds with the very ground from which they were taken. Instead of work being a delight, it would be drudgery. The couple were also removed from the holy land. Adam and his wife lost the gift of that special park. They found themselves expelled from the place of life and joy.

7.
The origin of distress and death

Please read Genesis 3:9-24

The judgement of God

Paradise now became a courtroom and the keeper of the grounds a criminal on trial. There are two parts to the judgement scene.

1. The trial (3:9-13)

Before the Judge passed sentence, he questioned the rebels — first the man and then the woman. The right order of authority was re-established, which the tempter had sought to undermine.

Firstly, God called to Adam, **'Where are you?'** (3:9). He was not ignorant of where they were hiding. This was a summons to come out of hiding and explain themselves. The man incriminated himself by his reply. He wanted to hide his nakedness from the God who had made him (3:10). God then asked two further questions arising out of his reply: **'Who told you that you were naked? Have you eaten from the tree of which I commanded you that you should not eat?'** (3:11). While admitting he had eaten the forbidden fruit (**'I ate'**), Adam sought to pin the blame on his wife (**'She gave me the fruit of the tree'**) and by implication on God himself (**'... whom**

you gave to be with me' — 3:12). To shift the blame onto someone or something else is a common way to evade responsibility. This is so typical of humanity.

When God turned to the woman and asked, **'What is this you have done?'** she also tried to cover up her sin by blaming the snake: **'The serpent deceived me, and I ate'** (3:13). Did the snake cause the woman to sin, and did she then in turn cause the man to sin? No! The tempter merely provided the occasion and opportunity, but he did not cause them to sin. Adam and his wife of their own free will chose to disobey God. The woman took the initial step without reference to her husband and the man completed the whole sorry episode by taking the decision to join her in the rebellion. They both sinned and compounded their sin by blaming others. We are responsible for what we do, or fail to do, and we shall be judged accordingly. Blaming our background, our parents, our genes, or our society, for our own wrong choices is ruled out of court by God.

As we think of the guilt of both Adam and Eve, two passages from the New Testament come to mind.

Romans 5:12-19 emphasizes the place of Adam as the head of the old humanity. The guilt of Adam is clearly presented to us in Genesis. He was not an innocent party, but as head of the household he took a determined decision to follow his wife and disobey God. It was therefore to the man that God first addressed his questions and it was to the man that God pronounced the death sentence with which he had threatened him earlier. Adam stands at the head of the human race in two senses: firstly, he is the *natural* head of the race (Acts 17:26); and, secondly, he is, as Romans 5 stresses, its *federal*, or representative, head (1 Cor. 15:21-22). The whole of humanity is bound up with the sin of Adam. We all stand guilty and condemned 'in Adam' and we all die 'in Adam'. Praise God for the second representative figure, the last Adam, who heads up the new humanity!

In *1 Timothy 2:13-14* Paul's point is to express the creation order of man first, then woman. However, the woman was not an innocent victim of man's wrong choice. She led the way and the man followed. The rebellion included reversing God's order, for the woman wrongly took the initiative and the man consented to it. Despite protests to the contrary, the New Testament stresses that male leadership in home and church life is not merely cultural but based on the creation order ordained by God (1 Cor. 11:2-16; 14:34-36).

There was no questioning of the snake. No attempt was made to arouse in the devil a sense of guilt or to elicit a confession. He was already an unrepentant rebel beyond redemption, who had deliberately set out to draw these newly created people from God. The devil was not allowed to give an account of himself. It was the woman who was given the last word when she accused the snake of deceiving her.

2. The sentence (3:14-19)

The questions have been asked and the excuses made. At the beginning of human history, every mouth was stopped and all eyes were on the Judge as judgement was pronounced. Right up to the present moment, we all experience the effects of those punishments. At the end of human history, the final judgement will take place, and the effects of that will last for ever. Never dismiss God's judgements. We are all experiencing them every day of our lives: 'For we have been consumed by your anger, and by your wrath we are terrified' (Ps. 90:7). God wishes us to learn from them and to embrace his love in Jesus Christ.

The culprits were addressed in ascending order of authority.

The snake (3:14-15)

God spoke to the snake because it was a devil-possessed snake. In the presence of God, the devil was reduced to silence and forced to listen to the divine judgement. The tempter is a creature and held responsible before God for his actions. Though the snake had not caused the woman to sin, he was culpable. The woman was right to accuse the snake of deceiving her, but wrong to make it an excuse for her own action. God's opening words to the snake, **'Because you have done this...'** (3:14), pick up the woman's accusation. The tempter's presence in the garden was for an evil purpose. He came there to lie, deceive and sow seeds of doubt.

While the snake is described in verse 1 as 'more cunning than any beast of the field', he is now **'cursed ... more than every beast of the field'**. This verse implies that the whole animal kingdom, domesticated and undomesticated, was affected by this rebellion (see Rom. 8:22). The snake, however, was subjected to a greater curse than the rest of the animals. Up to this moment only blessings had been pronounced. For the first time we read of a curse. A curse is the opposite of blessing. The curse on the snake involved two related parts.

First, he was told:

On your belly you shall go,
And you shall eat dust
All the days of your life

(3:14).

The characteristic feature of the snake is described. It writhes in the dust scavenging for food. All creatures that move on their bellies are regarded as unclean (Lev. 11:42). The snake is the largest and most typical of such creatures.

What is literally true of the snake became symbolic of the devil's punishment. God was actually pronouncing judgement on the Evil One. Whatever curse God may have uttered when the devil first rebelled, God here passed sentence on him in the hearing of those who had been tempted by him. The snake slithering on the ground, licking the dust, is a powerful picture of the devil's cursed position. As we see in the next verse, this tragic event in the garden was no defeat for God. It was all in God's good plan and fulfilled his purposes.

The snake's position and movement came to be symbolic of those who are cursed, humiliated and brought low. Reptiles do not actually eat dust, but eating or licking the dust is a graphic way of conveying the idea of submission and defeat. Nations 'shall lick the dust like a serpent; they shall crawl from their holes like snakes of the earth' (Micah 7:17).

The second part of the curse refers to continual conflict and ultimate defeat:

And I will put enmity
Between you and the woman,
And between your seed and her Seed;
He will bruise your head...

(3:15).

We might have supposed that the curse would result in there being no offspring. Blessing, as we saw from the creation account, involved being fruitful and multiplying (1:22,28). This curse, however, did not include being unproductive. The snake is to have **'seed'**, or offspring. The hostility that already existed between God and the snake was from now on to involve human beings. There would now be perpetual warfare between humans and snakes. In the new creation, Isaiah sees an end to this hostility when 'The nursing child shall play by the cobra's hole, and the weaned child shall put his hand in the viper's den' (11:8). But the snake will for ever assume a lowly position (Isa. 65:25).

Those who suggest that this verse is simply supplying a reason for the natural reaction that women have to snakes completely misread the text. The enmity between humans and snakes is a picture of a much deeper and sinister hostility. As we have seen, God is pronouncing judgement on the devil. An announcement is made of spiritual warfare in this world. We shall not understand the references to spiritual warfare in the rest of the Bible if we do not grasp what is said here. God himself is the author of this hostility: **'I will put enmity'**. The Evil One may have thought that he had won an easy victory. He had captured our first parents and with them their descendants too. But God intervenes. The hostility is not inspired by corrupt, evil hearts. It is not a case of evil breeding evil, with strife and infighting taking place. This animosity is inspired by God. God is committed to this battle. What is more, God has a plan of victory in which human beings will be on God's side over against the Evil One, as we shall see below.

The woman (3:16)

God now turns to the woman and solemnly announces her punishment. Though the word 'curse' is not used, that is what it is. As in the case of the snake, there are two parts to it, one relating to her children and the other to her husband.

In the first place, it is clear that, despite her sin, there is no withdrawal of the blessing to be fruitful and multiply. The previous verse has suggested that the woman will produce offspring. Now we are told that she will give birth, but it will involve much pain. **'Your sorrow and your conception'** is probably a way of saying 'your sorrow *in* conception'. The blessing of bearing children is to become bitter and burdensome. Without modern medical helps, giving birth is a highly traumatic and harrowing experience for most women. When the Bible wishes to express severe trouble it will often describe it in terms of a woman undergoing the pangs of childbirth (e.g., Isa. 13:8).

The second part of the punishment concerns the woman's relationship to her husband. Another blessing is adversely affected. The marriage relationship will continue, but it will suffer disruption: **'Your desire shall be for your husband and he shall rule over you.'** Clearly this cannot mean that the husband will be the leader and the wife will be submissive to her husband, for this was her position before the rebellion. In the New Testament Christians are encouraged to maintain this order. What we have here is a punishment for sin. It is a punishment that fitted her crime. She had acted independently of her husband in listening to the snake, taking the forbidden fruit and encouraging him to eat.

The punishment is open to at least two possible interpretations: it either refers to the woman's craving for her man, whatever his demands, so that she becomes his slave; or it may mean her urge to so control and manipulate her husband that he will need to exert effort in mastering her. This latter suggestion is supported by Genesis 4:7, where sin's 'desire' (same word) is for Cain and he must master it. The punishment, then, is describing either the exploitation of women by men or the beginnings of the battle of the sexes. On either view the harmonious relationship of love is wrecked, to be replaced by exploitation, subjection and struggle.

These are the realities of life. People's dreams of a perfect marriage are soon shattered. It is all part of the vanity of this world, of the curse which God has inflicted. Christians in their home situations are urged to overcome this curse by the Spirit and to follow the pattern laid down in Genesis 2:20-25 and seen in the relationship of Christ and the church (Eph. 5:22-33). The curse does not encourage people to treat one another badly or prevent advances in medicine. It simply announces and describes what will be. When God expresses his anger by abandoning people to their shameful practices he is not excusing or encouraging them in their sin. It follows, then, that in the same way as husbands and wives are encouraged to live joyfully together (Eccles. 9:9), so it is not wrong to seek to alleviate the pains of childbirth.[1]

The man (3:17-19)

As sentence is passed on the man, attention is drawn to his sin. The reason he is punished is **'because you have heeded the voice of your wife'** and has eaten prohibited fruit. Adam was not deceived by the devil but sinned wilfully. His fundamental error was to obey his wife rather than God. Again, there are two parts to the punishment.

Firstly, he had eaten the forbidden fruit, so *his punishment fitted the crime*: **'In toil you shall eat from it.'** In order to live he must eat, and so his punishment will be a continual reminder of his sin. The word for 'toil' in Hebrew is the same one that is used of the woman's pain in childbirth (3:16). Both in the bringing about of life and the ongoing process of sustaining life, there will be 'blood, sweat and tears'. A curse is pronounced concerning the ground, or land. Instead of producing only what was pleasant to the sight and good for food (2:9), it would now bear **'thorns and thistles'**. These are among the 'plants of the field' (see 2:5). This, along with the reference to **'the herb of the field'**, gives the first hint that the couple will be leaving the lovely garden for the uncultivated and desolate areas of the earth (Hosea 10:8). A land blessed is a land well-watered and fertile (Deut. 8:7-10; 33:13-16). A land cursed is one which is deprived of such blessings (Deut. 28:16-40). Again, this emphasis on 'land' becomes an important biblical theme and paves the way for the end-time hope of a new earth.

Secondly, in his struggle with the ground, *the ground will overcome him*. While in one sense man's **'return to the ground'** appears natural, for **'Out of it you were taken'** (see 2:7), it is clear that this is part of man's punishment. He had been originally threatened with death if he disobeyed God's command. **'Dust you are, and to dust you shall return,'** reminds us of the judgement on the snake. Man is reduced to dust and the snake moves in the dust. They are both brought to the same end. 'Then the dust will return to the earth as it was' (Eccles. 12:7). The final victory over the devil includes being raised from the dust of the earth (Dan. 12:2). Death is an enemy, associated with the devil. It is the last enemy to be destroyed (Heb. 2:14; 1 Cor. 15:21-26).

The grace of God

Despite the doom and gloom there are two indications of God's mercy and grace in this chapter.

1. The promise of a seed (3:15)

The judgement on the snake includes a precious promise. It is the first glimmer of the gospel. That is why theologians call it the *protevangelium*, 'the first good news'.

What does **'her Seed'** and the snake's seed mean? The term 'seed' is of special interest. It is one of the key words in the book of Genesis, occurring fifty-nine times. In modern English versions it can be translated as 'descendants', 'children', 'family', 'offspring', 'semen', 'line' and even 'people'. Like the English word 'sheep', the Hebrew word for 'seed' can be singular or plural. The 'seed' of the woman can, therefore, be taken either in a collective sense for descendants in general, or for one descendant in particular (12:7; 21:13). In some cases there is ambiguity and we should not be surprised if both ideas are present at the same time.[2] The snake's 'seed' includes all who belong to his rule. John the Baptist called the religious leaders of his day a 'brood of vipers', and Jesus followed this up by saying that they belonged to their 'father the devil' (Matt. 3:7; John 8:44).

The enmity between the devil's seed and the woman's seed suggests a collective struggle between the devil's descendants and the woman's descendants. God has always had descendants of the woman who have been opposed to the devil and his evil agents. These two opposing forces have existed in our world from the time of the Fall.

The final phrase, however, **'He shall bruise your head,'** strongly supports the view that the reference is to a particular individual. Interestingly, it does not say that the seed of the woman will bruise the seed of the serpent, but that the woman's seed will bruise the serpent itself. This is another indication that more than a mere snake is in mind. The verse speaks of the great adversary of humanity being given a deadly wound on the head, whereas the woman's 'Seed' receives a wound to the heel that is not fatal.

The woman herself seems to have taken God's word to refer to an individual, for we find Eve saying in the next chapter, 'God has appointed another seed for me instead of Abel, whom Cain killed' (4:25). The rest of Genesis keeps on emphasizing the importance of a special 'seed'. This 'seed' is connected to a chosen family line through Shem, Abraham, Isaac and Jacob. By the end of the book it is clearly associated with kingship (49:8-12) and Joseph becomes a type of this future royal Seed who will come from the line of Judah. The rest of the Old Testament builds on this until we come to the fulfilment in the coming of the Messiah.[3]

Just as the Evil One is distinguished from his posterity, so there will be one from among the human race who will crush the head of the ancient serpent. Jesus is *the* Seed. He has conquered, but not without a fierce fight. He was wounded and crushed so that, through his death, he might destroy him who had the power of death, that is the devil (Heb. 2:14-15).

> Bruised was the dragon by the Son,
> Though two had wounds, there conquered one —
> And Jesus was his name.[4]

All Christ's enemies shall be under his feet and shall lick the dust (Ps. 72:9; 1 Cor. 15:25). The victory won by Christ will also be experienced by all who belong to him (Rom. 16:20). It is amazing that God should give this truth as he passed sentence on the devil. This was the last thing the devil wanted to hear. How wonderful are God's purposes!

2. God's provision of clothes

God's grace is also evident in the fact that **'The LORD God made tunics of skin, and clothed them'** (3:21). Their awareness of being naked was an indication of their guilt and shame. They tried to cover themselves, but they were still naked and afraid of God (3:10). In God's presence their own paltry and desperate efforts were totally inadequate. They wanted to hide among the trees. If they were to be properly and decently covered, God must clothe them. For human beings to approach God it was necessary to have clothes provided and approved by him. In place of the skimpy belt of fig leaves, God chose tunics, or shirts, of skin. These tunics, as other passages suggest, were like robes worn next to the skin. The skin of animals covered their own skins. What a contrast! Adam and Eve simply strung together leaves which they had plucked from a tree, whereas God used the skins of dead animals to cover human guilt and shame. It showed how easy-going and cheap were the human efforts to deal with sin, and how thorough-going and costly was God's way. It involved the 'shedding of blood', something which is later emphasized in the ceremonial laws. 'This act of God in the taking of animal life laid the foundation for animal sacrifice.'[5] Adam would never have thought of doing such a thing. 'To us life is cheap and death familiar, but Adam recognized death as the punishment of sin. Death was in early man a sign of God's anger. And he had to learn that sin could be covered not by a bunch of leaves snatched from a bush as he passed by and that would grow again next year, but only by pain and blood.'[6]

Clothing is a theme running throughout Scripture in con-nection with the essential truth of the gospel and is associated again with blood sacrifice in the last book of the Bible (Isa. 61:10; Matt. 22:11-14; Rev. 7:9). All attempts at putting our-selves right before God are useless. We cannot cover up the results of our sin. Only God can properly clothe the guilty sinner. Promise and type give way to fulfilment and reality in Jesus, whose obedience and sacrificial death hide all our sins and enable us to stand upright in God's presence.

> Jesus, thy blood and righteousness
> My beauty are, my glorious dress.
> In flaming worlds in these arrayed,
> With joy shall I lift up my head.
>
> (Nicolaus von Zinzendorf)

The human response (3:20-21)

Adam **'called his wife's name Eve'**, a form of the word for 'life'. He would have had every reason for calling his wife 'death'. He had blamed her for his own sin and, in the light of God's judgements, he could well have expressed his frustration by associating her with the sentence of death. As he listened to the punishments to be inflicted he obviously noted the rays of hope. There was no comfort in the sentence pronounced on himself, but he recognized that there was to be an ongoing life in this world. God promised them children and told them that from such life there would come victory over the tempter. Adam took heart from these blessings contained within the curses and held on to them. In the middle of the death sentence there was the promise of life and hope. This is what the gospel is — light in the midst of darkness, life in the midst of death, blessing in the midst of curse. As we look at Calvary, the place of curse, of damnation, darkness and death, God has made it the place of blessing, glory, light and life. Whereas the first name that Adam gave his wife pointed back to her origin ('out of Man' — 2:23) this new name served to remind her of her destiny (**'the mother of all living'**).

The naming of his wife also reasserted his authority over her. The proper order in the home, which the Evil One had sought to destroy, was re-established. The husband's God-appointed leadership role is expressed in the context of the gospel hope, a point underlined in Ephesians 5:22-33 and 1 Peter 3:1-7. It is by the gospel that the curse is broken and the relationship between the sexes can exist as God originally intended.

Adam and Eve also allowed themselves to be clothed by God. While this action would have continually reminded them of their sinfulness, it also displayed the grace of God. It confirmed his promises and established an ongoing relationship with the sinful, shamefaced couple.

The punishment inflicted (3:22-24)

God again deliberated with himself: **'Behold, the man has become like one of us, to know good and evil'** (see 1:26;

6:3,7; 8:21-22; 11:6-7). The Lord could not have addressed
the holy angels in this way, for they are not morally autonomous creatures. They always take their directions from God.
Human beings had acted independently of God and decided to
disobey God. The snake's promise was partially true (3:5).
Only in the sense of deciding what was right without reference to a higher authority were they like God. It was a worthless prize. Acting independently of God's revealed will brought
them under God's curse. The use of the word 'man' here suggests that Adam represents his wife. It emphasizes his role not
only as head of his family, but as head of humanity.

1. Barred from free access to the tree of life

Apart from the tree of knowledge, the couple had been able to
eat freely from the trees of the garden, including the tree of
life. Eating from this tree was an expression of their life with
God. Their disobedience had brought about a severance in
that relationship. They were sinners under sentence of death.
God prevented them partaking of the tree which symbolized
fulness of life. The way he did so powerfully demonstrated
their cursed position. Again, the snake's strong assertion that
they would not die if they ate the forbidden fruit was a hollow
claim. They did not lose their physical lives immediately but,
instead of knowing that fulness of life associated with God in
paradise, they experienced expulsion, deprivation and the loss
of that free access into God's presence which is eternal life.

2. Exiled from the garden

The Garden of Eden was like the holy sanctuary where God
was uniquely present in all his life-giving power. Nothing unclean could live in that environment. Adam and Eve did not
leave the garden out of choice; they were thrown out. **'Drove
out'** is a much stronger verb than 'sent out' and is used by

Moses of the removal of the Canaanites from the land of promise (Exod. 23:28-31). The couple were driven from the holy
place like unclean lepers expelled from the holy camp of Israel. For an Israelite to be driven from the camp was far more
catastrophic than physical death. Israel's ultimate punishment
for disobedience was removal from God's land (Deut.
28:63-68). The couple experienced exile from the good land.

Such tragic happenings powerfully pointed to spiritual realities. It was not a case of play-acting. These things were for
real. They were experiences which the couple physically felt
and they expressed dramatically what it was like to live under
God's curse. This is humanity's position apart from the grace
of God. By birth we are all dead in trespasses and sins, aliens
and outsiders, with God's wrath hanging over us (Eph. 2:1,12;
John 3:36). The final curse is to be 'outside' the holy city with
all who are morally unclean. This is the second death (Rev.
21:8; 22:15).

3. No re-entry

The measures God took to prevent them from re-entering the
garden were also symbolic. We have seen how the garden was
a prototype of the Israelite camp and tabernacle. This again
comes to mind when we read of the **'cherubim ... to guard
the way to the tree of life'** (3:24; cf. Exod. 26:1,31; 1 Kings
6:29). The ceremonial law underlined what was first dramatically portrayed to Adam and Eve. Sin has caused a barrier
between ourselves and God and has shut us all out of the place
where God has chosen to reveal himself and to call his home.
Sin pollutes, and nothing unclean can enter God's heaven.
There is now no easy access to God. The cherubim are associated with God's presence (Exod. 25:18-22; 1 Kings 6:23-28)
and the **'flaming sword'** with God's holy judgements (1 Chr.
21:16). It was made abundantly clear that there would be

immediate death for any outsider trying to gain entrance to God's holy sanctuary and to the tree of life.

The Israelites were later taught that God could be approached and life gained through the offering of sacrificial animals. It is no coincidence that immediately preceding this scene is the account of God's clothing Adam and Eve. No Israelite with knowledge of the Mosaic sanctuary and sacrifices could fail to see the connection between God's clothing the couple and the means for overcoming the barrier preventing access to God and life. The priests had to be clothed properly to hide their nakedness as they offered sacrifices in the tabernacle (Exod. 20:26; 28:42).

All these divinely appointed symbolic actions pointed forward to the Son of God who became a human being to represent us and be our substitute. He is the Seed of the woman, who has not only gained the victory over the tempter but has gained access for sinners into God's presence. Every aspect of the original curse he endured. Thorns were placed on his head. He knew what it was like to be an exile when he suffered outside the camp and cried out on the cross, 'My God, my God, why have you forsaken me?' (Heb. 13:12; Mark 15:34). Our Lord also experienced the deadly sword of God's wrath piercing his heart. In this way he has opened up the way for sinners to have eternal life and to look forward to a new earth where there will be no more curse, where God will freely meet with his people and they will have a right to the tree of life. This was symbolically expressed when Jesus cried, 'It is finished!' and the veil of the temple was torn from top to bottom (Mark 15:37-38; John 19:30). If we belong to Jesus we can come boldly to God (Heb. 10:19-22). The garden sanctuary with its tree of life was deliberately preserved by God, at least for some time, not only to remind them of what they had lost, but to suggest this hope of a return from exile.

8.
The origin of human worship and culture

Please read Genesis 4:1-26

In this chapter we learn about the first children (4:1-2), the first worship (4:3-7), the first murderer and the first martyr (4:8-16), the first godless society (4:17-24) and the first religious revival (4:25-26). The spotlight falls on Cain and his descendants, with a brief reference to godly Abel at the beginning and to a godly community at the end. We see the awful progress of sin and what it does to family and society. Yet, despite human depravity, the chapter bears witness to the grace and goodness of God.

Cain and Abel (4:1-16)

The account begins with Cain's attempt to come to God and ends with him going away from God. We are warned not to go 'in the way of Cain' (Jude 11). It is the way of unbelief and apostasy. Rather, we are to follow the example of Abel, who 'obtained a good testimony through faith' (Heb. 11:2,4,39).

Cain's godly background (4:1-2)

He was born into a God-fearing home. Adam and Eve were sinners, but they were not pagans. It is a great blessing to be brought up in a godly home, to be shown the way of salvation, to be encouraged to pray and worship the Lord. Parents are urged to bring up their children in the training and instruction of the Lord (Eph. 6:4).

Eve's spirituality is expressed in her reaction to the birth of her first-born son. At one level the baby was the result of the sexual union of Adam and Eve: **'Now Adam knew Eve his wife, and she conceived...'** (4:1). The Bible uses the word 'know' to describe this union. Among human beings sex is not just blind instinct but a conscious, intimate act and something which rightly belongs to man and woman within the marriage bond.

But though this baby was the result of such union, Eve was aware of something more. She called her son 'Cain', a name which sounds similar to the Hebrew word for 'acquire' or 'gain'. She had 'gained' a man from the Lord, or with the Lord's help.[1] While giving birth she would have felt for the first time the effects of God's curse on her personally. Her labour pains would have reminded her of God's judgement. But God had brought her through the sufferings and the name 'Cain' expressed her faith in the Lord. This curse associated with bearing children does not exclude mothers from God's salvation if they continue in the faith (1 Tim. 2:15).

Adam and Eve had another son, Abel. Nothing is made of his name in the text of Genesis, but Abel means 'breath' or 'vanity'. It was prophetic and a reminder of the frustration and fragile nature of physical life in this world under the curse. The word is developed by the 'Preacher': 'Vanity of vanities ... all is vanity' (Eccles. 1:2). This is a theme which runs through Scripture. 'Man is like a breath; his days are like a passing shadow' (Ps. 144:4). 'For what is your life? It is even a vapour that appears for a little time and then vanishes away' (James 4:14). For the godly as well as the ungodly, life in this world is subject to the effects of the Fall (Rom. 8:20-23).

As a background to what follows we are told that Cain was **'a tiller of the ground'**, like his father (4:2; cf. 2:15; 3:23) and that Abel was a **'keeper of sheep'**, like Jacob's sons (47:3).

Cain's religious worship (4:3-5)

Modern anthropologists have had to reassess their former views. They have been impressed by the fact that, even in those cultures cut off from monotheistic beliefs, there is the consciousness of a Supreme Being lying behind all their animistic and polytheistic ideas. The Bible tells us quite clearly that human beings originally worshipped the one true creator God. Cain and Abel brought offerings **'to the LORD'**. The two brothers had been taught by their parents the importance of honouring God in their lives and the need to bring sacrificial offerings.

The time

'And in the process of time' (Hebrew, 'at the end of days' — 4:3). It may be that we are to think of the brothers bringing their offerings at the end of a year's work, or at the end of the agricultural year.[2]

The offering

It is clear that Cain and Abel knew more about offerings than the text suggests. We are only given the minimum of information, but Moses wishes us to read these early incidents of sacrifice in the light of the later revelation. The two brothers brought gifts that were in keeping with their respective occupations. Cain offered a sacrifice from his vegetable and fruit harvest. It was a most obvious offering to bring. The law later speaks of such offerings as acceptable to God. As a shepherd, Abel brought an offering from his flock. The mention of the fat suggests that he killed some of his flock in order to make this offering.[3]

The result

We are not told how the brothers were made aware of God's reactions. Divine approval is often shown in Scripture when God sends fire to burn up the sacrifice (Lev. 9:24; 1 Kings 18:38; 2 Chr. 7:1). The important thing is that God accepted Abel and his offering and did not recognize Cain and his offering. This resulted in Cain's becoming very angry, and it showed on his face.

The reason

Why was Cain's offering rejected and his brother's accepted? This is no academic question but of crucial importance for us today. There is a right and a wrong way to worship God. Being brought up in a Christian home does not guarantee that our worship is automatically acceptable to him. It is possible for the worship to be correct and yet for the person worshipping not to be in a right position before God. In the case of Cain there was a rejection of both the person and his offering. Maybe there was something wrong with the gift as well as the giver. We can make a number of observations.

Firstly, Abel, Adam's second son, offered first-born animals to the Lord (4:4). On the other hand, Cain, who was the first-born son, offered neither firstlings nor first-fruits. The law was later to stress that when corn, vegetables and fruit were offered the first-fruits were important (Exod. 22:29). Abel offered **'their fat'**, which was considered the choicest part of the animal (Lev. 3:16). The narrative suggests that, while Abel offered the pick of the flock, Cain merely offered some of the produce of the land. Already we see a different attitude. Our inner spiritual condition can show itself in the way we serve the Lord. Is it the case with us that anything goes? Do we offer to God what costs us little? David said, 'Nor will I offer burnt offerings to the LORD my God with that which costs me nothing' (2 Sam. 24:24).

Secondly, the first-born son had an important place in ancient Near-Eastern family circles, as we see from the lives of Isaac and Jacob. On the other hand, God often accepted the second-born above the first-born: Isaac not Ishmael; Jacob not Esau; Ephraim not Manasseh. This is the case with Abel. God often chooses what the world regards as second-rate. He takes the weak and the despised so that 'no flesh should glory in his presence' (1 Cor. 1:26-29).

Thirdly, it is significant that Abel, the second-born, should have offered firstlings from his flock and that he should have been the one who was accepted. The law indicated that the first-born son belonged to God and it laid down rules for redeeming the first-born by offering the firstlings of the sacrificial animals (Exod. 13:2,13-15). Was God teaching Cain and Abel that there is forgiveness and acceptance only through the shedding of blood? We are told in Hebrews 11:4 that it was by faith that Abel 'offered a more excellent sacrifice than Cain'. Now faith is never a leap into the dark. It is always exercised in the context of divine revelation. It is a response to God's Word. Abel's offering was not a good idea of his own. Why would Abel deliberately kill one of God's creatures as a sacrifice to God? Death may be familiar to us, but it was not so for that first family. They ate vegetables and fruit. The first experience of killing was when God clothed Adam and Eve with the skins of animals. The way of covering shame and nakedness, the way of acceptance before God, was via the sacrificial death of another. Abel learned this from his parents and he believed what God had revealed to them. To worship God sinners must come through the way God has ordained. It was revealed to Moses that without the blood of sacrifice there was no atonement (Lev. 17:11).

Fourthly, the fact that Cain was angry showed his wrong spirit and his unwillingness to accept what God was teaching them both. Cain had no right to be angry at God's ruling. The Lord is absolutely free within his infinite being to do exactly what he pleases. If he chooses to accept one and reject another, that is his prerogative. We sinful creatures have no right to complain. God is not a prisoner to our views. We find this as hard a lesson to learn as Cain did. Is God unfair? Not at all. Will you find fault with God? (Rom. 9:10-24). Cain did not deserve any favour or blessing from God. How many religious people are like Cain in their reaction to the message which tells us that we can be accepted by God only through the atoning blood of Christ, and in no other way?

Cain's slavery to sin (4:6-8)

Cain was angry not only with God, but with his brother. The Lord's reply to Cain's anger reveals the love of God. He was out to win the rebel. He pointed to the way of forgiveness and salvation and warned Cain of the danger he was in. Cain, however, refused to humble himself and to accept the way God had appointed. Instead, he became more and more a slave to his own passions and lusts. Sin is likened to a wild animal ready to pounce. There was already anger in his heart, and God pointed this out. He also directed him to the way of escape. But Cain hardened his heart. What a power sin has over our lives if we do not have it dealt with by God! Cain would not even allow the Lord to talk him out of his sinful actions.

Cain's refusal to listen to God led him to murder his brother. Abel was the first human to die. His death was not the result of God's general judgement on sin, what we call natural causes. The first death was actually the result of one human being's killing another. It must have horrified Adam and Eve. What had they produced? It was a callous, ruthless, violent act. Cain committed the dreadful deed when the two brothers were both in the field, in the uncultivated open plain where the wild animals roamed. In the Sinai law, if a crime was committed in the open plain, out of range of help, away from the camp, it was proof of premeditation. No one would have heard Abel's cries for help. Oh the treachery, the deceitfulness of sin! How ugly it is!

The first murder was also the first martyrdom. It was the result of a religious crisis. The one accepted by God was persecuted by one who was not accepted. Jesus refers to Abel as the first person to die for his faith (Matt. 23:35). Here was the first evidence of that hostility prophesied earlier (3:15). Stephen was like Abel. He too was put to death for his faith. Christ's death was also due to religious hatred, but his death was not a martyr's death. While the blood of Abel and other martyrs cries for God's day of vengeance, the blood of Jesus cries salvation to all who believe. Christ himself experienced the day of vengeance as he hung on the cross so that persecutors like Saul of Tarsus might have forgiveness and salvation. The blood of Jesus 'speaks better things than that of Abel' (Heb. 12:24). Nevertheless, God will punish all unrepentant sinners on the Day of Judgement (Rev. 19:2).

Cain's punishment (4:9-16)

The scene is again reminiscent of the law court scenario in the previous chapter. The Judge questions the criminal, sentences him and executes the sentence. How the Lord came to Cain and spoke to him we do not know.

Probing (4:9)

The Lord's question, **'Where is Abel your brother?'**, encouraged the culprit to own up. Hearing a question like that would make most people wince and go bright red if they were guilty. When Adam was challenged by God (3:10), at least he told the truth even if he tried to blame others. But Cain told a bare-faced lie: **'I do not know.'** He followed this up with an impertinent question of his own in order to cover up his tracks: **'Am I my brother's keeper?'** Cain's question betrayed a heart already hardened through the murder of his brother. He denied outright the responsibility he ought to have had for his younger brother. We have responsibilities to blood relatives, to the family of God and to our neighbours in general. John, in urging his hearers to love one another, uses the story of Cain as an example of people who do the very opposite. He hated his brother. The Christian is not to have such hatred, for 'Whoever hates his brother is a murderer' (1 John 3:11-12,15).

Prosecuting (4:10)

The Judge who sees all and knows all confronted Cain with his crime: **'What have you done?'** Cain could not hide his action. God declared that Abel's blood **'cries out to me from the ground'**. We speak of wrongs that 'cry out' to be put right. In the Bible victims of injustice are described as crying out to God for vindication and vengeance (Exod. 22:22-23,26-27; Rev. 6:9-10). For the first time we are introduced to the word 'blood'. Blood is associated with human and animal life: 'The life of the flesh is in the blood' (Lev. 17:11). Blood spilt suggests a violent death such as murder or sacrifice. For the first time a human life was taken through a brother's anger and hatred. It was a most heinous crime, for it expressed hatred of God, seeing that humans were created in God's image. To be 'guilty of blood' was to be guilty of murder. The shedding of human blood was regarded in the law as the most polluting of all things. Such blood-shedding polluted the land. Paradoxically, 'According to the law almost all things are purged with blood, and without shedding of blood there is no remission' (Heb. 9:22). Blood sacrifice has already been assumed in connection with the proper covering of Adam and Eve's nakedness and in Abel's offering. All were pointers to the Lamb of God, Jesus Christ, who offered the one perfect sacrifice to atone for sin, even the sin of murder.

Punishing (4:11-12)

Cain was cursed **'from the earth'** (or 'ground', as in 4:10). While Adam, and humanity in general, experienced the effects of the divine curse *on* the ground, Cain himself was directly cursed *from* the ground. His punishment was appropriate to him as a tiller of the ground. The ground would **'no longer yield its strength'** to him, meaning it would produce very little. He would also become **'a fugitive and a vagabond'**, a homeless, wandering vagrant on the earth. As Adam and Eve were exiled from God's garden, so Cain experienced another type of exile. His punishment meant that he was banished from the ground. He was not literally put to death for his crime (cf. 9:6). It was, nevertheless, a death sentence. This is clearly suggested in Cain's reply. He was driven from the fertile ground, from his home and also from the gracious presence of the Lord (4:14,16; cf. 2 Sam. 13:37-38; 14:23-24). Like so many of the incidents in these early chapters, Cain's punishment has a symbolic element to it. It is a vivid presentation of hell. Hell means exclusion from the new earth and from the face of God. It is to be deprived of all that is comfortable and restful, and to be tormented continually.

Protesting (4:13-14)

Cain was not pleading for forgiveness, as some commentators have suggested. The context gives no indication of a humble, repentant spirit. Cain regarded his punishment as worse than death. It is ironic that the one who had recently killed his brother was afraid of someone killing him. Kidner comments, 'Cain's protest is ... in contrast to the penitent thief's admission that "we receive the due reward of our deeds"' [4]

Protecting (4:15)

Though Cain's curse was drastic and symbolic of death, it was not the ultimate punishment. In this world God's wrath is always mixed with love. Cain's sentence was not reduced as a result of his protest, but he did receive God's protection from premature death. Any members of the family who engaged in revenge killing would themselves be punished: **'Vengeance shall be taken on him sevenfold.'** Seven in the Bible symbolizes completeness. Those taking revenge would feel the full weight of the divine anger. In this way God undertook to restrain human sinfulness and put an end to further bloodshed. While God, in his wrath, abandons people to their sinful desires (Rom. 1:24,26,28), he also, in his mercy, curbs human wickedness. What the mark or sign was that God gave to Cain we have no idea, but it had the effect of giving him protection. God is merciful and displays his kindness towards unrepentant sinners. He gives them every opportunity to change and seek the Lord (2 Sam. 14:14).

Parting (4:16)

The man who had been sentenced to be a wanderer (Hebrew, *'nad'*) settled in the Land of Wandering (**'Nod'**). He moved 'east of Eden' and away from all that would remind him of God. Cain can be compared to Judas Iscariot, who **'went out from the presence of the Lord'** into the night (4:16; John 13:30). Like Cain, Judas was one of the serpent's 'seed' (John 13:27; 1 John 3:12). He serves as a warning to all professing Christians. Let us firmly take hold of God's way of acceptance through the merits of Christ's blood and righteousness.

The godless society (4:17-24)

The chapter turns to Cain's descendants. As always in Genesis, the descendants of the non-elect sons are recorded before the elect line. Ishmael's line is considered before Isaac's and Esau's before Jacob's.

'Where did Cain get his wife from?' has been, and still is, one of those questions raised by scoffers to ridicule people who accept these early biblical accounts as historical. In return we could question the evolutionary atheist about similar issues. How did reproduction evolve in the animal world? Dawkins admits that 'There are many theories of why sex exists, and none of them is knock-down convincing... Maybe one day I'll summon up the courage to tackle it in full and write a whole book on the origin of sex.'[5] A true scientist will admit to much ignorance in his particular field of study. We need never feel embarrassed about admitting that we do not know the answer to every problem in the Bible. On the question of Cain's wife we are informed that Adam and Eve had many sons and daughters (5:4) and we do not know how long after the birth of Cain the incidents recorded in chapter 4 took place. It is very possible that Cain could have married one of his sisters, or even a niece of his.

The Bible does not underestimate human ability to achieve great and notable works and to help relieve some of the effects of the curse. Here we learn three things about early attempts at civilization.

1. Citizenship

Cain **'built a city'**. We must not think of a city like London or New York. In Old Testament times the word 'city' applied to any human settlement, whether great or small. Cain had obviously been trying to set up home in the Land of Wandering. Perhaps he thought that with a wife and a new baby it was time to settle down. He therefore made the first effort to erect a permanent settlement for his family. The city was named after his son Enoch. Cain was looking to a future and he saw it in his son. He had great hopes for him, as many people have today in their children. The verb in the original suggests that Cain did not complete what he began: 'He was building a city.'[6] Cain's judgement meant that he never did settle down. He had no contented life. How easy it is to think that life will be different if we can only get a settled job, get married, have a family, move to a new area! But it never works like that. Human restlessness can never be ultimately satisfied by seeking change in our outward circumstances. The true need is for a change at the centre of our lives. What Cain needed is what we all need — a new heart, a radical change in our innermost being (Deut. 10:16; 30:6). Our Lord insisted, 'You must be born again' (John 3:7).

The Bible can be seen as 'a tale of two cities'. Here we see the beginnings of an attempt to build a lasting settlement to the glory of man. The end of such endeavours is described in Revelation 18. On the other hand, God is building a city which will be a monument to his glory (Heb. 11:16; Rev. 21:10 – 22:5). To which city do you belong?

2. Cultural activity

The attempts at forming a settled community led to rapid advances by the descendants of Cain in the arts of civilization. Though human beings are under God's curse as a result of the great rebellion, they have many godlike characteristics. The picture we are given is of human beings picking themselves up and seeking to better their situation, both in rural and urban areas. With **'Jabal'** we have the origin of the Bedouin lifestyle, the semi-nomads who live in tents and make a living by rearing animals (4:20). He was not merely a shepherd but a livestock breeder, trading in a wide variety of beasts to assist humans in travel and employment. All this represents cultural advance. **'Jubal'** is described as the ancestor of those who have musical ability (4:21). **'Harp and flute'** are more sophisticated varieties of what would be better translated 'lyre and pipe'. These are among the oldest and simplest types of musical instruments. Finally, we read of **'Tubal-Cain'**, who was involved in bronze and iron work (4:22). The word translated **'instructor'** actually means 'sharpener' or 'hammerer'. Long before smelting and forging, surface deposits of iron and copper were hammered out and filed down. We should not underestimate the great advances made in those early days.

We admire human creativity and ingenuity. Such inventions have helped to make life bearable and alleviate many of the effects of the curse. The godly and the ungodly alike are beneficiaries of these advances. What unbelievable progress was made during the twentieth century! But whereas the godless world boasts in its own achievements and seeks to make a name for itself, the godly are to recognize that every good gift comes from God and desire to give God the glory.

The reference to **'the sister of Tubal-Cain'** is intriguing (4:22). Nothing further is said about her. It is a reminder that we are dealing with real people who actually existed.

Corrupt society

In this society there was no thought of God. While there may have been certain restraints at first due to people's having a general reverence for God, as time went on this would have dimmed. By the sixth generation we have a person who seems to have thrown aside all restraint — an attitude summed up in Lamech's song of hate, violence and revenge. However clever, inventive and knowledgeable human beings become, they cannot handle their own lusts and passions.

Sin affected married life: **'Lamech took for himself two wives'** (4:19). Bigamy and polygamy go against the pattern which God set down at the beginning.

Not only did society become more sexually permissive, it became ever more violent. In contrast to Adam's love poem (2:23), we have Lamech's cruel verse (4:23-24). We are not to think that Lamech had killed two different people. The same event is being described in two ways according to the manner of Hebrew poetry.[7] Lamech's **'seventy-sevenfold'** vengeance must be interpreted in the light of his boastful first words. It means that he had a very high opinion of himself and had taken it upon himself to gain revenge by retaliating far in excess of any wrong received. Unlike his ancestor Cain, who sought divine protection, he was self-sufficient and ruthlessly vindictive. God curbed this spirit by introducing punishments that fitted the crime (9:6; Exod. 21:23-25). When people live without regard for God they soon lose a proper respect for human life. On the other hand, Jesus urged his disciples to forgive, not just seven times, but 'seventy times seven' (Matt. 18:21-22).

The godly community (4:25-26)

In contrast to the previous paragraph, we find that God is central. He is remembered, trusted and worshipped.

1. The first ray of hope — a special 'seed' (4:25)

God used Adam and Eve's children to show them something
of what he meant by the cryptic words to the snake (3:15).

Firstly, in the murder of righteous Abel by his brother, they
had begun to see something of the hostility between the snake's
brood and the woman's seed, but Eve saw in the birth of Seth
God's activity to overcome the snake's intentions. She said in
faith, **'For God has appointed another seed for me instead
of Abel'** (4:25). The name **'Seth'** sounds similar to that for
'set' or 'appoint'. In 3:15 God said he would 'put', or 'set',
hostility between the snake's seed and the woman's seed.

Secondly, it is interesting to compare Eve's comment on
the birth of Cain with her remark over the birth of Seth. Instead of saying, 'I have gained another man with the Lord's
help' (cf. 4:1), she now says, **'God has appointed another
seed...'** 'Seed' in place of 'man' picks up the word 'seed' in
3:15. Eve was aware that God was remembering his promise.
She was looking forward to a special 'seed'. The whole of
Genesis is taken up with developing this theme of a particular
family line.

Thirdly, killing the righteous 'seed' and raising up another
'seed' to replace him is a picture of what happened to the
fulfilment of God's promises in Jesus. Cruel hands killed him,
but God raised him up. Other examples of this theme are to be
found in Genesis. Abraham offered his unique son, Isaac, and
in a sense received him back from the dead (Gen. 22; Heb.
11:17-19). Joseph was taken for dead and yet rose to a position of pre-eminence.

2. The second ray of hope — spiritual revival (4:26)

While the forces of spiritual darkness were at work in the descendants of Cain, the unseen hand of God was active in

keeping his promises and carrying out his purposes. To Seth a son was born and **'He named him Enosh'**, a name often suggesting human frailty and weakness (see Ps. 8:4; 103:15). But the significant thing is not so much the boy and his name as the fact that during his lifetime, **'Men began to call on the name of the Lord.'** At a time when the worldly civilization was out to make a name for itself and boasting of its enterprises and achievements, there were those who worshipped the Lord.

The Hebrew suggests there was a general calling on God. What is recorded is nothing short of a revival of true religion. Before the cultural revival in the days of Lamech and his sons we have this revival of spiritual life. What does it mean 'to call on the name of the Lord'? The word 'name' has occurred frequently thus far. Everyone and everything was given a name and under authority. But we are not told that God was given a name. He is under the authority of no one. Rather, everything owes its existence to God. The word 'name' in the Bible often refers to a person's nature and characteristics. It stands for all that the person is. Calling on 'the name of the Lord' means calling on God himself. To 'call on' God's name is a familiar expression in Genesis (12:8; 13:4; 21:33; 26:25). In these contexts it is used as a technical term for worship. It is associated with the offering of sacrifice. The chapter began with Abel offering an acceptable sacrifice to God. Because Cain's unacceptable worship was rejected, Cain persecuted to death the true worshipper. Nevertheless, God revived his work in the days of Enosh so that many people were worshipping, as Abel had worshipped, in a way that was acceptable to God.

While Cain and his descendants were setting up their humanistic city, another city, a heavenly one, was developing. People were being brought together for the first time in public worship. This worship was associated with the line of Seth, who replaced Abel. There is no indication, however, that the calling on God was confined to the descendants of Seth. The

cultural advances associated with Cain's family would have
been known and experienced by all including Seth's line. Likewise, when God revived his work among his people it probably had wide-ranging effects on society at large. This has
been the case throughout history. Times of spiritual awakening bring many hardened sinners to seek God's salvation and
there is a general fear of God. 'Whoever calls on the name of
the LORD shall be saved' (Joel 2:32; Rom. 10:13).

Part 3:
What Adam produced (5:1 – 6:8)

9.
The original register of births and deaths

Please read Genesis 5:1-32

The heading, **'This is the book of the genealogy of Adam'**, reminds us that a new major section of Genesis begins at this point. In this section we have the list of a special family line from Adam to Noah (5:1-32) and a statement of what conditions were like in the time of Noah, with an announcement of universal judgement (6:1-8).

The main theme of chapter 5 is the reign of death and the hope of deliverance. In chapter 4 we were given the names of some of the descendants of Cain, but nothing was said about their ages or the time of their death. Here we have the first register of births and deaths. Just as a registrar's certificate has a special layout, so this list follows a rigid pattern: the father's age on the birth of his son; the number of years the father lived after the son's birth; his age at death. Our attention is drawn in particular to three entries: those for Adam, Enoch and Noah.

Introduction (5:1-2)

The heading (5:1a)

Besides introducing a new section, the heading shows us the importance of particular families. The recurring phrase, **'the**

genealogy of', helps to bind the book of Genesis together and keeps reminding us that God has a plan through a special human line of descent. It acts as a big signpost encouraging us to look forward to the promised 'Seed' (3:15). Many false hopes would be shattered before the promise materialized. Eve's first-born son, for instance, turned out to be one of the devil's brood. The headings, however, keep nudging us to look to the fulfilment of God's purposes. At the end of the previous section the first hint was given that Abel was a pointer to the promised 'Seed' and that Seth was God's provision of 'another seed' in place of Abel. This new heading, therefore, focuses on Adam and what he produced through Seth. The genealogy traces a single line of descent from Adam to Noah. Later, another list will take us in a straight line from Noah's son Shem to Terah, the father of Abraham (11:10-26). This special line is shown to exist through God's gracious activity and will finally result in blessing for all who call out to the Lord for salvation (Acts 2:21-39).

To the usual heading there is added, **'This is the book of ...'** 'Book' can cover anything from a short legal certificate to a work the size of Deuteronomy (Deut. 24:1; 31:24-26). We read in Numbers 21:14 of 'the Book of the Wars of the LORD'. This was a written source from which Moses quoted. It may be that Moses used a written document here too. The genealogical lists, written on tablets of clay or stone, may date from an earlier time than that of Moses, or may have been collected together and written up into a separate book under his direction. It is possible that Moses made use of this same collection later in 9:28-29 and 11:10-26 when he picks up at the point where he left off in 5:32. All this reminds us that the formation of Scripture involved considerable human effort. It was not all given directly from heaven like the Ten Commandments. All Scripture is God-breathed and is exactly what God wanted to say, but it often involved God's servants in hard, painstaking work. Remember what Luke tells us about the production of his Gospel (Luke 1:1-4).

A summary statement (5:1b-2)

This recalls the words of Genesis 1:26-28 and prepares us for what follows.

Firstly, a contrast is drawn between the statements that **'God created man'** (5:1; cf. 1:27) and that Adam 'begot a son' (5:3). There is a world of difference between God's creative activity and human creativity. God created Adam and Eve, whereas Adam and those following him were procreating.

Secondly, the reminder that God created man **'in the likeness of God'** (5:1; cf. 1:26-27) parallels the statement that Adam fathered a son 'in his own likeness, after his image' (5:3). Despite the great rebellion, the truth needed to be re-emphasized that men and women were created in God's image. The image, though marred as a result of the Fall, was not obliterated entirely. It was passed on from father to son by natural reproduction (see 9:6).

Thirdly, the fact that God **'blessed them'** (5:2; cf. 1:28) is illustrated in the genealogy from Adam to Noah, which includes the refrain, 'He had sons and daughters' (5:4,7,10, etc.). Again, in spite of the Fall, human beings were blessed with many children and long life. This was typical of God's blessing in Old Testament times (Job 42:16-17).

Fourthly, we learn that God **'called their name Mankind'** (5:2); this parallels the statement in verse 3 that Adam **'named his son'** Seth. Just as Adam and Eve gave a name to their son, so God named Adam. We have not been told this before. The Hebrew word *'adam'* can be used as the proper name for the first man, 'Adam', or to refer to people in general, 'humankind'. In verses 1 and 3 it clearly means 'Adam', but in verse 2 both ideas are present. Kidner comments on 'the fact that though the male, as head, bore the name of the race, it takes the two sexes together to express what God means by "human" '.[1]

The whole introduction, taken with what follows, plays another important role. It depicts God as a Father. God fathered a son by creation while Adam fathered a son by procreation. Human beings are 'the offspring of God' (Acts 17:28-29). Seth bore the image of Adam, his father, while Adam bore the image of God. Luke reminds us that Seth was the son of Adam and Adam was the son of God (Luke 3:38). God's fatherly care is expressed by the reference to God's blessing his children and ensuring a future for them. As the genealogical table in chapter 10 will show, God is the Father of all humanity through Noah's sons, who are descendants of Adam. It is interesting, however, that it is in connection with the chosen line that we have this emphasis on God as Father. This is the line that leads to Abraham and his 'seed'. God is especially the Father of those who believe.

Notwithstanding human disobedience and its effects, God commits himself to blessing them through 'the seed' of the woman. The New Testament reminds us that the promised 'Seed' is Jesus Christ and through faith in him, we 'are all sons of God' and can call God 'Father' (Gal. 3:26 – 4:7).

Ten generations (5:3-32)

Going through this chapter is like walking through a cemetery. It can be quite a fascinating experience looking at old tombstones. A lot can be learnt just from examining the names and the ages of people. Imagine tiptoeing through the graveyard of those who died at the beginning of human history. What do we learn?

The names and ages of the men

In the first place, some of the names are very like the ones we read of in the previous chapter. **'Cainan'** (5:9-14) is similar to 'Cain'; **'Jared'** (5:15-20) to 'Irad' (4:18); **'Mahalalel'** (5:12-17) to 'Mehujael' (4:18); **'Methuselah'** (5:21-27) to 'Methushael' (4:18). There is also an **'Enoch'** and a **'Lamech'** in both tables (4:17-19,23-24; 5:18-31). This does not indicate that the two lists have become confused, as some scholars maintain. We all know how certain names become popular and then go out of fashion. At one time in Britain it was popular to name girls after flowers — Rose, Lily, Iris, Daisy. It should not be a surprise to find similar happenings in ancient times.

Secondly, the continual reference to **'sons and daughters'** bears silent testimony to the divine blessing (1:28; 5:2). Despite the curse God was gracious. If only people realized it, it is God who sees to it that there are succeeding generations. Untold things could go wrong to wipe out the whole human race. If it is through God's anger that we are consumed (Ps. 90:7) it is also true that it is through his mercies that we are not consumed (Lam. 3:22).

Thirdly, the precise details, concerning both the man's age at the time of the birth of the son who is next in line and his age at death, emphasize that we are dealing with real, not mythological, people. When Luke came to write up the family tree of Jesus, he went back to the people mentioned in this chapter. They are as real as Mary and Joseph and Jesus himself. Many of the names we know nothing more about, other than that they lived, had children and died. History is made up for the most part of people like that. It is unlikely that any of us will ever get our names into the history books — only a brief epitaph on a tombstone at best, another name in the registrar's book of births and deaths, just the bare fact that we existed on Planet Earth in the twenty-first century. Nevertheless, each one of us is known to God and bears the divine image, however blurred it may be.

While we pass by so many names which mean nothing to us, there are some which cause us to pause. Adam is an obvious case. What a remarkable find! We have found the epitaph of the first man who ever lived on the earth! It reads: **'All the days that Adam lived were nine hundred and thirty years; and he died'** (5:5). Adam had a unique beginning, but his end was the same as that of everyone else in the graveyard — 'He died.' This is what God had said would happen for disobeying his command. As we pass among the tombstones, the sight becomes monotonous and depressing. Seth died aged 912; Enosh died aged 905; Cainan died aged 910; Mahalalel died aged 895. Their bodies returned to the ground from which they were taken — dust to dust, ashes to ashes (2:7; 3:19).

What great ages they all lived! Jared lived to be 962; Methuselah died at the age of 969. The ancient Sumerians also kept genealogical tables. Texts have been found which list ancient kings who are said to have reigned for thousands of years before the Flood. They bear witness to a tradition that men lived much longer before the Flood than after. The Bible gives us the true figures.

Whether we are meant to use the ages of these men to work out when Adam was created is a debatable point. Henry Morris recognizes the possibility that there may be gaps in the genealogies.[2] It is significant that in this chapter we are given ten generations from Adam to Noah. This might suggest that we only have a representative list of names to cover the period from the creation to the Flood. Biblical writers do miss names out for various reasons. The most well-known example is Matthew's genealogy of Jesus. He arranges the table into neat groups of fourteen names each. In order to achieve this during the monarchy period, he misses out Uzziah's father, grandfather and great-grandfather (Matt. 1:8) His purpose is not to give a full list but to show that Jesus is of the right genealogical line. Whether there are any missing names in Genesis 5 it is impossible to say. What is certain is that the men's ages were not given for us to work out the exact date for the beginning of creation, as Archbishop Ussher tried to do with his figure of 4004 B.C. The ten names of real people from Adam to Noah are primarily given to show God's chosen line through Adam's son Seth. Their great ages indicate that hundreds, and perhaps thousands, of years separated the time from Adam to Noah. The numbers also indicate that, however long they lived, death caught up with them.

In looking at the great ages of these men, it is interesting to note that they all fall short of a thousand. Many of those named lived for over 900 years. Methuselah, who lived the longest, fell short of a thousand by only thirty-one years. Is there any significance in this? As actual objects and events were used to convey spiritual truth in Genesis 3 and 4, the numbers in this chapter may be carrying a symbolic meaning. John's Apocalypse encourages us to believe this to be so. Many of the items in the early chapters of Genesis appear in the last book of the Bible and it is there that we find reference to the thousand-year period (Rev. 20:1-7). Being the cube of ten, a thousand conveyed the idea of perfect wholeness, or a total amount (Ps. 50:10; Deut. 7:9; Eccles. 6:6). The figure also suggested a vast number or period of time (Deut. 1:11; Ps. 90:4). It is used symbolically in Ezekiel 48 and Revelation 7. To die at one hundred came to be symbolic of an untimely death (Isa. 65:20). Genesis 5 may be emphasizing that, despite their long lives, these people died prematurely. They really did live to these great ages, but the figures are also symbolic of the truth that they all fell short of God's best. They died while they were still in their hundreds. God did not allow any of them to reach the thousand mark. They failed to attain their full potential. Adam's disobedience meant that human beings would always fail to reach the proper span of life. Instead of going on with God into the millennium, their lives were cut short. No one lived and reigned with God a thousand years. Death reigned and the Evil One had gained the victory. Despite God's continued blessing in granting many descendants, death had the last word.

With this background in mind, the book of Revelation demonstrates how the seed of the woman gains the victory over the Evil One and that Christ and his people reign while Satan is bound. The saints are resurrected to live a thousand years (Rev. 20:4). They reach the proper span of life. Through his death, Christ has destroyed 'him who had the power of death, that is, the devil' (Heb. 2:14). Jesus said, 'I am the resurrection and the life. He who believes in me, even though he dies, he shall live. And whoever lives and believes in me shall never die' (John 11:25-26).

Enoch

But, wait, a gravestone is missing! Can anyone find Enoch's tomb? There is no epitaph concerning him. In the registrar's office there is a record of his birth, but nothing about his death. The only information we have is that he was last seen aged 365 (5:23). What happened to Enoch? In contrast to the usual phrase, **'and he died'**, the Bible tells us that **'He was not'** (5:24). It means that Enoch did not experience death. This is confirmed by what follows: **'... for God took him'**. Enoch broke the monotonous line of those taken by death. Death did not take Enoch; God took him. He was taken 'so that he did not see death' (Heb. 11:5). Can you imagine Enoch's friends and family searching for him, just as the sons of the prophets tried looking for Elijah when he was taken? Fifty men searched three days for Elijah without success (2 Kings 2:17). Something similar must have happened when Enoch disappeared.

Enoch's name is the seventh in the list, a point made by Jude (Jude 14). The seventh position is often specially favoured in biblical genealogies and this was certainly true of Enoch. Additional information is given in his case which points us forward to Christ.

Firstly, it was demonstrated to those ancient people that *God*, not death, *was the final and ultimate power*. There is a close connection between sin, Satan and death. Death is the result of that first sin. The devil was involved in that sin. He lured humanity into sin and death and he holds them in slavery (Heb. 2:14-15). In Enoch's case, God showed his power over Satan, sin and death in anticipation of what he would do through 'the Seed' of the woman.

Secondly, *Enoch's life in this world was very short compared with the others in the list*. He only lived on earth for 365 years. We have the interesting situation of a father who lived the shortest time producing a son who lived the longest. If there is symbolism in the ages of those like Methuselah who failed to live a thousand years, then Enoch's age could also have symbolic meaning. 365 is the number of days in a solar year. This suggests that his life was a rounded whole. The earthly life of the seventh man may not have been half as long as that of his father or his son, but it was certainly complete, whereas theirs fell short. **'All the days of Enoch'** added up to a recognized period of time, a year of years. Enoch's life on earth fulfilled its course. Though he did not stay long in this world, he was removed in the full vigour of his life at the appointed time. How like our Lord he was in this! At the age of about thirty-three Jesus was taken up to glory. His life on earth was short. It did not even reach half of the seventy-year allotted span (Ps. 90:10), yet it was complete and fulfilled in every way. He finished the course set out for him. He was received up at the appointed time (Luke 9:51; John 12:23).

Thirdly, *Enoch had the privilege of being taken up bodily into the immediate presence of God*. In this he points us forward to our Lord's ascension. Jesus did have a tomb, but his body did not lie in it for long. He arose from the dead and ascended to the right hand of the Father. The words on the tomb are not, 'Here lies Jesus Christ,' but 'He is not here; for he is risen, as he said' (Matt. 28:6).

Fourthly, God indicated to those people of long ago that *there is a life beyond this present, earthly existence*. Enoch did not stop living, but he did not go on living in this world.

What happened to Enoch also indicated that *there is a bodily existence beyond this present world order*. His translation anticipates the day when the last trumpet will be sounded and the dead in Christ will rise first and when we who are alive will be changed. We shall be caught up to meet the Lord in the air and so we shall ever be with the Lord (1 Cor. 15:51-52; 1 Thess. 4:16-17). For us this hope is built, not on the negative, 'He was not, for God took him', but on Christ's death, resurrection and ascension. We have a surer basis for our future hope. Equally, there is no excuse for unbelief.

What was the secret of Enoch's life on earth? It is emphasized, through repetition, that **'Enoch walked with God'** (5:22,24). This is in contrast to Adam, who hid when he heard the sound of God walking in the garden (3:8). The same expression is used to describe Noah, Abraham and Isaac (6:9; 24:40; 48:15). The prophet Micah reminds all God's people of their duty to walk humbly with God (Micah 6:8). The phrase suggests a special intimacy with God. Enoch enjoyed a personal relationship with God. It is interpreted later as pleasing God (Heb. 11:5-6). 'Walking with God' is associated with those who experience God's favour and blessing. It refers to those who are in a right relationship with God and worship him alone.

They are ones to whom God reveals himself, to whom he makes special promises, and in whom God confides and shares secrets.

Instead of saying that Enoch 'lived' three hundred years, and fathered children, as in the other cases, it states that **'Enoch walked with God three hundred years and begot sons and daughters'** (5:22). 'Walked with God' is substituted for 'living'. This was life for Enoch, fellowship with God. It did not stop him engaging in family life. He was no hermit or monk. On the other hand, he did not make the things of this world his life, not even his family. God was his life. This life with God could not end. To prove it God took him. As one commentator puts it, 'He changed places but not company.' The psalmist could say:

> … I am continually with you;
> You hold me by my right hand;
> You will guide me with your counsel,
> And afterwards receive me to glory
>
> (Ps. 73:23-24).

Enoch is an example of someone who found that life in its fulness was associated with fellowship with God and pleasing God. God is the fountain of life and in his presence is fulness of joy (Ps. 36:9; 16:11). Enoch's translation to heaven was a reminder of God's gracious intention to undo the effects of the curse.

Lamech

Another stone of note in our imaginary graveyard is that raised to Lamech. How different is this Lamech from the one of Cain's line! The fascinating thing about Lamech's epitaph is what he said when he named his son Noah. **'Noah'** means 'rest', but it sounds similar to the word for 'comfort'. So there is a play on

words when Lamech expresses the hope that Noah **'will comfort us concerning our work and the toil of our hands,
because of the ground which the** Lord **has cursed'** (5:29;
cf. 3:17). Lamech was very aware of the pain that life under
the curse had brought. Every time he worked the land he was
conscious of the curse. But Lamech treasured the promise that
God had made in 3:15. He was looking for one who would
bring relief from the curse.

Noah did not bring the consolation for which his father
hoped. Nevertheless, he did become a pointer to the future
deliverer (1 Peter 3:20-21). Lamech did not live as long as
most of the other men in the list. He was 777 years old when
he died. This was his true age, but the threefold sevens also
suggest that his death was not untimely. Seven is an important
number, gaining its significance from the seventh day of the
creation week. Among other things, seven denoted completeness. His age informs us that Lamech completed his allotted
span on earth. Though he might have been expected to live for
another 150 years, his life was not suddenly cut short like those
who perished in the Flood. Lamech did not live as long as his
father Methuselah, yet this is not considered a special judgement. Abraham did not live as long as his father Terah, nevertheless, he is said to have reached a ripe old age ('in a good
old age, an old man and full of years' —25:8). The same was
true of Lamech.

Noah

With the mention of Noah the standard formula is changed. It
does not say, 'and Noah lived ...', but **'And Noah was five
hundred years old...'** Also, not one son but three are named
— **'Shem, Ham and Japheth'**. Why all three are mentioned
will become clear later. The expected statement concerning
the remainder of Noah's life does not appear until 9:28-29.

Inserted into the genealogy at this point is the account of the Flood. The Flood forms part of the history of the chosen line. It is part of the history of redemption. What is significant, however, is that the Flood did not destroy any member of the chosen line mentioned. Noah's father died five years before the Flood. If there are no gaps in the names, Methuselah would have been Noah's grandfather and he died in the year of the Flood. Noah and his sons passed safely through the Flood.

10.
The origin of the Flood

Please read Genesis 6:1-8

The passage shows how human depravity increased to the point
where it became necessary for God to act to destroy what he
had created. It also draws attention to God's grief and grace.

Life in the pre-Flood period (6:1-4)

Who were 'the sons of God'?

Most scholars would agree that this is one of the most difficult
passages of the Old Testament to interpret. The main problem
revolves around the identification of the **'sons of God'**. Does
the term refer to angels, to the godly line of Seth, or to rulers?
We shall consider the various options before taking a fresh
look at the evidence. What does the phrase mean?

1. Angels

This is an ancient interpretation. The phrase 'sons of God' is a
recognized way of referring to supernatural beings (Job 1:6;
38:7). On this understanding, they were angelic beings who
had in some way contracted unions with the daughters of human
beings. 2 Peter 2:4 and Jude 6 are said to support this view.

While liberal scholars have accepted it as a clear example of myth in Genesis,[1] many evangelicals have rejected it on the authority of Jesus' words that angels are sexless creatures who neither marry nor are given in marriage (Matt. 22:30).

2. Rulers

Some of the old Jewish Aramaic paraphrases, the Targums, understand *elohim* (God or gods) in the sense of judges or rulers (see Exod. 21:6; Ps. 82:1,6). Thus 'sons of the *elohim*' would be high-ranking men or princes who obtained wives. This interpretation has been revived and associated with ancient Near-Eastern views on divine kingship and royal harems.[2] The main objection is that, although rulers are sometimes called 'gods', they are not referred to in the plural as 'sons of God'.

3. The line of Seth

Ancient and modern Christian expositors have understood the phrase to mean men of the godly line of Seth. The verse, 'You are the children [literally 'sons'] of the LORD your God' (Deut. 14:1), supports taking 'sons of God' as referring to the chosen line of Seth. **'Daughters of men'** are then said to be women of the line of Cain. There is thus a breakdown in the separation between the godly and the ungodly. The law of Moses warns Israel against mixed marriages (Deut. 7:3). This view falters in that the exact phrase 'sons of God' is not used in Hebrew for godly humans. It is also not at all clear that the expression 'daughters of men' refers to women of Cain's line.

4. Rulers possessed by angelic beings

It is possible that a combination of these views is the right one. Did fallen angels possess the bodies of human rulers? In the ancient pagan world kings were regarded as offspring of the gods and called 'sons of the gods'. Supernatural evil powers could well have been in league with those who exercised authority in those days. We know from Daniel 10:13 and 20 that powerful spirit beings ('princes') are at work behind the world rulers. Ephesians 6:12 reminds us that 'We do not wrestle against flesh and blood, but against principalities, against powers...' On this understanding, the reason for the awful judgement becomes obvious. Evil spirits were overstepping their boundaries and human beings were seeking in their own way to become divine. The words **'saw'**, **'beautiful'** (literally 'good') and **'took'** (6:2) echo 3:6 and suggest that these beings were transgressing as Eve had done in eating the forbidden fruit. As Adam acquiesced in his wife's sin, so the daughters and their parents were party to these sinful unions. The descendants of Seth of whom we read in chapter 5 were as much involved in this as the line of Cain in chapter 4. Human wickedness had taken a new turn for the worse. They had opened themselves to demon possession.

The mention of **'giants'** *(Nephilim)* who were **'mighty men'** and **'men of renown'** (6:4) has been used to add support to this view that unnatural unions existed among the rulers of the day. The Greek term from which the English word 'giant' comes is used to describe those produced by the union of the gods with humans. By adding **'also afterwards'** to **'in those days'**, Moses reminds us that there were similar giants around after the Flood. They appear in the report given by the spies (Num. 13:33). That demon-possessed rulers should produce unusual offspring would be consistent with known examples in more recent times of people who have dabbled in this forbidden realm. With the resurgence of paganism in Western society and the widespread use of drugs, those already in the kingdom of Satan are increasingly opening themselves to the influence of evil spirits. This understanding of the passage should be treated seriously and not lightly dismissed.

5. An alternative understanding of the passage

It is impossible to be dogmatic, but a further look at the evidence suggests another option. These verses, it must be remembered, do not begin a new section. The passage should be interpreted in the light of what has immediately preceded it. Despite the great rebellion, the command to 'be fruitful and multiply' (1:28) was not rescinded. Chapter 5 has emphasized how human beings were multiplying on the earth. This new paragraph takes up this point with the words: **'Now it came to pass when men began to multiply on the face of the earth...'** (6:1). It also draws our attention to the fact that **'Daughters were born to them.'** This again links up with the previous chapter where we have the constant refrain concerning the birth of 'sons and daughters' (5:4,7,10, etc.). Cain's genealogy makes no mention of daughters. The first verse of chapter 6 may thus be summarizing what has been presented in chapter 5, just as 2:1 summarizes Genesis 1. In fact, the next verse could also be part of the summary. **'Sons of God'** (6:2) is a succinct way of describing those created in the image of God. We saw how Genesis 5:1-3 points to God as the Father of humanity, and particularly of those who belong to the chosen line. Verse 2 may be saying no more than that the descendants of Adam, the offspring of God, especially this special line through Seth, were fulfilling the command to marry and have children. As today, the men were interested in beautiful women and they chose those whom they liked. Genesis often draws attention to a woman's good looks (12:11,14; 24:16; 29:17). The phrase **'took wives for themselves'** is the normal way of referring to marriage (4:19; 11:29; 12:19; 25:1). In describing the events prior to the Flood, our Lord does not mention anything out of the ordinary. It was precisely the ordinariness of the activities that is highlighted: 'For as in the days before the flood, they were eating and drinking, marrying and giving in marriage, until the day that Noah entered the ark, and did not know until the flood came and took them all away...' (Matt. 24:38-39). Life at that time went on normally, 'but in arrogant independence of God'.[3]

The statement that **'They bore children to them'** (6:4), completes the picture that in those days, despite God's curse, couples were very fertile. God blessed them with many children. These children grew to become the famous and valiant men of that period. Other ancient Near-Eastern documents bear witness to people of great reputation and influence on the earth prior to the Flood. The reference to the giants (the *Nephilim*) on the earth may be no more than an indication of time. There are a number of asides in the writings of Moses and this may well be one of them (see Deut. 2:10-12,20-23; 3:11,13-14). It would mean that the beginning of verse 4 should be in brackets: **'(There were giants in those days, and also afterwards.)'** The text does not actually state that the giants were the fruit of the union between the sons of God and the daughters of men. As there were giants in Moses' day, so there were people of great stature around in the period before the Flood. Neither does it follow that **'Those were the mighty men...'** alludes to the giants. The word **'those'** most naturally refers to the offspring in the immediately preceding sentence.

God's Spirit and human frailty (6:3)

This is another difficult verse to interpret. It is interesting that it comes between the statement concerning these marriages and the children born as a result of the unions. We are introduced to God's thoughts: **'My Spirit shall not strive with man for ever, for he is indeed flesh.'** 'Spirit' could mean the Holy Spirit, or 'the spirit of life' which is in every creature (6:17). The verb translated **'strive'** is only found here in the Old Testament. Modern research would support the ancient Greek translation (i.e. that of the Septuagint), 'remain'.

Whichever way we understand the disputed words, the verse indicates that human beings cannot exist on earth without God. **'Flesh'** emphasizes human frailty. Without God it is impossible for humanity to survive. Human life in this world will not go on for ever. If God's Spirit is meant, the verse is suggesting that there is a limit to God's patience. The Holy Spirit will leave humanity to its lostness. On the other hand, if the reference is to God's life-giving spirit then it is merely confirming the truth that has been so poignantly expressed by the refrain 'and he died' in chapter 5.

The final part of the verse is also problematic: **'Yet his days shall be one hundred and twenty years.'** Is God granting a reprieve of 120 years before his Spirit is removed and disaster strikes, or is he announcing a shortening of the average lifespan? If the first part of the verse is referring to an impending judgement where all human life will come to an end, then the 120 years could be a time of respite. 1 Peter 3:20 speaks of the patience of God waiting in the days of Noah. God warned and waited before he executed his judgements. In his other letter, Peter reminds us that 'The Lord is not slack concerning his promise ... but is longsuffering towards us, not willing that any should perish' (2 Peter 3:9).

On the other hand, after the great ages that have been recorded in chapter 5, God could be indicating that those long lives were to be exceptions rather than the rule. In case anyone should think it possible for humans to reach a thousand years, or live on for ever, the drastic reduction in the average lifespan announced here puts an end to such thoughts. The rest of Genesis shows how the great ages became increasingly shorter and Deuteronomy 34:7 records how Moses himself died at the age of 120. We live at a time when many are obsessed with their bodies. All kinds of treatments are on offer to prevent ageing. With the advances in medical science there is no doubt that people in the Western world are living longer.

The hope is that science will one day overcome death itself. Some have drawn up wills for their dead bodies to be kept refrigerated in the hope of being revived through human ingenuity. This verse puts an end to such notions.

Summary

There are basically two main options:

> 1. The passage is describing the state of affairs which gave rise to God's decision to wipe out the whole human race. Intermarrying of the godly with the ungodly, or the unnatural involvement of the spirit world with humans, was the reason for the divine judgement. This judgement would not fall immediately. It would be delayed 120 years.
>
> 2. The passage is not describing the reasons for the Flood but summing up the situation presented in the previous chapter. It also indicates God's intention to reduce the human lifespan from near the 1,000-year mark to a mere 120 years.

The reason for the Flood (6:5-8)

It is now that we are told the reason why God acted to remove human beings from the face of the earth. These concluding verses prepare us for what will be developed in the next section. Every verse centres on 'the LORD'. It is the Lord who sees, who is sorry, who passes sentence, and who shows grace.

The sight (6:5)

'Then the LORD saw that the wickedness of man was great in the earth and that every intent of the thoughts of his

heart was only evil continually.' This is a dreadful description of humanity in its rebellion against God. There are no
redeeming features. The last reference to God's 'seeing' was
in 1:31. Then everything was very good. What a contrast with
the present situation! Now he sees only evil in the human heart
and the effects of that evil in human behaviour. The root of the
problem is the heart, the seat of human personality. 'Out of
[the heart] spring the issues of life' (Prov. 4:23). The doctrine
of total depravity teaches that, as a result of the great rebellion, the whole human race, in every part of its make-up, is
affected by sin. The human will, thought-processes and emotions are contaminated by sin. This does not mean that every
individual is as bad as it is possible to be. This verse, therefore, is not telling us that human beings had become totally
depraved, for that is what they were from the moment sin
entered the world. What it is indicating is that human sinfulness had sunk to new depths and that people's thinking was
absorbed with nothing but evil. Every idea and scheme was
corrupt. There are degrees of evil. The people of Sodom were
'exceedingly wicked and sinful against the LORD' (13:13). There
are sins which tip the balance and demand immediate retribution. In the days of Abraham, God said that 'The iniquity of
the Amorites is not yet complete' (15:16).

The sorrow (6:6-7)

**'And the LORD was sorry that he had made man on the
earth, and he was grieved in his heart.'** Everything said
about God naturally has to be expressed in ways that we can
appreciate. In the previous verse we found no difficulty with
the idea of God 'seeing', even though we know that God is
without a body. Sometimes, as in this passage, the language is
very bold. God 'was sorry', or 'repented' (cf. 1 Sam. 15:11).
We must be careful not to draw the wrong conclusions. This is
a very obvious case where we must compare scripture with

scripture. In Numbers 23:19 Moses records God's word through Balaam: 'God is not a man, that he should lie, nor a son of man, that he should repent' (cf. 1 Sam. 15:29). God can never be accused of being capricious, disillusioned, or continually changing his plans in response to human unpredictability. This statement is a powerful way of emphasizing the seriousness of the situation. Of course God was not taken by surprise by this development on earth. It was already accounted for in his eternal purposes. But human action is no play-acting. A situation now existed on earth which demanded drastic action. God is not indifferent to human sin. The verse expresses the reaction of the righteous God towards humanity's gross wickedness. It is exactly because God is unchangeable in his character and attitude to sin that there is this response to the depths of depravity found on earth.

God is not only without body and parts; he is also without passions. The word translated **'grieved'** expresses a very strong human emotion. It is used of a forsaken woman 'grieved' in spirit (Isa. 54:6) and of David's reaction when he heard of Absalom's death (2 Sam. 19:2). If God were a human being this is how he would have felt (Ps. 78:40; Isa. 63:10). It suggests deep anger and anguish. These Old Testament ways of expressing God's attitudes and reactions prepare us for the New Testament depictions of Jesus. He is God in the flesh and we see him angry, deeply moved, weeping and lamenting on account of human sin and its effects (Matt. 23:37; Mark 3:5; John 11:35,38). Similarly, the Holy Spirit is said to be grieved by Christians.

God's attitude stands in contrast to the hope expressed at Noah's birth. There is a play on words in the original which it is not possible to convey in English. When Lamech named his son, he used three words ('comfort', 'work' and 'toil' — see 5:29) which are akin to the words 'sorry', 'made' and 'grieved' (6:6). While Lamech was looking for relief from the curse of work and painful toil, the Lord was regretting his work of making man and was painfully indignant.

The sentence (6:7)

The Judge of all the earth passed sentence: **'I will destroy man whom I have created from the face of the earth.'** God does not deal in half measures. This is a universal punishment of catastrophic proportions. The word translated 'destroy' is used of blotting out names from records (Exod. 32:32-33), wiping dishes (2 Kings 21:13) and 'blotting out' sins (Ps. 51:1; Isa. 43:25). On this occasion, God decrees that it is those who commit the sins who will be blotted out. The reference to **'both man and beast, creeping thing and birds of the air'** reminds us of the creation account (1:30). There is to be a complete reversal. The God whose power created human and animal life now expresses the determination to destroy.

> Know that the Lord is God alone,
> He can create and he destroy.
>
> (Isaac Watts)

God does punish sinners and the verse reminds us of the future universal judgement by fire (2 Peter 3:6-7).

The special favour (6:8)

The section, like the previous one (4:25-26), ends on a note of hope: **'But Noah found grace in the eyes of the LORD.'** For the first time the word 'grace' is used, although the idea has been present from chapter 3. An awful sentence of doom has been pronounced on the creatures that inhabit the earth. Surely if God destroyed all humanity the Evil One would have won and God's promises concerning the 'seed' of the woman would have come to nothing. Here, however, is a ray of hope. Noah became a trophy of God's grace. The hope that Lamech had in his son was realized in a way very different from what he had imagined.[4]

For someone to find grace in God's sight means that God is gracious to that person. In this kind of context, 'grace' refers to the attitude or action of a superior towards one who is of little or no significance. It expresses kindness that is undeserved, or favour towards the unworthy (18:3; 39:4; 50:4). Such grace is never won or earned. Noah was the recipient of God's unmerited favour. The last word in this section is not sin and judgement, but God's grace. 'But where sin abounded, grace abounded much more' (Rom. 5:20). Just as, in the middle of the judgement passage in chapter 3, God spoke words of grace concerning the woman's 'seed', so in this judgement paragraph, grace is shown to a 'seed' of the chosen line. Clearly God was acting to fulfil his promises. When the serpent appeared to have gained the hearts of all humanity, and nothing but their entire destruction seemed inevitable, Noah experienced God's grace. The next section will explain what this meant for him. Here is another step in God's redeeming purposes which come to full realization in God's chosen 'Seed', Jesus Christ.

Part 4:
What Noah produced (6:9 – 9:29)

11.
Judgement and grace

Please read Genesis 6:9-22

There are people living under the constant threat of a major earthquake or volcanic eruption who refuse to move, hoping nothing will happen. Every day that passes with no evidence of activity makes them more confident and less afraid. They get used to the threat, shrug off all the warnings and despise the offers of help and safety. This is how so many react to God's message concerning the judgement to come (2 Peter 3:3-10). It seems to have been the same in Noah's day.

Another major division begins with the heading: **'This is the genealogy of Noah.'** The first part presents Noah the righteous man saved from the curse of the Flood (6:9 – 9:17), while the second shows Noah in a drunken state as a result of which his grandson is placed under a curse (9:18-29). This is what Noah produced, warts and all.

Every civilization has a tradition about a great flood. Here we are given the authentic, accurate version of events. The biblical account stresses three things:

1. It was God who sent the Flood that destroyed the world.
2. It was God who saved Noah and his family by means of the ark.

3. It was God who promised never to flood the entire world again.

The sun always seems brighter, more dazzling, when it peeps through a mass of ominous thunder-clouds. We are told at the close of the previous section of God's intention to wipe out the whole human race on account of its wickedness. However, the last word is not one of judgement but grace. It is this that shines brightly through the whole of the present section of Genesis. God kept his word so that the line of promise continued.

A righteous man (6:9-10)

1. What this does not mean

It would be easy to jump to the conclusion that God was gracious to Noah and saved him because he was a good man. After being told in verse 8 that Noah found favour with God, are we not informed in verse 9 that **'Noah was a just man, perfect in his generations'**? Yet this would be a completely wrong deduction. God was not gracious to Noah because he was good. Rather, Noah was a righteous man because of the grace of God. There are at least three reasons for saying this.

Firstly, the word 'grace' forbids us to think that Noah's goodness earned God's favour. Grace means 'undeserved kindness'.

Secondly, Moses safeguards the truth of God's unmerited favour towards Noah by drawing a line under verse 8. We are not allowed to interpret the text to mean that verse 9 is the explanation of verse 8. Verse 9 begins with a new chapter heading and focuses on the consequences of God's grace towards Noah. Usually the sons of the person mentioned in the heading follow immediately (see 5:3; 10:1; 11:10; etc.). In Noah's case, we are told of his character (6:9), then of his sons (6:10). What Noah first produced by the grace of God was an upright, blameless life. 'When grace comes (verse 8) it produces the changed and distinctive life of the new man (verse 9).'[1]

Thirdly, the rest of the Bible forbids us to think that any sinner can merit or deserve God's blessings. It is 'not by works of righteousness which we have done, but according to his mercy he saved us' (Titus 3:5).

The grace which chose Noah to be a link in the line of promise and which saved him from destruction is the same grace which made him the man he was in that desperately evil society.

2. The kind of man Noah was

We are told three things about Noah:

In the first place, **'Noah was a just man.'** This means more than that he was fair-minded. It is the same word that is often translated 'righteous'. This is how the Lord describes him: 'I have seen that you are righteous before me in this generation' (7:1). A righteous person does what is pleasing to God. The grace that elects and saves is the grace that teaches and helps us to live righteous lives (Titus 2:11-12).

Secondly, he was **'perfect in his generations'**. This does not mean he was sinless. The word 'perfect' is used of sacrificial animals that are free of blemish. In other words, the term suggests that there was no noticeable blot on his character. He stood out head and shoulders above his contemporaries. As in the case of Job, there was a completeness about his life. Within that corrupt society he tried to keep himself unspotted from the world. It is a sad fact that where standards have fallen in society Christians have often followed the downward trend.

Paul urges believers not to copy the behaviour and lifestyles
of the sinful world (Rom. 12).

Thirdly, **'Noah walked with God.'** Here is the clue to why
he stood out and did not get sucked down by the pressures of
the world. Like Enoch before him (5:22,24), he lived in close
fellowship with God. This is the remedy against worldliness
— a personal, ongoing, vital relationship with God.

A ruined earth (6:11-13)

When he had formed the earth into a habitable place we are
told that 'God saw everything that he had made, and indeed it
was very good' (1:31). Now we find that **'God looked upon**
[or 'saw'] **the earth, and indeed it was corrupt'** (6:12). The
contrast could not be greater. Four times the word translated
'corrupt' or 'destroy' is used in these verses. It has the idea of
ruining something (see Jer. 13:7). The earth was **'corrupt'**, or
ruined (6:11,12), because all flesh **'had corrupted'**, or 'ruined',
'their way on the earth' (6:12). Thus God determined to
'destroy', or 'ruin', them along with the earth (6:13).[2] Here is
a clear case of the punishment fitting the crime.

God called human beings to be fruitful and multiply and
'fill the earth' (1:28). Instead, **'The earth was filled with
violence'** (6:11,13). What began with disobedience to God's
specific will was soon followed by man's inhumanity to man.
'Violence' is anti-social behaviour. It showed itself in the way
Cain killed his brother and in the vindictive spirit of Cain's
descendant, Lamech. A wrong relationship towards God leads
to wrong attitudes towards human beings, animals and the
environment generally. Modern humanists have often been able
to spread their views in places where societies have experienced the social and beneficial effects of the Christian message. When those effects wear off in a society that has rejected

the Christian message, the hollowness of the humanist philosophy becomes more apparent.

A remnant spared (6:13-22)

Here we have the first of four divine speeches which take up a large proportion of the Flood account (6:13-21; 7:1-4; 8:15-17; 9:1-17). Surprisingly, no words of Noah are recorded in the whole narrative up to 9:17. It is God who determines, commands and makes promises. Noah submissively carries out the will of God (6:22; 7:5,9,16).

Noah walked with God and was let into God's secret counsels. He was told what was to happen and how he and his family could escape the catastrophe. His faith was seen in his obedience to God's word (6:22). Hebrews 11:7 draws our attention to this: 'By faith Noah, being divinely warned of things not yet seen, moved with godly fear, prepared an ark for the saving of his household.' Building the ark would have provided a powerful witness both to his faith and to God's intentions. In this way he became by life and action a preacher of righteousness (2 Peter 2:5). Similar inside information was given to Abraham which led him to intercede for Sodom (18:16-33).

God's pronouncement (6:13,17)

The Judge of all the earth saw the situation and passed sentence. The phrase, **'The end of all flesh has come before me'** (6:13), is a Hebrew way of saying, 'I am determined to put an end to all flesh.' Because he is the sovereign Lord, he does not need to ask permission of anyone before pronouncing judgement. What he resolved to do he did. But it was not an arbitrary decision. The punishment was deserved and appropriate. There are echoes of this pronouncement in Amos' message: 'The end has come upon my people Israel' (Amos 8:2). Similar language is used by Ezekiel to describe the fall of Jerusalem: 'An end! The end has come...' (Ezek. 7:2). Such earthly judgements are pointers to the fact that 'The end of all things is at hand' (1 Peter 4:7; see also Matt. 24).

In verse 17 we are told for the first time exactly how God will punish the world and details are given of what it will mean: **'And behold, I myself am bringing the flood of waters on the earth.'** This is an exceptional flood and to highlight its uniqueness a special word, never used of any other type of flood, is employed. Apart from Genesis, the only other place where the word is found is Psalm 29:10. David reminds us of what is emphasized here when he says, 'The LORD sits enthroned over the Flood' (NIV). Even this massive flood was not for one moment outside God's control. He himself had the oversight of the whole event. In the New Testament the Greek term for the great Flood is the one from which we get the English word 'cataclysm' (Matt. 24:38; 2 Peter 2:5). It was a disaster of cosmic proportions. Suddenly and dramatically God acted to interfere with the normal order. What God did in the days of Noah he is going to do again, only the instrument used will not be water but fire (2 Peter 3:7,10-11).

Details are now given of what 'destroying' or 'ruining' the earth would entail (cf. 6:13). God, the author and giver of all life, was about to dramatically take away **'the breath of life'** from **'all flesh'** which is **'under heaven'**. This meant that humans, birds, animals, reptiles and insects would all die. Only life in the sea would be excluded.

God's pact (6:18)

Here is the first occurrence of the term **'covenant'** in the Bible. It is a word that is used for special agreements between two parties or groups (see 21:22-32). God condescends to employ these human arrangements to express important theological truths. When the term is used of God we cannot speak of the parties involved being on equal terms. There is no idea of a mutual pact. God does not enter into preliminary negotiations over terms and conditions. God's pact comes as a total package which human beings are called to accept. It is in that sense unilateral. God said, **'But I will establish my covenant with you.'** It is neither Noah's covenant with God nor a mutual covenant between God and Noah. 'I' and 'my' indicate that it is very definitely God's covenant.

When God states that he will 'establish', or 'confirm', his covenant with Noah it suggests that the covenant is already in existence.[3] Through the provision of the ark, God was assuring him of the special relationship that already existed between them. In other words, this verse is filling out the detail of the text which says, 'Noah found grace in the eyes of the LORD' (6:8). He was in the sphere of God's gracious activity.

God indicated to Noah what he was about to do. All flesh on the earth was to perish in the Flood (6:17). Noah was also flesh. Yet in this situation the grace of God reached out to rescue him. God implemented the covenant he had graciously made with Noah. The grace of God that set him apart from the world of his day and made him the man he was 'is saving grace, grace which protects and preserves him and his family from the judgement of God on a sinful world'.[4] So it is with God's people in every age. We are all part and parcel of a lost world and we all deserve to die the second death in hell. But God graciously meets us and brings us to himself and saves us from the wrath to come.

God's provision (6:14-16,18-21)

How would Noah and his family be saved? Would they suddenly disappear like Enoch? If that had happened the devil would have been victorious. There would have been no 'seed', no descendants left to fulfil God's promise made to Eve. The promised 'seed' of the woman must come. Noah was not the promised one. At best he was only a pointer to the 'seed'. It is this special descendant who is to gain the victory over the serpent. If God's promise was not fulfilled then the serpent would have won and there would have been no ultimate salvation for anyone, not even for Enoch or Noah.

The way in which God saved Noah and his family from the universal judgement not only enabled the chosen 'seed' to be born of a woman, but it provided a powerful illustration of the way God would rescue sinners from the ultimate judgement. The means God used to save humans and animals was through the building of an enormous coffin-like boat, called an **'ark'**.

Apart from the Flood account the only other occurrence of the Hebrew word for 'ark' is in Exodus 2:3,5. It is used of the basket of bulrushes in which baby Moses was placed. (A different word is employed for the ark of the covenant.) The name emphasizes that it was a very basic structure, its sole purpose being 'to provide shelter and orderly existence for a variety of creatures'.[5] This was no luxury liner. 'Vessel' would be a reasonable modern equivalent, especially one of the large container vessels.

Only enough information is given concerning the construction of the ark to impress upon us that it was sturdy, stable and seaworthy, and capable of carrying a huge load. The wood used is unknown to us. Like the ark in which Moses was hidden, it was covered with pitch. It had three decks and there was a gap between the roof and the sides of the ark all the way round to provide light and ventilation. This is the probable meaning of the **'window'** which is finished **'to a cubit from above'**. A cubit is about eighteen inches (forty-five centimetres). There was also a door in the side of the ark. Inside, the ark was divided into various rooms (literally 'nests'). Sectioning it off in this way not only contained the various animals, but also stopped everything rushing to one side of the craft and capsizing it. The whole structure measured about 450 feet (135 metres) long, 75 feet (22 metres) wide and 45 feet (13 metres) high.

Here was a most wonderful provision **'to keep alive'** (6:19,20) a remnant from both the human and animal world. Noah, his wife, his sons and daughters-in-law, along with a male and female representative of every bird, beast and creeping thing, were to be preserved alive in the ark. In some unexplained way the creatures would **'come'** (6:20) to Noah and he would **'bring'** them **'into the ark'** (6:19). The list of creatures and such phrases as **'after their kind'** and **'male and female'** call to mind the creation account (6:19-20; cf. 1:11,12,20-21,24,25,27). Likewise all the food to be eaten on board, which Noah was commanded to collect, echoes the wording about eating in 1:29-30. As the narrative unfolds we shall see that there is a sense in which God was bringing the world back to where it was before animals and humans were created and starting afresh. There is one big difference, however. The repopulation of the world after the Flood would not be from nothing, but from this remnant preserved in the ark.

As the little ark on the waters of the Nile kept baby Moses safe from drowning, so Noah's ark in the great Flood kept alive all who were within. This association presents Moses as a second Noah who escaped death to become, like Noah, the beginning of a new stage in God's purposes for the fulfilling of his promises.

There is a further striking connection with the time of Moses which suggests that this historical incident also has a symbolic meaning. The only other structure described in such detail in the Law is the tabernacle. Interestingly, the measurements of the tabernacle are similar to those of Noah's ark.[6] As the ark was God's provision for preserving life in Noah's day, so the tabernacle was set up to provide a similar function for the people of Israel. Both the ark and the tabernacle point forward to the great provision of life in the Lord Jesus Christ. When the judgement of God fell, Noah and his family were safe in the ark. It prefigures the saving work of Christ which Christian baptism symbolizes (1 Peter 3:21). The final judgement was experienced by Christ on the cross so that all who belong to him are safe from the coming day of wrath.

> Jesu, Lover of my soul,
> Let me to thy bosom fly,
> While the nearer waters roll,
> While the tempest still is high...
>
> Other refuge have I none;
> Hangs my helpless soul on thee...
> Cover my defenceless head
> With the shadow of thy wing.

(Charles Wesley)

12.
The great Flood

Please read Genesis 7:1 – 8:19

The Flood is made to stand out as an event of great significance in the history of the world. Moses writes up the details of what happened, not like a sea captain filling in a logbook, but with great skill and in an interesting way.

The Flood arrives (7:1-24)

1. The command of God (7:1-4)

The Lord, who had told Noah what would happen and had given him the plans for building the ark, now commanded him to embark: **'Come into the ark'** (7:1; cf. 8:16). God spoke to the one with whom he could have fellowship. In 6:9 we were told that Noah was righteous and unspotted among his contemporaries. Here there is a different emphasis. When God says, **'I have seen you are righteous before me,'** he is making clear that Noah was a justified man. He was right with God and did not stand condemned with the rest of the world. This was so purely as a result of God's grace to him. Noah trusted God's word for salvation so that he was in a right legal standing before God. His trust was seen in his life of obedience.

A godly family

God's call to enter the ark was addressed to Noah, as head of the household: **'Come ... you and all your household.'** It was a great blessing for Shem, Ham and Japheth to have such a godly father. Job had a similar influence over his family (Job 1:5). The New Testament makes a point of stressing the salvation of households. God often brings salvation to a household through the conversion of the parents. What a responsibility fathers and mothers have! What a privilege to be brought up in a godly home! Do not despise such an upbringing. On the other hand, do not take it for granted that because parents are saved their children are automatically saved. We are called individually to repent and believe the gospel. Noah's wife believed God and was saved, unlike Lot's wife, who looked back and was destroyed. Likewise, Noah's sons believed the word of God and, at one hundred years of age, they followed their father into the ark. Their wives also responded positively (7:13).

The animals

Noah was also commanded to take on board one pair of all kinds of creatures and seven pairs of all clean creatures. In writing up this account, Moses knew what God meant by clean and unclean animals (Lev. 11). The clean animals, birds and insects were the ones that could be eaten. Obviously Noah knew the difference and animal sacrifice was practised from the time that Adam and Eve first sinned.

God's interest in the animals was not merely to preserve the clean domesticated animals for human consumption and sacrifice. He was also interested in 'the beasts of the field', including the snakes, that they might reproduce and multiply on the earth after the Flood. God is concerned for the welfare of people and animals (Jonah 4:11). There are strict instructions on how to treat animals in the law of Moses. The fact that human beings are unique does not mean we can treat animals as we like.

The timing

Having commanded Noah to enter, God gave more detail concerning the timing of the Flood. Only seven days were left and then it would rain for forty days and forty nights. A week of grace was given to get all on board. One week becomes symbolic of the final period before the great consummation of all things (Dan. 9:27). We live in the 'last days' of that final week of grace. 'Now is the accepted time; behold, now is the day of salvation' (2 Cor. 6:2).

2. The obedience of Noah (7:5-16)

'The day when the old creation died is described with a gravity befitting the occasion.'[1] There is a clear parallel between verses 6-9 and 10-16. Without using precisely the same words, the main points are repeated for emphasis.

The date of the Flood (7:6,10,11)

One of the features of the Flood narrative is the precise dating of the various events. We are not only given the year and the month but the actual day of the month (cf. 8:4-5,13-14). The dates remind us that we are dealing with what actually happened in our world. It is also noteworthy that the seven-day-week pattern established at creation is followed here (7:4,10). Like the creation of the world, de-creation started on the first day of the week. The Day of the Lord is a day of judgement as well as a day of salvation.

How the Flood came (7:6,10,11-12)

'Fountains of the great deep' is a poetic expression (7:11; cf. Ps. 36:6; 78:15; Amos 7:4) describing how the waters of the abyss, which had been contained in some way, broke open. Similarly, the opening of **'the windows of heaven'** (cf. Mal. 3:10; Isa. 24:18) is suggestive of an unrestrained downpour. By releasing the waters below and above the earth, God was undoing the separating work described in Genesis 1:6-10.

Noah and his family enter the ark (7:7,13)

Four married couples entered the ark. There is no suggestion that they were forced to enter. Each came willingly. In 7:13 it does not merely say 'Noah and his sons', but **'Noah and Noah's sons'**, and they are named individually. Instead of 'Noah and his wife' (cf. 7:7; 8:18), it speaks of **'Noah's wife'**. In place of 'the wives of his sons' (cf. 6:18; 7:7; 8:18), we are told here that **'... the three wives of his sons ... entered the ark'**. Each came as a person in his or her own right. Peter is careful to draw our attention to this by stating that 'eight souls' were saved (1 Peter 3:20).

The animals enter in pairs (7:8-9,14-16)

The various groups mentioned (**'beast'**, **'cattle'**, **'creeping thing'** and **'bird'**) and the refrain (**'after its kind'**) echo the wording of the creation account. All that could breathe entered (7:15; cf. 6:17). **'Two by two'** is a general statement, as in 6:19. It does not contradict what we have been told in 7:2-3. They came in pairs, seven pairs of each clean animal and one pair of each of the other creatures. As God brought all the creatures for Adam to name (2:19), so he brought the male and female creatures **'into the ark'**.

God's command obeyed (7:9,16)

Noah did exactly **'as God had commanded'** (7:5,9,16). His obedience was an expression of his trust in God.

God closed the entrance (7:16)

In the ancient Babylonian account by Gilgamesh it was the man himself who closed the door. The biblical account emphasizes the Lord's action. When the time of grace came to an end, **'The LORD shut him in.'** For those inside, closing the entrance meant their salvation, but for those outside it meant their destruction. We are reminded of Jesus' parable where the wise virgins were ready and went in to the wedding 'and the door was shut'. The foolish, unprepared virgins arrived late and called out, 'Lord, Lord, open to us', but the Lord did not acknowledge them (Matt. 25:1-13). How dreadful to be locked out to endure eternal punishment!

3. The destruction by water (7:17-24)

What massive devastation floodwater can cause! The worst floods that are experienced today cannot be compared to the Flood of Noah's day. The great boundary between land and sea that God had decreed at creation was broken down.

The waters

We are told two things about the floodwaters.

Firstly, they **'increased'**, or 'multiplied' (7:17; cf. 1:28). Instead of human beings multiplying, the waters multiplied. Divine blessing gave way to divine curse. There was a sudden decrease in population as the waters **'greatly increased'** (7:18).

Secondly, they **'prevailed'** (7:18,19,20,24). This is a word that is used for success in battle (Exod. 17:11). The floodwaters **'prevailed exceedingly'** (7:19), like a victorious army. They covered all the mountains to a depth of fifteen cubits (twenty-two feet, or seven metres), allowing the ark to pass over them freely (7:20). The waters triumphed for 150 days (7:24), a figure that includes the first forty days of rain. There was no noticeable change until after this period had elapsed. Clearly, this was no local flood. The earth had returned to the watery state of Genesis 1:2.

Total loss of life

The narrative highlights three aspects of the destruction.

1. **'All flesh died that moved on the earth'** (7:21). The creatures that expired are listed in the order they were created. The Flood reversed God's act of creation.

2. **'All in whose nostrils was the breath of the spirit of life'** (7:22; cf. 6:17). Although this can refer to all the land animals, the use of the words 'nostrils' and 'breath' reminds us of the creation of man (2:7). The God who breathed into man's nostrils the breath of life now brought that life to an end. It is significant that it does not say that they drowned. This was not only a natural tragedy but a divine punishment.

3. **'All that was on the dry land'** (7:22) and **'all living things which were on the face of the ground'** (7:23) make it clear that all the creatures dependent on the dry land died. The verb **'destroyed'**, which can also be translated 'ruined' or 'wiped out' (7:23; cf. 6:7; 7:4), again stresses that the Flood was a divine judgement. What God threatened to do he did.

Salvation in the ark

The waters of the Flood that brought an end to all life on the ground had a different effect on the ark.

1. **'The waters ... lifted up the ark, and it rose high above the earth'** (7:17). The ark neither sank nor capsized. That great barge, three decks high, bursting with life, floated. Noah had built the ark according to God's directions and it served its purpose well. All who were within were kept alive and above water.

2. **'The ark moved about on the surface of the waters'** (7:18). It was able to travel freely and was not broken up on rocks.

3. **'Only Noah and those who were with him in the ark remained alive'** (7:23). In the middle of that great Flood, when 'all flesh' was destroyed, there was safety for all those in the ark. In the time of the Exodus, when the Egyptian army was destroyed by water, Moses and the Israelites were saved through water (1 Cor. 10:1-2). In the coming universal judgement, only those 'in Christ' will be safe.

The Flood abates (8:1-19)

The exact turning-point in the whole account is the statement: **'God remembered Noah...'** (8:1). It does not imply that God had forgotten him and suddenly called him to mind — quite the opposite. Noah had never been out of his thoughts. It speaks of action, of gracious intervention. What it means is that God was committed to rescuing Noah and was now ready to act to bring the Flood to an end. When God remembered the promises he had made to Abraham he rescued the Israelites from slavery in Egypt (Exod. 2:24; 6:5).

Noah and those with him in the ark were in a helpless condition, unable to do anything. Imagine being in a container vessel on the high seas for five months with no sign of entering port. The initial excitement of travelling on water would have worn off long ago. After the forty-day downpour had ended there was a further period of 110 days when nothing seemed to be happening. Had God forgotten them? Had he saved them in order to abandon them on the surface of an unending ocean? This was the kind of thinking expressed by the Israelites when the Egyptian army pursued them to the Red Sea (Exod. 14:11-12). There is no suggestion that such terror gripped Noah and his family, but they must have wondered what the next move would be. God kept his promise and acted to bring all those in the ark into a new world, just as later he acted to redeem his covenant people from Egypt and bring them to the promised land. God is committed to bringing all those who belong to Christ to the joys of heaven and his new creation.

1. God's action to decrease the water level (8:1-5)

God's loving concern extended not only to Noah but to the non-domesticated creatures — **'every living thing'** (8:1; cf. 1:25; 7:14) — and the domesticated **'animals'**. 'O LORD, you preserve man and beast' (Ps. 36:6). That solitary vessel, full of living creatures, was under the protection of God. He acted to restore the earth and repopulate it with the life kept safe in the ark in two ways.

First, we read that he made **'a wind to pass over the earth'**. The text does not speak of God's Spirit hovering over the surface of the waters, as in 1:2, but the Hebrew word for 'Spirit' is also the word for 'wind', thus echoing the earlier scene. God was not creating, but using the wind to return the earth to its former habitable state. God also used the wind to divide the waters at the Red Sea to form dry land (Exod. 14:21).

Secondly, he sealed the two sources from which the earth had been flooded (8:2), reversing what we were told in 7:11. They were **'stopped'**. The rain **'was restrained'**, reversing 7:12.

Thus the waters were no longer able to triumph. The source of their power was gone, so they retreated. They **'subsided'** (8:1), **'receded'** (8:3) and **'decreased'** (8:3,5). The waters returned to their appointed place (see 1:6-10). The same phrase, **'the waters receded'**, is used of the Red Sea returning to its former state (Exod. 14:26,28). In the case of the Flood, the waters did not return suddenly. They diminished gradually — **'continually'** (8:3,5). The process had begun to take place 150 days after the Flood started (8:3; cf. 7:24). Evidence that the water level had fallen fifteen cubits was felt when the bottom of the ark grounded on one of the mountains in the Ararat region (8:4; cf. 7:20). The area is now called Armenia and straddles the borders of eastern Turkey, southern Russia and northern Iran.

God is seen as the one who is over the waters (Ps. 29:10). He unleashed the waters and then recalled them to the boundaries set at creation. People fear the storm and the raging sea. The Bible uses the sea to symbolize God's sovereignty over the unruly forces of nature and the dark powers of evil (Prov. 8:27-29; Ps. 89:9-10; Rev. 13:1; 19:20). Jesus rebuked the great wind and said to the sea, 'Peace, be still!' Then, 'The wind ceased and there was a great calm' (Mark 4:39). Later Jesus walked on the turbulent sea and comforted the disciples by his presence (Mark 6:47-51). This is our God who 'plants his footsteps in the sea, and rides upon the storm'. In the picture that we have of the new creation there is no more sea to threaten that new world order (Rev. 21:1).

2. Noah's action to ascertain the water level (8:6-14)

Noah and his family must have felt like excited holidaymakers who, when they have landed at their destination, are eager to get off the plane or boat but are kept waiting for what seems like an age for the doors to open. It was not a few minutes but many months after the ark came to rest that all on board were allowed to disembark.

Forty days after the tops of the mountains became visible, Noah decided to open the window to release some birds. In ancient times birds were used for helping to find direction and to ascertain if land were near. Noah first sent out a raven, hoping it would give him some indication of how much further the waters had retreated. As the window was in the roof, he would only have been able to see the tops of the mountains. While the ritually unclean raven did not return, the dove that was released next found no resting-place and returned to Noah.[2] His tenderness in reaching out his hand to bring the bird inside highlights his care of God's creatures (see Exod. 23:4-5; Prov. 12:10).

A week later, Noah experimented with the dove again. This time it returned in the evening with a freshly plucked olive leaf, an indication that plants had begun to grow. A dove with an olive leaf in its beak is used as a symbol of peace. But here it is a symbol of new life as well as of peace. It meant that the time of judgement was over. It was no coincidence that the Holy Spirit chose to descend on Jesus at his baptism in the form of a dove. As the dove was a symbol of new life, so the Holy Spirit is the Spirit of life. He is associated with the Son of God in creation and re-creation.

Noah allowed a further week to elapse before releasing the dove again. This time it did not return. Noah then decided to have a good look round by removing **'the covering of the ark'** (8:13). He saw that **'The surface of the ground was dry.'** Though the earth was free from water, it would have remained soggy for some time. Not until a month later was the ground thoroughly dry.

As each new development in the creation story was carefully dated, so also throughout the account of the Flood very precise dates are given. The dates are connected to the days, weeks, months and years of Noah's life (7:6,11; 8:13). The Flood lasted in all one solar year of 365 days, or one lunar year of 354 days plus a further eleven days. Another interesting feature is the constant reference to the way Noah worked to the seven-day-week pattern established at creation (8:10,12; cf. 7:4).

3. God's command to leave the ark (8:15-17)

The God who called Noah to 'Come into the ark' (7:1) now said, **'Go out of the ark'** (8:16). Since the day Noah was directed to enter the ark, there has been no record of God speaking directly to him until now. Noah used his own ingenuity to discover what conditions were like on the earth during the period of waiting, but he did not move until God directed him. He did not run ahead of God, but patiently waited God's time.

God commanded Noah to bring out his family and all the other animals. The description of the various creatures **'according to their families'** (8:19) is akin to the initial creation account (1:21,24-25). We also have the general blessing to **'be fruitful and multiply on the earth'** (8:17). Those kept safe in the ark come into a new world to fill the earth as at the beginning.

4. Noah's obedient response (8:18-19)

Once more Noah is obedient to the divine command and proves again his trust in the Lord (cf. 6:22; 7:5).

As the Flood is used to prefigure the final judgement, so the new situation that emerged after the Flood is depicted as a kind of new earth. Those in the ark were not finally saved until they stepped back on dry ground. Likewise, believers in the Lord Jesus, saved and kept by the power of God, look forward to the day when they will step out with glorified bodies onto a new earth.

13.
A new beginning

Please read Genesis 8:20 – 9:17

On 20 July 1969 the *Eagle* lunar landing-module touched down near the edge of the Sea of Tranquillity. Neil Armstrong stepped out onto the moon's dusty surface and uttered those memorable words: 'That's one small step for a man, one giant leap for mankind.' The experience of the astronauts must have been a little like what Noah must have felt when he set foot on the earth. There was no one around to greet him, just an eerie silence. We have no record of his first words. No doubt he was well-pleased to be back on *terra firma*, but the text concentrates on Noah's humble, thankful spirit.

Noah's worship and God's response (8:20-22)

Noah's sacrifice (8:20)

Noah's first thoughts were Godward. He **'built an altar to the Lord'**. No doubt he was concerned to house his wife and family in this new situation, but the secret of a good home lies in putting the Lord first.

Adam's first full day was the one that God set apart as special (2:1-3). For Noah, his first day in the new world was a special day for worship. The day that Jesus rose from the dead, inaugurating a new era, is the day when he encourages his followers to meet for worship. Noah, by his action, paid homage to the Lord who had brought him into a newly cleansed world. Those who belong to Jesus Christ, who have been delivered from God's wrath and preserved by his grace, should be quick to come together on the Lord's Day to offer heartfelt praise and adoration.

Noah's action not only revealed a God-centred life, but it clearly indicated a thankful spirit. Often in the Old Testament, animal sacrifices were offered as expressions of gratitude and trust. The Bible spiritualizes these offerings. Psalm 141:2 reads: 'Let my prayer be set before you as incense, the lifting up of my hands as the evening sacrifice.' Believers are to 'continually offer the sacrifice of praise to God, that is, the fruit of our lips, giving thanks to his name' (Heb. 13:15). We come together especially on the Lord's Day to express corporately our thanks and to encourage one another to live every day a thankful, trustful life.

Noah **'offered burnt offerings on the altar'** which he had built. Here is the first record of the building of an altar. We also have the first mention of burnt offerings. Noah took some of the clean animals and birds that he had on board for the burnt offering. This was the most important of the sacrifices mentioned in the law of Moses. The entire animal was burnt on the altar (Lev. 1:1-17). As the whole sacrifice was consumed by fire and the smoke ascended, so it symbolized the total dedication of the worshipper to the service of God. This aspect of the sacrifice is taken up by Paul when he urges Christians to present their bodies 'a living sacrifice' (Rom. 12:1).

God's acceptance of the sacrifice (8:21)

Noah's sacrifice was also a propitiatory offering. As the smoke ascended, **'The Lord smelled a soothing aroma.'** Here, again, we have human action applied to God. Such expressions are called anthropomorphisms. This expression describes in a graphic way God's acceptance of the offering and the offerer. There was nothing automatic or mechanical about this. When the curses of the Sinai covenant are spelled out, God indicates that he 'will not smell the fragrance of your sweet aromas' (Lev. 26:31). The phrase, 'a soothing aroma' (see Lev. 1:9,13,17), highlights the special significance of this sacrifice. It suggests that it is a sacrifice to appease God's wrath.

This offering was not Noah's own idea. God instituted sacrifice (3:21; 4:4-5). What is later spelled out clearly in the law of Moses was already known to people at the time of the Flood. Francis Schaeffer points out that we constantly come across situations in Genesis 'where men have knowledge that we would not expect them to have. In other words, God has taught them things that are not recorded in Scripture.'[1]

Noah not only knew the difference between clean and unclean and animal sacrifice in general, but he also knew that fellowship between a holy God and sinful humanity was only possible through propitiatory sacrifice. This truth runs throughout the Bible and points to the one great sacrifice offered at Calvary. In his love for humanity God has provided for the removal of his wrath (1 John 4:10). 'God sent Jesus to take the punishment for our sins and to satisfy God's anger against us' (Rom. 3:25, *New Living Translation*).

God's decision (8:21-22)

'**Then the LORD said in his heart ...**' is another example of God's resolving to do something (cf. 6:3,7). Two items call for attention in God's response to Noah's action.

Firstly, in direct contrast to 6:5-7, God now determined not to '**destroy every living thing**' as he had done. Why is there this change on God's part? Is it because God realized he had acted wrongly in blotting out the entire human race? Was God frustrated over the fact that **'The imagination of man's heart is evil from his youth'**, and did he give in to the situation? The answer to each of these questions must be 'No'. Though no one deserves to live on the earth a moment longer, God is gracious. The changed situation is bound up with the 'soothing aroma' of Noah's sacrifice. Job offered propitiatory sacrifices for his children and his 'comforters' (Job 1:5; 42:8), but Noah's priestly action had universal significance. The peace that Noah established through his offering was symbolic of the atoning work of the 'Seed', our great High Priest, Jesus Christ. He has 'made peace through the blood of his cross', and by so doing has reconciled 'all things' in heaven and earth to himself (Col. 1:20). Christ's death is the means by which the new creation is secured and the consequences of the original rebellion are completely eradicated.

Secondly, the promise not to **'curse the ground for man's sake'** is not a removal of the curse pronounced in 3:17. The Flood was a curse over and above the one issued by God after Adam's rebellion. What God is intimating here is that he will not curse the ground any further despite the sinfulness of the human heart. God is not saying there will be no disasters of any kind in the world, but that there will be no flood of such magnitude ever again.

To emphasize that there would be no similar disruption to the created order before the final Judgement Day, God gave the promise of fixed seasons and regular daily cycles. This uniformity we all enjoy and it is on the basis of it that scientists can observe, analyse and predict. It is not by any natural necessity that there is this rhythm in nature, but by the deliberate will and faithfulness of God. God, not Gaia (Mother Earth) or immoral pagan practices, brings fertility and seasonal variations.

Although Noah came out into a new world, it was still the old creation. It was still under the initial judgement. Nature continued to be 'red in tooth and claw' and humans were depraved in the whole of their beings and subject to the decaying effects of the curse. The new beginning could at best only foreshadow the reality of the new creation. The assurance of continuity and uniformity applies **'while the earth remains'**. The present earth is not to go on for ever. God's gracious promise will last until the Day of the Lord comes when 'both the earth and the works that are in it will be burned up'. Out of that conflagration will come 'a new earth in which righteousness dwells' (2 Peter 3:10,13). The new situation into which Noah came after the Flood is the world in which we live. It is one which is running down, 'groaning' and full of sinful people like ourselves. The world to come, for which Jesus shed his precious blood, will be perfect in every way, with no possibility of sin ever entering it again.

God's universal covenant (9:1-17)

Preaching to the idolatrous people of Lystra, Paul and Barnabas urged them to turn to the living God, the Creator of heaven and earth. They reminded their hearers of the evidences of God in the created order, highlighting God's goodness in giving 'rain from heaven and fruitful seasons, filling our hearts with food and gladness' (Acts 14:15-18). In other words, the people were being informed of the promises that God made to Noah. Despite God's goodness we fail to honour and thank him (Rom. 1:21).

God's intentions to maintain the created order (8:20-22) are amplified and expressed to Noah in the form of a covenant. The announcement of a special agreement with Noah was first made before the Flood (6:18). It was because of God's grace towards him (6:8) that Noah had this covenant relationship with God. God had implemented the covenant by saving

Noah, his family and all the creatures that came into the ark. Further details of what that covenant involved are presented in these verses.

1. *Covenant blessing and covenant law* (9:1-7)

Creation blessing

As God blessed Adam and Eve, so **'God blessed Noah and his sons'**, commanding them to **'Be fruitful and multiply, and fill the earth'** (9:1,7; cf. 1:27-28). Noah is like a second Adam. He heads up the human race after the Flood. But although there is this fresh start, humans have a sinful nature (8:21) which needs to be curbed.

Changed conditions

Human beings were originally called to rule over the animal kingdom as God's representatives (1:26,28). We are now told that these creatures will experience **'the fear of you and the dread of you'** (9:2). This suggests hostility. Similar phraseology is used to describe Israel's presence among its neighbours: 'God will put the dread of you and the fear of you upon all the land where you tread' (Deut. 11:25). There was no animosity between humans and animals at the beginning. The first mention of enmity occurs after the Fall (3:15). Those kept safe in the ark would soon start hurting and destroying one another. The wolf and the leopard would worry the lamb and the goat, and children would be bitten by snakes. Only in the new creation will the situation be different (Isa. 11:6-9; 65:17-25; Hosea 2:18).

Following the great Flood, Noah and his family might have thought that life was easily disposable. A great destruction of human and animal life had taken place. Did this mean that life was cheap? God's covenant with every living creature indicated that he still held all life to be precious. He instructed Noah and his descendants to respect and preserve it.

Permission to kill for food

For Noah, as for Adam, God provided an abundance of food: **'I have given you all things, even as the green herbs'** (9:3; cf. 1:29). Again, the situation is different. At the beginning, human beings were vegetarian. Now they were permitted to eat meat. **'They are given into your hand'** (9:2) implies that humans have the power of life and death over the animals. No distinction is made between clean and unclean (7:2,8). Later, the Mosaic law forbade Israel to eat unclean animals. This regulation introduced under the old covenant was removed under the new (Acts 10:9-16; Mark 7:19).

Respect for all life

While permission is given to eat the flesh of **'every moving thing that lives'**, there is a restriction on how the flesh is to be eaten: **'But you shall not eat flesh with its life, that is, its blood'** (9:4). Blood pumping through the veins of an animal is a symbol of life. To feel a strong pulse and to hear a beating heart, these are sure signs of life. As the blood represents the life of the animal, abstaining from blood shows respect for life and the source of all life. They were not to act like wild animals tearing at freshly killed meat. Strict rules applied under the old Sinai covenant for draining the blood of an animal that had been killed (Deut. 12:16,23-25; Lev. 17:10,14). Israel's attitude in killing and eating meat set them apart from their neighbours and impressed upon all the fact that God was the author and sustainer of life. Even animal life could not be taken without God's permission.

This ruling must also be seen in the context of sacrificial blood. God allowed the shedding of animal blood to atone for human sin (Lev. 17:11). The sacrificial blood symbolized a substituted life taken to cleanse from sin's defilement and to cover God's anger (Lev. 16:14-19). All these animal sacrifices were symbolic of Christ's once-for-all, perfect sacrifice for sin. Whereas the blood of animals brought outward, ceremonial cleansing, the blood of Christ cleanses the guilty conscience and brings us into the heavenly presence of God. Now that the precious blood of Jesus has been shed for our sins, we do not need to consider the death of animals in sacrificial terms. In the early days of the church, Gentile believers were asked to refrain from consuming blood so as not to offend Jewish converts (Acts 15:20,29). Love for fellow believers involves consideration of those with sensitive consciences.

When we obtain our meat and poultry from the supermarket, all neatly pre-wrapped, we are apt to forget that a life has been taken. This passage is a reminder that all life is God's property and he alone has the right to sanction the killing of animals. Under this right it is sometimes necessary to cull species and to curb pests and vermin. It is contrary to the spirit of this regulation to engage in blood sports. Certainly, cruelty to animals is against the principle of this text. As a result of Christian influence such sports as bear-baiting, dog- and cock-fighting have been banned in the United Kingdom. Such organizations as the Royal Society for the Prevention of Cruelty to Animals (RSPCA) owe their existence to the effects of the Evangelical Awakening in the eighteenth century.

The unique value of human life

Whereas the blood of an animal may be shed but not eaten, the blood of a human being must not be shed at all. A distinction is clearly made between the life of an animal and the life of a human. After all the violence that existed before the Flood, and the great destruction of human life during it, God made provision for the protection of human life: **'Surely for your lifeblood I will demand a reckoning'** (9:5). The threat to human life by animals is dealt with first. While humans are given the right to kill animals, animals do not have the right to do the same to humans. If an animal kills a human it must be destroyed. We find this principle prescribed in the Sinai law. If an ox gores a man to death then the animal must immediately be killed (Exod. 21:28-32). The UK law concerning dangerous dogs is in keeping with what we have here. Human life is uniquely valuable. Situations are emerging today where there is greater respect and interest in preserving animal life than human. There are those who are obsessively interested in preserving animal and plant life under threat of extinction but have no interest in, or are even actively supportive of, the slaughter of thousands of unborn children.

Why should the human species be treated differently from animals? If human beings are only 'naked apes' there is no adequate answer. Yet every thinking person knows how revolting it is to see humans being treated like animals. It is the Bible which gives the only answer that is both right and reasonable. Human beings have been made **'in the image of God'** (9:6). They are related to God in a way that animals are not (see 1:26-27).

'No sin', writes Gordon Wenham, 'shows greater contempt for life than homicide.'[2] Not only must animals that kill humans be destroyed, but humans who murder other human beings (9:5). Again, a distinction is made between animals and humans. Animals, even those biologically close to humans, such as apes or chimpanzees, are not our brothers. The reference to **'brother'** reminds us of what Cain did to his brother. Every unlawful killing of a fellow human being is like the killing of Abel by his brother Cain.

Capital punishment and civil government

A murderer must pay the ultimate penalty for the ultimate crime. The punishment must fit the crime.[3] In the period before the Flood, people like Lamech were taking vengeance and exacting more than was due. God now sought to bring some order into a world of sinful people. This rule was incorporated into the Sinai legislation (Lev. 24:17-22).

In the case of the violence operating before the Flood, God took it upon himself to judge human beings by wiping them off the face of the earth. While he may continue to punish murderers directly, God also shares this authority with those created in his image. **'For in the image of God he made man,'** not only stresses the shocking nature of the crime, but is the only justification for people having the right to execute the death penalty.

What we find here is the origin of law and order in society. God has ordained civil authority and has given officers of state the right to punish wrongdoing (Rom. 13:1-7). Some have misunderstood the Sermon on the Mount, supposing that Jesus was seeking to reform the legal principle established here (Matt. 5:38-42). Jesus was not addressing those responsible for maintaining law and order in society. He was speaking to his disciples. In our personal relationships Christians are not to have a spirit of retaliation. Jesus' words must not be taken out of context. God has ordained that the state should judge wrongdoers, instead of individuals taking the law into their own hands and avenging themselves by exacting a penalty that is far in excess of the crime.

There are those who argue that capital punishment for murder is immoral. For the state to kill a murderer is to act no better than the murderer, they claim. There is all the difference in the world, however, between taking life for selfish and personal reasons and taking life in the cause of justice. We need to appreciate, firstly, God's right over life and death. It is God who gives this right to civil authorities to take the life of a murderer. The ultimate crime against humanity deserves the ultimate penalty. If we think only in terms of deterrents and cures we have removed the criminal from the sphere of justice. Failure to take seriously what a criminal deserves and only to consider what will cure him or deter others will result in the total abolition of justice. The history of our world is littered with cases of people being tortured and killed, not because they deserved such treatment, but in order to pacify public opinion or to enforce a warning. If a criminal is to receive a fair and moral sentence for his crime it must be in terms of retribution. The great Judge of all the earth has determined that for murder the death penalty is the only just punishment. Though God has ordained earthly rule and authority, it is bound to be imperfect. The best of institutions are run by people who are sinful and fallible. Mistakes are sometimes made, but this in no way invalidates the principles laid down here.

All this illustrates God's justice and the Day of Judgement. Rebellion against God is a capital offence. Unlawfully killing someone who bears the image of God is a monstrous crime. It clearly exposes the human heart's rebellion against God. It deserves the sentence of death. The true horror of sin was seen in the death of the Son of God. When people rebel against God it is not long before they treat in the same way those formed in God's image. This is again seen most graphically in the experience of Jesus Christ. An innocent, lovely human life was put to death for no just reason. What is more, the best system of law devised by man at that time failed miserably. Though Christ's blood was shed judicially by lawful human government, it was utterly unjust. A Roman court of law sentenced an innocent man to be crucified in the interests of self and society. Yet this grave miscarriage of justice did not stop

Paul and Peter insisting that we should honour heads of state and acknowledge that all civil authority owes its origins to God. It was in the purposes of God that Christ should be killed. He brought good out of this great evil. The ultimate crime became, through God's wisdom and grace, the supreme sacrifice. Christ experienced the ultimate punishment and paid the supreme price to rescue the worst of sinners. There is hope even for murderers.

2. Covenant promise and covenant sign (9:8-17)

The promise that God would never bring such universal disruption 'while the earth remains' (8:20-22) is now incorporated into the covenant that God had made with Noah (6:18).

The word 'covenant' occurs seven times in these verses. Both Isaiah and Jeremiah refer back to this covenant as they stress the certainty of God's future purposes and promises for his people (Isa. 54:9-10; Jer. 33:25-26).

The contents of the covenant

God pledges, **'Never again shall all flesh be cut off by the waters of the flood; never again shall there be a flood to destroy the earth'** (9:11).

The significant features of the covenant

It is unilateral. God is the initiator of this covenant. He imposes it. Often in human covenants the parties involved enter into mutual agreements. This is not the case in divine covenants: **'I establish my covenant with you'** (9:9,11).

It is universal. God not only makes this covenant with Noah and his sons (9:8), but with his **'descendants'** (literally, "seed")

after him and **'with every living creature'** that is with him
(9:9-10). He speaks to those who are in fellowship with him
and who can understand the commitment that God is making.
But the covenant promises not only concern Noah and his
sons, they include those not yet born and those who are incapable of appreciating the divine assurances.

It is unconditional. The pledge that God makes is not dependent on human beings or animals fulfilling certain obligations.
No conditions are laid down.

It is unending. It is described as **'the everlasting covenant
between God and every living creature of all flesh that is
on the earth'** (9:16). It is everlasting in the sense described in
verse 11. It is made **'for perpetual generations'** (9:12).

The sign of the covenant

The rainbow is the covenant sign. When God initiates a covenant he often appoints confirming signs. Circumcision became the sign of God's covenant with Abraham (17:11). The
Sabbath was the appointed sign of the old covenant that God
made with Israel at Sinai (Exod. 31:12-17). Circumcision and
the Sabbath were already in existence before they were used
by God as covenant signs. The same may be true of the rainbow. It is certainly going beyond the text of Scripture to insist
that rainbows did not exist before the Flood. On the other
hand, it is possible 'that completely new physical conditions
existed after the time of the flood and that the rainbow was a
new thing. The Bible does not tell us, and either way would fit
what these verses say.'[4] The point is that the rainbow has had
from that time onward a special significance. God says, **'I set
my rainbow in the cloud, and it shall be for the sign of the
covenant between me and the earth'** (9:13). The sun shining

on the rain clouds, giving that glorious spectrum of colour, became a very powerful confirmation of God's covenant.

The rainbow was not only appointed *by* God but *for* God. God says **'that the rainbow shall be seen in the cloud; and I will remember my covenant... The rainbow shall be in the cloud, and I will look on it to remember...'** (9:14-16). The rainbow sign is in the first instance for God's benefit. This is another example of anthropomorphic language. God needs no external reminder. The effect of putting it in this way is to emphasize that God will never go back on his word. John saw a rainbow surrounding God's throne, a sign of God's glory, mercy and of a new creation (Rev. 4:3).

It is not left to human beings to perform this covenant sign. In the case of other covenant signs like circumcision God calls on his people to implement them. Everything about this sign is an encouragement to Noah that God will stand by his commitment. Despite what the devil and humans might do, and despite terrible natural disasters that might happen in the future, God will never allow the whole earth to be flooded again.

The presence of the sign would in itself have brought no comfort. It was the explanation of the bow's function as a sign of the covenant that brought reassurance to Noah and his family. Imagine dark, threatening clouds covering the skies bringing a downpour of rain just prior to God's covenant announcement. It might well have filled Noah and his sons with foreboding as they remembered the recent judgement. But then the sun came out and a rainbow was formed. At that moment God spelled out the contents of the covenant and pointed to the rainbow as the sign of his gracious promise.

The rainbow has become one of the main symbols of those interested in 'green' issues. Unfortunately, many do not appreciate the true meaning of the sign. They live in fear of what might happen through human greed and the effects of global warming. The rainbow is the sign of God's mercy towards this planet. When we see the rainbow we can praise God that he has kept his promise down thousands of years. We can also be assured that he will continue to keep his promise until the day of final judgement.

The purpose of the covenant

Why should God go to all this trouble? Why keep the planet going one second longer? This covenant must be seen in association with God's promise in the Garden of Eden, concerning victory over the devil and salvation for humanity. God had promised to enter the fray to save humanity and the whole creation from the evil effects of sin and Satan (3:15). In order to realize these plans God made this covenant with the present creation. Nothing like a universal catastrophe must be allowed to take place again until God fulfilled his purposes through the 'seed' of the woman. Only when God has gathered to Jesus all his chosen ones out of every nation will this world order come to an end. The present creation is groaning, awaiting the coming in of the new (Rom. 8:18-23). Be wise, turn and believe the gospel before the final Day of Judgement!

14.
Canaan cursed

Please read Genesis 9:18-29

These verses make sad reading. How we wish Moses had ended the section with the account of God's covenant! If the Flood story had been a fairy tale it would no doubt have ended with Noah and his family living happily ever after. In fact, the ancient Near-Eastern text of the great flood which comes closest to the biblical account has the hero Utnapishtim enjoying immortality immediately after the flood. We love happy endings and feel cheated if the story does not end satisfactorily. But real life is far more complicated, and the Bible records life as it is. A common failing among us when writing or reading biographies is to pick out what suits us and ignore the rest. Anything which is embarrassing, or which spoils the picture, we tend to leave to one side. The Bible is an honest book. It does not hide the faults and imperfections of even the holiest of its characters.

Adam and Noah

Like Adam at the beginning, Noah was in a new world. They were both tillers of the ground. Both took fruit that did them no good. Nakedness and shame are associated with their actions and the sin of both affected their descendants.

While there are these similarities, there are obvious differences. Unlike Adam, Noah was not in an original state of innocence before he sinned. Noah was also suffering the effects of Adam's sin. Adam sinned in a perfect environment, whereas Noah sinned in a world which, although cleansed by the Flood, was still under the original curse. The sin of Adam affected the whole human race; on the other hand, Noah's sin permanently affected only one branch of the family. Both the similarities and the differences indicate that Noah belonged to the first Adam. The human race would have to look beyond Noah to the second man, the Last Adam.

Transition (9:18-19)

We are introduced again to Noah's three sons **'who went out of the ark'**. This time we have the added information that **'Ham was the father of Canaan.'** This alerts us to the main point of the episode. This final piece not only shows that the best of God's saints have feet of clay. It concerns the destiny of Noah's sons (9:25-27), and the introductory verses provide the necessary background. In addition, the words, **'From these the whole earth was populated'** (9:19), prepare us for the next major section of Genesis (10:1 – 11:9). They give advance notice that Noah's sons did fulfil the command 'to multiply and fill the earth' (9:1,7). All this is necessary for understanding how God fulfilled his promise made in Eden concerning the 'seed' of the woman.

Noah's drunken state and his sons' response (9:20-23)

Before the curtain falls on Noah and his sons, an incident is recorded which casts a blot on the character of this otherwise upright man.

The sins of Noah and his son Ham

Three sins are discernible.

1. Drunkenness

Verse 20 is often rendered in a way that suggests that Noah was the first to till the ground. But this was something that Adam did even before the Fall. What this verse says is that Noah, 'the man of the ground', was the first to plant a vineyard, or simply that **'Noah, the farmer, began to plant a vineyard.'**

No blame is attached to Noah for planting a vineyard or using the grapes to produce wine. The law of Moses encourages the purchase of wine or similar drink for festive occasions (Deut. 14:26). Wine is also used to accompany the burnt and peace offerings (Num. 15:5-10). Psalm 104:15 speaks of it as a gift from God to gladden people's lives. The Bible also indicates its use for medical purposes (Luke 10:34; 1 Tim. 5:23).

At the same time, this passage is the first of many in the Bible on the dangers of alcohol. If this was the first occasion for Noah to make and taste wine, it may be that he was not aware of what it would do to him. The fact is that he over-indulged himself and became drunk. Israel was constantly warned of the dangers of drinking too much wine: 'Wine is a mocker, intoxicating drink arouses brawling' (Prov. 20:1). Jesus warned against drunkenness (Luke 21:34) and Paul mentions it in his lists of vices typical of the ungodly world (Rom. 13:13). In order to keep in a ritually clean state, those who took a Nazirite vow were to abstain from alcohol. Likewise the priests were forbidden to drink when officiating in the holy sanctuary.

Drink is one of the great evils of society. It contributes towards the break-up of many marriages, to hooliganism at football matches and other anti-social behaviour. It is one of the main causes of absenteeism at work. The problem is world-wide. Things have not changed over thousands of years. In relating this incident at the beginning of a new era, it is as if God is letting the world know what will be one of the external characteristics of human sinfulness.

2. Immodesty

Associated with drunkenness is Noah's sin of immodesty. The Bible does not go into elaborate details. It is not like the tabloid newspapers, which take delight in giving the lurid details to satisfy the perverse minds of their readers. Enough information is given to indicate the sorry consequences of over-indulgence. Look what it did to this man of God who before the Flood walked with God and stood out blameless in that godless, violent society! How sad to see a man of God reduced to this pathetic state!

Sexual misconduct and drunkenness go hand in hand. Habakkuk 2:15 pronounces judgement on

> ... him who gives drink to his neighbour,
> Pressing him to your bottle,
> Even to make him drunk,
> That you may look on his nakedness.

Drink takes away people's inhibitions and enables them to throw off God-given restraints. It also makes a person vulnerable to attack and subject to further sinful behaviour (Lam. 4:21). God instigated the use of clothing to properly cover the shame we feel and to inhibit sexual misconduct. Our decadent Western society is obsessed with sex and drink. It is reminiscent of the Canaanite world, which at the time of Israel's exodus from Egypt was ripe for God's judgement.

3. Dishonouring parents

Noah's condition led his son into the sin of dishonouring his father, the subject of the Fifth Commandment (Exod. 20:12). Ham showed disrespect by looking at his father's shame and then by making it known to his brothers (9:22). Instead of quickly covering up his father's shame, he feasted his eyes upon it and gossiped about it to his brothers. Ham's action only added to his parent's disgrace. However old we are, the rule remains: 'Honour your father and mother' (Eph. 6:1-2). It also means that when our parents become old and senile we shall continue to be careful to treat them with respect and not joke about them to others.

In Ham we have the first indications of a society that delights in what is immodest and shameful and takes pleasure in pornography. Corrupt minds feed on scantily dressed or naked bodies in suggestive positions. The modern media have made their millions through pandering to human lust. In the process they have increased the demand and have become a major corrupting influence on society. No society can continue for long in this way. All the great civilizations of the past have disintegrated through internal moral collapse.

The righteous action of Shem and Japheth

The quick action of the other two brothers is wholly commendable. Here we are given practical help in dealing with what is shameful and improper. Notice the way their action is emphasized. In contrast to the very brief statement concerning Ham's action, verse 23 is full of detail and repetition. The repetition slows down the account to enable us to appreciate the honourable action of Shem and Japheth. It was clearly an awkward task as they walked backwards into Noah's tent with a cloak over their shoulders to cover their father's nakedness without looking at him.

Their whole approach was the very opposite to that of Ham: **'They did not see their father's nakedness.'** Even though Noah had brought dishonour upon himself, they treated him with respect. Children must honour their parents even when they see that their parents have brought shame upon themselves. We are not to gloat over the sins of others, nor to add to their shame by our own behaviour. All humans must be honoured, even the most depraved wretches.

This account also teaches us the need to take drastic, unusual action in order to remain clean in our own thoughts. We might think the way in which Shem and Japheth acted was 'over the top'. While it may seem extreme to us we should remember that Jesus said, 'If your eye makes you sin, pluck it out. It is better for you to enter the kingdom of God with one eye, than having two eyes, to be cast into hell fire' (Mark 9:47). We are taught to hate 'even the garment defiled by the flesh' (Jude 23).

Noah's prophecy (9:24-29)

Noah awoke out of his drunken stupor and became aware of Ham's sin. Either he knew intuitively, or someone told him. Ham is described as **'his younger son'**. The Hebrew has 'little son', which is an idiomatic way of expressing the superlative — 'the youngest son'. After realizing what had happened, Noah pronounced a curse on Ham's son and a blessing on his other sons.

What Noah uttered was not due to the influence of drink. The text makes this quite clear by emphasizing that he awoke, not so much from sleep as **'from his wine'**. He was in his right mind. Instead of being under the influence of wine, he came under the influence of God's Spirit.

Canaan cursed

There was nothing magical about this curse. Noah's words
are revelation from God and become effective through God's
power. The curse meant abject slavery for Canaan: **'A servant of servants he shall be to his brethren'** (9:25). The
phrase 'servant of servants' is another Hebraic idiom to express the superlative, like 'king of kings'.

The most striking thing about Noah's pronouncement is
the lack of any reference to Ham. Shem and Japheth are named
later in the blessing, but Ham is nowhere mentioned. Instead
of Ham's being cursed for what he had done, the curse fell on
his son, Canaan.[1] Why should this be? The curse is repeated
three times. Its fulfilment is certain. Some have suggested that
Canaan was involved with his father in dishonouring Noah,
but there is no hint of this in the text.

We need to see the curse on Canaan in the light of the blessing pronounced on Shem and Japheth. It is generally agreed
that the blessing looks beyond the time of Noah and his sons.
We are being prepared for the next section, where the three
sons become the heads of the three great branches of humanity. When Noah speaks of Shem, he is thinking of him as the
head of a particular racial grouping. The same is true of Japheth.
Thus, the blessing pertains to a time later than that of Shem
and Japheth. If this is appreciated, it will not be so startling to
find a descendant of Ham being cursed rather than Ham himself. In addition, although the curse is on Ham's son, Canaan,
it is directed to him as head of that particular branch of Ham's
line that became known as the Canaanites.

When this part of God's Word was written, the Canaanites
were notorious for their sexual misconduct (see Lev. 18). By
the time of the Exodus their sins had reached such a point that
they were ripe for God's just retribution to fall on them. God
used Israel to punish the Canaanites. Joshua was told that they

were to be devoted to the Lord for destruction. Those who escaped destruction became servants to Israel, just as Noah's curse indicated.

The curse on Canaan is a prophecy that looks beyond the time of Noah and his three sons. These sons become types of their descendants. Ham's attitude towards his father became a type of what would develop and be so abominable in that branch of his family represented by his youngest son. Thus the curse on Canaan represented God's just sentence on the sins of the Canaanites.

It is necessary to point out that this was not a curse on the whole Hamite race. Regrettably, this passage has been applied to all the black people of Africa. Many Dutch and American Reformed Christians have, in the past, propagated the view that blacks are inferior, less intelligent and doomed to be the white man's slave. It was the theological justification for the slave trade and later for the apartheid policy in South Africa. These deplorable ideas indicate how careful we must be when interpreting Scripture. How easy it is for culture, prejudice and prevailing worldly wisdom to colour our thinking and understanding of the Bible!

Shem and Japheth blessed

While Ham's disrespect for his father brings down a curse on only one group of his descendants, the honourable action of Shem and Japheth brings blessing to many. The prophetic nature of this benediction is the first of many such pronouncements in Genesis (cf. 27:27-29; 48:15-20; 49:2-28).

Shem has given us the words 'Semitic' and 'anti-Semitism'. The unusual way in which the blessing is formulated stresses that the line of promise, which we detected before the Flood, will run via Shem's descendants. It is not Shem who is blessed, but **'the LORD, the God of Shem'** (9:26). The benediction is in the doxology. As the curse was not directed to Ham but to Canaan, so the blessing is directed not to Shem but to 'the LORD' (Jehovah). Noah is associating God in a very special way with Shem. Shem is blessed by having the God of creation and redemption as his God. 'Happy are the people whose God is the LORD!' (Ps. 144:15). God's blessings can only be enjoyed by being united to God. The essence of divine blessing is to be in a personal relationship to God (John 17:3). The special association that God had with Shem would be seen later when the line was narrowed down to a particular family, and God would be known as the God of Abraham, Isaac and Jacob. Eventually the blessing would find its ultimate fulfilment in Jesus Christ, who is of this same line. All who belong to Jesus Christ are blessed. 'Blessed be the God and Father of our Lord Jesus Christ who has blessed us ... in Christ' (Eph. 1:3). This truth shows how the final part of the blessing relating to Japheth finds its ultimate fulfilment.

Japheth is to share in this blessing. In order to emphasize the point there is a play on his name: **'May God enlarge'** *(yapht)* **'Japheth'** *(Yephet)* (9:27). What Noah must have hoped for at his birth by giving him the name Japheth ('enlargement') is now confirmed in this prophetic blessing. The following chapter records how the descendants of Japheth spread far and wide over the face of the earth (10:2-5). There is a second part to Japheth's blessing: **'and may he dwell** [literally, "tabernacle"] **in the tents of Shem.'** An ancient Jewish interpretation believes that God is the subject of this part of the sentence. It is true that God did indeed dwell in the middle of Israel's tents: 'I will dwell [literally, "tabernacle"] among the children of Israel and will be their God' (Exod. 29:45; see 40:34-38). This same God 'dwelt [literally, "tabernacled"] among us' in the person of his Son, Jesus Christ (John 1:14).

Although this understanding is appealing, the more obvious sense of the words would suggest that what we have here is a continuation of Japheth's blessing. The descendants of Japheth are to dwell in the tents of those of Shem. In this context, to live in someone's tent involves sharing in that person's life or destiny (see 24:67; Ps. 84:10). The descendants of Japheth are to share in the fortunes and blessings of Shem. We have seen that the heart of Shem's blessing is spiritual. It involves being in a personal relationship with God. The nearest we get to any fulfilment of this in the Old Testament is during the era of David and Solomon. People from other nations came to Jerusalem to admire the God-given blessings (1 Kings 4:34; 10:13,23). However, this period of Israel's history was only an imperfect type of the true and ultimate fulfilment. Noah's prophecy points to the spiritual blessings of the gospel enjoyed by the Gentile nations as well as the Jews. Amos speaks of rebuilding

> ... the tabernacle of David,
> Which has fallen down...
> So that the rest of mankind may seek the LORD,
> Even all the Gentiles who are called by my name,
> Says the LORD
>   (Acts 15:16-17, quoting Amos 9:11-12).

Conclusion (9:28-29)

We are reminded of the genealogy in chapter 5. There is one interesting variation to, and one important omission from, the familiar pattern that we find in that chapter. Instead of saying, 'after he begot ...' (5:7,10,13, etc.), the text tells us that **'after the flood ...'** Noah lived 350 years. The passing of time is marked, not by the usual references to human births, but by the great Flood, which involved a new beginning. It separated the old world from the new.

The striking omission is the phrase that always appears after the time reference informing us that 'He begot sons and daughters' (5:16,19,22,26, etc.) This draws our attention to the fact that Noah only had three sons. He had no other children after the Flood. This means that all humanity is descended from these sons, Shem, Ham and Japheth. It prepares us for the next section, which will begin with what these sons of Noah produced.

Noah walked with God, and God graciously preserved him from that watery judgement so that it could be written that **'Noah lived after the flood'**. Yet Noah was not the promised 'seed'. Though he came through into a new situation, with all its possibilities for a fresh start, sin had not been eliminated and the original curse still hung over humanity. Noah, the first man of the new beginning, lived 350 years after the Flood, **'and he died'** (9:29). Death continued to reign. **'So all the days of Noah were nine hundred and fifty years.'** Human hopes were dashed, and yet God had made a commitment, of which the rainbow was a sign, to give stability to the earth. He made this pledge precisely because of the curse he had pronounced on the devil which involved blessing for humanity. In order to keep that promise he had saved Noah and his family.

But what of the future? Where are we to look for the fulfilment of God's original promise? Which branch of Noah's family will produce the woman's Seed who will bruise the head of the serpent? The future hope is again seen in the midst of sin, shame, dishonour and curse. Blessing comes through the line of Shem. The final, and most amazing, example of God's bringing blessing out of a cursed situation, and good out of gross wickedness, is the cross of our Lord Jesus. This is the goal to which these happenings in Genesis point.

Part 5:
What Noah's sons produced (10:1 – 11:9)

15.
The origin of nations

Please read Genesis 10:1-32

Living in a large city like London often means there is an international flavour when Christians gather for worship. It can be a moving experience to be in fellowship with representatives of different nations. It is a little foretaste of the scene described by John of that innumerable throng from 'all nations, tribes, peoples, and tongues, standing before the throne and before the Lamb, clothed with white robes' (Rev. 7:9-10). In order to appreciate the full significance of that future scene, this section of Genesis is vitally important. It also provides the background to so many of the Bible's references to the nations.

The heading again calls to mind the promised 'seed'. Instead of a single person, the three sons of Noah are named. We read, **'This is the genealogy of the sons of Noah: Shem, Ham and Japheth.'** It alerts us to the wide-ranging nature of what follows. Many races and nations are mentioned. The section is in two parts: the table of nations (10:1-32) and the tower of Babel (11:1-9).

Introduction to the table of nations (10:1)

Noah's sons did not have any children until after the Flood. The following table shows how they multiplied and repopulated the earth. God will not allow the earth to be depopulated again until the end comes. There have been plagues which have wiped out millions of people, but God does not allow them to overtake the whole world. Probably the worst was the bubonic plague, known as the 'Black Death', which ravaged Europe in the fourteenth century and killed nearly half the population. The AIDS epidemic is of deep concern at present and millions are affected worldwide; nevertheless, God is committed to supporting human life on the earth. He gives skill to scientists in their efforts to control disease. Where divine judgement is deserved and the status quo is shaken, divine mercy and faithfulness act to stop total destruction.

The table is divided into three parts, according to the three sons of Noah. The total number of names descended from them adds up to seventy, not counting the names in brackets in verse 14 which do not belong to the main list. Seventy is a familiar number in Scripture (see Exod. 24:1; Num. 11:16). It became a traditional round number and symbolic of a large group. This suggests that the list of names was never meant to be exhaustive. It is a representative list. For the most part it mentions peoples and nations that would have been known when Moses was writing. 'Its cosmopolitan outlook suggests an author well-informed about world affairs and possibly connected with a royal court.'[1]

We are being prepared for the promises that God made to Abraham (12:3; 18:18). Before Abraham we have seventy nations mentioned; after Abraham his 'seed' numbers seventy (46:27). While Adam produced seventy nations through Noah's sons, Abraham, like a second Adam, grew to seventy through Jacob's sons. The one chosen from the nations produced a number that represented all the nations (see Deut. 32:8). This again points us forward to Jesus, the Last Adam, who is of the seed of Abraham and brings God's promises to a grand and ultimate fulfilment.

The table also draws attention to the special blessing associated with Shem's descendants (9:26-27). The order of the list — Japheth, Ham and Shem — is not what we are used to seeing. Neither is it the order according to age, for Japheth is the eldest (10:21) and Ham the youngest (9:24). As we progress through Genesis we find that the line of promise is always dealt with last. Cain's line was first considered, before the descendants of Seth. So here, the genealogies of Noah's other sons appear before the chosen line of Shem.

Japheth's descendants (10:2-5)

Seven sons are mentioned and seven grandsons. The list is already selective because only the grandsons by two of the sons, Gomer and Javan, are given. You will forgive a Welshman' s interest in Gomer because he is identified with the later Cimmerians from which *'Cymry'* ('Welshmen') is said to derive! (see Ezek. 38:6). The nations mentioned are, from a Middle-Eastern perspective, on the outer fringes of the world. They live to the north, west and east of the land of Canaan. Noah prophesies that God will enlarge Japheth (9:27) and this is seen to be fulfilled, for his descendants inhabit vast portions of the earth.

There is a summary statement in verse 5 concerning Japheth's line, and two terms found here become significant later. One is **'coastland peoples'** (or 'isles') and the other is **'nations'**, or **'Gentiles'**. Prophets and psalmists look forward to the establishment of God's righteous rule over the whole earth, which the devil has usurped. The Servant of the Lord 'will bring forth justice to the Gentiles' and 'The coastlands shall wait for his law' (Isa. 42:1,4). Messiah's reign will stretch from sea to sea. 'The kings of Tarshish and of the isles will bring presents,' and 'All nations shall serve him' (Ps. 72:10-11).

God's people in Old Testament days must have wondered how
this could possibly come about. They had a brief, small preview in the days of Solomon, when we are told that 'All the
earth sought the presence of Solomon to hear his wisdom,
which God had put in his heart. Each man brought his present'
(1 Kings 10:24-25). In Jesus we have a greater than Solomon.

> Jesus shall reign where'er the sun
> Doth his successive journeys run;
> His kingdom stretch from shore to shore,
> Till moons shall wax and wane no more.
>
> (Isaac Watts)

Ham's descendants (10:6-20)

Much more space is devoted to this line than to Japheth's because many of those grouped among the descendants of Ham
were close neighbours of Israel, or were among those who
affected Israel in a big way. Some of the names mentioned are
not regarded by linguists and anthropologists as Hamites, but
the classification is not always according to language and race,
but according to lands and tribal groupings, or because of their
associations with Israel. Through intermarriage certain groups
would have been able to trace their lineage to more than one
line (see Assyria/Asshur in 10:11,22).

The four sons of Ham are named: **'Cush, Mizraim, Put
and Canaan'** (10:6). Again, the numerical pattern of listing
descendants in sevens is evident in the first name. Five sons of
Cush are mentioned, together with two grandsons through
Raamah (10:7). This again indicates that Moses has been
selective.

'Cush' represents the peoples of Arabia, Ethiopia and the
Sudan. It is clear from this, as 9:25-27 has indicated, that not
all Ham's line was cursed. Many of his descendants would

partake with Japheth of the blessings to come. Again, the gifts
and testimony of the Queen of Sheba in the days of Solomon
become a type, or preview, of the universal rule of God through
Messiah. 'The kings of Sheba and Seba will offer gifts,' and
'The gold of Sheba will be given to him' (Ps. 72:10,15). Acts
makes a point of recording the conversion of the Ethiopian
eunuch (Acts 8:26-39). **'Raamah'** is associated with Sheba
in Ezekiel 27:22.

The detail concerning **'Nimrod'**, who ruled territory **'in
the land of Shinar'** (Babylonia), is added for a special reason
(10:8-12). Five sons of Cush have already been listed. This
sixth son is considered separately because he was an important figure in this early period and what is said of him provides
further light on the incident recorded in the next chapter. What
we are told indicates the justness of God's reaction to the Babel
incident. There are four points, in particular, which are worthy
of note.

1. The name **'Nimrod'** means, 'We shall rebel,' which
may suggest that he was behind the rebellion against
God.

2. The description, **'a mighty one on the earth,'**
reminds us of the violent days before the Flood (6:4).

3. His connection with **'Babel'** prepares us for the
following chapter.

4. He had a name for being a **'mighty hunter before
the LORD'** (literally 'mighty of game before the LORD').
The other great hunter in Genesis was Esau, who despised his birthright. 'Before the LORD' recalls the statement that the earth was corrupt 'before God' (6:11). It
suggests that Nimrod stood out head and shoulders
above his contemporaries. He is 'the archetype of Mesopotamian ideals of kingship', where pride in building,
fighting and hunting was the order of the day.[2]

Nimrod was responsible for the early developments in Mesopotamia which led to the great civilizations of that region: **'And the beginning of his kingdom was Babel, Erech, Accad and Calneh, in the land of Shinar. From that land he went to Assyria and built Nineveh...'** Babel is associated with the Babylonians; Erech is one of the earliest Summerian cities; while Accad and Nineveh are cities of Assyria, the latter becoming the capital of the Assyrian Empire. Nimrod is thus a second Cain, living in opposition to God, and yet possessing natural gifts and abilities to produce order and stability in society.

The linking of Assyria with Babylon is also significant. Micah the prophet couples Assyria with the 'land of Nimrod' (Micah 5:6) and Isaiah considers them together in his oracle against Babylon (Isa. 13:1 – 14:27; see also Num. 24:24). We are already being prepared in Genesis for the later symbolic associations of Babylon with human pride and wickedness which God will ultimately destroy. Nevertheless, there is blessing for rebellious Ninevites who repent and turn to the Lord, as was seen in the days of Jonah.

'Mizraim' is the Hebrew name for Egypt. The sons of Egypt are mentioned, not as individuals but groups of people or tribes. This is shown by the plural ending *'-im'* in their names, such as **'Ludim'** and **'Anamim'**. Egypt, of course, figures prominently in the history of Israel and Genesis ends with God blessing Egypt through Joseph. Isaiah prophesies a time when both Egypt and Assyria will be one with Israel. The Lord will bless them saying, 'Blessed is Egypt my people, and Assyria the work of my hands, and Israel my inheritance' (Isa. 19:24-25). Mercy triumphs over wrath as the descendants of Ham find blessing by being associated with Israel's God.

No descendants are given for **'Put'**. The prophecy of Nahum mentions it as a country allied to Egypt (Nahum 3:9). It is commonly identified with Libya.

Finally, the line of **'Canaan'** is presented in some detail. All the tribes described as occupying the land of Canaan in the days of Moses and Joshua are noted. Though the Canaanite language (Ugaritic) belongs to the West Semitic language group, the Canaanite people are clearly not Semitic (Shemite) as far as their roots are concerned. The text also defines the boundaries of where the Canaanites lived (10:19). Moses is anticipating God's word to Abraham concerning Canaan (13:14-17; 15:18-21) and the later conquest of the land by Israel. The table of nations already defines what will become known as the promised land. In the days of Abraham we are repeatedly told that the Canaanites or the Amorites lived in the land (12:6; 13:7; 15:16,21). The cities of the plain which were destroyed in the days of Abraham are also listed as part of the boundary line of Canaan — **'Sodom, Gomorrah, Admah, and Zeboiim'**. These cities were the first to experience the curse that God had pronounced on Canaan.

Shem's descendants (10:21-31)

To impress upon us the importance of this family line, it is given a special introduction. Instead of saying, 'The sons of Shem were...' (cf. 10:2,6), it begins: **'And children were born also to Shem...'** Attention is drawn to this son and his family. We are also reminded of Shem's relationship to Japheth: **'the brother of Japheth the elder'** (10:21; cf. 9:27). Though Japheth is the oldest brother, he will be blessed by his association with Shem. The introduction also highlights one particular family of the line of Shem: **'... Shem, the father of all the children of Eber'**. Eber is a descendant of Shem's son **Arphaxad** (10:24-25). It is from this family that Abraham will be born. Eber is related to the word 'Hebrew', a term often used by people of other nations to describe Abraham and the

Israelites. For instance, we read of 'Abram the Hebrew' (14:13; see also Exod. 1:15,19; 2:7).

Abraham and the Israelites are descendants of Peleg, the son of Eber. Peleg's family tree is not given at this point, for that will be the subject of the next section (11:10-26). What we are told is that **'In his days the earth was divided.'** This is probably a reference to what happened at the tower of Babel (11:1-9). The mention of the thirteen sons of Peleg's brother, Joktan, completes the list of Shem's descendants. As for the other sons of Shem, only the descendants of **'Aram'** are listed (10:23). It is because of the close links that Abraham's family had with the Arameans (or Syrians) that more information is given (see the references to 'Bethuel the Syrian' and 'Laban the Syrian' in 25:20). When presenting the first-fruit offerings to the priest, the Israelites were taught to recite, 'My father was a Syrian, about to perish, and he went down to Egypt...' (Deut. 26:5).

Conclusion (10:32)

The final verse forms the grand conclusion, linking up with the first verse and the other summary statements (10:5,20,31). What, then, is the overall purpose of the chapter?

Firstly, the chapter stresses that *the human race*, despite linguistic and geographical differences, *is really one family* (10:32). This unique table of nations reminds us that there is no super race. When nations become powerful they often begin to feel they are of different stock to the rest of humanity. Paul reminded the proud Athenians that God 'has made from one blood every nation of men to dwell on all the face of the earth' (Acts 17:26). Israel, too, needed to be reminded of this fact (Deut. 7:7).

Secondly, the chapter bears witness to *the differences that do exist*. It is a fact of life that the human race is divided by race, language and land, and this raises the question of the reason for such division. The next chapter provides the answer.

Thirdly, the phrase **'after the flood'** occurs at the beginning and end of the chapter. We are not allowed to forget this judgement on rebellious humanity. The phrase also indicates God's grace. There is an 'after'. From one of Noah's descendants will arise a woman's 'Seed' who will destroy the one described by Jesus as 'the ruler of this world' (John 12:31).

Fourthly, we notice that Moses has inserted into the list several additional notes. These notes call attention to *what God will do in judgement in the future*. The first relates to Nimrod and indicates that God was not overreacting when judgement fell on Babel. There are also notes concerning 'the Philistines and Caphtorim' (10:14), the Canaanites, Sodom and Gomorrah and the other cities of the plain (10:15-19), all of whom experienced God's righteous wrath.

Finally, the chapter *prepares us for the story of Abraham's call* and God's promise that through his descendants all families of the earth would find blessing. This promise is fulfilled in Jesus Christ (2 Cor. 1:20), who is the Saviour of the world (John 4:42). The Great Commission of Jesus to his people is: 'Go, therefore, and make disciples of all the nations...' (Matt. 28:18-20). Today, it is possible to find people of almost every nation of the world calling 'on the name of Jesus Christ our Lord, both theirs and ours' (1 Cor. 1:2). The day of grace is still with us and there are more to be gathered in.

16.
The origin of languages

Please read Genesis 11:1-9

It is estimated that there are 6,000 languages spoken worldwide. Most of these languages fall into family groups, such as the Indo-European, Hamito-Semitic (including Hebrew, Arabic and some African groups), Sino-Tibetan, Malayo-Polynesian, Uto-Aztecan (native American groups) and the Finno-Ugric (including Finnish and Hungarian). There are some languages, such as Basque, which defy classification. The whole subject is fascinating and there are many matters which linguists are at a loss to explain. What we are told in these verses is that the multiplicity of languages was the result of supernatural activity.

Three great judgements have affected the whole of humanity. The first was the result of the Fall, the second was the Flood and the third was the communications breakdown at Babel.

A question of order

Why is the Babel account placed here and not before the table of nations? Different lands and languages are mentioned in chapter 10 before we are given the cause and explanation. A number of good reasons have been suggested for this order:

In the first place, it clearly emphasizes that the creation blessing, reiterated after the Flood, was fulfilled. The sons of Noah were fruitful and filled the earth (see 9:1). It would have been more difficult to present this point if God's judgement at Babel had been related first.

Secondly, it indicates that God's judgements in this world are set against the background of his kindness towards his creatures. While God's anger is revealed against all human sin, it must be viewed in the context of the stability promised in God's covenant with Noah.

Thirdly, the judgement at Babel is placed immediately before the account of the line of promise (11:10-26). This is deliberate in order to indicate that the answer to human sinfulness lay in God's covenant with Abraham. The account of Babel lies between two genealogical lists. In these lists, our attention is drawn particularly to Eber's two sons Peleg and Joktan, for it was in their day the earth was divided. It is the non-elect line of Joktan that is listed in chapter 10, ending with the note concerning 'the mountain of the east' (10:26-30). The east is often associated with going away from God. It is in the east that the Tower of Babel incident occurs (11:2). Eber's line through Peleg is the subject of the next section and ends with the mention of Terah and Abram, who moved from the east towards the land of promise (11:10-26,31; 12:5). In this way the focus continues to be on the fulfilment of God's special promise of a 'Seed' who will crush the head of the old serpent and save God's people from their sins.

Relating the story

There are five brief scenes, and the central one, the Lord's visit (11:5), draws our attention to the turning-point in the whole incident.

Introduction (11:1)

'Now the whole earth had one language and one speech.'
The 'whole earth' means all the inhabitants of the earth (see
9:19). There is nothing surprising in our being told that the
descendants of Noah all spoke the same language. People who
have a common origin will naturally speak a common language.

Scene I (11:2)

People were on the move, journeying **'from the east'**. This
would be better translated 'eastwards'. These early settlers
had migrated from the Ararat region (present-day northern
Turkey and Armenia) to **'a plain in the land of Shinar'** (or
Sumer), a fertile area in Mesopotamia. Cain went east of Eden,
away from God's presence (4:16) and Lot was to travel east
away from Abram (13:11). It is possible that we are intended
to recognize this move eastwards as being wrong and something that will result in judgement on the people.

Scene II (11:3-4)

The development of a godless civilization reminds us of the
activities of Cain and his descendants (see 4:17). The world
after the Flood was no different from the world before the
Flood. The same errors were repeated. Human beings made
their plans without reference to God.
    **'Come, let us make bricks... Come, let us build our-
selves a city...'** We have a very interesting and accurate description of the building techniques in southern Mesopotamia
at this time compared with those in Egypt and Canaan. Lacking significant quantities of stone, they began to manufacture
bricks. They hardened mud bricks in the fire and **'had asphalt
for mortar'**. The Gulf region is still rich in oil deposits. Crude

oil lies close to the surface in many places. They used the tar, or bitumen, to cement the bricks together.

Their purpose in developing these skills was in order to build **'a city, and a tower whose top is in the heavens'**. These people had big plans. They wanted the tower to be a kind of uniting-point between heaven and earth. By their own efforts they were trying to bridge the gulf, to meet God, to have contact with God and to be like God. This was the original temptation in the Garden of Eden — to be like God, but without reference to God and independently of him. Humanity, in its rebellion against God's authority, is for ever trying to grasp at becoming like God.

Towers became very popular in the Babylonian region. They were the ancient equivalent of our 'skyscrapers'. Remains of a number of them exist to this day. They are called ziggurats. The great temple tower of Marduk in Babylon was discovered at the end of the nineteenth century. It rose to a height of 100 metres (over 300 feet). The tower referred to in Genesis may have been a prototype of these later towers which became temple shrines to the gods worshipped in that area.

Everything about the project was man-centred. The use of **'us'** and **'ourselves'** emphasizes that this building was their idea and for their own benefit. We have not changed. The Empire State Building in New York, the world's tallest building when it was erected in 1931, was later dwarfed by the twin towers of the World Trade Centre, which rose to a height of 412 metres, or 1,350 feet, until their destruction in September 2001. Cities all over the world have copied these monuments to human achievement. They have become status symbols. Malaysia has since outdone the United States by erecting an even higher structure, the Petronas Towers in Kuala Lumpur. No doubt we shall hear of other countries trying to get into the *Guinness Book of Records* with even taller towers.

Their self-centredness is also depicted in their boastful statement: **'Let us make a name for ourselves.'** This is the height
of impiety, for it is usurping God's prerogative. In the Bible it
is God alone who makes a name for himself. He alone has the
right to see that his name is glorified, for there is no one greater.
Moses and the godly men who came after him were aware of
the way God had made a name for himself at the time of the
Exodus (Isa. 63:12; Neh. 9:10; Jer. 32:20). It is in us all to
want to become famous and to have a reputation for having
done something great. What God said to Baruch he says to
us: 'Do you seek great things for yourself? Do not seek them'
(Jer. 45:5). The important thing is to work for God's honour.
He is the greatest and he will reward those who put him first.

God also has the right to make great whom he wills. He
promised to make Abraham's name great (12:2) and David's
(2 Sam. 7:9). These men were descended from Noah's son
Shem, and 'Shem' means 'name'. God had already promised
to make Shem great by associating himself with him and his
line: 'Blessed be the LORD, the God of Shem.' These men whom
God made great were preparing the way for the coming of
Messiah, who is also of this line from Shem through Abraham
and David. They are types of the one whose 'name shall endure for ever' (Ps. 72:17). Jesus Christ has the right to the
name that is above every name. He is Jehovah, to whom every
knee shall bow (Isa. 45:22-25; Phil. 2:9-11). Jesus alone is the
one who unites heaven and earth. He is the temple, and only in
him can we be united to God and have fellowship with him.
Every other way is doomed to failure, as we see in this incident.

Finally, the reason for the whole enterprise, we are told,
was **'lest we be scattered abroad over the face of the whole
earth'**. They tried to congregate in one area, contrary to the
divine command to fill the earth. By building the tower they
may well have been trying to protect themselves from another
judgement like the Flood. By building this tower to heaven

they may have thought they could get above, and out of reach of, what God might do to them. The irony is that they were condemned to suffer what they tried to prevent. God, the one whom they were opposing, was the one who caused them to scatter.

Scene III (11:5)

This is the turning-point in the whole story. We move from the earthly scene to the heavenly and view the whole episode from God's vantage-point. The tower, which people thought would reach to heaven — why, God could hardly see it! So insignificant was it that God must come down to look at it! Anthropomorphic language is being used again. When we read that **'The LORD came down'**, we are not to think that God necessarily had to come to earth to see what was going on. By using human actions to express God's evaluation of the situation the text vividly portrays how trifling and puny are the things of which people boast. We pride ourselves in our great achievements, but what do they amount to in God's estimation? To the one 'who sits above the circle of the earth ... its inhabitants are like grasshoppers' (Isa. 40:22).

> Why do the nations rage
> And the people plot a vain thing?...
> He who sits in the heavens shall laugh;
> The LORD shall hold them in derision
>
> (Ps. 2:1,4).

Scene IV (11:6-7)

In Scene II we found human beings saying, 'Come, let us make... Come let us build...' Now we have God expressing his intentions: **'Come, let us go down and there confuse their**

language.' God did not topple their tower; he confused their communications. This community scheme, where God was not only left out but directly opposed, was taken seriously by God. 'God in judgement decrees that the centrifugal forces will have their way. If you will live without God as the centre, you will have no centre at all.'[1]

God's deliberations with himself and the phraseology used remind us of the pronouncement in 3:22. Building the tower, like eating from the tree of knowledge, is seen as a prelude to something worse, which God cannot for one moment tolerate: **'This is what they begin to do; now nothing that they propose to do will be withheld from them.'** Just as people cannot rebel against God and at the same time partake of life, so God will not allow human beings unlimited freedom to do their own thing. Using a similar combination of words, Job confessed to the Lord, 'I know that you can do everything, and that no purpose of yours can be withheld from you' (Job 42:2). Human beings, precisely because they are created in the divine image, are capable of planning and executing incredible projects. Because they are sinners such planning or plotting has to be restrained. God puts a brake on human rebellion. He will not allow it to reach the proportions evident prior to the Flood. No similar worldwide judgement is to take place before the Second Coming of Jesus Christ. In this respect, the judgement at Babel includes a gracious provision for the long-term preservation of life. God sent the communications problem as a restraining influence in a world bent on acting contrary to God. Such restraints will be removed prior to Christ's return (2 Thess. 2:6-8).

The first person plural (**'us'**) provides another indication in these early chapters that there is a community of persons within the oneness of God (cf. 1:26). It is this divine community which acts to destroy the united anti-God community so that the divine plan for the salvation of sinful people might not be thwarted.

Scene V (11:8)

In Scene I we saw people on the move, coming to live in one place. Now people were forced to move as a result of God's action. Human plans were frustrated and what was feared most happened: **'So the LORD scattered them abroad from there over the face of all the earth.'** Without the ability to communicate through a common language, it was quite impossible for them to co-operate. Empires can only be built where there is a common language. Today we are closer to a centralized world government than we have ever been since the days of Babel. Nations are gathering together into large economic units, and global networks increase to everyone's benefit. One can appreciate how all this could be used by the great end-time 'lawless one' who will dominate the entire world. The totalitarian regimes of the past are but precursors of the final world empire prior to our Lord's coming to judge.

Conclusion (11:9)

This verse summarizes the results of God's judgement. The inhabitants of the earth, whose ideas of unity, security and well-being ran counter to God's commands, were brought to confusion and forced to scatter, so that the city they were building remained unfinished. **'Therefore its name is called Babel.'** Our word 'Babylon' is the Greek form of the Hebrew 'Babel'. The Babylonians understood the name to mean 'the gate of god' *(bab-ili)*. By a play on words, the Bible presents the real significance of the name — 'confused, mixed up'. That which was meant as a showpiece of human enterprise and technology, and as a meeting-point between heaven and earth, became a reminder of divine judgement on human pride and autonomy.

Pride of man and earthly glory,
Sword and crown betray his trust;
What with care and toil he buildeth,
Tower and temple, fall to dust.
  But God's power,
  Hour by hour,
Is my temple and my tower.

(Robert Bridges)

The message of Babel

The British journalist Libby Purves read the Babel narrative in
the light of the war in Kosovo.[2] She acknowledged the frustration felt by many philosophers over the breakdown in communication between people, leading to separation and conflict. Like so many who bewail the folly of human inability to
co-operate, she dismissed the God of the Bible and his diag-
nosis of the human predicament. Instead, she placed her confidence in the ability of people to change things for the better.
What a futile hope!

'Communication' is one of the 'in' words of our age. Good
communications help to break down barriers and prevent mis-
understanding and isolationism. Babel is about lack of communication, and it is seen as a divine judgement. The united
action of rebellious humans was curbed so that God might
fulfil his plans to overcome the Evil One and redeem a people
to himself through the promised seed.

In Scripture Babel, or Babylon, stands for world power
in opposition to God. Nimrod, the symbol of personal prowess and rebellion against God, is associated with Babel and
other well-known cities which were later to become centres of civilization and godless rule. Isaiah the prophet describes another king of Babylon in satanic terms (14:13-15).

In Nebuchadnezzar's dream of the great image that was smashed by the stone that became a mountain, the head of gold represented Babylon. Today there is little to show of that great city; its famous hanging gardens lie in ruins in the sand. It is no accident that the last book of the Bible uses Old Testament references to Babylon (Isa. 13-14; 47:1-11; Jer. 50-51) to speak of worldly opposition to God and his people (Rev. 17-19). In contrast to Babylon, the great harlot who is left naked and destroyed, we have the picture of the new Jerusalem, the bride of Christ.

The stone which became a mountain and filled the whole earth in Daniel's vision is the rule established by Jesus. Our Lord's parable of the mustard seed underlined the truth of Daniel's interpretation. From small, unimpressive beginnings God's rule spreads far and wide and triumphs (Matt. 13:31-32). Associated with this is the idea of a new society, the city of God, made up of people from all nations united in the worship of God. There is to be an undoing of the Babel judgement. The prophets foretell the end of the confusion and speak of a time when Egyptians will be called God's people and speak the language of Canaan (see Isa. 19:18-25; Zeph. 3:9-10).

When certain Greeks came looking for him, Jesus began to speak of his death. He said, 'Now is the judgement of this world; now the ruler of this world will be cast out. And I, if I am lifted up from the earth, will draw all peoples to myself' (John 12:20-22,31-32). After his resurrection, Jesus commanded his disciples to preach 'repentance and remission of sins ... in his name to all nations' (Luke 24:47; Acts 1:8). This they did after they received divine power.

On that Pentecost Sunday when the promised Holy Spirit filled those first believers, there was in the streets of Jerusalem a great reversal of the Babel incident. Instead of confusion and scattering, the language barrier was broken down and people from different parts of the world heard the wonderful

works of God in their own tongue. In his account of that remarkable day, Luke is careful to note that there were representatives from 'every nation under heaven'. Descendants of Shem,
Ham and Japheth are listed. A new multi-national, multi-racial,
multi-lingual society was born comprised of those who trusted
Jesus for salvation. Instead of division and separation, these
believers were together (Acts 2:1-47).

Pentecost is a foretaste of that grand and glorious day when
sin will be completely eradicated and perfect unity restored.
All who belong to the Lord Jesus Christ will be of one language, living in perfect harmony in that city which has foundations, whose builder and maker is God (Heb. 11:10,16; Rev.
21:2,24-27). This is the 'city of God' of which 'glorious things
are spoken', where people of various nations will be recorded
as having been born.

> I will make mention of Rahab [Egypt] and Babylon to
>   those who know me;
> Behold, O Philistia and Tyre, with Ethiopia:
> 'This one was born there.'...
>
> The LORD will record,
> When he registers the peoples:
> 'This one was born there'
>
>   (Ps. 87:1-7).

It is God's gospel which genuinely unites people.

Part 6:
What Shem produced (11:10-26)

17.
Semitic origins

Please read Genesis 11:10-26

It is one of the disciplines and blessings of working through a book of the Bible in a consecutive way that it forces us to consider passages that do not have an immediate appeal. This little section of names and ages fulfils an important function and provides us with an opportunity to review the previous chapters and prepare for what lies ahead.

Introduction

The opening words, **'This is the genealogy of ...'**, remind us that we are beginning a new section. The phrase occurs eleven times throughout Genesis and could be translated, 'This is what *x* produced.' In no way can it mean, 'This is the origins of *x*.' It is not dealing with ancestors, but with offspring.[1] In 2:4 it is used metaphorically for what heaven and earth produced. Thereafter, it is used literally.

Each time the phrase appears it acts like a section heading. It would be wrong, however, to think of these introductory words as mere section markers. They are there to emphasize the great purpose of the book of Genesis. These headings have the effect of binding the whole book together and focusing our minds on the promises of God. They act as major signposts encouraging us to look forward to the fulfilment of God's purposes for this world. Genesis highlights the importance of 'seed', or 'offspring'. It is therefore most appropriate to have this introductory expression drawing our attention to a family line. The very structure of Genesis calls us to look to a seed that God will use to gain victory over the devil and his offspring.

The family tree

People in the West are again interested in their roots. There are helps galore in the form of books and courses. For those in a hurry, or too busy to bother, researchers will do the work for you at a price. To a previous generation, and in many cultures today, such activity would have been unnecessary. The family tree was known and passed on accurately by word of mouth from parent to child. Where they came from mattered a great deal.

The ancient world had the same interest. Here we have another example of a family tree. It reminds us that we are dealing with real people in real situations. Genesis is not a book of fairy tales. The genealogies are there because the people named really existed. These men are all links in a chain that would eventually lead to the Saviour of the world.

There are two types of family tree in Genesis. One type concentrates on presenting the trunk of the tree. It lists the descendants who belong to the main family line. We call this a linear genealogy, where A fathers B, B fathers C, and C fathers D (see 5:1-32). In the other type, the trunk often gets lost in the branches. Family members and their descendants are named who are not belonging to the principal line. This is known as a segmented genealogy, where D fathers E, F and G; E fathers H, I and J; F fathers K, L and M; and G fathers N, O and P (see 10:1-29).

This short section contains a linear genealogy. It lists Shem's descendants and is similar to the family tree we have already read in chapter 5. The Bible uses genealogies to cover large periods of history in a brief and succinct way. Chronicles, for instance, can take us from Adam to David in the space of a few chapters. But these genealogies do much more than that. They point out important family lines and highlight significant details. The linear genealogy in chapter 5 took us quickly from Adam to Noah, establishing the main line of descent and emphasizing the universality of death. It paused a moment to stress the importance of fellowship with God which not even death can sever.

The present genealogy moves us rapidly on from Noah's son Shem to Abraham's father, Terah. Scholars often insist that ten descendants of Shem are listed here, following the same pattern as the genealogy in chapter 5. But the number is nine. In order to achieve the extra name they assume that Noah or Abraham must be included. The ancient Greek translation of the Old Testament, the Septuagint (*LXX* for short), was also keen to have a balancing list of ten names. It achieved this by inserting a 'Cainan' between Arphaxad and Salah, or Shelah (see verses 12-13). Luke includes this name in his genealogy of Jesus (Luke 3:36). All this suggests again that we may not have a complete list of names from Shem to Terah. It might be an appealing idea to think of Abraham as a baby being cuddled by Noah, his great-great-grandfather to the tenth generation, but there is no indication that this was the case. In fact, the Bible tells us that Abraham came from a pagan background (Josh. 24:2).

It might be objected that, if there are gaps in these statements, then the Bible is in error when it states that A was x years old when he fathered B, and B was y years old when he fathered C, and so on. This is not the case. It was an accepted procedure in genealogical tables to miss out names. If we

compare Ezra 7:1-5 with 1 Chronicles 6:3-14 there are a
number of omissions. The same is true when we compare
Matthew's genealogy of Jesus with Old Testament lists (cf.
Matt. 1:8 with 1 Chr. 3:11-12). We must allow for the possibility of a similar reading between the lines in the Genesis family trees. The following pattern will help to understand what
sometimes happens: 'A lived x years and fathered a son from
whom B was a direct descendant. After he fathered a son from
whom B was a descendant, A lived y years and fathered sons
and daughters.' Thus it may be that Reu lived thirty-two years
and fathered a son from whom Serug was a direct descendant
(11:20).

A chosen people

This list of names is given, not to calculate time, but to draw
attention to a special family line. The names are links in a chain
from Noah's son, Shem, to Terah, Abraham's father.

In the previous chapter Noah's three sons appeared in the
heading and the tribes and nations arising from them were set
out in some detail, Shem's family included. The lists had the
effect of showing that all three sons experienced the creation
blessing that had been reissued after the Flood. In Shem's case,
five sons were named and we see how they branched out in all
directions. This chapter concentrates on the trunk of the tree.
Only the main line of descent from Shem is given. But why is
Shem's name in the heading and why are we drawn to Shem's
descendants?

To answer this question we must go back to 9:26-27. There
we read that God associated himself in a special way with
Shem. God was known as 'the God of Shem'. Later, he would
be known as the God of Abraham, Isaac and Jacob. It suggests that God had entered into a special relationship with

Shem. Promises were made to him. In this sinful world it is wonderful to see God's love reaching out to people who do not deserve any kindness. There is a message of hope for this sad world of lost human beings. God made a promise at the time of Adam's initial rebellion (3:15) and it is the purpose of Genesis to show God keeping that promise. Of the three sons of Noah, it is Shem who is in the line of promise.

In chapter 10:21-31 Shem's descendants are listed, showing how various branches of the family became separate nations and peoples. These verses in chapter 11 narrow the line to reveal the special family to whom promises have been made. Eber, one of the descendants of Shem, is a significant name in the previous list (10:21,25). He is the ancestor of the Hebrews and the father of Peleg and Joktan. Here in chapter 11 only Peleg is mentioned because he is the one in the line of promise. Despite the great confusion and scattering over the earth that happened in Peleg's day, God did not forget his promise, nor were his plans thwarted by this judgement. The special line continues.

The men whose names appear in this representative list were not necessarily the first-born sons of their fathers. We saw this in the case of Shem himself. He was the middle son. According to 10:22, Arphaxad was the third of five sons of Shem, but now we are shown that he was in the line of promise. We know nothing further about such men as Reu or Serug. Their names seem strange and unfamiliar to us, but they are significant to God. As far as this world is concerned, these men are nobodies. They have not made a name for themselves like Nimrod. It reminds us that God has chosen the powerless, the insignificant and those whom the world considers unimportant so that no mere mortal can boast in God's presence (1 Cor. 1:27-29). God's electing love should cause every Christian to humbly give all the glory to the God of all grace.

On such love, my soul, still ponder,
Love so great, so rich and free;
Say, while lost in holy wonder,
  'Why, O Lord, such love to me?'
    Hallelujah!
Grace shall reign eternally.

                                              (John Kent)

The Flood

For the last time in Genesis the great Flood is mentioned. Shem
fathered Arphaxad **'two years after the flood'** when he was
'one hundred years old' (11:10).

Shem's age at this time is a cause for comment. We are told
that Noah was 500 years old when he fathered his three sons
(5:32) and 600 years old when the Flood came (7:6). If his
sons were triplets this would mean they were all 100 years old
at the time of the Flood. But this verse tells us that Shem was
100 years old **'two years after the flood'**. It is possible that
the earlier dates are approximations, rounded to the nearest
hundred, and that this is a more exact date. Another suggestion is that Japheth, being the eldest, was born in Noah's 500th
year and Shem, the second son, was born two years later.

In 10:1 we were told that Noah's three sons all had sons
'after the flood'. That time reference is repeated here. It indicates that Shem, the son of the special family line, obeyed
God's command and experienced the same creation blessing
as his brothers (see 9:1; 1:28). At the same time, the birth of
Arphaxad, two years after the flood, marks the dawn of a new
era, in which God has not forgotten his promises. Shem may
well have had Elam and Asshur immediately after the Flood
(see 10:22), but as far as Genesis is concerned it is the birth of
Arphaxad that is significant. He is the child of promise.

The human lifespan reduced

By the time we reach the end of this list of names, people were living much shorter lives. Noah was 950 when he died (9:29), whereas Nahor, the father of Terah, was 148 (11:24-25). Associated with this reduction in their lifespan, the age when they had the son of promise is much earlier. While Noah was about 500 years old when he had his sons (5:32), Shem was 100 years old when he fathered Arphaxad and Terah seventy when he fathered Abraham, or Abram, as he was then called. Arphaxad was only thirty-five when he fathered Salah, while Nahor was twenty-nine when Terah was born. Many of them were having children, like people today, in their twenties and thirties. This will become an important point to bear in mind when we come to the story of Abraham and his concern for a family. God promised to give him a son in his old age and it is clear that from at least the age of seventy a person could be considered old.

A bridge passage

The section gathers up what has gone before and prepares us for what is to follow. It acts as a bridge between the primeval history in chapters 1-11 and the patriarchal period commencing with Abraham.

We shall not understand the call of Abraham, the election of Israel to be a light to the nations and the coming of Jesus, unless we appreciate these early chapters. They teach that God is sovereign. He is the beginning of all things, and human beings are created in his image. We are also shown why people are the way they are now. All are sinners in rebellion against God as a result of that initial rebellion in the garden of God. The sad state of the world left to its own ingenuity resulted in the crisis of the Flood. But God acted in grace to save Noah and his family. Soon more divine wrath was expressed towards sinful humanity at the Tower of Babel. Confusion, division and scattering over the face of the earth resulted, and the tribes and nations of the world, with their own languages and cultures, developed. An enemy is ultimately responsible for the mess, although human beings are held accountable for their actions. We only have the vaguest of hints in Genesis as to who that enemy is. Temptation entered the garden from outside, from a serpent, a beast of the field who spoke with a human voice. It was at this point that the first glimmer of gospel hope appeared. God declared war on this serpent and a promise was made that through the seed of a woman the serpent's head would be bruised. Those great signposts at the beginning of each new section of Genesis point us forward to the fulfilment of this divine victory through a human 'seed'.

This little section, with its signpost and linear genealogy, reminds us of God's covenant with Shem. God curses human rebellion and restrains the evil intentions of the human heart. Nevertheless, hope lies in this God who condescends to be known as the God of Shem. All is now ready for the account of Abraham's call and the promises made to him which will result in blessing for all nations. These promises find their fulfilment in Jesus Christ, whose family is traced back to Abraham and Shem. He is the Saviour of the world. He has won the decisive battle with that old serpent, the devil, that the kingdoms of this world might become the kingdoms of our God and of his Christ. The only hope for a confused and divided world is in God's promised Seed, Jesus Christ.

Part 7:
What Terah produced (11:27 – 25:11)

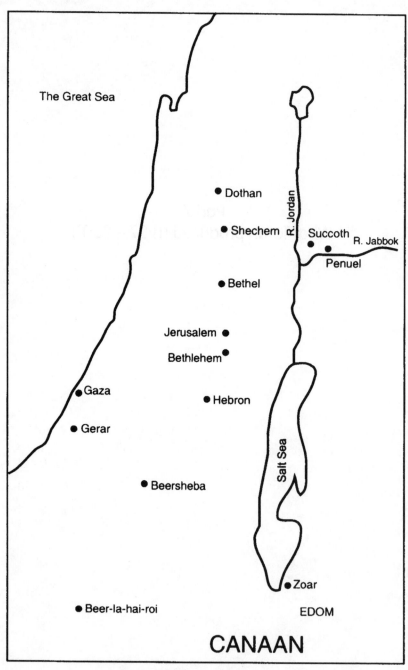

Canaan in the time of the patriarchs

18.
The origin of the holy nation

Please read Genesis 11:27 – 12:9

This section brings us to the second main part of the book. It tells us about the great ancestral fathers of Israel, Abraham, Isaac and Jacob, and Jacob's twelve sons. We are not given biographies of these men. Details of their lives are presented to show how God furthers his saving purposes through the most unlikely individuals.

Many people today have returned to thinking like the ancient Greeks. They assume that there is no direction to life, that we are governed by impersonal forces outside of our control. But it is very difficult to live consistently with this understanding of existence. We all yearn for significance and meaning. It is not wrong to do so. The universe is not controlled by impersonal powers and there is a purpose to life. This is because, as Genesis explains, there is a personal God who is good and over everything. History is going somewhere. God has a plan for the salvation of sinful humanity and Genesis shows that plan being worked out in its early stages.

Family background (11:27-32)

There are a number of reasons why we are given these verses.

1. A turning-point

A major turning-point in the history of humanity is introduced with this reference to Terah. Adam stands out as the original head of the human race. Noah is presented as the head of a new beginning after the Flood. Now God is seen acting to fulfil his promises through Terah's family.

In each of these three cases it is significant that Genesis names three sons. Only three sons of Adam are named and the line of promise extends from Seth. Noah, a descendant of Seth, had three sons and it is through Shem that the chosen line continues. Terah is a descendant of Shem and has Abram, Nahor and Haran.

From this point, instead of looking at universal, worldwide events, we are brought to consider one family and how it inter-acts with other nations.

2. The father figure

These verses introduce us to the head of an extended family. Why is Terah highlighted? Abram is the man we would have expected because he is later described as the father of the Jewish people and of the family of faith. 'This is the genealogy of Abram,' would seem to be more appropriate than **'This is the genealogy of Terah'**.

One reason for the prominence given to Terah is that he is the head of various branches of the family mentioned in the following chapters. He is not only the father of Abram and Sarai (20:12), but the grandfather of Lot, the great-grandfather of Rebekah, Isaac's wife, and the great-great-grandfather of Leah and Rachel, the wives of Jacob. The roots of the nation of Israel revolve around what Terah produced. Both his sons and daughters are important.

It is also characteristic of these sections for the heading to mention the father, while the rest of the section focuses on the offspring. In 25:19, for example, the heading mentions Isaac but the contents concern his sons Jacob and Esau. Nevertheless, in each case, the father mentioned in the heading is still the head of the family. It reminds us that the heading means 'This is what Terah produced.' Those versions that translate 'This is the account of...' convey the wrong impression.

Again, we should bear in mind that, though Terah's death is recorded in 11:32, he might well have lived to see the birth of Isaac. It would seem that Terah died just two years before Sarah, when Abraham was 135 years old. If this is so, then he was indeed the father figure for most of the period covered in this section. It is because Terah plays no further part in the story after the family reached Haran that Moses briefly summarizes his life and records his death in chapter 11. Sometimes Genesis will trace one line through to its end before returning to the main theme. When Stephen, in his address to the Jews, referred to Abraham's moving from Haran to Canaan after Terah's death, he was indicating the precise point in the text where the account is found (Acts 7:4).[1]

3. Prominent people

'**Abram**' is possibly the eldest son of Terah.

'**Lot**', whose father, '**Haran**', died young, '**before his father Terah**' (11:28), is the subject of a number of incidents in the life of Abram. Abram took responsibility for this son of his deceased brother.

'**Sarai**', later called 'Sarah', occupies a very important place as '**Abram's wife**' (11:29). A significant detail is added that will heighten the tension later over Abram's future descendants: '**But Sarai was barren; she had no child**' (11:30).

The importance of **'Nahor'** and his wife, **'Milcah, the daughter of Haran'**, will become clear in connection with finding a wife for Isaac. Milcah was Terah's granddaughter and Nahor was Terah's son. This means that Nahor married his niece.

The only name which does not figure in the subsequent narrative is **'Iscah'**, the sister of Milcah (11:29). Although Haran died young, he still had a number of children. He not only fathered Lot, he was also **'the father of Milcah and the father of Iscah'**. This serves to underline the plight of Abram, who had no children.

4. Good intentions

While Terah took his family from **'Ur of the Chaldeans to go to the land of Canaan'**, we find that **'They came to Haran and dwelt there'** (11:31). This is where most of the extended family settled. They planned to go to Canaan. That was the goal. But they stopped at Haran. Travelling round the fertile crescent, Haran is approximately halfway between Ur and Canaan in what is now Turkey, near to the Syrian border. They would have journeyed up the river Euphrates along the trade route.

Terah had headed in the right direction but he did not make it to the intended destination. He had moved, and yet he had not moved. Haran was similar in culture and religion to Ur. To move from Haran to Canaan would have meant moving into unfamiliar surroundings. For Terah to journey on to Canaan would have involved going against the tide of opinion. It was the tendency in those days to migrate from West to East. Thus Terah made his home in Haran and died outside the land of promise.

Life and salvation are associated with God's promise of a special descendant, a chosen 'Seed'. This promise, as we shall see, is connected to the land of promise. Terah lost sight of

God's promises. Perhaps you have been moved to alter course in life. Once you had no time for God and you never read the Bible. But then came a change. You are now reading the Bible and going to church. But you have come to a full stop. To go further would involve awkward decisions and going against the tide. Will you end your days still belonging to the old life? Or will you take hold of God's promises and trust Jesus Christ?

Abram's experience of God (12:1-9)

Of all the people whose lives are recorded in the Bible it is Abraham (or Abram, as his name was at this time) who is called 'the friend of God' (James 2:23; Isa. 41:8; 2 Chr. 20:7). Jews, Christians and Muslims have a special interest in Abraham. He is particularly significant in God's plan for the salvation of the world.

1. Abram's background

We live 2,000 years after Christ's birth. Imagine living 2,000 years before Christ. That is about the time when Abram was born.[2] Many assume that because people lived in those far-off times, everything must have been very primitive. Nothing could be further from the truth. For hundreds of years before Abram, a great civilization existed in the area called Mesopotamia, between the Tigris and Euphrates. Looking at the area around Ur today, all is a barren waste and has been for many centuries. 4,000 years ago and earlier, things were very different. Ur was an important centre associated with the Sumerians from the third millennium B.C. The city and its suburbs extended for about four square miles (10 km. square) with a population not far short of half a million. Art treasures from the royal tombs have come to light which show the skill of the people. The city boasted a supermarket, a library and a school.

We even have pupils' exercises and teachers' reports. During periods of peace and stability, life in Ur would have been very comfortable for the average person and luxurious for the privileged few.

By the time Moses came to write up this account, he described the place as **'Ur of the Chaldeans'** (11:28,31) to distinguish it from other settlements of the same name. 'Ur' means 'city'. The Chaldeans moved into the area after Abram's time. 'Chaldean' is used later as a synonym for 'Babylonian' (see Isa. 13:19; 47:1). It is generally agreed that Ur is to be identified with the mound el-Muqayyar on the Euphrates some 220 miles (350 km.) south-east of modern-day Baghdad.

On the religious front, the people of Ur worshipped many gods, but the chief deity was the moon-god. A great temple-tower, a ziggurat, was built in his honour. Associated with the religion were rituals which involved magic and prostitution. In Joshua's farewell address to Israel, he speaks of Abram's family worshipping other gods (Josh. 24:2,15). In fact, several members of the family have names which suggest adherence to moon-worship, such as Sarai (Sarratu was the wife of the moon-god) and Milcah (Malkatu was the god's daughter).

This was Abram's background. Alexander Whyte has put it bluntly: 'The first Jew was a Gentile. The first Hebrew was a heathen.'

2. God's choice

Although Abram, like the rest of his family, deserved eternal damnation, God chose to save him and to give him many wonderful promises. Stephen states: 'The God of glory appeared to our father Abraham when he was in Mesopotamia, before he dwelt in Haran' (Acts 7:2). Why did God reveal himself to Abram? There was nothing special about him. Yes, he was in the line from Shem. But Shem had many children; Nahor, the father of Terah, had many sons and daughters; and Terah had other sons besides Abram. The only answer is that God willed to do so. When Moses was explaining why God chose Israel, he could only express it in what philosophers would call circular argument. He loved Israel and chose them because he loved them (Deut. 7:7-8). This is not human logic. It is the logic of divine grace.

God chose Abram because in love he chose to do so. It was completely undeserved. This is true in the life of everyone who belongs to Jesus Christ. There is nothing in any of us to commend us to God, yet God graciously sets his love upon individuals and chooses them to be to the praise of his glory (Eph. 1:3-6). All this is tremendously comforting, as well as humbling. If God waited until someone showed some interest or made the first move, no one would be saved. Jesus said to those who found his words hard, 'Therefore I have said to you that no one can come to me unless it has been granted to him by my Father' (John 6:65). If anyone is saved it is the result of God's undeserved love and choice.

3. God's call

'Now the Lord had said to Abram' (12:1). God first revealed himself to Abram when he had no faith. It was no doubt as a result of this revelation that his family left Ur. Instead of going on to Canaan, they settled in Haran. Haran was a strategic trading centre that was also noted for its worship of the moon-god.[3]

Many commentators have censured Abram for stopping at Haran and not breaking straightaway with his family and roots.[4] There is, however, no hint in the text that Abram was acting like Lot in Sodom, lingering when he was told to get out. We must be careful not to make a sermon point from silence. It may well be that Abram was waiting God's timing in order to move on. There can be good and honourable reasons for delay and waiting. A preacher or missionary may have made an initial response to God's call and yet find that he has to wait patiently for the right moment to proceed further. For Abram, that moment is described in chapter 12.

The translation, **'Now the LORD had said to Abram,'** assumes a call in Ur. It is better, however, to see these opening words as a fresh revelation to Abram in Haran. 'Said' rather than 'had said' would be the usual way of reading the Hebrew.

The call is clear and crisp. **'Get out'** (literally 'go by yourself'), suggests that Abram is to be his own person, making his own decisions. This involved leaving Haran (**'your country'**), leaving his clan, which had settled in Haran (**'your family'**) and leaving his close relatives (**'your father's house'**). Abram had not done this before. He was being called to 'go it alone'. It was a life-changing call to renounce all and follow the Lord. This same call is heard in the New Testament. Jesus put it bluntly: 'He who loves father or mother more than me is not worthy of me' (Matt. 10:37). This call is not given without gospel content. We are called to believe the gospel. The gospel is found in the promises made to Abram.

4. Abram's response

Obedience of faith

'So Abram departed as the LORD had spoken to him' (12:4). Abram believed what God had said to him and the evidence of that faith was seen in his obedience to the divine call. Biblical faith is not a leap into the dark. It is trusting God and his word. This faith showed itself in obedience. You are never too old to believe God's word and act upon it. Abram was seventy-five years old when he responded to God's call.

Example of faith

'**And Lot went with him**' (12:4). Lot could have settled down
with the rest of Terah's family in Haran. But he went out in
faith with Abram. Abram's faith in God clearly influenced his
nephew. Our faith in the Lord should be an inspiration and
example to others.

Life of faith

Abram left Haran '**to go to the land of Canaan. So they
came to the land of Canaan.**' Terah moved in the right direction but never arrived. Abram actually came into Canaan.
Many have good intentions and start well but never arrive at
the intended destination. Jesus speaks in the parable of the
sower of those who receive the word with gladness but because 'they have no root in themselves ... endure only for a
time' (Mark 4:16-17).

   We are also told that Abram '**passed through**' Canaan from
top to bottom. This he did, not secretly or furtively, but with
all his servants and possessions (12:5,6). He probably entered
by way of Damascus, along the shores of the Sea of Galilee,
on '**to the place of Shechem**' (12:6), then '**east of Bethel**'
(12:8) and down '**towards the South**' or the Negev (12:9).
All Abram's movements were symbolic of taking possession
of the land. He passed through it as if he owned it. His action
was an acted prophecy of the time when Israel would later
take possession of the whole land from the Canaanites. Likewise, the Christian lives by faith. Though we enjoy many benefits here and now, the heavenly inheritance is reserved for us.
'Blessed are the meek, for they shall inherit the earth' (Matt.
5:5).

Assurance of faith

God spoke to Abram again and renewed the promise concerning the land (12:7). On this occasion we are told that God **'appeared to Abram'**. God was gracious and gave Abram this encouragement. God by his Spirit continues to assure Christians of their heavenly home (John 14:23; 1 Peter 1:8-9).

Confession of faith

Abram did not set about building a city or a tower to draw attention to himself. Instead, he built an altar to the God who had revealed himself to him (12:7,8). Calling on the name of the Lord at the altars he built near Shechem and Bethel was an expression of Abram's faith in God's promises. He worshipped the God who had disclosed himself to him. This very public confession of his faith in the living and true God was a witness to the pagan world around. **'The Canaanites were then in the land'** (12:6). Before the watching world we are to proclaim our faith in the God who is there and who has revealed himself in the person of his Son.

God's promises (12:1-3,7)

The covenant promises are made in the context of the command to go out in faith. There is no thought of God's entering into a mutual agreement with Abram. God does not come with a proposal that if Abram is prepared to leave home, then God will bless him. We have one solemn command followed by seven promises. Notice the 'I wills'. God is not presenting possibilities but firm resolutions. The blessings far outweigh the demands. There is no comparison between the command to leave all and follow the Lord and the good things God has in store for those who love and obey him.

1. Blessing

In the sense used here, blessing is the opposite of cursing: **'I will bless those who bless you, and I will curse him who curses you'** (12:3). God's covenant with Israel at Sinai included blessings and curses. They are associated with physical, tangible items such as long or short life, wealth or poverty, peace or war, good and bad harvests, fertility or barrenness. 'What modern secular man calls "luck" or "success" the OT calls "blessing." ' [5] Spiritual and eternal blessings are often hidden in the physical. To know God and to be in a personal relationship to him is the highest blessing of all. These are blessings which Adam lost in the Garden of Eden, but which Enoch experienced and which God promised: 'I will walk among you and be your God, and you shall be my people' (Lev. 26:12). God so blessed Abram that he became the prime example of what blessing is and the mediator of blessing to others. Abram was blessed by God during his lifetime (see 24:34-36). However, the extent of the divine promises presented here would only begin to be fully realized with the coming of God's Son.

2. A great nation

'I will make you a great nation' (12:2). What a promise to make to a seventy-five-year-old man who had no children! The *Oxford Dictionary* defines a nation as 'a community of people of mainly common descent, history and language, etc., forming a state or inhabiting a territory'. What makes a nation great? Is it a large population? Certainly this is one ingredient, and God promises Abram: 'I will make your descendants as the dust of the earth' (13:16). Is it a large amount of territory that makes a great nation? Land is an important factor, and God promises Abram an area stretching from the borders of Egypt to the Euphrates (15:18). Britain was called 'Great Britain' when the English and Scottish crowns were united in

1603. What made Britain truly great, however, was its God-consciousness and respect for the Bible. 'Righteousness exalts a nation' (Prov. 14:34). Moses informed the people where true greatness lay: 'For what great nation is there that has God so near to it, as the LORD our God is to us...? And what great nation is there that has such statutes and righteous judgements as are in all this law which I set before you this day?' (Deut. 4:7-8).

3. A great name

'I will ... make your name great' (12:2). A 'great name' in this context means a famous name. Cain wanted to make his son's name great and the builders of Babel wanted to make a name for themselves. In order to counter human arrogance and selfish pride, God planned to make famous a person of his own choice, one who would draw attention to the greatness of his own name. God alone is great and he is worthy to be celebrated and acclaimed by his creation. He desires his name to 'be great among the nations' (Mal. 1:11). It is when God is known that his greatness is appreciated. 'In Judah God is known; his name is great in Israel' (Ps. 76:1).

Even in his own lifetime Abram's name became great. The only other person given a great name by God in Old Testament times was David (2 Sam. 7:9). It points forward to great David's greater Son, of whom it was announced, 'He will be great' (Luke 1:32).

4. A catch-word for blessing

'And you shall be a blessing' (12:2). This again is a very strong statement of intent, like the previous 'I wills'. The promise is often taken to mean that Abram will be a source of blessing to others, but that is what the final promise states. The exact phrase is used again in Zechariah 8:13: 'Just as you were a curse among the nations ... so I will save you, and you shall be a blessing.' Zechariah is referring to the fact that the nations had been using the name 'Israel' in their curses (see Deut. 28:37; Ps. 44:14). But the prophet is indicating that instead of a swear word, the nations will use the name as a blessing. They will employ a formula such as, 'May God make us like Israel!'

God is promising that Abram's name will be used in a similar way. People will automatically couple his name with blessing and will say, 'May God make me like Abram!' (cf. 48:20: 'May God make you as Ephraim and as Manasseh!').

5. Divine protection

'I will bless those who bless you, and I will curse him who curses you' (12:3). The bond between the Lord and Abram was to be a close one. Those who dealt well with Abram would experience God's favour; those who acted in a hostile way, God would curse. They would be punished. This is a guarantee of protection far more personal than anything Cain knew. God is identifying himself with Abram and indicating that he is on Abram's side. Abram was chosen to enjoy this special relationship with God. The way to life and blessing is shown to be in association with Abram.

6. The mediator of blessing to others

'And in you all the families of the earth shall be blessed' (12:3).[6] The final promise brings the passage to a triumphant and universal conclusion. When this promise is repeated, instead of 'families' it speaks of 'all the nations of the earth' (18:18). Not every individual is promised blessing through Abram, but all the clans and nations, such as those mentioned in that representative list in chapter 10, will find blessing. One single person is chosen and blessed in order that all nations might be blessed. This would be illustrated even within the lifetime of Abram. When the promise is reiterated after his great test of faith, 'in you' becomes 'in your seed' (22:18). The promise finds its ultimate fulfilment in Jesus Christ (see Acts 3:25-26; Gal. 3:8-9,16). We are beginning to see how the curse that fell on humanity as a result of the Fall will be removed. The 'seed' is associated with Abram (or Abraham, as he would come to be known).

7. The gift of land

'To your descendants I will give this land' (12:7). The promise of land is already implied in the command to go 'to a land that I will show you' (12:1). Here it is made quite definite. Land is closely associated with Abram's 'seed'. He will have descendants who will be given the land as a gift from God. The promise of 'seed' and 'land' dominates the book of Genesis. The other books of Moses show how the 'seed' of Abraham is moulded into a nation at Sinai. Under Joshua the nation is given the land of Canaan and in the days of David and Solomon the earthly glory of the nation is seen. But that did not exhaust the scope of these promises. The prophets look beyond the days of David and Solomon to more wonderful things to come when Abraham's seed would inherit the world (Rom. 4:13).

Isaiah prophesies a day when Israel will be a blessing in the land with Egypt and Assyria (Isa. 19:24-25). The New Testament shows how Abram's 'Seed' removes the curse which all nations and individuals deserve, so that 'the blessing of Abraham might come upon the Gentiles in Christ Jesus' (Gal. 3:13-14).

19.
The land of promise

Please read Genesis 12:10 – 13:18

After the amazing promises of the previous paragraph, a big question mark now hangs over the land. There is also concern over Abram's life and wife and, by inference, Abram's 'seed', and instead of being a blessing, Abram brings judgement on others. By the close of the passage, however, the promise concerning land and innumerable descendants is reiterated and faith in God renewed.

Abram in Egypt (12:10 – 13:4)

It comes as a shock to read of this unheroic performance by Abram. He had shown great faith in leaving his father's home to live a semi-nomadic life. Now that he was in Canaan, a different type of testing experience came his way that showed up moral weaknesses in his character. Life in Canaan was not a bed of roses. It reminds us that the Lord has not promised believers an easy ride in this world (Acts 14:22).

1. Abram's faithlessness

The circumstances (12:10)

Abram moved to 'the South', to the Negev (12:9). This part is very dry and barren today, but archaeology has shown that there were villages dotted about this region and a much better rainfall existed in the area at one time. Nevertheless, famine could still occur and Abram found himself in a situation where there was a lack of food.

After all we have been told about the land of promise, this is a surprising move. No sooner had Abram come into the land than he was moving out of it. From a life of wandering up and down Canaan, he was now contemplating settling in Egypt for some time. Egypt was the natural place to turn to in times of famine. It was severe famine which later prompted Jacob and his sons to do the same, as God would subsequently reveal to Abram (15:13). There is nothing in the text to suggest that Abram was wrong to go there. It provided a foretaste of what Jacob and his descendants would experience. In addition, it reminded Israel that Canaan at best was only a type of the heavenly country (Heb. 11:13-16).

The deceit (12:11-13)

The sin was not in going to Egypt, but in what Abram schemed to say while he was there. On the borders of Egypt, he suddenly had a dreadful thought: 'What if the Egyptians take a liking to my wife? They will kill me and take her.' Fear for his own safety led him to practise deceit. To get round the problem, he had a bright idea to which Sarai agreed: **'Please say you are my sister'** (12:13). This was not an outright lie, for Sarai was Abram's half-sister. They had the same father but a different mother (see 20:12). But it was a half-truth which covered up the central fact that she was his wife.

Perhaps Abram was trying in his own feeble way to keep alive the promises that God had made to him. If the Egyptians killed him in order to take his wife, what would become of God's promise concerning descendants and future blessing? Instead of trusting the Lord in the situation, he resorted to dishonest practices which would lead others into grave sin. God does not expect us to sin in order to further his purposes.

As so often happens, when our plans appear to be producing good results, unforeseen circumstances complicate matters. Abram had probably assumed that if an Egyptian wanted to marry Sarai, supposing her to be Abram's sister, negotiations would take some time which would allow him to escape with Sarai. What he had not allowed for was that **'The princes of Pharaoh also saw her and commended her to Pharaoh'** (12:15). Abram was powerless to prevent her from being brought into the royal palace to became part of Pharaoh's harem. Abram was duly presented with gifts. Bride money was given him for Sarai (12:16). But what must Abram have thought as he sat alone in his home? He had gained in wealth but he had lost his wife. Our sins have a nasty habit of getting us into trouble just when we thought everything was working out well. 'Be sure your sin will find you out (Num. 32:23).

Why was there such interest in a sixty-five-year-old lady? **'The Egyptians saw the woman, that she was very beautiful'** (12:14). If we have a problem here it is not with the text but with ourselves. Our ideas of womanhood and beauty may well be very different from theirs. This is certainly the case as we move from culture to culture in our world today. On the other hand, because Sarai had had no children she may have looked much younger than her age would suggest.

Embarrassment and expulsion (12:17-20)

How often have Christians complained that the ungodly sin and get away with it, while they sin and are found out! We should be thankful that this is the case with Christians. God does not want his people to remain in a backslidden condition: 'For whom the LORD loves he corrects, just as a father the son in whom he delights' (see Prov. 3:11-12; Heb. 12:5-7). How embarrassing, though, when the ungodly are used to correct the godly! A plague hit the pharaoh's palace and he became aware that something was very wrong. Finally, he learned the truth that Sarai was married to Abram. The latter was then called before the pharaoh and sternly reprimanded. The questions that Pharaoh put to Abram and his statement, **'I might have taken her as my wife'** (12:19), express his distressed state. We understand that adultery was generally regarded throughout the ancient world as a great sin deserving the death penalty. For a believer to be rebuked by a pagan over such a serious moral issue brings great dishonour to the cause of God in the world. Abram could say nothing in his own defence. He had been found out and was made conscious of his guilt.

An expulsion order was put on Abram. He was told to take his wife and get out of the country. The punishment of being sent away from the plenty of Egypt (12:20), along with the question, **'What is this you have done...?'** (12:18), reminds us of God's question to Eve (3:13) and the expulsion from the garden of plenty.

Fellowship restored (13:1-4)

Can you imagine how Abram must have felt as he made his way out of Egypt with his wife, his herdsmen and Lot? Instead of trusting God and confessing his faith in that pagan environment, he had turned to his own plans and deceitful practices and had been disgraced by the Egyptian ruler for his sinful behaviour. We do not read of Abram having fellowship with God in Egypt and he was given no assurances of faith.

Nevertheless, this sad experience led him back to the Lord. Abram retraced his steps **'from Egypt'** to the Negev (**'the**

South') and on **'as far as Bethel'**, to the place where he had
camped soon after his arrival in Canaan and **'to the place of
the altar which he had made there at first'**. There he worshipped the Lord. 'Whenever we backslide there is nothing
else to do but to come back by the old gateway of genuine
repentance and simple faith.'[1]

2. God's faithfulness

One of the themes running through the history of these early
fathers of Israel is the threat to the promises that God made to
Abram in 12:1-3,7. We shall often find that it is not the enemies of God, but God's chosen people themselves, who are
the cause of problems. But each time God remains faithful and
acts to safeguard the promises. The Lord intervened in Egypt
to rescue Abram and Sarai out of the mess they were in.

Though the pharaoh had acted in ignorance, he was still
guilty of taking another man's wife, and so **'The LORD plagued
Pharaoh and his house with great plagues'** (12:17). At the
same time, the plague had the effect of protecting Abram and
Sarai. It would appear that the pharaoh did not violate Sarai
and he took no revenge on Abram, but allowed him to leave
with all his possessions.

The protection that God had promised is shown in this situation and it makes Abram's original fears seem so unfounded.
Testing times come, and we are tempted to look away from
the Lord. Fears so grip us that instead of trusting God we can
only see the problems. We forget the goodness and faithfulness of God and we end up bringing more trouble on ourselves. Praise God that, even when 'we are faithless, he remains faithful; he cannot deny himself' (2 Tim. 2:13).

Moses need not have recorded this incident in Egypt because we have a repeat performance by Abram before
Abimelech and the Philistines and then by Isaac (see 20:1-18;
26:6-11). Why record in detail such similar events? They

emphasize the sinfulness of the human heart, even the hearts of God's saints. But they do more: they press home the faithfulness of God in keeping his promises.

As Moses writes up this part of redemption history under divine inspiration, he records it in such a way as to parallel to some extent what happened later. Typology is an important item to remember in the interpretation of Scripture. We often think of it in relation to Old Testament people, events, places and utensils which find their antitypes in the New Testament. It is clear, however, that one item can typify another within the history of the Old Testament period. The incident concerning Abram in Egypt prefigures, or anticipates, the events leading to the exodus from Egypt. Abram, like Jacob, was brought into Egypt on account of famine and treated well by the pharaoh. In both cases the Lord struck the pharaohs with great plagues which led to Abram, and later Moses, being summoned into their presence. The pharaoh said to Abram, **'Take … and go'** (12:19) which is exactly what was said to Moses and Aaron in Exodus 12:32. In both cases they were **'sent … away'** by the Egyptians (12:20; Exod. 12:33) and enriched **'in livestock, in silver, and in gold'** (13:2; Exod. 12:35,38). Despite the obvious differences, there are enough similarities to indicate that Moses wishes us to see certain parallels between them. Why has he done this?

Not only is the history of Israel in Egypt foreshadowed in Abram's experience, it is prophesied in the time of Abram (see 15:13-14). Typology, like prophecy, encourages the people of God to look forward to coming events central to God's purposes. In typology we see the kind of way God acts to bring about the fulfilment of his promises.

Here is a remarkable wonder and it bears witness to the sovereignty of God over all history and events. These historical events, and the people involved in them, all fit into a plan. There is nothing haphazard or undetermined, and yet the people are not puppets manipulated by God, but individuals who make real decisions and act according to their own inclinations. Through such people and their experiences God pointed to later events. This is why they are recorded as part of Scripture. Within the Old Testament period, the Exodus was God's great act of revelation and redemption. What happened when Abram was in Egypt thus became symbolic of, and a pointer to, that greater and more significant event in the days of Jacob and Moses. But, as Isaiah indicates later, this great Old Testament saving event itself becomes symbolic of the more wonderful redemption from slavery to sin and Satan through the promised 'Seed'.

People and events which are typological of what is prophesied for the future are an aid to faith. Incidents that actually happened in the past and people who really existed, when used as types of future realities, encourage the people of God to wait with certain hope. It is the great purpose of the Bible to reveal God's saving activity in Christ. Sometimes we can get lost in the details of the text. It is good to step back and see the Bible as a whole, and how the contents fit together so remarkably to make us wise about salvation.

Abram and Lot (13:5-18)

As a result of Abram's experience in Egypt, there was a new desire to seek the Lord (13:1-4). The life of faith, however, is rarely straightforward. Now that fellowship with God had been restored it did not mean the end of frustrating and testing experiences. The land is again at the heart of a new problem that faced Abram.

1. A prosperity problem (13:5-6)

God had blessed Abram and Lot in very tangible ways (13:2,5) and it was this blessing that created the problem. It is often true that the more prosperous a person becomes, the more problems there are in managing his or her affairs. Abram and Lot at first lived like semi-nomads, moving about from place to place to find pasture for their ever-increasing flocks and herds. But they preferred to settle down somewhere in the land. The word 'dwell' is a key word in this chapter (13:6,7,12,18). Abram and Lot wanted to **'dwell together'** but they were prevented from settling in any one place for too long because they had so many possessions (13:6). There were also other people in the land, for we read, **'The Canaanites and the Perizzites then dwelt in the land'** (13:7). No doubt these original inhabitants occupied the best parts, leaving Abram and Lot to find pasture where they could. The land of promise was proving a difficult place in which to dwell.

2. A dispute develops (13:7)

A quarrel broke out among the herdsmen of Lot and Abram. We can all think of examples of the difficulties that can arise living in close proximity to other people and sharing the same facilities. It only takes some trivial matter to spark off a big incident. There was no tension at this time between the new-comers and the original inhabitants. This was an 'in-house' dispute, but if it were not settled satisfactorily it would make them more vulnerable to attack from the Canaanites.

3. A suggested solution (13:8-9)

Abram, the head of the household, took the initiative. He did not want this quarrel spreading from the herdsmen to the owners. They were members of the same family, **'brethren'**, in the sense of 'kinsmen' (13:8). For Abram, the ideal would have been for them to dwell peacefully together in the same area. But he was wise enough to see that the present situation did not allow them all to dwell in one spot. He therefore suggested a peaceful separation: '**Is not the whole land before you? Please separate from me.**' Abram's generosity is seen in allowing Lot to take first choice: '**If you take the left, then I will go to the right; or, if you go to the right, then I will go to the left**' (13:9). Abram manifests here a very different attitude from his behaviour in Egypt. A tendency to manipulate had given way to a magnanimous spirit. Instead of jealously guarding what was his by right, he gave it away in the interests of peace. At one level, it seemed a foolhardy thing to do. He was prepared to give the land to Lot. Yet, at a deeper level, it was an act of faith, for Abram knew that, whatever happened, God would give him the land. This expression of faith reached a climax in Abraham's willingness to offer up his only son and heir.

There are a number of biblical principles Christians can learn from Abram's example.

In the first place, *meekness and a peaceable spirit* are not qualities generally evident in our self-centred world, but they are to be the characteristics of a true believer (Matt. 5:5,9). Christians are called to pursue peace with all (Heb. 12:14).

Secondly, *believers are still sinners and full of weaknesses and frailties*. The ideal of perfect unity is there before us. It is the Lord Jesus Christ who has brought Christians together as brothers and sisters. Old barriers of race and religion are broken down. 'Behold, how good and how pleasant it is for brothers to dwell together in unity' (Ps. 133:1). Nevertheless, occasions do arise when peaceful coexistence is not possible any longer. In such last-resort situations, amicable separation is preferable to all-out war. To allow an issue to develop into open conflict brings dishonour to the name of Christ. We live surrounded by enemies of the gospel who are delighted when Christians are at war with each other. Better to separate while brothers are still talking than when there is open hostility. While

Abram and Lot went their separate ways, they were still at peace with each other.

Putting the interests of others before our own interests is another biblical principle we learn from Abram's example. So many disputes among believers are due to selfish ambition and self-interest. Abram took the heat out of the situation by not standing for his rights, but allowing his nephew to take first choice. That attitude is seen most perfectly in the life of our Lord. He put the interests of others before his own. Christ Jesus made himself 'of no reputation'; he made himself nothing. He did not stand on his honour, and his people are called to do the same. 'Let nothing be done through selfish ambition or conceit, but in lowliness of mind let each esteem others better than himself' (see Phil. 2:3-11). Such an attitude helps 'to keep the unity of the Spirit in the bond of peace' (Eph. 4:3).

4. *A disastrous decision* (13:10-13)

There is a hill about ten miles north of Jerusalem, near Bethel, from which Abram and Lot would have had a good view of the southern part of the Jordan valley as it flows into the Dead Sea. The fertile nature of **'the plain of Jordan'** is described in glowing terms. It was **'well-watered everywhere ... like the garden of the LORD'** (13:10; cf. 2:10). The plain of Jordan is also described as **'like the land of Egypt'**. The Nile ensured that Egypt had plenty of water for irrigation.

Lot viewed the scene, saw the great advantages, took up Abram's offer and **'chose for himself all the plain of Jordan'** (13:11). But as Shakespeare reminds us, 'All that glisters is not gold.'[2] He made a selfish and faulty choice and the way the narrative is written emphasizes how wrong it was.

1. **'Lot lifted his eyes and saw...'** (13:10). Having already drawn our attention to the Garden of Eden, these

words immediately remind us of Eve, who 'saw that the tree was good for food, that it was pleasant to the eyes...' (3:6). Just as Eve's look aroused desire which allowed her to forget God, so Lot's look blinded him from considering other factors. Without any concern for Abram, he looked, he saw and he **'chose for himself'** the fertile area (13:11).

2. The words, **'before the LORD destroyed Sodom and Gomorrah'**, cast a shadow over the scene (13:10). That area which appeared so well-watered and lush would not always be so. The additional phrase, **'as you go towards Zoar'**, also draws our attention to the forthcoming destruction of Sodom. Zoar was the city to which Lot and his daughters fled. The final outcome of the choice is hinted at here.

3. Lot turned his back on the whole of Canaan and chose the border region (see 10:19). In fact, Moses draws a contrast by writing, **'Abram dwelt in the land of Canaan, and Lot dwelt in the cities of the plain'** (13:12). It was not part of the promised land, but an area destined for destruction.

4. As we noted earlier, the word **'east'** (13:11) is often associated in Genesis with a move away from God (3:24; 4:16; 11:2). This real movement in an easterly direction is another indication that this was a wrong move.

5. Lot **'pitched his tent even as far as Sodom'**, and we are informed of the kind of people who lived there: **'But the men of Sodom were exceedingly wicked and sinful against the LORD'** (13:12-13). This is what the whole world was like before the Flood (see 6:5).

All these details underline the folly of Lot's choice. What Lot considered to be the paradise of God was a cesspool of iniquity. Calvin comments, 'Lot, when he fancied that he was dwelling in paradise, was nearly plunged into the depths of hell.'[3] It should be a warning to every Christian when choosing a place to live or seeking employment, not to look merely at the scenery or the material advantages.

5. A gift guaranteed (13:14-17)

The Lord is no man's debtor. God says, 'Those who honour me I will honour, and those who despise me shall be lightly esteemed' (1 Sam. 2:30). Abram may have wondered if he had done right. We all know what it is like to have second thoughts after doing the honourable thing.

The Lord graciously spoke to Abram after **'Lot had separated from him'** (13:14) to assure him of the promises he had previously made. The way the narrative is written impresses upon us the importance of the Lord's promises, showing how blessed Abram really was. There are certain parallels between Lot's movements in response to Abram's generous proposal and what the Lord called Abram to do. 'Lot lifted his eyes and saw' (13:10) is answered by God's telling Abram, **'Lift your eyes now and look'** (13:14). Lot was offered **'the whole land'** by Abram (13:9), yet God says to Abram, **'All the land which you see I will give to you'** (13:15). After these parallels there is one great contrast made. Lot chose a border region that was destined for destruction (13:10), whereas Abram was assured of the whole land of Canaan **'for ever'** (13:15).

Linked with the land is the promise of 'seed'. God emphasized what he had intimated earlier: **'And I will make your descendants as the dust of the earth...'** (13:16). These promises, as we see from the New Testament, go beyond the natural and nationalistic sense. All who are in Christ are descendants of Abram and are inheritors of the world (Rom. 4:11-13; Ps. 37:9-11; Matt. 5:5).

The Lord urged Abram to **'walk in the land through its length and its width'** (13:17). Doing this would be a symbolic gesture of ownership. God was calling him to walk the walk of faith. We too are called to do the same, but not in the sense of walking round cities to claim them for Christ. Paul tells us that all things are ours in Christ. Though this world is destined to be destroyed by fire, from its ashes a new earth will be formed where we shall reign with Christ. 'We walk by faith, not by sight' (2 Cor. 5:7).

6. *A right response* (13:18)

Abram moved south again to the Negev **'and dwelt by the terebinth** [or "oak"] **trees of Mamre, which are in Hebron'**. There were a considerable number of trees in Mamre (23:17), providing shade and showing evidence of a good water supply. This is where Abram remained for most of his life and where he and his family were buried.

For the third time we are told, **'Abram built an altar ... to the LORD'** (see 12:7-8). Wherever he settled, Abram was concerned to provide a place of worship. It is as we acknowledge God and seek him in prayer that we shall find blessing, be a means of blessing to others and find grace to wait for God to fulfil all his good promises.

20.
War and peace

Please read Genesis 14:1-24

The first recorded war in the Bible, some twenty centuries before Christ, was in the Middle-East region. Twenty centuries after Christ it is still a volatile area. Despite all the outward changes over four millennia, human nature is basically the same and nations still fight each other. In this world of war, safety and peace are to be found in the God of Abram.

Abram saves Lot (14:1-16)

From a local dispute between herdsmen we move to the world of international politics and Abram becomes a force to be reckoned with. It is striking that the conflicts described are along the borders of the promised land. Trouble blew up where Lot had chosen to settle, whereas Abram lived peaceably in the land.

1. Initial conflict (14:1-4)

The ancient equivalent of Saddam Hussein of Iraq, along with neighbouring allies, invaded the cities of the plain. An alliance of four kings descended on the very area which resembled the Garden of Eden. Like Lot, they were no doubt attracted to this prosperous spot. Since the Fall, no paradise on earth is free from trouble. Human greed grabs what it can and will use whatever force is necessary. The four kings were: **'Amraphel, king of Shinar'** ('Babylonia' — see 10:10; 11:2), part of modern Iraq; **'Arioch king of Ellasar'**, a place identified with an area of modern Turkey or in northern Syria; **'Chedorlaomer** [the alliance leader; see 14:4] **king of Elam'**, part of modern Iran; and **'Tidal king of nations'**, an inclusive term for northerners from the Hittite region of modern-day Turkey.

These kings had conquered the five city-states named in the previous chapter. The names of four of the five defeated kings are listed. **'Shinab'** means 'Sin (the moon-god) is father' and **'Shemeber'**, 'The name is powerful'. Both these names are what we would expect to find in that pagan society. As for the names of the kings of Sodom and Gomorrah, they are most unusual. **'Bera'** means 'in evil' and **'Birsha'** 'in wickedness'. Their names draw attention to the immorality associated with their cities.[1]

As a result of the devastating defeat, the five kings and their city states were brought into subjection to Chedorlaomer and were obliged to pay tribute to him. After twelve years of suffering such indignity they had had enough, so **'In the thirteenth year they rebelled'** (14:4).

2. The second conflict (14:5-11)

A year later, Chedorlaomer called on his old alliance partners to regroup and together they invaded the area a second time. Before they punished the offending kings, they attacked all the neighbouring kingdoms. The route they followed took them along the well-known 'King's Highway' (Num. 20:17). Entering the Transjordan region from the north, they subdued first **'the Rephaim in Ashtaroth Karnaim'** (in Bashan), **'the Zuzim in Ham'** (south of Ashtaroth) and the areas later inhabited by the Moabites and Edomites. The confederation then made its way down to the tip of the Red Sea ('**El Paran**'). '**Then they turned back and came to En Mishpat (that is, Kadesh).**' They also attacked '**the Amalekites**' and '**the Amorites**' along the southern borders of Canaan. All these peoples and places are associated with Israel's wanderings under Moses' leadership (Exod. 17:8; Num. 10:12; 13:26,29; 20:22; 34:4; Deut. 2:10-22).

The five kings from the cities of the plain took the offensive. Led by the King of Sodom, they engaged the enemy coalition of four kings where they had done so previously, '**in the Valley of Siddim**', which is identified as '**the Salt Sea**' (14:3,8). It would appear that the southern end of the Dead Sea is the most likely place. The area was full of bitumen or '**asphalt pits**' (14:10). The battle went against the five kings, so that '**The kings of Sodom and Gomorrah fled**' and hid in the pits,[2] while '**The remainder fled to the mountains**', which rise very steeply on either side of the Dead Sea. Sodom and Gomorrah were completely overrun and the invaders made off with as much booty as they could carry and many prisoners (14:11,16,21).

3. Lot taken captive (14:12)

The main reason for recording this incident is that it impinged on the life of Abram. His nephew, Lot, who was now living '**in Sodom**', had been taken captive. He found to his cost that the pleasant plain was not such a good place to live after all. His wealth had been taken and he was being marched off in the direction from which he had first emigrated with his uncle. When Christians backslide and allow themselves to be ruled by worldly thoughts, God may use drastic means to bring them to their senses. He shatters their peace in order that they might learn not to put their trust in this world's goods.

4. *Abram to the rescue* (14:13-16)

This third conflict scene is one which the four conquering kings least expected. As they made their way home with the goods and captives, they no doubt felt very pleased with themselves. They had taught those rebellious rulers a lesson they would not soon forget.

While all this was happening, Abram was dwelling comfortably by the trees of Mamre, the Amorite, with whom he had sworn an agreement, along with Mamre's brothers, Eshcol and Aner (14:13).[3] He may have been aware of troop movements in the south, but it was from someone who had managed to escape capture that he learned of Lot's plight. A less gracious and understanding person would have given up on Lot and left him to it. Abram, however, bore him no grudge. When he heard the bad news, he immediately set about mobilizing his 'trained' men, 318 of them (14:14). Together with his Amorite allies (see 14:13,24), Abram headed quickly to the northern borders of Canaan and defeated the invaders in a surprise night attack, pursuing **'them as far as Hobah, which is north of Damascus'** (14:15). He was then able to rescue Lot and his possessions, as well as all the other goods and people captured from Sodom (14:16).

It was an amazing victory, completely overshadowing the previous victories of the invaders. What has been said concerning Chedorlaomer and his allies makes Abram's expedition even more remarkable. Through this most unexpected means the adversaries were overthrown. Abram's selfless spirit brought blessing, not only to his immediate family but to the people of Sodom, as well as stability to the whole area. As the second half of the chapter shows, Abram's name became great and was associated with blessing. In a small, symbolic way, Abram was already experiencing the fulfilment of God's initial promises to him (see 12:1-3).

Lessons from this conflict

From Abram's military encounter we pause to consider two issues.

1. Encouragements and pointers

This account would have been a great encouragement to Moses and Joshua as they skirted the borders of the promised land and prepared to enter it. Christians too can find reassurance. Victory over God's enemies and ours is promised to those who trust him and are obedient to his Word. 'And this is the victory that has overcome the world — our faith. Who is he who overcomes the world, but he who believes that Jesus is the Son of God?' (1 John 5:4-5). We are overcomers because of Jesus and this passage leads us to him. Abram's victory reminds us of the woman's 'Seed' who will decisively defeat the devil. It points us to Abram's great descendant who came to rescue, not only those of his own race, but people of all nations. We praise God for Jesus, who came to deliver us from our captivity to sin and Satan. These powerful enemies are defeated through the most unlikely and feeble means, the cross of Christ. All who are saved through faith in him are 'more than conquerors' (Rom. 8:37).

2. Christians and war

War is part of life in this fallen world. Christians should not be surprised when conflicts occur. War is a great evil and one of the consequences of sin. James reminds us that wars arise through sinful desires (James 4:1-2). If people cannot get what they want through fair means they will resort to foul. We tend to isolate war and treat it as something unique, but it is a larger and more frightening expression of the fighting that is seen between individuals in the home, between opposing parties in society and even within the fellowship of the church.

Is there such a thing as a just war? The Bible makes it clear that the state has the task of keeping order and part of its duty is to punish criminal behaviour. If this is so on a regional and national level, there is a place for keeping order on an international level. As police are given the authority to go to war against the criminal and bring him to justice, so it is sometimes necessary to go to war against an aggressor, bring him to justice and restore what he has seized. This is what Abram did. Self-defence is another just reason for taking up arms to fight. But in all this activity the Bible's guide is that the punishment must fit the crime. Those engaged in a just war must themselves seek to act fairly and justly.

Is it ever right for a Christian to fight? Our Lord's words in the Sermon on the Mount concerning turning the other cheek and not retaliating apply to the Christian's personal relationships towards others. God's people are to exhibit the spirit of meekness such as Abram displayed towards his self-centred nephew. If a Christian decides to be a conscientious objector then it will be on other grounds than our Lord's teaching in Matthew 5:38-45. As members of society Christians do have duties towards the state. Our Lord calls us to give to Caesar what belongs to him (Matt. 22:21). If it is the state's duty to resist evil-doers and bring them to justice then, just as Christians in the police force will be at war against criminals, so there is no reason why Christians should not be in the armed forces to fight against foreign aggressors. Christians are caught up in the evils of society. On the other hand, the Christian church is not to resort to earthly weapons to advance the kingdom of God. 'The weapons of our warfare are not carnal but mighty in God for pulling down strongholds' (2 Cor. 10:4).

Abram meets two kings (14:17-24)

The climax of the account is Abram's meeting with the kings of Sodom and Salem. Even without radio or e-mail, word soon got round. His victory was being celebrated before he arrived home.

A welcome party, headed by the King of Sodom, went out to meet the all-conquering hero in **'the Valley of Shaveh (that is, the King's Valley)'**.⁴ There is a 'King's Valley' mentioned in 2 Samuel 18:18 which is situated just over two miles south of Jerusalem. If this is the same valley then the King of Sodom would have travelled some distance to greet Abram. What was the reaction of this defeated king to victorious Abram? We are deliberately left guessing and in the meantime we are introduced to another king whom we have not met before, **'Melchizedek king of Salem'** (14:18).

1. The King of Salem

Melchizedek means 'My king is righteous.'⁵ Salem is another name for Jerusalem (Ps. 76:2). Canaan at this time had a number of settlements, and leaders emerged who ruled over these self-governing communities, which scholars call 'city-states'. The cities of the plain were of this type. Melchizedek was the ruler of the city-state of Salem and came out to greet Abram, bringing a present of **'bread and wine'**. This was the kind of gift presented to kings. When Jesse sent a present to King Saul it included bread and wine (1 Sam. 16:20). Having conquered the enemy kings, Abram could rightly claim a position of authority in the region. Melchizedek recognized this and honoured him as a king.

Like many ancient Near-Eastern rulers, Melchizedek combined the offices of king and priest. As priest of **'God Most**

High' *(El Elyon)*, he blessed Abram. The actual words of the blessing are recorded. We notice that the priest-king acknowledged God as the **'Possessor of heaven and earth'** (14:19). In this context 'Possessor' is another term for 'Creator' (Deut. 32:6). Here is a representative of the families of the earth blessing Abram. God had made Abram's name great in the sight of the Canaanite rulers, and people had found blessing through him (see 12:2-3).

2. Abram's response to Melchizedek

Abram responded in an accepted and fitting way. He gave him a tenth of all the goods he had captured from the enemy (14:20). Wenham informs us that 'Tithing was an old and widespread custom in the ancient orient.'[6] Kings and priests were offered tithes. Abram did not give this tithe as a tax, but as a spontaneous offering in virtue of Melchizedek's priestly blessing. He recognized Melchizedek as a representative of the God whom he worshipped.

3. The King of Sodom

The difference between King Melchizedek, 'king of righteousness' (Heb. 7:2) and King Bera, king of 'evil', could not be greater. Whereas the King of Salem gave a present fit for a king, the King of Sodom brought no gift. Melchizedek blessed Abram; not so the King of Sodom. Instead, Bera's brief word demonstrated that he had not come primarily to thank Abram, but to make sure Abram understood that the booty belonged to him. The king's words betray an ungracious attitude: **'Give me the persons, and take the goods for yourself'** (14:21). He came making his demands as if he still owned everything. It was Abram who had the right to both the goods and the people and to distribute the booty as he wished. The King of Sodom had no rights. He had lost everything to the enemy.

4. Abram's response to Bera

Abram made it clear that he would take to himself not so much as **'a thread to a sandal-strap'** (14:22-23) of the booty. The phrase **'lifted my hand'** indicates, as it does today, that a solemn oath had been sworn (see Dan. 12:7). Only what the young men had already eaten on the campaign had been taken. He also acknowledged that his Amorite allies had a right to a share of the plunder. What rightly belonged to Abram he freely and willingly gave to the King of Sodom. He did not wish to give the king any grounds for thinking he had made Abram rich (14:23). In swearing by **'God Most High, the Possessor of heaven and earth'**, Abram identified himself with what the King of Salem had said. He acknowledged that it was the Lord who had delivered his enemies into his hand.

Important issues arising from this incident

1. Attitudes to God's kindness

The King of Sodom's attitude

This incident did not humble the people or their king. They were already an evil and sinful people ripe for judgement. Yet God, before bringing the 'end-time' destruction, gave them a warning through this traumatic incident. Not only that — he brought the King of Sodom into contact with those whose trust was in the Creator God. Instead of repenting and seeking the God of Abram, he treated the saviour of the situation in an arrogant way. The Lord had said to Abram, 'I will bless those who bless you, and I will curse him who curses [or disdains] you' (12:3). Here is an example of one who treated Abram disdainfully. This was the sin that tipped the scales. The Sodomite king rejected the one through whom he could have found true peace.

Before the final judgement, God warns by sending lesser judgements to bring us to the end of ourselves in order that we might cry to him for mercy and salvation. The sin of sins is to spurn God's love and reject those who witness to his goodness. God associates himself with his people. Our attitude towards those who love God and his Son, Jesus Christ, betrays our attitude to God himself. To reject Jesus, the Saviour of the world, is to reject the only hope there is from the coming day of wrath.

The King of Salem's attitude

He blessed Abram and was himself blessed. Here was someone not of the seed of Abram who recognized God's hand at work in the life of Abram. He embraced the God of Abram. This is an encouragement to us to do the same and to find blessing in the God of Abram, who is also the God and Father of our Lord Jesus Christ.

Abram's attitude

His victory over the kings, and his obvious importance in the eyes of the leaders in the surrounding area, did not go to his head. He was humble enough to receive blessing from the King of Salem, to recognize his superiority in matters spiritual and to acknowledge that God had given him the victory. To the King of Sodom, who owed him nothing and treated him shabbily, Abram showed a generous spirit and testified to the Lord (14:22). 'He who glories, let him glory in the LORD' (1 Cor.

1:31). Christians are also urged to do good to those who ill-treat them.

2. Tithing

Tithing has been associated in church history with legalism, taxation and state interference. Nonconformists in England and Wales were often forced to pay tithes to churches and clergymen they did not recognize, a situation that existed in some areas late into the twentieth century. Under the old covenant tithing was made compulsory but there is no direct teaching on the subject in the New Testament. Our Lord, like the prophets, denounced the self-righteous who were meticulous in tithing their herbs but neglected the weightier matters of the law (Amos 4:4-5; Matt. 23:23).

On the other hand, those blessed by the Priest who is 'according to the order of Melchizedek' are clearly urged to show their gratitude by giving at least a tenth of their wealth to the Lord. Abram was under no compulsion to give. It was a spontaneous offering, an expression of a thankful heart. This is to be the attitude of the Christian (Matt. 10:8). There is, however, a place for giving regularly, not only for special needs (1 Cor. 16:1-4), but for the support of the ministry. It is in this context that a principle concerning tithing can be drawn from the law of Moses that is of continuing validity. The tithes were specifically for the support of the full-time workers in the tabernacle. In the New Testament men are called and set apart to preach the gospel and they are to be looked after financially. Jesus said that the 'labourer is worthy of his wages' (Luke 10:7; see Gal. 6:6). A clear parallel exists between those who ministered in the tabernacle and those who minister in the church of God. Tithing enables gospel ministers to be paid regularly and adequately.

3. Melchizedek

His beliefs

Was Melchizedek a polytheist who served the chief god of the Canaanite pantheon, El, 'the most high god'? Or was he a pagan saint, a priest of a pagan religion who had a genuine faith in God? Or was he an anonymous believer who worshipped in ignorance the true God under the name of El? Such questions are being asked, not only by those who believe that all religions lead to God, but by those who suggest that the unevangelized may not be in such a hopeless and lost state as Christians have formerly supposed.[7]

It is a dangerous procedure to build a theology concerning anonymous Christians or pagan saints from such slender pieces of evidence. Melchizedek is not only an enigmatic figure but an exceptional person. The Bible is quite clear that all have sinned and that the whole world lies in the grip of the Evil One. All are by nature under God's wrath and deserve hell, and all need to hear and respond to the gospel if they are to escape the coming wrath.

Not having any background information concerning Melchizedek, we cannot assume that he was a pagan priest. In fact, the evidence points in another direction. He was a priest of God Most High and knew him as the Maker of heaven and earth. Abram himself used the title 'Most High' when referring to God and associated it with the name 'LORD' or 'Jehovah' (14:22). This is not syncretism. It was not a case of joining two religions together. The God whom Melchizedek worshipped and served is the God of Abram, who later revealed himself to Moses as 'I AM'. 'God Most High' is used by Moses and the psalmist to emphasize God's authority over the nations (Num. 24:16; Deut. 32:8; Ps. 83:18).

However defective Melchizedek and Abram may have been in their understanding of God and their attitude to other gods, one thing is clear: they had both been given knowledge of the true God and knowingly worshipped God (14:20). As God revealed himself to Abram we must understand that he had revealed himself to this priest-king in Jerusalem. Melchizedek not only knew about the true God, but he trusted this God, was in his service and loved the people of God.

Salvation history

There was a belief among Jews of the New Testament period that Melchizedek was an angel. On the other hand, among Christians it has often been suggested that he was a pre-incarnate appearance of the Son of God. There is nothing to support the angelic view, and as for the Christian idea, Hebrews 7:3 tells us that Melchizedek only resembles the Son. The Genesis text gives us no warrant for thinking of him as a divine person.

This saintly figure who united the office of priest and king in the ancient city of Jerusalem is treated as a type of Christ. Abram, the father of the faithful, acknowledged this person as a priest of the supreme God. Moses, the great law-giver and prophet of the old dispensation, gives him a prominent place before Aaron is mentioned. David, the first king of Israel who conquered and ruled from the place once occupied by Melchizedek, prophesied that his greater descendant would be a priest as well as a king 'according to the order of Melchizedek' (Ps. 110:1-4). David was implying that the priestly line through Levi and Aaron, prescribed in the law, would be set aside. Jesus drew attention to Psalm 110 in his confrontation with the Jewish leaders concerning the Messiah (Mark 12:36-37). The writer of the epistle to the Hebrews leaves us in no doubt that Jesus is the reality of which the priest-king of Salem was a type (Heb. 5-7). What is said, and left unsaid, about Melchizedek (there is no reference to his parents or ancestors) is all significant in pointing us to our great High Priest. Jesus is the true King of Righteousness and Peace, who is without beginning and whose rule and priest-hood have no ending. He ever lives to intercede for us. With the coming of Jesus, the inferior order of priests of Levi's line must give way to this superior order.

21.
Justification by faith alone

Please read Genesis 15:1-21

We think of Moses as the great Old Testament figure who foreshadows Christ in his offices of Prophet, Priest and King. In this chapter we are introduced to Abram's role as a prophet who received God's Word, a priest who prepared a sacrifice and a king who was promised victory and much land. But Abram is not only an early type of Christ; he is held before us as a model believer.

Abram's faith (15:1-6)

Faith, as we have seen, is not a leap into the dark. It is trusting the good word of God.

God spoke to Abram (15:1-5)

Why did God say to Abram, **'Do not be afraid'**? It is common for people to fear when God reveals himself. In addition, the question that Abram put to God shows where his fears lay: **'Lord God, what will you give me, seeing I go childless...?'** (15:2). Abram's question draws our attention to the central concern of the chapter — God's delay in fulfilling his promise. God's people have always had to live with apparent delays. But God reveals truth to his people to allay their fears and to encourage faith in promises that are not immediately fulfilled. The righteous live by their faith in God's word, for 'The vision is yet for an appointed time... Though it tarries, wait for it' (Hab. 2:3).

1. God's first word (15:1)

Abram's position as a prophet is clearly emphasized in this divine visitation. The introductory phrase, **'The word of the LORD came to Abram'** (see also 15:4), is a typical way of introducing revelation from God through the prophets (see Jer. 1:4; Hosea 1:1). Moses prepares the later generations of God's people for the prophetic voice in Israel (see 1 Sam. 3:1,21; 15:10). It first came to Abram, the father of the nation. The Hebrew word translated **'vision'** is a rare word (see Num. 24:4,16) and is an added indication that this is a divine revelation. In the vision it is the Word of God that is revealed.

'I am your shield' confirms what Melchizedek had said in praise of 'God Most High', who had 'delivered' the enemy into Abram's hand (14:20).[1] 'I am your shield' is to be understood in the light of the second phrase, **'your exceedingly great reward'**. In Ezekiel 29:19 the word 'reward' is used of a soldier's wage which would be taken from the spoils of battle. Abram is promised a prize far in excess of anything he might have gained by keeping all the enemy spoil for himself. God, the great victor and deliverer of his people, has 'led captivity captive' and 'received gifts among men... Blessed be the Lord, who daily loads us with benefits' (Ps. 68:18,19). Paul uses these verses to describe Christ's victory over the enemy: 'When he ascended on high he led captivity captive, and gave gifts to men' (Eph. 4:8). Psalm 84:11 speaks of 'the LORD God' as 'a sun and a shield', and immediately follows this with the truth that:

> The LORD will give grace and glory;
> No good thing will he withhold
> From those who walk uprightly

2. Abram's reply (15:2-3)

This is Abram's first recorded prayer. He opened his lament with the words, **'Lord GOD'** (literally, 'my Lord Jehovah'; see also verse 8).[2] Though he was deeply frustrated, Abram showed proper respect when approaching God. It was not that he was ungrateful, but his faith in the promises already made to him (12:1-3; 13:16) meant he could not rest content. 'A lesser man would have basked in the comfort of verse 1.'[3]

God's revelation to him spurred him to protest: **'What will you give me, seeing I go childless…?'** This pitiful cry is not the dejected outburst of an Elijah depressed after the excitement of victory. This is the cry of a man of faith who could not be satisfied with all God's blessings when one small but vital ingredient remained unfulfilled. What good were all the promises concerning a great nation when he had no son? How could he be blessed when he had no children? (cf. 9:1). It seemed humanly impossible for him to have a child by his wife Sarai, for we have already been told that 'Sarai was barren; she had no child' (11:30).

This ache in Abram's heart is something that has been felt by all God's people throughout history in connection with the execution of God's promises. The psalmist cried, 'O Lord, how long?' While we rest in the glorious future promises, we cannot rest content with the present state of affairs. As Daniel fasted and prayed after reading God's Word, so God's people today must continue to plead for a revival of true religion in our countries.

> How shall thy servants give thee rest,
> Till Zion's mouldering walls thou raise?

Till thine own power shall stand confessed,
And make Jerusalem a praise?

(Philip Doddridge)

If God's promise of future 'seed' was to be fulfilled, Abram figured that it would have to be in some other way than through Sarai. Abram put forward the first of a number of ideas for solving the problem. On this occasion he brought his idea to God. One way out of the impasse would be to adopt Eliezer of Damascus as his heir. After all, he was a member of his household, **'one born in my house'** (literally 'a son of my house').[4] Up till now God had not told Abram how he would have descendants. Abram's suggestion, therefore, must not be seen as displaying any lack of faith. An adopted son could have been the legal heir. Similar procedures operated at that time among the Hurrians (or Horites).[5] Abram believed God's promise concerning the future and brought this accepted custom to God as one possible way forward.

3. God's answer (15:4-5)

God emphatically put an end to any idea of Eliezer as an adopted son: **'This one shall not be your heir.'** Abram's faith is further instructed by this revelation. He is to have a child of his very own: **'One who will come from your own body shall be your heir.'** There will be more heart-searchings to come. Will the child be born to Sarai or not? But for now Abram is given this special revelation that the 'seed' will definitely be his own flesh and blood.

God then strengthened his faith. It was at night that God came to him and it provided the opportunity for his word to be confirmed by the sight of the stars. God had told him that he would have descendants 'as the dust of the earth' (13:16). Now he is told that they will be like the stars in the sky (15:5). Later they are compared to the sand on the seashore (22:17).

This promise finds its ultimate fulfilment in the countless numbers who have looked to Jesus Christ for salvation. Abraham is 'the father of all those who believe' (Rom. 4:11).

God justified Abram (15:6)

1. Saving faith

Abram's response to this special revelation was that **'He believed in the LORD.'** This is the first occurrence of the word 'believe' in the Bible and the one place in the Old Testament where faith is counted for righteousness. We can understand why this verse is quoted frequently in the New Testament (Rom. 4:3,20-24; Gal. 3:6; James 2:23).

Abram believed God's word. God revealed truth to him and he accepted it. We cannot say that we believe God if we do not believe his revealed word concerning 'the Seed'. Abram could not rest content with the other promises until he had certainty about 'the seed'. The other promises remained detached without the promise of a 'seed'. That 'Seed' is Christ, in whom all the promises of God find their 'Yes' and 'Amen'. Without Christ the other promises cannot be appropriated. Many want the blessings of heaven and God but they do not want Christ.

Abram believed in the Lord. This suggests personal commitment. Abram rested in the Lord who had made these wonderful promises. It is possible to assent to the gospel truths without trusting the Lord. Trust involves personal reliance on the Lord.

Abram kept on believing. The form of the verb found here suggests continual trust. It was not a passing phase in his life.

This was no temporary faith. True saving faith is no spur-of-the-moment action. Faith rests on Jesus Christ alone for salvation for time and for eternity.

2. Justification

The second part of the verse tells us that **'He accounted it to him for righteousness.'** Though the subject in the first half of the verse is Abram, it makes more sense, and has New Testament approval, for God to be the subject of the second half. It was God who accounted Abram's faith to him for righteousness.[6]

'Normally righteousness is defined in terms of moral conduct ... and might well be paraphrased as God-like or at least God-pleasing, action.'[7] Abram, however, does not do righteousness but has righteousness credited to him by God. It was Abram's faith that was reckoned to him for righteousness. Does this mean, as many Jews of New Testament times thought, that Abram's faith was seen by God as a righteous act? If this were the case the verse would be teaching that faith is an acceptable alternative to righteousness. Neither Moses, Paul nor James teaches that the act of believing becomes a substitute for a lack of personal righteousness. The word **'accounted'** also forbids us to view righteousness as an equivalent compensation for some meritorious action. It is made perfectly clear by Paul in Romans 4:4-5 that righteousness is not a reward for Abram's 'work' of faith. God reckons, or credits, this righteousness to him as a gift in response to Abram's trust in God's promise. Abram's faith is not to be seen as a work which God is pleased to treat as a righteous act, but as reliance on God's promise concerning the 'Seed'. It is the divine promise which is the important item. Faith in the promised Saviour is not a substitute for righteousness, but the means God uses to declare sinners righteous.

Some modern scholars suggest that the phrase 'to credit as righteousness' means 'to be brought into a covenant relationship'. This is to go beyond what the text says. Covenant membership is a by-product of justification and not the heart of the matter. The verse teaches that the divine Judge acquitted Abram the sinner and accepted him as righteous, because righteousness had been placed to his account. The negative side of this is expressed by David: 'Blessed is the man to whom the LORD does not impute [or credit] iniquity' (Ps. 32:1-2). The justification of sinners involves a great exchange. Whereas sin is not reckoned to the person, righteousness is (2 Cor. 5:21). The sins of believers were put to Christ's account and he paid the price in his atoning death. In union with Jesus Christ, believers also have placed to their account the moral righteousness of Christ, who has fulfilled all God's righteous requirements. He is our righteousness (1 Cor. 1:30). This is the truth concerning justification by faith alone that Luther rediscovered and which started the religious Reformation in the sixteenth century.[8]

Only the righteous can be acquitted. God will by no means clear the guilty. But no one is righteous in himself. All have sinned and all our so-called righteous acts are filthy rags in God's sight. On what basis could God account not guilty those who are guilty sinners? How could God pronounce righteous those who are not righteous? Abram's faith was in God's promised 'seed', and this was accounted to him for righteousness. It is on the same basis that we are justified today. That promised 'Seed' is Jesus Christ. The Old Testament people of God looked forward to the coming of the promise; we look back on what Christ did for us on the cross. We must all rely solely on Christ to put us right with God.

God's faithfulness (15:7-21)

In this scene the word 'covenant' is the key word (15:18; cf. 6:18; 9:9-17). The essence of God's covenants is this: that God enters into special relationships with people, gives them promises and goes on oath to keep those promises. God inaugurated a special relationship with Abram so that the divine plan for the salvation of sinners might go ahead and that all nations might be blessed through Abram's 'seed'. Though the word 'covenant' has not been used in connection with Abram until this point, it is clear that this is what God's relationship with Abram was (see 12:1-3; 13:14-18). God confirmed his covenant promises in a special ceremony.

The covenant ritual

The Lord promised to give Abram the land of Canaan for an inheritance (15:7). Abram then asked, **'How shall I know that I will inherit it?'** (15:8). In response, God instructed him to bring clean animals and to cut each carcass into two pieces. The dove and the pigeon were not cut. All this reminds us of the law concerning the offering of sacrificial animals and birds (Lev. 1:6,17). However, instead of the animals being placed on an altar and burnt, the pieces were placed in two parallel rows opposite each other (15:9-10). When birds of prey swooped down on the carcasses, Abram shooed them away (15:11). Then at sunset, on the second day, when the vultures had gone to rest, an uncanny, **'deep sleep'**, **'horror and great darkness fell upon'** Abram (15:12). This was God's doing. The same 'deep sleep' that descended on Adam before Eve was formed now fell on Abram (see 2:21). In addition, an awesome dread seized him as he found himself in the presence of the great, mysterious God. 'Darkness', often associated with the divine glory cloud, was a feature of God's presence at the time of the Exodus (Deut. 4:11). It was as Abram was in this situation that:

> 1. God informed him of the Egyptian bondage and the Exodus after 400 years, in the fourth generation (15:13-16);
> 2. God **'passed between those pieces'** in the form of a **'smoking oven and a burning torch'** (15:17). Fire and smoke (or cloud) are associated with the presence of God (Exod. 13:21; 19:16-18).

What was the reason for this unusual activity? Some think that God was indicating in a striking way that he was among his people and would certainly give the land to Abram's descendants. But, surely, there is more to it than that? The next verse supplies the answer: **'On the same day the Lord made a covenant with Abram'** (15:18). A covenant ritual had taken place. The Hebrew idiom for 'made a covenant' is literally 'cut a covenant' and we can see why. Animals were cut in two and those making the covenant passed between the pieces. This is what sometimes happened in the ancient Near East. The parties to a treaty would walk between sacrificial animals that had been cut in half. In the final days of the kingdom of Judah, there is reference to a similar covenant ritual (Jer. 34:18-20). By this means the participants graphically indicated their intention to keep the agreement.

In this incident, God condescended to use a human treaty ritual to make the point clear to Abram that nothing would stand in the way of God's fulfilling his promise. This ritual emphasized three things:

1. God's initiative in calling for animals to be sacrificed (15:9)

The sacrificial slaughter of animals in the Bible is not an idea that human beings have invented in order to twist God's arm.

In pagan worship, people offer sacrifice to try to get the gods on their side. In the religion of the Bible, God directs what people are to sacrifice. Abram did exactly what God asked him to do.

2. God's action in making the covenant (15:18)

In the actual ritual, God was the sole actor. After cutting up the animals, Abram was put out of action (15:12). He was only allowed to be an observer, not a participant. Abram heard God solemnly declare what would happen to his descendants and that the land would be given to them. It would stretch from **'the river of Egypt'** (not the Nile but the brook or wadi near Gaza; see 1 Kings 8:65) **'to the great river, the River Euphrates'** (15:18). It was during the reigns of David and Solomon that this promise had its Old Testament fulfilment (1 Kings 4:21). This high-water mark in Israel's history itself becomes symbolic of the future kingdom of Messiah. With the coming of *the* Seed of Abraham, Jesus Christ, the promise of land takes on cosmic dimensions (see Rom. 4:13; Matt. 5:5; Rev. 11:15). The ritual indicated that he was prepared to receive the curse if the promises were not implemented. In this spectacular way God went on oath to keep the promises spelled out to Abram.

3. Sacrificial death was associated with covenant-making

This would become even more obvious in the setting up of the covenant at Mt Sinai (Exod. 24:8).

This covenant ceremony is only a preparation and type of what happened when the new covenant was inaugurated. God was the initiator of it. In place of the old Sinai agreement Jeremiah prophesied that the Lord would make a new covenant with his people (Jer. 31:31-34; Heb. 8:7-13). The new covenant involved blood sacrifice. But instead of symbolic rituals we have the reality when Christ died on the cross (1 Cor. 11:25). Jesus Christ took sole responsibility for keeping the covenant. He actually became a curse for his people by experiencing God's wrath on account of their sins. All who are united to Christ will never experience the curse they deserve and are assured of the eternal inheritance (Heb. 9:15).

The Exodus foreshadowed

The special covenant ceremony recounted here has convinced a number of modern scholars that it depicted symbolically what would happen at the time of the exodus from Egypt. But the meaning of the symbolic actions is spelled out in the prophecy.

The symbolic action

Firstly, the clean sacrificial animals that Abram was told to bring and slaughter were the very ones ordained in the law to be offered in place of the people. In other words, the animals represented the Israelites, and the birds of prey represented the unclean Gentiles who would seek to afflict the people of God.

Secondly, the clean animals had to be three years old. This means the animals were in their fourth year and the prophecy tells us that Abram's descendants would return in the fourth generation.

Thirdly, Abram's action in driving away the vultures looks forward to the Exodus, when Israel would be delivered from the unclean Gentiles who had thought to exterminate them.

Fourthly, the darkness, the smoking oven and burning torch are a reflection of the fire and darkness that accompanied God's presence at the time of the exodus and on Mt Sinai (Exod. 14:20; 19:18; 20:18; Deut. 4:11).

Fifthly, God's action in passing between the sacrificial animals represented his presence among his people in the cloudy pillar and fire.

The prophecy

Abram had asked, 'Lord GOD, how shall I know that I will inherit it?' (15:8). The Lord replies, **'Know certainly...'** (15:13). The prophecy makes clear two things.

Firstly, it assured Abram that *his descendants would inherit the land of Canaan, but not before a long period of suffering and slavery* (15:13-16). They would be strangers and oppressed in a foreign land for **'four hundred years'** (15:13). This is a round number, for the exact figure is given later as 430 years (Exod. 12:40). **'But in the fourth generation they shall return'** to Canaan (15:16) is not a contradiction of the previous figure. 'Generation' in this passage means 'lifetime', so that 400 years is equivalent to four generations. Levi, for instance, one of Jacob's sons who went down into Egypt (first generation), had a son called Kohath (second generation), a grandson Amram (third generation), and a great-grandson Moses who led the people out of Egypt (fourth generation; see Exod. 6:16-20).

The statement that **'The iniquity of the Amorites is not yet complete'** (15:16) is most remarkable. God is 'slow to anger' and gives ample opportunity for people to repent. The Amorites, though one tribal group in the land (15:21), here stand for all the inhabitants of Canaan. Though all sin deserves immediate judgement, the Canaanites had not arrived at the point where God's tolerance could bear with them no longer.

This verse also reminds us that the invasion of Canaan by Israel under Joshua's leadership was not aggression but an act of justice. It was not for Abram, powerful though he had become, to go out and conquer Canaan. God's people were called to wait God's time. In the process it would cost them centuries of hardship before the time was ripe. 'Holy wars' carried out supposedly in the name of God today are pure aggression and have nothing to do with God's justice. He has given no authority for one nation to invade another in the name of religion. As far as God's kingdom is concerned, it is spread not by force of arms, but by the preaching of the gospel.

Secondly, it assured Abram that *he would not suffer the oppression.* The phrase **'go to your fathers'** (15:15) is a Hebrew expression for death. Abram is promised a peaceful death. This is the first occurrence of the word **'peace'** *(shalom)* in the Bible. It suggests that Abram would die in safety. Death at a **'good'**, or ripe old age, is how Job and David, as well as Abraham, ended their lives (25:8; Job 42:16-17; 1 Chr. 29:28).

> For he who dies believing
> Dies safely through thy love.
>
> (Paul Gerhardt)

Valuable lessons for us

Besides the importance of the exodus theme in God's purpose, this passage also highlights two points.

1. Delay and suffering are part of God's plan

Abram was shown that the apparent slowness of God and the suffering that his descendants would experience were no threat to the divine plan. Rather, he was taught that it would be through suffering that God's people would enter into the inheritance. David learned through suffering and exile to wait God's time (1 Sam. 16-31; 2 Sam. 5:1-5). Isaiah prophesies that through suffering the Servant would be exalted (Isa. 52:13 – 53:12). Suffering before glory is the theme of Peter's letter (1 Peter 1:6-7,11; 4:12-13; 5:1,10).

2. Death is no barrier to peace and future blessing

It may seem strange to us that God, having promised Abram many descendants and that the land would be his, should now make clear to him that the promises would not be fulfilled until long after his death. How could he die in peace when so many of the promises lay in the future? The secret is that he believed God, saw the fulfilment from afar and rejoiced in the future 'Seed' (John 8:56; Heb. 11:13-16,39-40). He looked beyond death to a day when he would participate in these blessings. Like Abram, all who believe in Jesus for salvation look forward to that better, heavenly country.

22.
Hagar's son

Please read Genesis 16:1-16

Have you been tempted to help God along? We have all heard the saying, 'God helps those who help themselves.' It is quoted as if it were gospel truth. The Bible, however, teaches that God helps those who cannot help themselves. This chapter shows the unhappy consequences of trying to force God's hand. At the same time we see how God cares for the helpless and furthers his plans, not only in spite of, but through the folly of human sin.

Human faithlessness (16:1-6)

Central to the story of Abram is the promise of a son. Most of the incidents in his life have a bearing on this important subject. They are not set down haphazardly, but carefully chosen so that only what is relevant concerning the promised 'seed' is presented. Some of the incidents create suspense and we begin to wonder whether the promise will ever be fulfilled.

Why was God taking so long to fulfil his promise? Was it to teach Abram and Sarai patience? Learning patience was a by-product of the long wait. The fundamental purpose for the apparent delay was to convince them and us that the promised 'Seed', the future deliverer, would be of supernatural origin. Abram and Sarai were taught through the incidents in their lives that the promised 'Seed' would not be born through the will and schemes of human beings, but by the power of God. We marvel at the divine wisdom. God has not only worked through the rough and tumble of human history to fulfil his promises in Jesus Christ but, through the folly of human impatience and lack of trust, to present pictures and types of the coming Messiah.

1. Sarai's feelings

Up to this point we have viewed the lack of a son from Abram's side. He had been told that he was to have a son of his very own. Imagine how Sarai must have felt on hearing this news. It would have led her to suppose that she was the one preventing the promises from being fulfilled. By now she would have given up hope of ever being the mother of Abram's son. There was nothing for it but to wait to die. Perhaps Abram would marry again and that would result in the promises of God being fulfilled.

2. Sarai's plan

It was Sarai's turn to have a bright idea. No doubt she kicked herself for not thinking of it sooner. It was the ancient equivalent of surrogate motherhood. Sarai had a maid called Hagar. She would give her servant girl to Abram as a wife. Any son born out of the union would still be regarded as Sarai's and Abram would have a son who was really his own flesh and blood. So Sarai said to her husband, **'See now, the LORD has restrained me from bearing children. Please, go in to my maid; perhaps I shall obtain children by her'** (16:2).

The plan seemed sound and acceptable. There was nothing to oppose it. The custom of those days allowed it. Jacob's wives both made use of it later. Various laws from those times mention it. Hammurabi, an early Babylonian king (*c.* 1750

B.C.), produced a code of laws. Law number 146 refers to a
wife giving a female slave to her husband to bear children.
Clay tablets from the site of the ancient town of Nuzi (now in
Iraq) are more explicit. A wife who bears no children could
give her husband a slave-girl. With custom and law on their
side, it seemed the most reasonable thing to do. In addition,
time was against them. Abram was now eighty-five, approaching eighty-six (16:16). Expediency, reason, law and custom
all agreed that this was what they should do. What is more, it
worked! Abram got his own child. Not only that, the new
baby was a boy. The plan must have been right, for everything
came together to produce the desired result! Perfect guidance,
you might think.

3. Wrong move

Sarai's scheme, however, was not right. Sometimes guidance
does come through circumstances all coming together in perfect harmony, but not always. How do we know that it was
not right in this instance? There are a number of clues.

Firstly, the way Moses draws a parallel between this incident and the account of the Fall indicates that Sarai's plan was
wrong. God said to Adam, 'You have heeded the voice of
your wife' (3:17). Here we read, **'Abram heeded the voice
of Sarai'** (16:2). Again, we are told that Eve 'took' and 'gave
to her husband'. Here we read that Sarai **'took'** Hagar and
'gave .... to her husband'. Although there was no specific
prohibition as in Genesis 3, nevertheless Abram and Sarai's
entire thinking and action showed a lack of trust in God's ability to keep his promise.

Sarai's proposal ran counter to God's original plan for
humanity. Genesis 2:24 makes it clear that it was God's will
that men and women should live in monogamous relationships.
The fact that God allowed polygamy and legislated in divorce
cases did not mean that he approved of such behaviour. In the

case of divorce we are told that God hates it (Mal. 2:16). Jesus reminds us that it was because of the hardness of the human heart that such activity is allowed, but 'From the beginning it was not so' (Matt. 19:8).

Thirdly, the result of this 'good idea', in terms of its effect on family life, clearly indicates to us how wrong it was. Hagar soon became pregnant and then a war started in the home. She became proud and despised her mistress, for it appeared that she was to be mother to the long-awaited heir. Sarai, in turn, became jealous and it led her to blame her husband: **'My wrong be upon you!'** (16:5). Abram's reaction was to wash his hands of any responsibility: 'She's your maid; you do with her as you like.' So Sarai began treating her harshly and this eventually ended with Hagar's running away.

4. The folly of going ahead of God

We can learn some important lessons from all this. It is possible to convince ourselves that something is right when in fact it is going against the revealed will of God. In very many cases, the clear will of God is there in the Bible but we do not like it. Instead of trusting God and waiting his time, we try taking short cuts and running ahead, and in the end make more trouble for ourselves. Sometimes God may use sanctified common sense and circumstances to direct us in a particular course of action. What we must not do is to pit the providence of God against the revealed will of God. It has been known for Christians to convince themselves that they are doing the right thing in marrying non-Christians because of the way circumstances have brought them together. They have gone ahead and married despite the Bible's clear teaching, only to regret their actions at a later date.

When you are tempted to take a course of action irrespective of God's revealed will, think again. Remember what an awful thing it is to rebel against the Lord who died to save you. Take a long, hard look at the possible consequences of such action. Sin breeds sin and results in tragic divisions.

In the difficult area of childlessness we again must be careful that we do not start playing God and tampering with his plans for our lives. There are legitimate medical procedures that can be tried but there comes a time when we have to call a halt. This can be very hard, especially when the law of the land and reason might dictate that we press on experimenting till we get the desired results.

Divine faithfulness (16:7-16)

With Hagar having fled from the home, Abram and Sarai might well have considered that the problem they had brought upon themselves had suddenly resolved itself and they were now back to square one. Our folly is rarely so easily settled. Sin, particularly of a sexual nature, can have long-term effects. It leaves wounds that can take years to heal and even then they may leave scars that remain for the rest of a person's life. Sometimes the results of former sins can turn up and haunt us later when we least expect it. No doubt President Clinton thought that former unconfessed immoral acts were past and forgotten. If Abram and Sarai imagined they could forget about Hagar, they were in for a rude awakening. God in his wisdom and providence saw to it that Hagar was restored to the household. The spotlight now falls on Hagar and God's dealings with her.

1. Hagar's feelings

Hagar was an Egyptian and it would appear that when she ran away her intention was to return to Egypt. She was in the desert area **'on the way to Shur'**, which borders Egypt (16:7). Having run a long way, she was now parched and tired. Imagine it, a pregnant woman all alone, dejected and rejected, making her way back to her native country, wondering what would become of her.

As she tried to refresh herself at a spring of water, she was refreshed even more with the presence of the Lord. What a wonderful phrase that is: **'Now the Angel of the LORD found her'**! (16:7). God came to meet her at the point of her deepest need. How often God has done that in human experience down the centuries! He has found unbelievers when they were at their lowest and brought them to himself. The Lord has come to his wayward people when they were in distress, to comfort them and set them on the right path again.

2. The Angel of the LORD

This is the first reference to an angel in the Bible. The word often means a human 'messenger', although it can refer to a heavenly created being in the service of God. There is good reason to believe, however, that this 'angel' was not one of those ministering spirits sent to do God's will but a special appearance of the Lord himself.

In the first place, Hagar is said to have **'called the name of the LORD who spoke to her, You are the God who sees'** (16:13). God personally came to her and spoke to her. She named the God who had seen her in her distress, 'the seeing God' *(El Roi)*.

Secondly, 'the Angel of the LORD' later appeared to Moses in the burning bush and we are told that God spoke from the bush (Exod. 3:2-4; Deut. 33:16). Again, the Angel of the Lord is associated with the pillar of cloud and fire which was the visible expression of God's presence (Exod. 14:19). This is the Angel of God's presence who accompanied Israel throughout their desert wanderings (Isa. 63:9). These references in Exodus show that Hagar had a similar experience of God to that of Moses and the Israelites.

Thirdly, Hagar's words, **'Have I also here seen him who sees me?'** (16:13) are more accurately translated, 'Have I also here seen after [in the sense of "the back of"] the one who sees me?' God said to Moses when he desired to see his glory: 'You will see my back parts; but my face shall not be seen' (Exod. 33:23).

All manifestations of God are associated with the Second Person of the Trinity. The invisible God revealed himself visibly through his Son who finally became incarnate as the man, Christ Jesus.

3. God and Hagar

God graciously showed himself to this proud Egyptian maid. How kind God is! The God who called out to Adam and Eve after they had disobeyed God came to this girl in her distress. She may have been a mere servant girl, a foreigner, but God was interested in her. He addressed her personally by name and as someone responsible for her actions. His call to her also reminded Hagar of her position. She was **'Sarai's maid'**. The questions put to her were not for God's benefit (16:8). He knew exactly where she had come from and where she intended to go. God not only confronted her as her Judge, demanding an account of her conduct, but as her heavenly Friend concerned for her welfare.

Her reply draws attention to the opposition she had experienced, but also to the fact that she had done wrong. She was seeking to escape from her mistress, the one to whom she belonged. Her words, **'I am fleeing from ... my mistress Sarai'** (16:8), prepare for the Lord's next instructions: **'Return to your mistress, and submit yourself under her hand'**

(16:9). She must not run away. She belonged to Sarai and she was bearing Abram's child. The first step towards knowing God's blessing is the call to submit. Hagar was not the last to run away from the harsh realities of life. Running away never solves personal problems. The way out is to turn around and come back. The way to win is to submit and to do God's will as revealed in the Bible. We have an example in the New Testament of a slave who ran away but who was found by God through the ministry of Paul. The slave Onesimus became a Christian and was a great help to the apostle. Paul, however, sent him back to his master, Philemon, with a letter of commendation. That was where he belonged.

4. The promise of 'seed'

Hagar would have found it hard to return. Instead of a letter of commendation the Lord gave her a remarkable prophecy to take back and to encourage her as she walked the road of obedience. The prophecy is in three parts.

A promise (16:10)

There is an initial promise concerning the distant future: **'I will multiply your descendants** ["your seed"] **exceedingly…'** This future promise also meant that there was hope for the present. As we read this divine revelation, we are left guessing whether God will, after all, use Hagar to fulfil his promise concerning a future 'Seed' who will bruise the serpent's head and bring blessing to the nations.

A pronouncement (16:11)

While Hagar already knew she was pregnant, she was told she was carrying a son and that he was to be called Ishmael ('God hears'). The son to be born to her would remind her of the God who heard her cries when she was afflicted by Sarai.[1] What the Egyptian slave-girl experienced at the hands of Sarai would later be meted out to the descendants of Abram and Sarai by the Egyptians, where the same word, 'affliction' or 'oppression', is used (Exod. 3:7; 4:31). God's announcement to Hagar also reminds us of what was said to Mary: 'You will conceive in your womb and bring forth a son, and shall call his name Jesus' (Luke 1:31). The God who rescued Hagar and the Israelites came to save his people from the affliction and bondage to sin and Satan.

A prediction (16:12)

In this oracle of destiny Ishmael will be **'a wild man'** (literally, 'a wild donkey of a man'). The donkey's proverbial stupidity is not in mind here. Rather, the picture is of an animal that has not been domesticated, who 'scorns the tumult of the city; he does not heed the shouts of the driver' (see Job 39:5-8). It suggests that Ishmael and his descendants will live an independent, nomadic life in the desert. He will always live in close proximity to his brothers and yet always in opposition to them. If Hagar has been kicked around as a slave-girl, God makes clear that this will not happen to her son and his descendants. In a sinful world the prophecy only expresses how sin multiplies. The Arabs today claim descent from Abram through Ishmael.

5. The response of faith

God's intervention at this critical moment in Hagar's life had an immediate and positive effect on her. Her first concern was not her own interests but the God who had met her.

She worshipped the true God who had revealed himself to her

Later, when Israel heard that the Lord had 'looked on their affliction', they 'bowed their heads and worshipped' (Exod. 4:31). Hagar's worship took the form of a confession: **'You are the God who sees.'** There is adoring wonder that God should take notice of her, even though she had had a proud, bitter spirit. She had run away from the one family in all the world who had been specially blessed by God, yet the love of God would not let her go. She had no doubt been brought up to believe in the gods of Egypt who could neither see nor hear. In Abram's household this girl from pagan Egypt would have heard of the Creator God who had revealed himself to her master. Now she had personally experienced this living God who sees as no one else can see, right into our very hearts. It is a salutary reminder that there is no creature hidden from his sight, but all things are naked and open to the eye of him to whom we must give account (Heb. 4:13). To unbelievers that is a frightening thought. But to a girl who was feeling dejected and lonely, the realization that the true God is not remote, that he does care, was most wonderfully reassuring. The response of every believer to this God should be one of worship. 'Blessed be the God and Father of our Lord Jesus Christ, the Father of mercies and the God of all comfort' (2 Cor. 1:3).

Her second statement suggests that she was also amazed that God had revealed himself to her: **'Have I also here seen him who sees me?'** Hagar had been granted the privilege of seeing God. When other people came face to face with the holy God they expected to die. To see God and live was considered remarkable and an expression of God's grace. The comment, **'Then she called the name of the LORD who spoke to her...'**, makes it clear that the God whom Hagar had seen was, in fact, Jehovah. The Lord who met Moses and rescued

Israel from the Egyptian oppression had met Hagar. This same God actually took human nature and lived on earth as the man, Christ Jesus. As we read the Bible with the eye of faith, we view our God and Saviour and look forward to seeing him face to face.

She witnessed to the God who had met her

To commemorate the event, Hagar herself, in all probability, named the place **'Beer Lahai Roi'**, which means 'Well of the Living One who sees me' (16:14). We are told it was **'between Kadesh and Bered'**, but the exact spot is uncertain. It was a great blessing for her to have seen the spring of water, but it was a greater blessing that the Lord had seen her and that she had been spiritually refreshed. The place was from that time onwards a permanent reminder of God's gracious care towards this needy woman. Hagar wanted others to know the God who had personally come to her and blessed her. Christians are encouraged to witness to the grace of God who has saved them and keeps them.

She obeyed the God who had met her

This is implied in the final verses of the chapter. Strengthened in body and spirit, Hagar returned to Abram's household and, as God had promised, she gave birth to Abram's son. The fact that Abram named the child **'Ishmael'** meant that Hagar had told him the whole story. It was probably Abram who gave weight to the idea of calling the place 'Beer Lahai Roi'.

6. Sarai's hard lesson

There is no mention of Sarai in the final verses. All the emphasis falls on Abram, Hagar and Ishmael. Three times they are mentioned together (16:15-16). The plan was that any child Hagar bore would belong to Sarai. Though her little scheme had succeeded in producing a son, Sarai did not consider Ishmael to be hers. She seems not to have taken part in the celebrations or the naming of the child. But the child's name, Ishmael, 'God hears', would have continually convicted her of her own lack of faith. God's grace to Hagar would also have spoken to Sarai. Instead of crying out to God and looking for him to act, Sarai had devised a solution of her own that proved disastrous. We too must remember that God sees and hears and answers the prayers of his people. God's people are called to trust and wait patiently.

7. Abram's son

At eighty-six years of age Abram at last had a son. The question is whether he was to be the child of promise. God had made known to Hagar something of Ishmael's future and that his descendants would **'not be counted for multitude'** (16:10). Abram himself had already been promised innumerable descendants. Was this another confirmation to him? As we shall discover, Abram and Sarai would have to wait another thirteen years before God made clear to them what his purposes were.

23.
Sarah's son and the covenant sign

Please read Genesis 17:1-27

We come now to a crucial moment in the history of God's dealings with Abram and Sarai. 'Covenant' is the key word. It is used thirteen times in this chapter. Promises that have already been made become more specific. The new elements include Sarai's part in the fulfilment of the promises, reference to a royal line, the 'everlasting' nature of the covenant and the demands inherent in the covenant.

God's promises concerning land, protection, many descendants and blessing for the nations all revolve around the promise of a special 'seed'. Yet this was the very thing Abram and Sarai did not have. Sarai was barren. Various human means to obtain the promised son had been overruled by God. For the first time we are told that Sarai herself will give birth to Abram's child.

Divine revelation and human response

Chapter 17 begins by telling us that **'the LORD appeared'** to Abram (see 12:7).

The time of the revelation

Abram was ninety-nine years old when he had this gracious
visitation (17:1,24). He was eighty-six when Ishmael was born
(16:16). Thirteen years had gone by with no divine communication. Calvin suggests that the long delay was designed as a
discipline by God for taking Hagar as his wife. Life had gone
on and Ishmael was now into his teens. His mother had been
given special promises concerning Ishmael, and Abram and
Sarai had perhaps grown used to the idea that he was the son
of promise. We can well imagine the whole family settling down
to the idea that God in his providence had overruled their foolish scheme and was using it to fulfil his purposes. Suddenly,
the Lord appeared to Abram.

The way God revealed himself

We are not told how God revealed himself. The only detail of
interest is that when he had finished talking to him, **'God went
up from Abraham'** (17:22). This suggests that God appeared
in the form of the Angel of the Lord (see 16:7). It was a pre-
incarnate appearance of the Son of God.

The content of the revelation

Abram not only saw an appearance of God, but God talked to
him (17:22). This was the crucial thing, not what God looked
like. It is interesting that even when the Lord became incarnate we are not given any description of his physical
appearance.

The reaction to the revelation

There are three main parts to God's word and at the end of
each we are given Abram's response (17:3,17-18,23-27).

God's initial word (17:1-2)

Abram is reminded of who God is.

1. God's character — 'I am Almighty God'

The Hebrew words for 'God Almighty' *(El Shaddai)* are
well known. *El* is equivalent to our word 'God'. Six times
Shaddai occurs in Genesis and each time it is associated with
God's power, with his ability to transform situations, particu-
larly where humans are completely helpless and vulnerable.
'Almighty' is a good translation.

El Shaddai was a precious divine name to the fathers of
Israel. God said to Moses: 'I appeared to Abraham, to Isaac,
and to Jacob, as God Almighty' (Exod. 6:3). *El Shaddai* was
to these men what *Yahweh* (Jehovah) was to Israel and what
Jesus is to Christians.

God revealed himself as *El Shaddai* to transform Abram
and Sarai's hopeless situation. When we are at the end of our
tether, let us remember *El Shaddai*, the all-powerful God. He
is our refuge and strength and works all things for the good of
his people.

2. God's will — 'Walk before me and be blameless'

The God who had called Abram to follow him from a pagan
society sets before him the kind of life he is to lead. Life is a

pilgrimage and we are either journeying without God or with him. Enoch and Noah both knew what it was to 'walk about' with God. This is a figurative expression for living a godly life. Christians are called to live in fellowship with God (1 John 1:7).

Walking **'before'** God suggests that no other god must come between us and God. The first commandment is: 'You shall have no other gods before me' (Exod. 20:3). We, like Abram, are called to worship him alone (see 1 John 5:21).

In addition, walking before God means living with the consciousness that he is there. Do you remember as a child being taken by your parent or guardian to the park? You felt quite safe knowing someone you loved was watching. Perhaps you strayed some distance on your own, then panicked, thinking no one was there. Yet all the time loving eyes had you in sight. At other times when you sensed danger you would run into those arms of love for safety. As Christians we are sometimes apt to forget that God is there. How wonderfully assuring to know that God does see and care for his people! The devil may roar like a lion, spiritual pit bull terriers may come at us, but we are safe in Christ. Let us resolve with the psalmist: 'I will walk before the LORD in the land of the living' (Ps. 116:9).

Abram was called to be perfect, or **'blameless'**. This again is the calling of every child of God. Jesus said, 'Be perfect, even as your Father in heaven is perfect' (Matt. 5:48). As we walk before God and do his will, the more we shall be seen to be like God. Noah walked with God and was perfect among his contemporaries. There was no obvious flaw in his character (6:9). Though we are not sinlessly perfect in this world, we are urged not to sin and to grow to maturity. God has chosen us that we should be holy and without blame before him in love. It is the destiny of all who belong to God through Jesus Christ to be like God in moral perfection.

*3. God's promises — 'And I will make my covenant between
me and you'*

God had already made a covenant with Abram (see 15:18). It
may be that it is reaffirmed here because of Abram and Sarai's
rash action in using Hagar. If that is the case, it is similar to
God's reaffirmation of the Sinai covenant after the golden-
calf incident (Exod. 19:5; 24:7-8; 34:10).

The covenant promises, summarized in the words, **'I will
... multiply you exceedingly'**, are spelled out in the verses
that follow. What is of interest are the demands inherent in the
covenant. As God's original promises were made in the context of a command to go out in faith (see 12:1-3), so here
there is a link between God's call to live a godly, blameless life
and the making of the covenant. The **'and'** indicates purpose
or consequence. We could translate it like this: 'Walk before
me and be blameless, *so that* I may make my covenant between me and you.' Again, there is no thought of God's entering into a mutual pact with Abram. God was not imposing
prior conditions before reaffirming the agreement. Nevertheless, submission to God's will on Abram's part was essential
to the relationship. This chapter highlights divine sovereignty
and human responsibility. The God who called Abram, and
who also calls us to live before him and be perfect, is God
Almighty who will bring to pass what he has purposed. This is
the God who 'brought up our Lord Jesus from the dead ...
through the blood of the everlasting covenant'. May he, as he
did in Abram's life, 'make you complete in every good work
to do his will, working in you what is well-pleasing in his sight'
(Heb. 13:20-21).

Abram's response (17:3a)

'Then Abram fell on his face.' This is the proper response to the divine revelation. It is one of reverence and submission. This is the essence of true worship. Self is brought low; God is everything. Our consciences are awakened in his presence; our minds are instructed by his Word; our hearts are moved by his grace; and we surrender our wills to his purpose.

God's second word (17:3b-16)

It was while Abram was lying with his face to the ground that God continued talking to him. Three significant messages are given.

1. The first message concerns God — 'As for me...' (17:4-8)

The 'I wills' emphasize the divine promises and actions. Abram's change of name is the sign of the certainty of God's word. The promises contain two main points.

Many descendants (17:4-6)

Firstly, the use of the word **'fruitful'**, like that of 'multiply' in verse 2, recalls the general blessing to Adam which was re-stated after the Flood (1:28; 9:1). Abram, like Adam and Noah, 'stands at the beginning of a new epoch in human history.'[1] In Abram's case, God Almighty promises to make him excep-tionally (**'exceedingly'**) fertile.

Secondly, three times God promises that **'nations'** will arise from Abram. As a sign that he will be **'a father of many nations'**, his name is changed from Abram ('Father is exalted') to Abraham, which is similar in sound to the Hebrew for 'Father of a multitude'. In the New Testament Abraham is described as 'the father of all those who believe' in Jesus, whether Jew or Gentile (Rom. 4:11; Gal. 3:29). To those who prided themselves on their physical descent from Abraham, John the Baptist reminded them that 'God is able to raise up children to Abraham from these stones' (Matt. 3:9; Luke 3:8; cf. John 8:33-40). Even in Genesis the word 'father' need not be restricted to physical descent. Abraham was the 'father' of all those in his household who were identified with this covenant, whether actually born to him or not (17:23-27).

Thirdly, we are told for the first time that Abraham's 'seed' is to include a royal line — **'and kings shall come from you'**. Genesis will show how these promises were partially fulfilled. Abraham became the father of the Edomites, the Ishmaelites and the Midianites as well as of Israel. Kings of Edom are mentioned (36:31-39) and future kingship in Israel (36:31) is anticipated in the life of Joseph and prophesied concerning the royal line of Judah (49:8-12). While the promise is further anticipated in the era of David and Solomon, the complete realization comes with the Messiah, Jesus Christ (see Rev. 7:9).

An eternal commitment (17:7-8)

This covenant is to be permanent — **'an everlasting covenant'**. Despite the emphasis on Abraham's responsibilities, God will see to it that this agreement will not fail. How different this is from the covenant made with Israel at Sinai! Failure was written into the latter. The Sinai covenant looked beyond itself to a new covenant which would be lasting (Deut. 30:1-6; Jer. 31:31-34; Heb. 8:7-13). The new covenant incorporates the everlasting covenant with Abraham and the permanent covenant made with David (2 Sam. 7:12-17; Isa. 55:3).

It is to be personal. God **'will be their God'** (17:8), and will be a **'God to you and your descendants after you'** (17:7). It expresses a unique relationship between God and Abraham, and those who belong to Abraham's special line (see 17:19-21). This commitment by God can be followed through the Bible. When he rescued his people from Egyptian slavery, God said, 'I will take you as my people, and I will be your God' (Exod. 6:7). The blessings belonging to the old Sinai agreement included the promise: 'I will walk among you and be your God, and you shall be my people' (Lev. 26:12). Paul applied these words to Christians (2 Cor. 6:16). He could do this for at the heart of the new covenant we read, 'I will be their God, and they shall be my people' (Jer. 31:33). In John's vision of the new creation he heard the words: 'Behold, the tabernacle of God is with men, and he will dwell with them, and they shall be his people, and God himself will be with them and be their God' (Rev. 21:3).

It involves possession. For the first time God himself specifically calls the land **'Canaan'**. It is to be their **'everlasting possession'** even though Abraham is still **'a stranger'** in the land. Like the everlasting bond between God and his people, this everlasting possession must be seen in the light of the rest of Scripture. It is symbolic of the new earth where God's people will reside to all eternity.

2. The second message concerns Abraham — 'As for you...' (17:9-14)

The 'you shalls' emphasize Abraham's actions and the sign of circumcision witnesses to the reality of the covenant bond.

The covenant requirement

Abraham and his descendants were called by God to **'keep my covenant'** (17:9). Covenant promises include covenant obligations. Alec Motyer writes, 'The law of God is written into the heart of the covenant idea.'[2] This is a principle that runs through the Bible. Those whom God calls into fellowship with himself, he commands. God Almighty is also the one who enables us to obey.

The covenant sign

Like the covenant idea itself, circumcision was not some new practice unknown before God introduced it. The custom of removing the foreskin from the male reproductive organ was practised long before Abraham's time among the peoples of western Asia and Africa. The earliest evidence to date for the custom has been found in northern Syria around 2800 BC. To prevent infection and to aid fertility were two reasons given by ancient authors for the practice. It is often associated with initiation rites, marking the transition to full adulthood. In some societies a form of circumcision is practised on females which is most cruel and often leads to medical complications. Circumcision as ordained by God was to be carried out on males only. Normally, it was to be administered to infants, eight days old (17:12).

The significance of the sign

Just as God invested the rainbow with covenant significance, so God took the practice of circumcision and invested it with covenant significance for Abraham and his descendants.

Circumcision is called the **'sign of the covenant'** (17:11). It was the mark of God's special relationship with Abraham and the sign of belonging to the covenant community.

The sign was so closely associated with the covenant that it was identified with it. God says, **'This is my covenant... Every male ... among you shall be circumcised'** (17:10). Then God adds, **'My covenant shall be in your flesh'** (17:13).

Not to have the covenant sign meant repudiating the covenant itself (17:14). It was not an optional extra but *the visual expression of the special relationship.*

It was primarily *a religious and moral sign.* Social, cultural or racial reasons were not the first concern. That is why from the beginning it was open to all, including foreigners. Everyone associated with Abraham was circumcised (17:12-13).

It showed *the equality* that existed between all who were in this relationship with God. If they were circumcised, the slaves who had been bought belonged to the covenant just as much as did those who were born into the household (17:12-13).

Although it was not intended as a nationalistic badge when it was first introduced, circumcision was clearly linked to *the special family line.* The covenant was established 'with Isaac' and his descendants and not with Ishmael (17:19-21).

Circumcision was not only a sign of God's commitment to Abraham and his 'seed', but of their commitment to God. They carried out the covenant sign. It expressed *their faith in God and obedience to his will.* Paul speaks of it as 'a seal of the righteousness of the faith' which Abraham had while still uncircumcised (Rom. 4:11).

The covenant sign meant a permanent mark in the flesh and spoke of *the permanency of the covenant:* **'My covenant shall be in your flesh for an everlasting covenant'** (17:13; see Ps. 105:10).

In that the sign involved the male organ of reproduction it was an appropriate reminder concerning one of the main ingredients of the covenant, *the promised 'seed'.* It is interesting that soon after Abraham was circumcised his wife became pregnant and Isaac was born (17:21).

The sign required cutting flesh and spilling blood (Exod. 4:25-26). It would have reminded Abraham of the cutting of the animals and *the shedding of blood* associated with the covenant ceremony in Genesis 15. The covenant was sealed in blood. Circumcision symbolized the covenant curse.

Anyone who did not carry out this sign came under God's curse, for it meant that person had broken God's covenant. Not to be cut in circumcision would result in being 'cut' in a more drastic way — **'that person shall be cut off from his people'** (17:14). To be 'cut off' often meant direct punishment from God (9:11; Exod. 4:24).

The covenant sign was spiritualized by Moses and the prophets. The Israelites were urged to circumcise the foreskin of their hearts and God promised that he would circumcise their hearts to love the Lord (Deut. 10:16; 30:6). Among Israel's immediate neighbours, the Philistines were alone in not practising circumcision. The 'uncircumcised' Philistines became typical of all who were sinful and unclean. Unfaithful Israel is described as uncircumcised in heart (Jer. 9:26). Stephen levelled this charge against the Jews of his day (Acts 7:51). Paul describes all those outside of Christ as 'dead' in their sins and 'the uncircumcision' of their flesh (Col. 2:13). On the other hand, the apostle indicates that all who belong to Christ, who have no confidence in the flesh, are the true people of the circumcision (Phil. 3:2-3). Again, 'He is not a Jew who is one outwardly, nor is that circumcision which is outward in the flesh; but he is a Jew who is one inwardly, and circumcision is that of the heart' and accomplished by the Spirit (Rom. 2:28-29).

An infant was to be circumcised on *the eighth day* after birth. The eighth day is the beginning of a new week. It would have spoken of the need of a new start, a new beginning, a new birth. If we follow this through into the New Testament, the eighth day is associated with Jesus, who is the resurrection and the life. He rose from the dead on the eighth day, the first day of a new week. Jesus Christ has put an end to the old blood ritual of circumcision by taking the curse on himself and offering the propitiatory sacrifice. Paul also writes that what matters in Christ Jesus is not whether we are circumcised or not, but 'a new creation' (Gal. 6:15; 2 Cor. 5:17). With the Old Testament teaching on circumcision, Jesus expected the rabbi Nicodemus to understand his illustration of the new spiritual birth from above.

Circumcision became *an integral part of the Sinai covenant* and only those who had been circumcised could partake of the Passover (Exod. 12:48; Josh. 5:1-10). It was so closely associated with the law of Moses that Jesus had to remind the Jews of his day that its origins were with the ancestors of Israel (John 7:22).

The initiatory sign of entry into the new covenant community is baptism. Like circumcision, this new covenant ordinance speaks of the new birth, of the 'circumcision made without hands' and of Christ's substitutionary circumcision for his people. Christ was not only literally circumcised when he was eight days old. Paul indicates that 'the circumcision of Christ' was associated with his death on the cross when he was 'cut off' from the land of the living' (Col. 2:11-12; Isa. 53:8). Christians, too, have been circumcised in Christ. United to him, believers have died his death and are now raised with him to new life. Baptism, like circumcision, can become a mere cultural, social or superstitious rite. Without the reality to which it points baptism too becomes an empty formality.

3. The third message concerns Sarai — 'As for Sarai' (17:15-16)

Promises are made concerning Sarai and, as a sign, her name is changed to Sarah. The meaning is the same, 'princess', but the slight change is enough to emphasize the truth of what God says. Like her husband's name, it is prophetic. It is a sign of God's promise to bless them with many descendants, including kings.

God now indicates that Sarah is to give birth to the promised son. God repeats the promises made to Abraham (see 17:6): **'She shall be a mother of nations'** and **'Kings of peoples shall be from her.'** Such repetition emphasizes that Sarah will be as much involved as Abraham in God's future purposes. God first indicated his intention to fight on the side of the woman at the time of the Fall. Through the various headings and genealogies we are pointed forward to a person of royal descent who will defeat the old serpent. The birth of a son to Abraham and Sarah is an important link in the chain that will eventually lead to King Jesus, the Saviour.

Abraham's response (17:17-18)

1. Actions — 'Abraham fell on his face and laughed'

When God first spoke to Abram he lay prostrate on the ground, and that was his position when God began speaking the second time (17:3). Hearing that God was going to bless Sarah with a son would have been reason enough for him to have raised his head in surprise. After hearing such amazing messages we can also appreciate why Abraham was back with his face to the ground. What we do not expect is to find him laughing. Many former commentators understood this to mean that Abraham was so overjoyed at hearing that Sarah was to bear him a son that he burst into laughter. When God restored his people from exile, their mouths were filled with laughter (Ps. 126:1-2). The excesses witnessed by those caught up in the 'Toronto Blessing' should not drive us to a position where we suppress spontaneous expressions of emotion in God's presence.

Some modern scholars have suggested that this was a mocking laugh and assume that the questionings in his heart express Abraham's doubts and unbelief. But Paul informs us that he 'did not waver at the promise of God through unbelief, but was strengthened in faith, giving glory to God' (Rom. 4:20). The fact that we are told that his faith needed strengthening does imply some weakness which each new revelatory word sought to help. The laughter may have indicated a measure of disbelief, but this is quite different to the snigger of unbelievers. Abraham is not like the scoffers who ridicule God's Word. There is not the slightest hint that Abraham was censured by God for his outburst. His laughter may have expressed mixed emotions. Joy and disbelief can exist together. They were present in the reaction of the disciples to the appearance of the risen Lord (Luke 24:41).

2. Thoughts — '... and said in his heart...'

The astonishing announcement took Abraham completely by surprise. God had not granted Abraham and Sarah children up to this point, so why should he do so at their time of life? Abraham believed God's promises, but he wondered how God would fulfil them. Abraham would soon appreciate what it meant for God to be 'Almighty God', just as centuries later it was revealed to Mary that 'With God nothing will be impossible' (Luke 1:34,37).

3. Prayer — 'Abraham said to God...'

In his prayer, it is surprising that Abraham makes no mention of the promised son through Sarah. Instead, his thoughts are towards the son he already has. **'Oh, that Ishmael might live before you!'** is the cry of a father concerned for the son he had come to regard as his true heir. Before Ishmael came on the scene, it was Eliezer his servant whom he considered to be his son and heir (15:2-3).

God's third word (17:19-22)

God's final word clears up Abraham's doubts and concerns.

1. A word concerning Isaac (17:19,21)

Abraham is rebuffed. The promised seed is not Ishmael. New information emphasizes that God does mean to bless Sarah.

Firstly, the child is to be called **'Isaac'** ('He laughs'). The name would be a perpetual reminder of 'the laugh, the promise and the miracle that made his birth unique'.[3]

Secondly, the covenant is confirmed with this son: **'I will establish my covenant with him for an everlasting covenant'** (17:19,21; see 17:7).

Thirdly, before he is born Isaac is assured of descendants and that the covenant will be reaffirmed with them (17:19).

Fourthly, the time of his birth is given: **'at this set time next year'** (17:21). God has an appointed time for everything. At the right moment, 'God sent forth his Son, born of a woman' (Gal. 4:4).

2. A word concerning Ishmael (17:20)

The opening sentence, **'And as for Ishmael, I have heard you,'** is a play on Ishmael's name ('God hears' — 16:11). God answered Abraham's prayer. Ishmael also would be fruitful and multiply **'exceedingly'** and become a **'great nation'**. Descended from him would be **'twelve princes'** or 'leaders' (see 25:12-18) corresponding to the leaders in Israel (see Num. 7:2,10-84). But there is no promise that Ishmael's line will be a blessing to others. He is not the child of promise. The Messiah will not arise from Ishmael's line.

Abraham's response (17:23-27)

Abraham's reaction was swift and decisive. The proof of his faith was shown in his immediate obedience to what God demanded of him. At the age of ninety-nine, Abraham got himself circumcised. He also circumcised all the male members of his household, including his thirteen-year-old son, Ishmael. What an important day that was! The repetition of the phrase, **'that very same day'** (17:23,26) stresses the significance of the event. It was like the day on which Noah entered the ark (7:13), or the day that Israel was brought out of Egypt (Exod. 12:41,51).

Though Ishmael was not of the special family line, he was a member of the covenant community. This prepares us for the truth that we are all sons of God through faith in Christ Jesus. 'For as many of you as were baptized into Christ have put on Christ. There is neither Jew nor Greek, there is neither slave nor free ... for you are all one in Christ Jesus' (Gal. 3:27-29).

24.
Sodom and salvation

Please read Genesis 18:1 – 19:38

These chapters recall Abraham's earlier concerns for Lot and the people of Sodom. It is all too easy to be so absorbed with our own personal concerns that we forget the needs of others. Though Abraham had enough troubles in his own family, it did not prevent him from being involved in what was going on elsewhere. We are also shown a man who lived in close fellowship with God. The central theme of Genesis, however, still dominates the scene — the promised 'seed'.

The heavenly visitation (18:1-15)

'Then the LORD appeared to him' reminds us of the opening words of chapter 17. With this information we can better understand what follows. We are left guessing for some time as to the identity of all the visitors. Abraham, however, recognized one of the men as the person who had appeared to him only a month or two earlier.[1] He directed his first words to him and addressed him in a way normally reserved for God. (**'My Lord'** has a form of spelling that is used for God.) Later, we find Abraham praying most earnestly to this same person.

The continual shift from the singular to the plural in the first fifteen verses is of special interest.[2] This unusual feature, along with the clear impression that the three men are associated with the appearance of the one LORD, has led Christians from earliest times to see the doctrine of the Trinity foreshadowed here. We can well understand why this chapter is one of the Lessons for Trinity Sunday in the Anglican *Book of Common Prayer*. Griffith Thomas, a former principal of Wycliffe Hall, Oxford, warns us 'not to read too much of such a New Testament idea into it'. But he does add that 'We are perfectly safe, and entirely warranted, in seeing in this unique manifestation an indication of certain essential distinctions in the Godhead which subsequently were fully revealed as the Trinity of the New Testament.'[3]

Abraham's encounter with heaven was **'by the terebinth trees of Mamre'**. This is where he had settled after Lot left (13:10,18) and where he learned the news of Lot's capture (14:13).

1. 'Entertaining angels unawares' (18:1-8,16)

No doubt Abraham had just finished his morning work and had settled down at his tent door for a quiet siesta. It was the hottest time of the day. He was probably dozing when he became aware that **'Three men were standing by him'**. Immediately he rushed to greet them and respectfully **'bowed himself to the ground'**. He offered them the usual courtesies of Eastern hospitality: water to drink, water to wash their feet, a place to rest under a shady tree and some light refreshments. The visitors agreed to stay.

Despite the midday sun, Abraham prepared a meal fit for a king. Abraham's **'morsel of bread'** turned out to be a full-course meal of roast beef with all the side dishes. Like a good host, Abraham stood at the table to serve his guests (18:8).

The New Testament urges, 'Do not forget to entertain strangers, for by so doing some have unwittingly entertained angels' (Heb. 13:2). When strangers turn up at our Sunday services, we should be eager to offer them a meal. When believers welcome fellow believers who are strangers to them, they are in fact welcoming Christ: 'I was hungry and you gave me food ... inasmuch as you did it to one of the least of these my brethren, you did it to me' (Matt. 25:35,40). In Abraham's case, he actually entertained the Lord himself and his angels.

Unlike so many of his natural descendants, Abraham received the Lord. Jesus challenged his hearers, 'If you were Abraham's children, you would do the works of Abraham' (John 8:39-40). When Zacchaeus welcomed the Lord into his home Jesus said, 'Today salvation has come to this house, because he also is a son of Abraham' (Luke 19:9). Can this be said of us?

It may be that the event had covenant overtones. The incident comes shortly after God's covenant with Abraham had been reaffirmed. We know that covenants between people in the ancient world often included sharing a meal (see 26:28-30). In the divine covenants, it is God who normally calls people to dine at his table (Exod. 24:1-11; Mark 14:22-26; 1 Cor. 10:16,21; 11:23-26). Here we find God in human form condescending to eat and drink at Abraham's table. It was a foretaste of the fellowship which God's people enjoy with the triune God. Jesus said, 'If anyone loves me, he will keep my word; and my Father will love him, and we will come to him and make our home with him' (John 14:23). Jesus challenges his covenant people: 'Behold, I stand at the door and knock. If anyone hears my voice and opens the door, I will come in to him and dine with him, and he with me' (Rev. 3:20).

Abraham was warm-hearted and entertained his guests with the choicest foods he could offer. Only the finest wheat-flour would do for the cakes (18:6). Only the top-quality bull calf was prepared for the table (18:7). We are also called to give of our very best in the service of the Master, which includes giving of our best to one another and to the life of the church.

2. Confirmation that Sarah is to have a son (18:9-15)

The reason for the presence of the heavenly visitors now becomes clear. Their question concerning Sarah was a way of notifying Abraham that they had something important for her to hear. It may have been the custom for the married woman to remain hidden in her tent when visitors were present. Though Abraham, representing his wife, was addressed, the message was for Sarah herself to hear. It is therefore wrong to think of her as eavesdropping. She was meant to be **'listening in the tent door'**, behind the divine speaker (18:10). When Elisha called the Shunammite woman she stood in the doorway while he prophesied that she would have a son (2 Kings 4:15).

It was the Lord himself who made the announcement: **'I will certainly return to you...'** (18:10). The phrase **'according to the time of life'** could mean 'at this time next year' which would parallel the phrase 'at this set time next year' (17:21). Elisha used the same phrase in his prophecy (2 Kings 4:16-17). God informed them that he would definitely **'return'**, meaning that he would graciously intervene and bless Sarah with a son.

Before Sarah's response is given, Moses inserts a word of explanation (18:11). Up to this point the emphasis has been on Sarah's barrenness. Now we are told that **'Sarah had passed the age of childbearing.'**[4] Sarah had moved beyond the stage of being barren. She had passed the menopause. Humanly speaking, it was now impossible for her to have a baby.

This explanation helps us to understand her laugh. It was not the scornful laugh of arrogant unbelief but the laugh of incredulity. Like Abraham she did not openly express her doubts but **'laughed within herself'** (18:12). **'After I have grown old** [or "After I have worn away"] **shall I have pleasure?'** suggests that she thought of herself like a worn-out garment. The Lord rebuked her gently and gave her the news that she would have a son at the appointed time (18:14).

Sarah was now afraid in the presence of the all-knowing God. She had not laughed out loud. To that extent she was correct. But the Lord reminded her that he could read her innermost thoughts and graciously used her laugh to confirm the prophecy. Her son's name was foreshadowed in her laughter. When God said, **'No, but you did laugh!'**, he was not only countering her denial, but saying in effect, 'Do not deny that you laughed, for I have made it into a sign that you will have a son called Isaac' (see 17:19).

Abraham and Sarah were taught that the coming of the promised 'seed' would involve the direct activity of God. Isaac, the type, was the result of a divine miracle in the womb of Sarah. Christ, the antitype, was born as a result of God's miraculous activity in the womb of Mary. God's question to Sarah, **'Is anything too hard for the LORD?'** (18:14), prepares us for the angel's message to Mary: 'For with God nothing will be impossible' (Luke 1:34-38). Every true Christian is the result of God's miraculous activity. The disciples asked Jesus, 'Who then can be saved?' Jesus replied, 'With men it is impossible, but not with God; for with God all things are possible' (Mark 10:26-27).

The destruction of Sodom and Gomorrah (18:16 – 19:29)

The account of the destruction begins and ends by viewing the cities from Canaan — **'looked toward Sodom'** (18:16; 19:28) — and by stressing that Abraham **'stood before the LORD'** (18:22; 19:27).

1. The friend of God (18:16-21)

In typical Eastern fashion, Abraham accompanied his heavenly visitors for some distance **'to send them on the way'**. In New Testament times Christians did this for gospel preachers (see Acts 21:5; Rom. 15:24). It was while Abraham was literally walking with God that God decided to tell him what he was about to do.[5] Abraham is called God's friend (Isa. 41:8; 2 Chr. 20:7; James 2:23). The idea is not of God's befriending Abraham, but of God's taking Abraham into his confidence like a friend.

There are some interesting parallels between what God says here and what Jesus said to his disciples: 'You are my friends if you do whatever I command you. No longer do I call you servants, for a servant does not know what his master is doing; but I have called you friends, for all things that I heard from my Father I have made known to you' (John 15:14-15). God gave three reasons for sharing with Abraham (18:17-19).

Firstly, *he had promised* that Abraham would become **'a great and mighty nation'**, and that **'all the nations'** would find blessing in him' (18:18; see 12:2-3), words which reach their ultimate fulfilment in Jesus Christ.

Secondly, *God had singled him out* (18:19). **'For I have known him'** means not only that God had chosen Abraham, but that he had a special relationship with him (see Exod. 33:17; Deut. 34:10; Amos 3:2). The same is true of all believers in Christ. 'The Lord knows those who are his' (2 Tim. 2:19). It is a knowledge that goes back to eternity (Rom. 8:29; 1 Peter 1:2).

Thirdly, God had in mind *the creation of a 'God-fearing community'* (18:19).[6] Abraham was called for the purpose of commanding all his household **'that they keep the way of the LORD'**. It is important that Christian parents teach their children God-like behaviour (**'righteousness'**) and encourage them to make decisions that are based on God's revealed will (**'justice'**). Jesus urges us to obey him and to share the gospel with others. Calvin comments, 'God does not make known his will to us, that the knowledge of it may perish with us.'[7]

The purposes of God come about through his people's obedience to his will (18:19). There is no doubt that God will bring all his promises to completion, for the God who commands is also the one who works within human lives to enable them to will and to do according to his good purpose (Phil. 2:12-13).

2. The revelation of God's mind (18:20-21)

'The LORD said' suggests that God now turned to Abraham to inform him of Sodom's state. The wording, **'I will go down now and see...'** (18:21) reminds us of previous acts of divine judgement (11:5,7). It is not that God was unaware of what was happening, or that he was coming to make sure his information was accurate. God condescended to speak to Abraham in a way that helped him (and us) appreciate that God is always fair and just in his actions. He does not act on rumour but sees for himself (18:21).

The **'outcry'** resulted from the wickedness of the place. Like Abel's blood, unpunished sin looks to God for vengeance. We live in a moral universe. People think they can get away with murder. They may escape human justice but there is no escape from God.

God's estimate of the situation (18:20) recalls the introduction to the Flood account (6:5). An ominous note is sounded in the phrase, **'They have done altogether'** (literally, 'completeness'), which is an idiom for 'They deserve destruction'. It is when their sin is full, or 'complete', that judgement falls. God is depicted as holding back and making sure that the crimes committed have reached a pitch where destruction is inevitable (see 15:16). The final phrase, **'If not, I will know'**, leaves open the possibility of a last-minute reprieve. God's judgements are never hasty. Any apparent delay is not a sign of indecision but of mercy. This also applies to the final judgement. God is 'not willing that any should perish but that all should come to repentance' (2 Peter 3:9).

3. *Pleading for the righteous* (18:22-33)

It was while two of the men made their way to Sodom that **'Abraham still stood before the LORD.'** God did not tell Abraham to pray, but personal friendship involves two-way communications. Abraham turned what he heard from God into prayer. As the Lord did not move on immediately with the other two, Abraham snatched the opportunity to present his requests. After hearing God's thoughts Abraham could have shrugged his shoulders and muttered, 'Serve them right!' Or he might have been tempted to rush home to his wife and friends with this inside information concerning Sodom's impending destruction. But no, he remained with the Lord and **'came near'** to pray. It was an eleventh-hour situation and he boldly pleaded for the people of that wicked city.

Jesus encourages his friends to pray (John 15:7-8,16). John Knox was a great intercessor. The last two days of his life were spent pleading with God on behalf of the church. Abraham, who had already pleaded successfully for Ishmael (17:18), prays earnestly for the honour of God and the salvation of others.

The honour of God

The prayer is based on the fact that God is a righteous God: **'Would you also destroy the righteous with the wicked?'** There are standards we expect from earthly judges. God is the perfect Judge. Abraham filled his prayer with arguments based on the character of God (18:23-25) and pleaded for God to be consistent with himself.

The blessing of others

This was the second intervention of Abraham on behalf of Sodom. He had acted to rescue Lot and the people of Sodom when they had been taken captive (14:16). Abraham does not mention Lot in this prayer. He was concerned not only for his nephew, but for others in that doomed city. In this Abraham is unique among the great intercessors of the Old Testament, such as Moses, Samuel, Amos and Jeremiah, who prayed for their own people only. Abraham points us to the great Intercessor of the new covenant, the Lord Jesus, who prayed for his enemies and taught his followers to do the same.

Abraham's prayer is an example of earnest, fervent and persistent praying on behalf of others. He began by asking whether God would spare the city if fifty righteous people could be found there, and then kept reducing the number till he came to ten.[8] The Lord indicated that he would not destroy the city for the sake of ten righteous people. It is often suggested that Abraham 'negotiated' God down from fifty to ten. The context is against this for it was God who encouraged Abraham to persist in prayer. Events proved that the righteous in Sodom numbered less than five. Only the Day of Judgement will reveal how blessed a country is to have a significant number of godly people living there.

The prayer displays great boldness, which is how Christians are encouraged to pray (Heb. 10:19-22). At the same time, a reverent and humble spirit is evident: **'I who am but dust and ashes have taken it upon myself to speak to the Lord'** (18:27; see also 18:30,31,32). Friendship with God does not mean being over-familiar and flippant.

4. Lot and the people of Sodom (19:1-11)

The men who left Abraham to go towards Sodom were certainly heavenly messengers (19:1; 18:22). This was not immediately obvious to Lot and the inhabitants of Sodom. Lot, like Abraham, greeted the visitors warmly and invited them to his home for refreshment. As they had come to investigate, we can understand why they wished to remain in the city square. Lot knew what the night-life of Sodom was like and **'strongly'** pressed them to stay under his roof until morning (19:1-3). In the event the men saw all they needed at Lot's front door.

It would appear that Lot had become an influential figure in the city, **'sitting in the gate of Sodom'**. Was this a sop by the King of Sodom in recognition of his uncle's intervention on behalf of the city? (see 14:16-24). Certainly, the angry crowd at Lot's door did not appreciate a foreigner like him acting as their judge (19:9). Though Lot was in a backslidden condition, his actions indicated that he was of a different spirit to the rest of the population. He was hospitable, kind and protective of strangers, like his uncle.

The response of the people of Sodom to the visitors revealed how depraved the society was. When Ezekiel pronounced judgement on Jerusalem he likened her to Sodom. The sins highlighted include pride, self-satisfaction, self-indulgence, lack of concern for the poor and needy, arrogance and sexual immorality. Sodom has given its name to that sexual perversion which is against the Creator's design. The verb to **'know'** is used for intimate relations between a man and a woman within the marriage bond (4:1,25). The people of Sodom had twisted this most precious union beyond recognition. Homosexual practices had become so common that **'old and young'** alike **'from every quarter'** of the city had ganged up together to gratify their sinful desires. In order to protect his guests, Lot offered his daughters, but they would not be deflected from their evil intention. Had it not been for the action of the heavenly messengers in striking them with blindness, the mob would have had their way.

The wickedness of the city was concentrated at the door of 'righteous' Lot. Here was the evidence that tipped the balance and made judgement inevitable.

5. 'Remember Lot's wife' (19:12-26)

There were five cities of the plain (14:2,8). Sodom is given more attention because it was the leading city and the place where Lot had settled. What is said concerning the depravity of Sodom also applied to the other cities. Of the five only Zoar was saved on account of Lot's pleas. Besides Sodom and Gomorrah the other two cities are also used by the Lord to warn Israel: 'How can I make you like Admah? How can I set you like Zeboiim?' (Hosea 11:8)

The heavenly messengers warned Lot of the impending destruction and urged him to speak to his family. Accepting the message himself, Lot set about persuading others. He risked his life by leaving the house at night to urge his **'sons-in-law'** to escape but they would not listen.[9] They thought he was **'joking'** (19:14).

'When the morning dawned,' the time of grace was all but over. Yet in those last moments, the **'merciful'** Lord snatched the hesitant Lot, his wife and daughters, and brought them out of the city (19:15-16). Lot's plea to be allowed to escape to the little city of Bela (see 14:2,8) also displayed God's grace. God promised not to destroy the city and held back the moment of judgement until Lot was safely inside (19:21-22). The place was thereafter known as Zoar, which is of the same Hebrew word group as **'little one'**, and a reminder of Lot's plea for the city (19:20,22).

When the punishment came it was swift and terrible (19:24-25). God rained, not water but **'brimstone and fire'** (burning sulphur). So spectacular and complete was the destruction that it is frequently mentioned in the Bible as a warning, especially of the end-time judgement (Deut. 29:23; Ezek. 38:22; Luke 17:28-30; 2 Peter 2:6; Jude 7). While the Flood speaks to us of a future world judgement, Sodom and Gomorrah teach us that the future judgement will be by fire:

> Upon the wicked he will rain coals,
> Fire and brimstone and a burning wind;
> This shall be the portion of their cup
>
> (Ps. 11:6).

Buried somewhere in the Dead Sea region lie the remains of the cities of the plain. It is a most unusual and uncanny place, a monument to God's judgement on human sin. The sea itself lies hundreds of feet below sea level and is full of salt. At the southern end there is a great mountain of salt 700 feet high and five miles long, known in Arabic as the 'Mount of Sodom'. Pillars of salt also arise from the ground and there is the stench of sulphur fumes in the air. God had turned paradise into hell (see 13:10).

Lot's wife, who had been so blessed by God and so near to safety, was caught up in the destruction. Her action in looking back was in direct opposition to the command: **'Do not look behind you or stay anywhere in the plain'** (19:17). Jesus said, 'Remember Lot's wife. Whoever seeks to save his life will lose it' (Luke 17:32-33). Lot's wife tried to hang on to her life in Sodom and lost her life in the great conflagration. We can know great privileges and yet still belong to the world and come under God's wrath. John Bunyan closes the first part of *Pilgrim's Progress* with this warning: 'Then I saw that

there was a way to hell, even from the gates of heaven, as well
as from the City of Destruction.'

6. *'God remembered Abraham'* (19:27-29)

Try putting yourself in Abraham's sandals as he got up early
and went to the spot **'where he had stood before the LORD'**
to plead for Sodom. What did he see? Instead of a paradise he
saw smoke, **'like the smoke of a furnace'** (19:28). Imagine
him saying to himself, 'I had relatives there. Have they all been
destroyed? Why did God give me the opportunity to pray for
Sodom?' At that time he would not have known of Lot's escape
and Zoar's reprieve.

Verse 29 impresses upon us that God did answer Abraham's
prayer. It draws our attention to God's activity. God *ruined*
the cities, *remembered* Abraham and *rescued* Lot.

There are many parallels between the account of the Flood
and the record of the destruction of the cities. Among the
similarities is the phrase, **'God remembered Abraham,'** which
is like 'God remembered Noah' (8:1). It is not an exact parallel, otherwise it would have read, 'God remembered Lot.' Noah
and Lot were the people saved from the judgement. The sub-
stitution of 'Abraham' for 'Lot' makes a very powerful point.
It emphasizes the grace of God in delivering Lot, not on account of his own righteousness, but through the intercession
of Abraham. Abraham's prayer had been used in God's purposes to save Lot. It directs us to the one who interceded for
sinners (Isa. 53:12; Luke 23:34). God remembered his Son
and rescued his people from the coming wrath.

We may be tempted to wonder if there is any point in praying. To think such a thought suggests a failure on our part to
appreciate the blessing of fellowship with God. Friends enjoy
communing together. We should be encouraged, however, that
God does remember our prayers. Though we may have to

wait and appearances may be deceptive, we can be assured that our prayers are answered and the Judge of all the earth will do right.

The origins of Moab and Ammon (19:30-38)

1. The history of Lot

He was a righteous man

This is Peter's estimate of Lot (2 Peter 2:7-8). He trusted God's promises and left all to come into the land of promise. Lot's righteous soul was disturbed by the Sodomites' filthy life-style (cf. Ezek. 9:4). He believed the divine warning and took risks to persuade others to leave the doomed city (19:14). The righteous will mourn over the state of society and yearn after conduct that is right in God's sight (Matt. 5:4,6).

He was a worldly-minded man

Lot made wrong choices based on worldly advantages rather than on God's Word. God disturbed his easy life, yet he continued to live in Sodom. Lot can be described as 'a firebrand plucked from the burning' (Amos 4:11). 'If the righteous one is scarcely saved, where will the ungodly and the sinner appear?' (1 Peter 4:18).

2. Lot's continued lack of trust (19:30)

What a faint-hearted, vacillating man he was! It was a 'blind anxiety of mind', as Calvin puts it, that made him flee to the mountains. It seems incredible that Lot could be so fearful of disaster overtaking him either in the hills or in the city when

God had rescued him from brimstone and fire. But Christians can be just the same. If we have known what it is to be saved from the hell we deserve, why should we fear lesser evils?

> [In Christ] ... we may boldly say,
> 'The LORD is my helper;
> I will not fear.
> What can man do to me?'
>
> (Heb. 13:5-6).

3. Lot's daughters (19:31-35)

This final narrative from Lot's life is almost a repeat of what happened to Noah after the Flood. Though Lot's daughters had escaped from Sodom, they brought the lusts of Sodom to the cave where they lived. Worldly-minded Lot was a poor example of a better way.

The girls wanted children — a perfectly natural desire — yet the way they went about it was all wrong. Instead of committing their situation to the Lord, they took matters into their own hands. Unlike Abraham and Sarah, they acted in a way which went against custom and law. They knew it was wrong and that their father would never agree, so they arranged to get him 'dead' drunk. The older girl devised the plan and encouraged her sister to join her.

Their filthy scheme worked and Lot had two sons to carry on the family line. The end, however, did not justify the means.

4. Lot's descendants (19:36-38)

Lot's death is unrecorded and his grave unknown. What a tragic figure! There was nothing to show for an earth-centred life. All that he had worked for had been burnt up. Our last picture of him is as a cave-dweller who was used by his own daughters.

The Bible warns, 'Do not love the world' (1 John 2:15). 'Keep [yourselves] unspotted from the world' (James 1:27).

What was Lot's legacy to the world? Moab and Ben-Ammi became two nations that despised the seed of Abraham. The Moabites tried to curse Israel using Balaam. They later seduced Israel into sexual immorality and false worship (Num. 23-25). The Ammonites were no better, for they joined Moab in hiring Balaam and refusing to assist Israel in their journeyings. For these reasons they were banned from having fellowship with Israel to the tenth generation (Deut. 23:3-6). The divine judgement is consistent: 'Surely Moab shall be like Sodom, and the people of Ammon like Gomorrah' (Zeph. 2:9). Yet, by God's grace a remnant from Moab will be among God's people (Jer. 48:47). In fact, Ruth the Moabitess becomes a link in the chain that leads to the Messiah.

25.
The child of promise

Please read Genesis 20:1 – 22:24

Binding these chapters together we find the subtle interplay of God's providences, promises and purposes. God is not defeated by human failure. What he has planned and promised will happen.

The promise in jeopardy (20:1-18)

1. The sin of a saint

We find God's friend out of step with God. The chapter is a mirror image of Abraham's experience in Egypt (12:10 – 13:1). These similar accounts have been taken as evidence of two different traditions of the same story. Such poor scholarship fails to appreciate the many differences between the two or the fact that the present account assumes the earlier incident. Scholars often lose sight of reality and cannot believe that Abraham would make the same mistake twice. We know from experience how easy it is to fall into the same sin.

Abraham moved south towards the coastal plain. Perhaps he needed to find fresh pasture for his flocks. He came to the area associated with the Philistines and settled in Gerar, south-east of Gaza. Because he felt vulnerable, he again passed off his wife as his sister (20:2,12; cf. 12:12-13). Abraham claimed it was his general policy to spread this lie and seemed to suggest it was God's fault for causing him to wander (20:13). The local chieftain took Sarah to become one of his wives. **'Abimelech'**, like the word 'Pharaoh', is not a personal name but a royal title. This local ruler was not as powerful as the pharaoh of Egypt and yet Abraham was afraid. He assumed that Abimelech and his people were completely godless and felt he should take protective measures (20:11). His attitude was a disgrace. Why was Abraham so worried that a ruler like Abimelech would be interested in an old woman of ninety? This account does not mention Sarah's beauty (cf. 12:11), but it may be that physical changes were taking place in preparation for the promised conception, so that she appeared younger than her age would suggest.

Abraham was quick to accuse others of what he was guilty of himself. He professed to fear God and assumed that the people of Gerar were not God-fearing (20:11). But at that time he feared man more than he feared God. Abraham was also forgetful of God's promise of protection from enemies. What a terrible example to the ungodly world when Christians act deceitfully! It brings dishonour to God and spoils their testimony.

2. The piety of a pagan

It is a humbling fact that people of other faiths can act in a more upright way than the people of God. Certainly Abimelech outshone Abraham here. This leads us to an important conclusion. The rightness or wrongness of a belief system does not finally rest on the behaviour of its adherents. What needs to be asked is whether the claims made for the religion will stand up to scrutiny. Although the human witness was a poor example, the God of Abraham is the one true God. This is the God who sent his Son to save us.

Abraham knew from his own pagan past how sin corrupts. He was also aware of what conditions were like in the cities of the plain. **'The fear of God'** is the Old Testament way of describing true religion. We can understand Abraham's concern (20:11). Unlike Lot, who did not seem to have any scruples about living in a sordid city, Abraham thought in terms of the fear of God. What could not be justified was Abraham's lack of faith. To his surprise he found there was more fear of God among the pagans than he imagined.

It may be that Abimelech already knew of Abraham's God. Nevertheless, God actually revealed himself to Abimelech in a dream. Abimelech's response indicated a humble, reverent attitude. His prayer, **'Lord, will you slay a righteous nation also?'**, is reminiscent of Abraham's plea for Sodom (20:4). Though he had acted in all innocence, Abimelech recognized his responsibilities and acted honourably. He offered gifts, not as bridal money, but as compensation for the wrong he had unintentionally done (20:14). Abimelech was generous to Abraham and encouraged him to live in his territory (20:15). Abraham also received **'a thousand pieces of silver'**. A labourer in those times would have received half a piece of silver a month in wages. This was final proof to all that Sarah had not been disgraced. She was 'vindicated' (rather than **'reproved'**) by the king, despite her part in the deception (20:16). Abimelech's ironic remark to Sarah, **'Behold, I have given your brother a thousand pieces of silver,'** stresses that he had been a victim of their dishonesty.

Abimelech was not a pagan saint, as some have suggested. He and his people may have been more saintly than the men of Sodom, but they were still sinners heading for hell. However, Abimelech obeyed God's special revelation by believing and repenting of his sin of ignorance. Though he deserved death (20:3), he was healed along with the rest of his household. He is an example, not of a pagan saint, but of a pagan who became a saint.

3. The grace of God

Divine grace overruled events so that Abraham might be the father of the promised seed and a blessing to many. Abimelech was struck down with a deadly disease and the women were made infertile (20:3,7,18). This judgement saved him from consummating the marriage with Sarah.

The grace of God changed the curse into blessing. Abimelech had prayed for mercy (20:4). But for the curse to be removed and for him to know life, he needed to identify himself with the one in whom all families of the earth are blessed. Abraham's prophetic calling was to intercede for this ruler. Poor representative that he was, Abraham was used to bring salvation to Abimelech and his family. In this he pointed forward to the great Prophet to come. It is through Jesus Christ that the curse is removed and we receive life. Our sinless Saviour has provided a covering for our open and secret sins and our sins of ignorance.

The promise fulfilled (21:1-34)

After all the disappointments, diversions and delays, the long-awaited son arrived.

1. The birth of Isaac (21:1-7)

The birth is announced in a brief and matter-of-fact way. It is the significance of the event that is brought to our attention:

1. The birth was not the result of human ingenuity but of divine activity: **'The Lord visited Sarah...'** (21:1).

2. It came about exactly as God had promised: **'as he had said ... as he had spoken ... of which God had spoken to him'** (21:1-2).

3. The promised son arrived at the right moment in God's plan, **'at the set time'** (see 17:21; 18:14).

4. The miraculous nature of the birth is stressed. They had a son in their old age (21:2,5,7). **'Who would have said to Abraham that Sarah would nurse children?'** (21:7).

5. Before the baby was conceived God told Abraham what his son was to be called (17:19). Abraham obeyed and **'called the name of his son who was born to him ... Isaac'** (21:3).

6. The birth was a cause of great happiness. There is another word-play on Isaac's name, 'He laughs' when Sarah says, **'God has made me laugh, so that all who hear will laugh with me'** (21:6). The laughter of incredulity gave way to the laughter of joy. The barren woman had become 'a joyful mother of children' (Ps. 113:9).

7. In obedience to God's command (17:12), Abraham **'circumcised his son Isaac when he was eight days old'** (21:4). This was the first time that Abraham had performed the ceremony on a baby.

The arrival of this miracle son was proof of God's ability to keep his word. Sarah's boy child also anticipates the one in whom all the promises of God find their fulfilment. The circumstances surrounding Isaac's birth would have taught Abraham and Sarah truth concerning the Messiah. In the brief account of the birth of Jesus we are again drawn to the significance of the event.

1. Jesus was born not through human planning. It was the result of divine activity.

2. The birth of Jesus happened exactly as the Lord had promised through his prophets (Matt. 1:22; Luke 1:54-55).

3. It was at the right moment in God's plan that the promised 'Seed' appeared, 'when the fulness of the time had come' (Gal. 4:4).

4. Mary's conception was miraculous. She 'was found with child of the Holy Spirit' (Matt. 1:18).

5. God indicated before the birth what the child would be called so that Joseph obediently 'called his name Jesus' (Matt. 1:25).

6. His arrival brought much happiness. Angels announced 'good tidings of great joy' for all people. The shepherds, Simeon and Anna praised God on seeing the baby (Luke 2:10,20,28-32,38). Wise men rejoiced at his star and worshipped (Matt. 2:10-11).

7. Jesus Christ was also circumcised on the eighth day according to the law (Luke 2:21).

Abraham saw and embraced Christ from a distance through Isaac, the type, and was glad. Have we trusted Christ? Are we rejoicing in the Saviour and encouraging others to do so? 'Joy to the world! The Lord is come!'

2. Expulsion of Ishmael (21:8-21)

After the joyful events of the birth, further celebrations took place when Isaac was weaned. In those days, as is still the case in some cultures, children were nursed at their mothers' breasts until they were at least three years old. To reach this age would have also been a significant achievement, as infant mortality was high. Abraham made a great feast to mark the occasion.

Abraham's other son, Ishmael, now a young man of about seventeen, found that he was no longer the centre of attention. Sarah caught him **'scoffing'** at her son (21:9). This is another play on the word 'Isaac'. Ishmael was 'isaacing' Isaac. Unlike verse 6, the form of the verb used here suggests a 'laughing' or 'playing' that was deceptive.[1] It was not harmless fun but revealed Ishmael's hostility towards the new arrival. Paul is quite right to state that Ishmael 'persecuted' Isaac (Gal. 4:29).

Sarah's motherly intuition rightly sensed what was going on. She used the occasion to her advantage to remove both the lad and his mother from the home. Sarah had nursed a grudge ever since her maid was found to be pregnant by Abraham, even though she was party to the arrangement. Nevertheless, on one thing she was right. She saw clearly that the son of the slave woman **'shall not be heir with my son'** (21:10; cf. 15:4).

Abraham was again caught in the middle. The slave-woman's son was his first-born son and God had promised to bless Ishmael. He was also aware that Sarah's attitude was wrong (21:11).[2] In this untidy situation, God intervened. On the previous occasion, Abraham had simply bowed to his wife's wishes (16:6). Here he had special guidance to accept his wife's counsel.

Through this sad scene the point is stressed that the elect line will run through Isaac, not Ishmael. It was to protect the promised seed that Hagar and Ishmael were removed from the home. But God did not abandon them. He confirmed the promise made earlier (17:20) and reassured Abraham, **'I will also make a nation of the son of the bondwoman, because he is your seed'** (21:13).

In marked contrast to Sarah's attitude, Abraham's concern for Hagar and Ishmael was shown by personally tending to their needs and sending them on their way (21:14). Christians are to be kind to all. 'Bless those who persecute you' (Rom. 12:14).

When Hagar and her son were dying in the desert for lack of water, God kept his word and **'heard the voice of the lad'** (21:17). Here is a play on the name 'Ishmael' ('God hears'; see 16:11). Though Ishmael had mocked the child of promise, in his desperation he had cried out to God. The Lord was gracious and saved him. Ishmael belonged to Abraham's God and God continued to be with the lad (21:20). He remained in the wilderness (16:12) and his mother took upon herself the duties of the absent father in providing him with a wife from **'Egypt'**, her own home country. It is an encouragement to know that God hears the prayers of the outcast and needy when they turn to him for help.

Paul uses the story of Hagar and Ishmael to show that it is those who belong to Jesus who are the true children of Abraham. Though they may boast of their natural descent, if people despise the promised Seed, they are children of the slave-girl. All those who rely on their good actions for salvation are not true children of Abraham. Nevertheless, the Hagars and Ishmaels of this world will find salvation if they put their trust in the Lord.

3. The treaty with Abimelech (21:22-34)

'At that time' (21:22) means that the following incident happened when Isaac was weaned and Ishmael was evicted. It is possible that Abimelech and his army commander, Phichol, had been invited to the 'great feast' that Abraham had arranged (21:8) and that, while they were at the party, they took the opportunity to make a deal with Abraham.

Difficulties for the people of faith

The problem of pasturing rights was a continuing headache. Abraham had recently dug a well for the needs of his household and animals. Abimelech's men, however, had seized it by force (21:25). Though Abraham had become a powerful figure in the area, he was a temporary resident in a foreign land (21:23). Jesus has promised that his people will inherit the earth but this does not make our present experience any easier. We live by faith as resident aliens and must pass through many testing times (1 Peter 1:1,6-7,17; 2:11).

Divine promises fulfilled

The first tangible evidence that God was beginning to fulfil his promises was the birth of Isaac. More indications that the promises were taking shape are associated with the Philistine leader. The fact that Abimelech wanted to make an agreement with him shows how important Abraham had become. God had, in a small way, made Abraham's name great. Not only that, but Abraham's name had become a symbol of blessing. Abimelech and his commander said, **'God is with you in all that you do'** (21:22). Again, through Abraham's prayer blessing replaced judgement.

God had also promised that he would give the land of Canaan to Abraham's seed (12:7). Yet Abraham was a temporary alien. Now we find Abraham gaining his first foothold in the land. Through his agreement with Abimelech, **'Beersheba'** belonged to Abraham. The place-name means 'Well of the seven', because of the seven ewe lambs that Abraham gave to Abimelech as a witness to the covenant. There is a play on words because *'sheba'* could also be a form of the verb 'to swear an oath'. The name 'Beersheba' would serve as a continual reminder of the sworn agreement they had made.

The covenant guaranteed that they would live in peace and that Abraham could call the well his own. Thus Isaac and Beersheba were two evidences of God's fidelity to his covenant with Abraham.

Gratitude to God

Both parties left thoroughly satisfied with the deal. The area where Abimelech lived was by Moses' day known as **'the land of the Philistines'** (21:32). Like the later sea peoples of the same name, it is possible that the Philistines of Abraham's day represented an early migration from the Aegean area. In recognition of God's goodness, Abraham did two things (21:33).

First, he **'planted a tamarisk tree in Beersheba'**. The tamarisk is one of the evergreens of the east, common in that southern part of Canaan, and provides good shade from the sun. A tree needs water and the place was associated with the water found there. The planting of this tree was a lasting reminder of God's provision. Evergreens are symbolic of life and divine blessing. The godly are likened to a tree whose leaf does not wither (Ps. 1:3; Jer. 17:7-8).

Secondly, he **'there called on the name of the LORD, the Everlasting God'** (cf. 12:8). This spot which he could call his own became his sanctuary. He honoured God as the Eternal God *(El Olam)*. The covenant oath with Abimelech reminded Abraham of God's unchangeable faithfulness to keep promises. The best agreements that people make fail through human frailty. But concerning God Moses can say, 'Even from everlasting to everlasting, you are God' (Ps. 90:2). Peace and security for people of all nations is promised to those who belong to the everlasting covenant that Jesus has established.

We are also told that Abraham **'stayed in the land of the Philistines many days'** (21:34). The land promised him was still not his. It was only a temporary residence and symbolizes the Christian's life in this world. With Abraham we embrace God's promises but confess that we are 'strangers and pilgrims on the earth', looking for that heavenly country (Heb. 11:13-16).

The promise sacrificed (22:1-24)

No other narrative in Genesis quite matches this account. It is brilliantly written. Beyond its literary merits, this true story contains deep theological truth. The only event to surpass it is the one to which it points, the story of the Christ who died for us.

1. Faith proved

Abraham's testing experience falls into three main scenes. Each scene begins with a call to Abraham and his reply, **'Here I am'** (22:1,7,11).

We are told that **'God tested Abraham'** (22:1) but Abraham was not informed of this. The situation is not dissimilar to Job's great trial. Neither Job nor his comforters knew that his sufferings were a special test of his faith in God. We do not always see the evils that befall us as tests. Tragedies are not packaged like examination papers with the word 'test' written on the envelope. We may never know the reason why we should suffer in a particularly distressing way. The Puritan Thomas Watson wrote, 'God is to be trusted when his providences seem to run contrary to his promises.' Job said, 'Though he slay me, yet will I trust him' (Job 13:15).

This call to sacrifice Isaac was not some sudden impulse which Abraham thought had come from God.[3] There are people who imagine that God has spoken to them and they convince themselves and others that it is right for them to do something outrageous. Anything we might feel God is personally saying to us must be tested by his written Word. This call to Abraham came from outside himself. It was a divine test. The word 'tempt' used to include the idea of testing (see the AV, 'God did tempt Abraham'). In modern English it conveys only a bad sense. God never incites people to do wrong, as James reminds us (James 1:12-15). It is Satan who tempts us to sin. God tests us for our good and for his glory.

What a dreadful command Abraham received from God! He was being asked to give up his pride and joy. Not only that, God was directing him to act contrary to all that God had previously said. Isaac was the son of promise. Abraham had dismissed his other son on God's instructions and now he was being asked to sacrifice this unique son in whom all God's promises rested.

It is quite remarkable how Abraham obeyed so readily. When he left the servants with the donkey at the foot of the mountain, Abraham told them to wait there: **'The lad and I will go yonder and worship, and we will come back to you'** (22:5). What faith! He was going to worship by offering Isaac on the altar. Though he believed God concerning his son, he was prepared to commit him to God. At the same time, he expected that they would both come down the mountain and meet up again with the servants. Abraham reasoned that 'God was able to raise him up, even from the dead, from which he also received him in a figurative sense' (Heb. 11:17-19).

The last stage of the journey would have been the hardest. Imagine the old man with the fire in his hand and his young teenage son carrying the wood making their way silently up the mountain. Eventually Isaac breaks the silence with a question that must have pierced his father's heart: **'Look, the fire and the wood, but where is the lamb for a burnt offering?'** (22:7). How was Abraham to answer? Some have assumed he merely evaded the issue with a pious reply — 'Don't worry, it is all in God's hands' — in the hope that Isaac would not ask any more awkward questions. But that is not how the text reads. It is a statement of faith at an important turning-point in the story: **'My son, God will provide for himself the lamb for a burnt offering'** (22:8). God has promised to give his people the right word for the occasion (see Mark 13:11).

At that crucial moment when Abraham's hand was raised to cut Isaac's throat, God intervened, saying, **'Do not lay your hand on the lad, or do anything to him'** (22:11-12). Abraham had passed the test. Like Job he was a man who feared God. The testing experience proved that his faith was genuine (22:12). James uses this example to show that his faith was living and active. Abraham's obedience indicated that he was in a right position before God (James 2:20-23).

2. God's pledge

This unique experience not only tested his faith; it also informed his faith. For the last time and in a most emphatic way the promises first made when Abraham left Haran (12:1-3) are confirmed.

God's promises are always the expression of his grace but they are presented here in the context of Abraham's trustful obedience. It is, God says, **'because you have done this thing, and have not withheld your son ... because you have obeyed my voice'** (22:16,18), that the promises are renewed. Abraham's obedient response was used in God's overall purposes. Divine grace and human responsibility come together. The same was true when the Son of God came into the world. Mary and Joseph were obedient servants of God through whom the great promise was finally and completely fulfilled. There is every encouragement to live the life of faith and to do what is pleasing to God.

God condescended to reach down to Abraham's level by going on oath to fulfil his promises: **'By myself I have sworn'** (22:16). This is the first divine oath in the Bible and the only one in Genesis. It is often referred to later (see 24:7; 26:3; 50:24).

The promises are expanded. **'In blessing I will bless you and in multiplying I will multiply...'** is a Hebrew way of emphasizing the verbs: 'I will certainly bless and multiply you' (cf. 2:17). Abraham's descendants will become extremely numerous, **'as the stars of the heaven'** (see 15:5; 17:2) **'and as the sand which is on the sea-shore'** (22:17). The promise that **'Your descendants shall possess the gate of their enemies'** (22:17) reminds us of the time when Israel under Joshua conquered the land of Canaan. But beyond that it looks to victory over the serpent and his 'seed' when the kingdoms of this world will become the kingdoms of our God and his Christ. The ultimate blessing is that through the promised **'seed all the nations of the earth shall be blessed'** (22:18).

3. The gospel proclaimed

The whole testing experience foreshadowed future developments in the life of the people of God and the coming 'seed'. Like Abraham, Israel was called to go on a three-day journey to sacrifice at a mountain (Exod. 3:18). There the Lord appeared and promised blessing to those who obeyed him. At the time of the Exodus we are told that every father in Israel was expected to dedicate his first-born son to the Lord and to redeem him by offering a sacrifice (Exod. 13:1-16). Redeeming the first-born sons of Israel recalled the night on which they left Egypt when all the first-born in Egypt died and all Israel were spared judgement on account of the blood of the Passover lamb. Isaac's rescue from death was like the sparing of the first-born sons of Israel. The ram that Abraham eventually offered in place of his son was like the Passover lamb that was killed in place of the first-born.[4]

This is the first detailed account we have of Abraham offering sacrifice. We are told that he offered a ram as a burnt offering, foreshadowing the practice laid down in the law of Moses. It anticipated the daily burnt offerings of lambs every morning and evening in the tabernacle. Is it a coincidence that the place where Abraham offered the ram — a mountain in **'the land of Moriah'** (22:2) — has the same name as the spot where Solomon's temple was to be built? (2 Chr. 3:1).

Isaac becomes a type of what is prophesied concerning Jesus, the Servant of the Lord. As Isaac did not resist his father, so the Servant was led like a lamb to the slaughter and actually became the offering for sin and rose bodily from the dead (Isa. 53:7-12; Acts 8:32-35).

Through this great testing experience Abraham saw, in a symbolic way, the truth concerning Jesus Christ, the unique Son of the Father. **'You have not withheld your son, your only son'**, the Angel of the LORD said to Abraham (22:12,16). Likewise, 'God so loved the world that he gave his only begotten [unique] Son' (John 3:16).

4. Divine providence

The great provision

The Hebrew for **'The LORD Will Provide'** is well known — *Jehovah-Jireh*. This name meant much to Hudson Taylor. It became the motto of the China Inland Mission (now called OMF). As *Jireh* is from the verb 'to see' we could translate the name as 'The LORD will see to it'. God 'sees' to the needs of his people. Abraham had said to Isaac, 'God will provide for himself [Hebrew, 'see for himself'] the lamb for a burnt offering' (22:8). God did see to it and Abraham was not allowed to offer his son. The **'ram caught in a thicket by its horns'** was the Lord's provision (22:13).

'As it is said to this day' (22:14) gives the whole story 'a certain timelessness'.[5] **'In the Mount of the LORD it shall be provided'** (or 'seen') looks back to the words of Abraham (22:8) and forwards to the time when the temple would stand on Mount Moriah. Jesus said to the Jews, 'Your father Abraham rejoiced to see my day, and he saw it and was glad' (John 8:56). The Scottish preacher Robert Candlish wrote, 'Thus the very transaction which so severely tried the faith of Abraham showed him all that his faith longed so much to see. He saw the day of Christ — the day of his humiliation and triumph.'[6] As we look to that mount called Calvary where the heavenly Lamb was slain for sinners, we can praise God for his wonderful provision. This is the Lamb who stands on Mount Zion with his redeemed people (Rev. 14:1-5). If God has gone to these lengths to save us we can be sure he will provide for us through our earthly pilgrimage. If God did not spare his only Son, 'How shall he not with him also freely give us all things?' (Rom. 8:32).

Nahor's family

Nahor's family tree is presented here because of the information received concerning Abraham's relatives in Haran (22:20-24). Abraham's brother, Nahor, and his wife Milcah had been blessed with many sons. Most of Milcah's sons we know little about. Uz and Buz are of interest in that Job came from the land of Uz and the young man Elihu came from Buz. It is Bethuel, the last-named son, who is the important figure. We would have expected Bethuel's sons to be named, such as Laban. Instead, we only find his daughter Rebekah mentioned.

We are also informed that Nahor had a concubine named Reumah who bore him four more sons. The names of her sons are later associated with towns and areas in what today is Syria and Lebanon. It was a common practice in the ancient world for men to have concubines. A concubine was a second-class wife with fewer rights than an ordinary wife. Apparently, no bride-money was involved so she was cheaper to acquire. It was another indication of how people had moved away from the ideal laid down by God at the beginning.

In all, Nahor had twelve sons. This contrasts sharply with Abraham, who had only one son by his wife and one by her maid. Later, Jacob, the grandson of Abraham, was to have twelve sons, four of whom would be born to concubines. While other family members were rewarded immediately with many descendants, those belonging to the chosen line lagged behind.[7] Nevertheless, God was working out his purposes, slowly but surely, within the special line of promise. This is how God has always worked and it is helpful for us to know this and not to become discouraged when progress seems slow.

The placing of information about Rebekah at this point teaches us another lesson about God's providential dealings with his people. Before Abraham began finding a wife for Isaac, God was already at work preparing the way. In God's ordering of affairs there are no accidents. God 'works all things according to the counsel of his will' (Eph. 1:11). We fret and worry too much. If we are his children through faith in Christ, then we can be assured that the Lord has our best interests at heart.

26.
Weddings and funerals

Please read Genesis 23:1 – 25:11

Three major events conclude this section of Genesis: the death of Sarah, Isaac's marriage to Rebekah and Abraham's death. God's Word comes to us in the context of home and personal experiences common to us all. In a world affected by God's curse, 'All our joy is touched with pain,' and 'Shadows fall on brightest hours ... thorns remain.'[1] These events also have a bearing on the ripening of God's purposes to end the curse and bring everlasting consolation.

The land of promise (23:1-20)

The report of Sarah's death and burial frames this very full account of Abraham's purchase of a burial plot.

1. Sarah's death

Sarah died aged **'one hundred and twenty-seven'** (23:1), thirty-seven years after giving birth to Isaac. She has the distinction of being the only woman in the Bible whose age is recorded. This in itself indicates her importance. Sarah, along with Eve and Mary, is one of the three most significant women in the history of redemption.

Like her husband, Sarah tried to walk ahead of God. Yet, despite such lapses, 'She judged him [God] faithful who had promised' and died 'in faith' (Heb. 11:11,13). If you want to die 'in faith' make sure you are living by faith.

Abraham's lifelong companion, who had trekked with him from Haran to Canaan and had experienced all the hardships and frustrations of an unsettled life for over sixty years, was now dead. Before she died they had obviously moved again from the comparative comfort of Beersheba to Kirjath Arba, later called Hebron (23:2; see Judg. 1:10).

Death is the great divider. In the marriage vows the promise is made to live together 'till death us do part'. Make every effort to live happily with your husband or wife so that when death comes you will have no regrets. Though her faults are also recorded, Sarah is held before us as an example of a godly woman who submitted to her husband (1 Peter 3:6).

It was a great loss both to Abraham and Isaac (23:2; 24:67). The greater the value, the greater the loss. Here we are told that **'Abraham came to mourn for Sarah and to weep for her'** (23:2). Abraham paid his respects to his dead wife in the customary way, which would have included tearing his clothes, shaving his beard, putting dust on his head and fasting. There were also real tears. Matthew Henry comments, 'It is not only lawful but a duty to lament the death of our near relatives.' There is a false piety which thinks it wrong for a Christian to shed tears and to show signs of mourning. The shedding of tears is actually one of God's amazing safety valves to release the shock of a great loss. To suppress such emotion is unnatural and dangerous. Those who treat death in a glib and light-hearted way should remember that death is the result of God's curse. It is a separation of what should never be separated — the soul from the body. On the other hand, Christians do not sorrow like those who have no hope. Tears flow just as Jesus wept at the grave of Lazarus. But we are assured that all who die trusting Jesus for salvation are present with him in heaven.

2. The purchase of the burial site

Purchasing a plot of ground for burial can be an expensive business. Here we have a very early account of a successful attempt at buying a cemetery. Abraham needed somewhere to bury his wife. Much space is given to this subject, which means it is of special significance.

The site which Abraham had in mind was a cave at the end of a field belonging to Ephron the Hittite (23:9). Both cave and field belonged to a district known as Machpelah **'which was before Mamre'** (23:17), that is Hebron (23:19). In the modern city of Hebron there is a mosque over the site of what is claimed to be the burial-place of Abraham and his family. Abraham only wanted the cave but an opportunity was given him to purchase the large field in which the cave was situated.

Abraham negotiated with the Hittites, the sons of Heth, who owned the site. The Hittite homeland was what is now modern Turkey and they became a powerful force by the eighteenth century B.C. It may well be that some of the Hittites had moved into Canaan centuries earlier for purposes of trade. These Hittites were associated with the Canaanites through Heth, a descendant of Canaan. They had integrated so well that they had taken local names like Ephron and Zohar.

The negotiations were carried out in a very civil and polite way and the deal was done before witnesses. Christians are to be wise in their use of money, follow local customs and be respectful. They should also make sure that there are witnesses to any agreements made.

At first the Hittites only offered to allow Abraham to bury where he wanted. They did not actually offer to sell any land. Abraham, however, was not prepared to accept the burial site as a gift. To do so would have put himself under obligation to them (see 14:23). Abraham made sure that any land was his by right of purchase and not a gift from one of the Canaanite tribes. Eventually, Ephron offered to sell the land and the cave at the inflated price of 400 shekels.

The importance of this purchase cannot be overemphasized. Here was the first step towards Abraham and his descendants receiving the whole land of Canaan. Our attention is drawn to the fact that Hebron is **'in the land of Canaan'** (23:2,19). We are reminded of what Jeremiah did on the eve of the Babylonian exile. He expressed his trust in God's future purposes by purchasing a parcel of land, confident that one day they would return and enjoy it. Abraham's action became a sign of what God would do in the future. That is why the burial spot figures so prominently, especially towards the end of Genesis (49:29-32; 50:13; 50:24-26).

3. The burial

This is the first record in the Bible of a burial. In those days it was common practice to bury in some kind of vault or cave. We should not make too much of the burials mentioned here and in many other parts of the Bible; otherwise we would be confined to burying in caves and tombs. Nevertheless, burial, by whatever method, is certainly more in keeping with the biblical revelation than cremation. For the people of God it is very symbolic of the body at rest, awaiting the resurrection morning. If it were possible to choose, then burial should be the preferred option. On the other hand, we should not make a big issue out of it when there is no explicit command in the Bible concerning the right way of disposing of a human body. The important thing is that the corpse is removed in a decent way, for it is the remains of someone created in the image of God.

A bride for the promised 'seed' (24:1-67)

The longest chapter in the book of Genesis deals with one subject, finding a wife for Isaac. Isaac was nearly forty years old and still did not have a wife. His mother had died and his father was an old man. Any father would be concerned for the future well-being of his son. But Isaac was not just any son. Divine promises had been given concerning the descendants of Isaac. How could these promises come about if Isaac was not married?

This fascinating account not only provides us with lessons for our own lives; it emphasizes the way God fulfils his purposes for our eternal well-being.

1. A model servant

Abraham's servant is an example of what our service to the Lord ought to be.

Faithful

This most senior of Abraham's servants was in charge of all his affairs. Abraham had total confidence in him. Some think he was Eliezer, but the text does not say so. He was completely devoted to Abraham, calling him **'my master'** (24:12,14). Christians are called to be servants of Christ. He is our Master and we swear allegiance to him.

Thoughtful

The servant did not give blind devotion. He raised legitimate questions (24:5). The Lord's servants are not called to follow the Lord with mindless enthusiasm. God gives us good reason for serving him and encourages us to be thoughtful in all our responses to his commands.

Godly

Conscious of his difficult assignment, he prayed to the God of Abraham for good success and that his master would know God's **'kindness'** (or 'covenant love' — 24:12,14). Abraham had ruled his household well (18:19). This servant had a personal faith in God, knew of God's covenant love, gave thanks for answered prayer (24:26-27,52) and was not afraid to witness to his faith (24:42-44,48). He is an example to us all of a life lived with reference to God.

Wise

The servant was skilful in the way he presented his case. He was dealing with wily people who struck hard bargains, as we know later from the account of Jacob's dealings with Laban. The servant showed remarkable patience and tact. Jesus calls his servants to be as wise as serpents and as harmless as doves.

Single-minded

Before he sat down to eat he insisted on telling Bethuel and Laban the reason for his arrival (24:33). When they encouraged him to stay, he replied, **'Do not hinder me ... send me away so that I may go to my master'** (24:55-56). The servant had a mission and he was determined to fulfil it as speedily as possible. In our service for the Lord we are called to be single-minded and not easily side-tracked.

2. The Lord's guidance

To be nearly forty and not married would have been unusual. Isaac was restricted, for he was not allowed to marry a Canaanite woman. The death of Sarah and the news from Haran brought matters to a head. It was Abraham who took the initiative. Isaac was a mere onlooker. Even for that culture he seems to have been unusually passive. On the other hand, Rebekah's lack of involvement during the negotiations between the servant and her parents was typical of Eastern custom. The story shows that this method of matchmaking, so unlike modern Western practice, when undertaken prayerfully, was clearly seen to be under God's control and it enabled the couple to accept the outcome willingly. In India, where Christian parents arrange their children's marriages, the wedding invitation includes the words: **'The thing comes from the LORD'** (24:50).

Whatever method is used for finding a marriage partner, it needs to be prayerfully and carefully considered. Again, parents do have a duty in preparing their children for marriage by giving them some understanding of the male and female psyche and helping them to develop marriage skills. The test that the servant applied suggests that he was looking for a person ready to go a step further than what was actually required.

The command not to marry those outside the family becomes a biblical principle. Jacob was instructed to find a wife from within Terah's family (28:1-2). Later, the law laid down the rule that the Israelites were not to marry the Canaanites (Deut. 7:3-4). The New Testament maintains this principle by urging Christians to marry 'in the Lord' (1 Cor. 7:39) and not to be 'unequally yoked together with unbelievers' (2 Cor. 6:14-18).

We gain help in this area of guidance from the way the servant acted. What he was looking for was not flashing lights or inner voices, but an ordinary human action that would reveal quality of character. Christians today often look for guidance that is dramatic and unusual. But God rarely guides in that way. More often than not guidance comes through ordinary providences and common sense.

'**Before he had finished praying**' (24:15) suggests that his prayers were answered immediately. God is very gracious and sometimes gives immediate answers. As we go on trusting him he teaches us other lessons and we learn to leave the timing to God. But it is good to remember that 'Before they call, I will answer; while they are yet speaking, I will hear' (Isa. 65:24). God is always more ready to hear than we are to pray.

Although the sign was quickly granted, the servant did not blindly accept first impressions. God does not bypass our minds. He has given us the Bible as our guide-book. It is not like a magic book for us to open at random and expect answers to pop up from the page. The Bible gives us principles, and we need to apply them to specific situations, look prayerfully to God and seek the advice of others. The servant had obeyed his master, prayed to God and could confess: '**As for me, being on the way, the L**ORD **led me to the house of my master's brethren**' (24:27). Bethuel and Laban also acknowledged the divine hand: '**The thing comes from the L**ORD**; we cannot speak to you either bad or good**' (24:50).

Rebekah '**became [Isaac's] wife, and he loved her**' (24:67). In arranged marriages love follows the union; in courtship marriages love is kindled before marriage. Arranged marriages must involve the consent of the couple. Rebekah gave her consent and Isaac willingly received Rebekah and freely chose to marry her. In whatever way we enter the married state, it is in the context of the marriage bond that we learn to love and respect our partners. It is a lifelong commitment. The first duty of husbands is to love their wives as Christ loved the church. It is the wife's duty to give herself to her husband in loving submission.

3. Faith in God's promises

God had pledged to bless Abraham (12:2). Here we are told that '**The L**ORD **had blessed Abraham in all things**' (24:1).

Later, the servant recounts the ways in which Abraham had been blessed (24:35). It was rare at that time to be in possession of camels, but the servant was able to take ten of Abraham's camels, which must have impressed the future in-laws. God had proved faithful, but the promises were only partially fulfilled. Abraham looked to their complete fulfilment. It was because of this that he was determined that a wife should be found for Isaac. What good was the land of promise if there were no descendants to occupy it? (see 24:7).

The last recorded words of Abraham are found in these verses. He enters history with God's promises ringing in his ears and he passes out of history with the same promises on his lips (24:2-9). Abraham was also confident of success, although he assured his servant that if the woman would not return with him he would be free from the oath (24:7-8).

It was because of these divine promises that the servant was instructed to make sure that his son married within the family and that on no account was Isaac to leave Canaan for Haran (24:3-4,6-8). There is much inbreeding. Blessing for the nations arises out of one family, the offspring of Terah. Terah was the father of Abraham and Sarah, the grandfather of Isaac, and Rebekah's great-grandfather on both her father's and her mother's side (24:15; 22:20-24). What was later forbidden in the law was allowed at the beginning of Israel's history. Later, as the servant left with Rebekah, they repeated the promises made to Abraham (22:17):

**Our sister, may you become
The mother of thousands of ten thousands;
And may your descendants possess
The gates of those who hate them**

(24:60).[2]

Rebekah showed the same faith that was first seen in Abraham. She was prepared to leave her father's household

and head for an unknown land and identify herself with the
God of Abraham and Isaac. Her simple yet firm response, **'I
will go'** (24:58), recalls Ruth's determination to go with her
mother-in-law:

> Wherever you go, I will go…
> Your people shall be my people,
> And your God, my God

(Ruth 1:16).

Such is to be our response to the gospel.

All was now in place for the divine purposes to move forward through Isaac. He was ready to take over from Abraham,
and Rebekah was the new Sarah whom Isaac brought into his
mother's tent. Isaac loved Rebekah and **'was comforted after
his mother's death'** (24:67).

4. Messiah's bride

The marriage union becomes a potent symbol of the Lord's
relationship with his people. This account of finding a bride
for Isaac takes us back to the origins of marriage in the Garden of Eden. There has been no similar marriage story between these two events. In that first account, we are told how
God brought the woman to Adam (2:22-24). In this chapter it
was through God's ordering of events that Rebekah was
brought to Isaac. Paul sees marriage as a type of the union
between Christ and his church, and he uses Genesis 2:24 to
indicate this. In the same way we can take this second and
very detailed description of how Isaac, who is himself a type
of the promised 'Seed', found a wife, as a pointer to the reality of the relationship between the Lord and his people. What
is more, God uses his servants to bring people to Christ. Concerning the Corinthian believers Paul could write, 'I have

betrothed you to one husband, that I may present you as a chaste virgin to Christ' (2 Cor. 11:2).

Abraham's last days (25:1-11)

In this final part of the section, the aim is not merely to complete the life of Abraham, but to draw attention to God's saving plan.

1. The descendants of Abraham through Keturah (25:1-4)

These verses come as a complete surprise. In chapter 24:1 Abraham was old and well-advanced in years, whereas here we have a report of his marrying another woman and producing many more sons.

There is a difference of opinion among the commentators as to when this marriage took place. It is natural to assume that Abraham's marriage to Keturah took place after Sarah's death. Abraham lived another thirty-eight years, time enough for him to get married again and raise another family. The God who gave him the strength to father a son when he was a hundred years old could have enabled him to produce other sons. It is quite in order to get married again after the death of a marriage partner. The New Testament encourages the practice and it is never considered disrespectful to the memory of the deceased.

The other view is that Abraham had married Keturah years before, while Sarah was still alive. This is an old view. The Geneva Bible of 1560 translates the opening phrase, 'Now Abraham had taken another wife...' (25:1), and adds a marginal note: 'while Sarah was yet alive'. The Hebrew can have that meaning and the fact that it is referred to at this point and not earlier should be no surprise, for incidents are not always

arranged in chronological order. Keturah is called a concubine (25:6; 1 Chr. 1:32). This would suggest that Sarah was
still alive and that Keturah was a second, inferior wife. Calvin
suggests that Abraham's marriage to Keturah took place after
Sarah had forced him to divorce Hagar. If Abraham could tell
the same lie more than once, then he could also get involved in
wrong relationships twice over. What would have been so-
cially acceptable did not mean it was acceptable in God's sight.
In God's plan, a man should have one wife and a woman should
have one husband.

The family tree of Abraham and Keturah only gives certain
information. They had six sons and it is the second and fourth
that are highlighted, Jokshan and Midian. The names of their
sons are given, together with the sons of Jokshan's second
son, Dedan. All the names are associated with Arabian and
Syrian desert tribes.[3]

The most significant name from the perspective of Israelite
history is that of the fourth son, Midian. The Midianites inhabited the desert regions surrounding Israel. They appear in the
story of Joseph (37:28,36). Moses married a Midianite (Exod.
3:1; 18:1-2). They became a threat to Israel in the period of
the judges. But all these sons of Keturah were distant relatives
of Israel. They all looked to Abraham as their illustrious ancestor. Abraham in this physical way did become the father of
many nations (17:4-6). But there would be a fulfilment of the
promise in a far richer and fuller way through the chosen line
of Isaac. The final verses again focus on Isaac's place in God's
purposes.

2. The distribution of Abraham's estate (25:5-6)

It was common for a man to divide his estate among his sons
before he died (see Luke 15:12). In our culture we appoint
executors to carry out the wishes of the deceased. It is wise to
make a will and we have a duty to provide for our family. If

there is more than enough then we may consider leaving property or money to further the Lord's work in this world.

Abraham ploughed his possessions into the godly line, giving **'all that he had to Isaac'** (25:5). It indicated that Abraham continued to show his trust in God's promises. Isaac alone was the heir to the inheritance. The sons of the concubines had no rights of inheritance and could have been sent away with nothing. But Abraham **'gave gifts to the sons of the concubines'** (25:6) and sent them to the east. 'Eastward' refers to those desert regions on the eastern edges of Canaan, and their descendants are later referred to as 'the sons of the East' (Judg. 6:3,33; 8:10). As we have noted previously, moving east is symbolic of moving away from God's blessings (see 4:16). These sons were sent away from the land of promise. Canaan was for Isaac and his descendants. God had a plan to carry out through Isaac and his descendants. Now that the plan has been fulfilled with the coming of Jesus, blessing can come to all nations. There is the promise of a better land, and of an inheritance that is eternal. The banished ones can return. Those afar off can come near. Isaiah sees the descendants of Keturah, Midian and Ephah, and 'all those from Sheba' coming back. Gentiles from every nation will come to Zion's light (Isa. 60:1-6). Sinners of all types may come (Luke 15:1-32).

3. The death and burial of Abraham (25:7-11)

Abraham's death (25:7-8)

Instead of the typical formula (see 5:5 etc.) more detail is given which emphasizes the importance of this man's life. Abraham was 175 years old when he died. He was seventy-five when he came to Canaan (12:4). This means he had lived 100 years in the land of promise. There was a completeness about his life which the statement concerning his death stresses.

Two words are used in Hebrew for Abraham's death — he **'breathed his last** ["expired"] **and died'** (25:8). The first emphasizes that the last breath of life had gone. He **'died in a good old age, an old man and full of years'**. This recalls the Lord's promise: 'You shall be buried at a good old age' (15:15). His life had been blessed and he died contented.

The phrase, he **'was gathered to his people'**, is not a reference to his bodily remains in the family tomb. What happened to his body is mentioned in the following verses. The meaning is that he continued to exist as a person with the rest of his ancestors, for there is an existence beyond death. Abraham was not buried; only his body. Death is an unnatural state for it means existing without the body. Abraham, however, died believing and looked forward to the complete fulfilment of God's promises, which he saw from a distance through the circumstances surrounding the birth, sacrifice and resurrection of his son Isaac. He looked, however faintly, to the final state, to the resurrection of the body. Jesus implied that Abraham is alive and awaiting the resurrection day. God 'is not the God of the dead but of the living, for all live to him' (Luke 20:37-38).

Abraham's burial

The burial was conducted by Isaac and Ishmael. Again, emphasis is placed on the burial site. Abraham was buried in the land of promise, in a piece of land that he had actually bought. He was to the end of his days a pilgrim on earth looking for the ultimate fulfilment (see 23:4; Heb. 11:13).

God's blessing on Isaac

Blessing, not the curse of death, has the final word in this section: **'God blessed his son Isaac'** (25:11). His family might have been tempted to say, 'Ah well, that is the end of an era. Abraham had all the blessings and promises and they have all died with him.' Not at all! Blessing continued along the chosen line. God remained faithful to his promises. His covenant love endures for ever (Ps. 136:3). Isaac points us again to Jesus, who has removed the curse so that 'the blessing of Abraham' might come to Jew and Gentile alike in Christ (Gal. 3:13-14).

Isaac moved from Mamre and went to live at Beer Lahai Roi, the place where he had been in the south (the Negev) to meet Rebekah (24:62). This area was associated with Ishmael and his mother (see 16:14). While Ishmael moved east, Isaac remained in the place of blessing. Every time he drew water from the well he would have been continually reminded of God, the fountain of life, who lives and provides. Our trust is in the same God through Jesus.

Part 8:
What Ishmael produced (25:12-18)

27.
Arab origins

Please read Genesis 25:12-18

'Now this is the genealogy of Ishmael' marks another major division. This is the seventh such heading in Genesis. They help to bind the whole book together and encourage us to look forward rather than backward. It is what the person produced that is important.

Why are we encouraged to look forward? This is a history book with a difference. In the nature of the case, history means looking back at what has happened in times past and assessing the importance of people and events. But in the case of Genesis we are urged to look forward. We are not allowed to stop and remain with the great father figures at the dawn of world history. They are stages in the history of redemption. The headings are like signposts encouraging us to look beyond these important people to the fulfilment of God's purposes. God had made a promise that the seed of the woman would bruise the serpent's head. There is a battle to be won. The great deceiver, who tempted our first parents and brought humanity under his power, is to have his rule broken so that God's kingdom might be established on earth. The headings keep reminding us that there is this future hope. While there are partial fulfilments of God's promises in Genesis and in the history of Israel, particularly in the time of David and Solomon, the complete fulfilment awaits the appearing of Jesus the Messiah.

How does this heading concerning Ishmael's descendants lead us to Christ? Ishmael's family line will not lead to the special 'Seed'. As Gordon Wenham has expressed it, Ishmael is like Cain, Ham or Esau, 'one of the cul-de-sacs' in divine history, a man who is bypassed in the unfolding of God's purposes. Why, then, is there a whole section given over to what Ishmael produced?

Promises fulfilled

Ishmael was **'Abraham's son, whom Hagar ... bore to Abraham'** (25:12), and he was the subject of divine promises. God spoke to both Abraham and Hagar concerning Ishmael's future.

To Abraham God said, 'I have blessed him, and will make him fruitful, and will multiply him exceedingly. He shall beget twelve princes, and I will make him a great nation' (17:20). Similar promises were made to Hagar (see 16:10; 21:18). This section records the fulfilment of those promises, for Ishmael had twelve sons who became princes, or chieftains, of twelve tribal groups. They give their names to settlements in the Arabian area (25:13-16).

What God did for Ishmael in fulfilment of his word he was to do for Isaac, as the following sections will show. The descendants of Abraham through Isaac would eventually become twelve tribes and be formed into a great nation.

Hagar was also given specific promises concerning her son, concluding with the words: 'He shall dwell in the presence of all his brethren' (16:11-12). This promise is picked up at the close of the present section, although it is not obvious in the translation: **'He died in the presence of all his brethren'** (25:18). The AV margin suggests that instead of 'died' we should read 'fall'. John Calvin, who was a good Hebrew scholar, comments that the word 'fall' sometimes signifies 'to lie down' or 'to dwell', a translation accepted by many modern commentators. The phrase would then read literally, 'He lived opposite all his brothers.' This could either mean that Ishmael, represented by his descendants, lived in close proximity to the descendants of Isaac, or that he lived in opposition to them.[1] The ambiguity may be deliberate to suggest both ideas. The Arabs claim descent from Abraham through Ishmael and we see the fulfilment of this prophecy where Arab and Israeli live in close proximity to each other and yet relations between them are turbulent.

What the entire section does is to record the fulfilment of all the promises made to Hagar and Abraham concerning Ishmael. The effect of this is to assure us that the Lord, who was faithful to those who were not of the chosen line, will certainly make sure that his much greater promises through Isaac are realized. We can also appreciate why the non-elect family line is considered first before the chosen line. If God's promises to Ishmael were fulfilled, then the promises to Isaac will not fail. This section, therefore, encourages us to look with eager anticipation to Isaac's family line which follows. The New Testament makes it clear that the promises are consummated in God's Son, our Lord Jesus Christ.

Grace abounding

As noted earlier, Ishmael means 'God hears'. God heard the cries of his mother and came to her assistance (16:11). Later, God heard the voice of Ishmael and saved him and his mother (21:17). The God of Abraham and Isaac was also the God of Hagar the Egyptian and her son Ishmael. Hagar knew this God as 'the God who sees' and who had relieved her thirst (16:13).

Despite the fact that Ishmael was not of the chosen line, this did not mean that he and his descendants were for ever outside the orbit of God's grace. They were not of the elect line in the sense that God did not use that family to bring the promised Victor into our world. The line that would lead to the coming of Messiah would be via Isaac, Israel and the Jews, not Ishmael and the Arabs. Jesus said that 'Salvation is of the Jews' (John 4:22). Though Jesus Christ belongs to the 'seed' of Isaac and David, 'according to the flesh', it was in order that all nations might find blessing and be saved. This includes Arabs. The same passage which speaks of the descendants of Keturah coming to the light of the gospel also includes Ishmael's sons Nebaioth and Kedar (Isa. 60:7). On the Day of Pentecost we read of Arabs in Jerusalem listening to the wonderful works of God (Acts 2:11). There are many Arab believers in the world today, despite persecution from their own people.

Much hostility still exists between Jew and Arab, as God's Word prophesied. Lasting peace can only be found when they become one in the Lord Jesus Christ. We need to pray for those who work in the Middle East to bring the gospel light to Jews and Arabs.

Any who may feel disadvantaged, or who regard themselves as outsiders, should find encouragement from this passage. The God who heard and answered the cries of Ishmael when he called to the Lord is the same God who hears and acts today.

> This poor man cried out, and the Lord heard him
> And saved him out of all his troubles...
> ... none of those who trust in him shall be condemned
> (Ps. 34:6,22).

Whoever you are and whatever your background, there is hope through the promised 'Seed', the Lord Jesus Christ.

Part 9:
What Isaac produced (25:19 – 35:29)

28.
The origins of Israel and Edom

Please read Genesis 25:19 – 28:9

The heading, **'This is the genealogy of Isaac, Abraham's son'**, reminds us that we are back with the chosen line. It also tells us not to stop with Isaac, but to look beyond this unique son to the one in whom all God's promises find their complete realization.

Our attention is drawn to what Isaac produced. Esau and Jacob are fascinating characters whose lives provide us with warnings of dangers to avoid and with encouragements to persevere in the faith. Above all, these gripping stories are there to highlight the wonders of God's grace and his faithfulness to his covenant promises despite the obstacles raised through human folly.

The birth of Jacob and Esau (25:19-26)

1. Bethuel

The reference to **'Bethuel'**, the father of Rebekah and Laban (25:20), takes us back to Isaac's marriage to Rebekah and prepares us for the account of Jacob's journey to Padan Aram.

2. Barrenness

Isaac was forty when he married Rebekah. According to the rabbis, men normally married before they were twenty. Then we read that Isaac was '**sixty years old**' when his wife first gave birth (25:26). Not only did he marry twenty years later than most men, but he was married for twenty years before they had children. Rebekah had left her father's home with the blessing of having many children ringing in her ears (24:60). It was a miserable position for any woman from the ancient Near East to be in; how much more so for people who believed the divine promises concerning many descendants! This is almost a rerun of the problem that confronted Abraham and Sarah.

Isaac and Rebekah could have gone in for the ancient equivalent of surrogate motherhood, but they did not. Isaac may appear to have been a rather passive figure, but in his favour it must be said that he did not make the mistake of his parents. He did not seek to force God's hand. It was a real test of faith as the years went by and they remained childless. In carrying forward his plans God also trains his people. His apparent delays are for their good.

'**Isaac pleaded with the LORD for his wife**' (25:21), which is what every Christian should do in a similar situation. It is what the church must do in its concern to see spiritual children and the revival of God's work. Twenty years is a long time to wait. Some have waited longer. Others have not lived to see their requests granted. Prayer that is based on his Word will be answered. God had promised descendants to Isaac (17:19), but Isaac did not know how or when. He did not shrug his shoulders in a fatalistic way and say, 'What will be will be.' Isaac pleaded with God and '**The LORD granted his plea, and Rebekah his wife conceived**' (25:21). God uses our prayers to fulfil his purposes.

3. Battle

No sooner had one problem been put right than another one arose, for **'The children struggled together within her'** (25:22). Pregnant mothers can sympathize with Rebekah in the difficulties she experienced. Some mothers have no problems, while others have all kinds of complications as they carry their unborn babies. The Hebrew word for 'struggle' is a very strong one. It can mean 'to crush' or 'smash'. This was a particularly unpleasant and painful experience, so that Rebekah cried out in anguish, **'If all is well, why am I this way?'** or 'If it is like this, why am I here?'[1] Her words suggest that she began to despair of life. The initial joy of realizing they were to have a child had been turned into despair. This was not what they expected. Sometimes God's answers are not what we imagined and we begin to wonder what God is doing. It throws us back on the Lord.

This is what Rebekah did. **'She went to enquire of the LORD'** (25:22)[2] and he indicated what was happening in her womb (25:23). The first part of the oracle emphasized the promises made to Abraham (17:16). Rebekah did not need 'a scan', for she learnt from the message to expect twin boys. She was informed that the trouble she was experiencing was the beginning of a conflict between two nations, one stronger than the other, and that the older twin would serve the younger. Knowing what was happening inside her would have helped her to bear the discomfort with more fortitude.

When Rebekah gave birth the prophecy was confirmed: **'Indeed there were twins in her womb'** (25:24). The way they were born prepared for all that was to follow. Because he was **'like a hairy garment all over'**, the first-born was called Esau ('hairy'). This information is important for what happened later (27:11). The reference to his coming out **'red'** points us towards Esau's other name, 'Edom', which sounds like the word for 'reddish' (25:25).

His twin brother came out with his hand clutching Esau's heel (25:26). He was struggling to catch up with his brother and not wanting to be last. He was given the name Jacob, which is a word-play on the word for 'heel' and 'supplant' (see 27:36). While Esau was named after his appearance, Jacob was named after his action. The struggle in the womb was continuing at birth and this was a sign that it would be ongoing.

The struggle between the twin brothers becomes another important theme in Genesis. We have seen something of it in the account of Cain and Abel and that of Ishmael and Isaac. In each case the younger and weaker is chosen above the older. God accomplishes his purposes through this struggle between the righteous and the unrighteous. The greatest conflict of all was at Calvary's cross, where the woman's Seed bruised the head of the serpent (3:15).

As for the choice of the younger over the older, another biblical principle shines out. God's blessings are not by natural right. Membership of God's family is not due to any claims we may think we have on God. It is due solely to God's grace. Paul uses this passage in Romans 9:10-13 when discussing the purposes of God in election. Unlike Ishmael and Isaac, Esau and Jacob were twins, having the same mother and father. Yet, despite the fact that Esau came out of the womb first, God bypassed Esau and chose Jacob. God is sovereign in our salvation. This truth also offers hope to the underdogs of society. God 'has chosen the weak things of the world to put to shame the things which are mighty; and the base things of the world and the things which are despised God has chosen ... that no flesh should glory in his presence' (1 Cor. 1:27-29).

Esau sells his birthright (25:27-34)

The conflict continued as the twins grew up and the situation was not helped by the actions of the parents.

1. The lifestyle of the twins (25:27)

Esau was an out-of-doors person — **'a man of the field'**. His home was in the uncultivated areas, with the wild animals. **'Esau was a skilful hunter'**, a man of adventure, who got his excitement from hunting down food in the wild. Jacob was quite the opposite. He remained in and around the campsite, in the cultivated part, with the domesticated animals. The word translated **'mild'**, or 'plain', usually means 'perfect', or 'complete'. It may suggest that Jacob was a more self-contained character than his brother. Whereas Esau needed the open countryside to gain satisfaction and 'a kick out of life', Jacob was more placid and level-headed.

This description of the two young men becomes symbolic of their spiritual state. It suggests that Jacob belonged to the people of God whereas Esau did not. The Garden of Eden was separated off from the uncultivated, open field where the non-domesticated animals roamed. Later, the tents of the Israelite camp were separated off from the unclean, open area outside the camp. Jacob belonged with his people in the camp, **'dwelling in tents'**, but Esau belonged outside. Jacob, like Abraham and Isaac, 'sojourned in the land of promise ... dwelling in tents' (Heb. 11:9). Unlike Esau, Jacob became a man of faith. God's promises meant more to him than physical pleasures.

2. Unwise parents (25:28)

How true to life today! It happens too often that the mother will take a liking to one child and the father to another. This does not encourage family harmony and spiritual growth.

Up to this moment, everything we have read about Isaac has been positive. He appears a perfect gentleman and a spiritually-minded man who waited on the Lord until his prayers were answered. But the best of gentlemen are sinners and here

we are told of one of his weaknesses which clouded his thinking and spiritual discernment: **'Isaac loved Esau because he
ate of his game'** (25:28). Isaac was not content with lamb,
goat or beef. He liked the taste of the wild meat that Esau
brought him. Isaac's love of exotic foods made Esau his favourite son and he no doubt made excuses for his undisciplined
lifestyle. His love of Esau made him oblivious to his spiritual
condition.

No reason is given why **'Rebekah loved Jacob'**. It may
have been because he was around the camp more than his
brother. On the other hand, it may have been because Jacob
was more interested in the promises that God had made to his
father and grandfather.

Here were two unwise parents who helped fuel the problems that already existed and which would increase between
Esau and Jacob. It is a warning to parents not to have favour-
ites. Treat your children fairly. Take care that some attractive
quality in one child does not cloud your mind and prevent you
from treating all your children equally.

3. Jacob gains the birthright (25:29-34)

Genesis abounds in word-plays, especially in association with
people's names. There are some very clever ones in this paragraph. **'Jacob cooked a stew'** (25:29). The word for 'cook'
is similar in sound to the word for 'hunt'. Esau **'was called
Edom'** because he was 'red' and on this occasion he yearned
for the **'red stew'** (25:30; cf. 25:25). The Hebrew brings out
the irony of the incident. Esau the hunter came in from the
open country like a ravenous wild animal looking for meat.
Jacob's cooking trapped the hungry Esau into selling his birthright. Jacob hunted the game he wanted and caught Esau when
he was most vulnerable.

It is ironic that Esau the hunter was famished. Perhaps he had had a fruitless mission and had caught nothing. He was hungry and exhausted and asked if he could gulp down some of the 'red stuff'. The cool, calm and collected Jacob had Esau where he wanted him and went for the kill: **'Sell me your birthright as of this day'** (25:31). Esau's response was desperate and somewhat melodramatic, **'Look, I am about to die; so what profit shall this birthright be to me?'** (25:32). Jacob was in the strong position and dictated the terms: **'Swear to me as of this day'** (25:33). The elder had been brought in submission to the younger. Esau gave in and swore an oath to give him the birthright. Thus he **'sold his birthright to Jacob'** for a bowl of lentil soup. His present need was satisfied, for **'He ate and drank, arose and went his way.'**

The account does not comment on Jacob's ruthless and manipulative spirit, a trait we shall notice again, but on Esau's attitude to his birthright. The comment at the end tells all: **'Thus Esau despised his birthright'** (25:34).

What was the birthright? It was the special status which belonged to the first-born son. It meant becoming the principal heir to the father's inheritance and head of the family on the father's death. While it was an important matter in ancient Near-Eastern culture generally, it was of special concern among those of this chosen family line. It involved divine promises. The covenant that God had made with Abraham and Isaac was tied up with the birthright. Jacob was interested in these spiritual blessings whereas Esau had no real concern. He treated his birthright as something worthless.

Esau is held up before us as a typical man of the world. He becomes symbolic of an apostate who tramples on the covenant blessings for the pleasures of this world. Esau sacrificed long-term spiritual blessings to satisfy short-term appetites. Immediate, temporal needs came before those unseen eternal realities. The people of faith, on the other hand, trust God and his promises. Although he went about it in the wrong way, Jacob's priorities were right. He was not short-sighted but followed in the footsteps of this family who embraced the promises from afar. Like Moses, he looked to the heavenly reward rather than the passing pleasures of sin and the riches of this world (Heb. 11:25-27). We are warned not to be like Esau, the spiritual fornicator and profane person, 'who for one morsel of food sold his birthright' (Heb. 12:15-16). Do not draw back but press on looking to Jesus.

Like father, like son (26:1-33)

Most of what is recorded of Isaac finds him in the shadow of either his father or his sons. Even in this chapter, which is the only one given over entirely to Isaac, he is constantly being compared to his father, or reminders of Abraham are being brought to our attention.

1. God's promises and the obedience of faith (26:1-6)

There was **'a famine in the land'** besides the one **'in the days of Abraham'** (26:1). It would seem that Isaac planned to do what his father had done and go down to Egypt (cf. 12:10). However, the Lord told him not to go there, but to remain in the land. As the Lord appeared to Abraham, so he did to Isaac and encouraged him with the promised blessings of the covenant (cf. 12:7). Isaac was living in land occupied by the Philistines, yet the Lord informed him that even **'all these lands'** (26:3-4) would belong to his descendants. The promise, guaranteed by God's **'oath ... to Abraham'**, also included the assurance of the Lord's presence: **'I will be with you'** (26:3; cf. 22:15-18).

The divine 'I wills' indicating God's intention to bless Isaac are followed by **'because'** relating to Abraham's obedience (26:5). How is it possible for God go on oath to guarantee the promises, and for those same promises to be based on Abraham's obedience? God fulfils his purposes whether human beings are obedient or not. But obedience is necessary for human beings to participate in those promises. If we are to enjoy God's benefits we must live in obedience to his Word. This truth would have been especially relevant when Moses urged Israel to keep the commandments of the law.

God's concluding words to Isaac present the divine estimation of Abraham's life: **'Abraham obeyed my voice and kept my charge, my commandments, my statutes, and my laws'** (26:5; see Deut. 11:1). Abraham is a model of the obedience to God's law which should characterize Israel and all God's people. Isaac was encouraged to obey and enjoy God's blessings, and this is what he did, for **'Isaac dwelt in Gerar'** (26:6). God's sovereignty and human responsibility go hand in hand. God will fulfil his purposes, either in association with us or despite us, but if we want to enjoy his blessings then we should 'trust and obey'.

2. Isaac's failure and God's unseen protection (26:7-11)

Though Abraham's name is absent from this paragraph, his folly is repeated. When the men of Gerar asked about Isaac's wife, **'He said, "She is my sister"; for he was afraid to say "She is my wife"'** (26:7; cf. 12:10-20; 20:1-18). Despite the fact that God had promised to be with him, Isaac was prepared to sacrifice his wife's honour for his own safety. Rebekah, however, was not taken from her husband and Abimelech was able to find out the truth of the deception without supernatural intervention. Abimelech saw Isaac and Rebekah displaying affection appropriate to husband and wife (26:8) and did the honourable thing. He did not want any of his people to become unwittingly guilty of adultery (26:10). Isaac and his wife were also given protection by the king (26:11). Isaac's sin could have led to divine punishment breaking out, as on the earlier occasion. But the unseen hand of God saved the situation.

It is a sad fact that God's people sin. We can be influenced both by the weaknesses as well as the strengths of our parents. Though children might in all sincerity vow never to follow the vices of their parents, it is all too common to see them grow up to repeat the sins of their parents. But what dishonour it brings to the name of Christ when Christians are seen by non-Christians to have acted wrongly! Our witness can be spoiled and God ridiculed. It should make us thoroughly ashamed and cause us to seek his forgiveness immediately. Thank God, he 'is faithful and just to forgive us our sins and to cleanse us from all unrighteousness' (1 John 1:9).

3. Isaac prospers and the Philistines are envious (26:12-22)

Despite Isaac's deception, the Lord was gracious and **'blessed him'** as he had promised (26:12; cf. 26:3). One proof of this was that **'Isaac sowed in that land, and reaped in the same year a hundredfold'** (26:12). Isaac also prospered greatly in that he had flocks and herds in abundance **'and a great number of servants'** (26:13-14). His prosperity brought other problems. The Philistines became envious and this led to harassment.

The agreements that Abraham had made with Abimelech were being conveniently forgotten or disregarded now that he was dead (26:18). Isaac was expelled from the area and he found that the wells his father had dug had been filled in by the Philistines (26:15-17). This was a stupid thing to do in an area which needed such water supplies, but it is typical of enemy action. It is equivalent to the scorched-earth policy seen in the Balkan region and central Africa.

Undeterred, Isaac arranged for his servants to reopen the wells his father had dug and **'He called them by the names which his father had called them'** (26:18). This was a wise move. It is sensible to dig where you know there is water, rather than to waste time and energy digging where you might not find any. Isaac followed his father in well-digging. While we are warned against following our parents' sins, we can be encouraged to follow their strengths. If your parents have found the water of life, what about you? The world would seek to blot out the true significance of the faith of our forefathers. Dig where the Reformers, the Puritans and the preachers of the eighteenth-century spiritual Awakening dug. Go to the fountain of life yourself and taste and see that the Lord is good.

Two of these wells that had been re-dug were the cause of fresh disturbances. Isaac was harassed by the herdsmen of Gerar. He did not fight over the wells, but moved on from one site to another (26:19-21). Whenever he was forced to move he renamed the well-sites to remind everybody of these skirmishes. One he named Esek ('quarrel') and the other Sitnah ('enmity').[3] At the third well Isaac was left in peace and he renamed it **'Rehoboth** ["roomy, open spaces"] **because he said, "For now the** Lord **has made room for us, and we shall be fruitful in the land"'** (26:22). In renaming the well, Isaac recalled God's promises. There are a number of chapels in Wales with the name 'Rehoboth'. They are reminders of God's blessings in time of spiritual revival when there was need to build larger places of worship to accommodate the people.

Throughout all these pressures, Isaac did not lose faith in God. Isaac was clearly a meek man. He did not go to war over the wells. This was not weakness, but a sign of strength, and showed a different spirit from that of the people of the world. Jesus said, 'Blessed are the meek, for they shall inherit the earth' (Matt. 5:5).

4. The Lord appears and Isaac worships (26:23-25)

The promises made to Isaac (26:3-4) are reaffirmed after he had moved back to Beersheba (26:23). God again assured him of his presence and once more the blessing was linked to his father Abraham. For the first time we hear God speak of himself as **'the God of … Abraham'** (26:24). He is the God of the covenant, a personal God who has fellowship with his people. Isaac responded like his father, for **'He built an altar there and called on the name of the LORD'** (26:25). Isaac's servants dug a fresh well at Abraham's old base.

5. God's presence acknowledged by the world (26:26-33)

Now that Isaac had prospered and become a force to reckon with in the region, Abimelech came with two of his chief men to make peace. Abimelech acknowledged that the Lord was with Isaac and had blessed him (26:28-29; cf. 21:22). A covenant meal took place (26:30; cf. Exod. 24:7-11), they swore an oath together and left **'in peace'** (26:31). Isaac was secure in the land, as his father had been. On that same day Isaac's servants struck water. Thus Isaac reaffirmed the name that his father had given to the place (26:32-33; cf. 21:31).

The life of Isaac pictured in this chapter expresses the truth of Solomon's words: 'When a man's ways please the LORD, he makes even his enemies to be at peace with him' (Prov. 16:7). These incidents in Isaac's life not only cause us to look back to Abraham but point us forward to a greater than Isaac. The true 'Seed' of Abraham did no sin: '… who, when he was reviled, did not revile in return; when he suffered, he did not

threaten, but committed himself to him who judges righteously'
(1 Peter 2:23). He bore the awful insults of the enemy and the
consequences of our sins, in order to obtain a righteous peace
and worldwide acclamation. Christians are called to be meek.
'If it is possible, as much as depends on you, live peaceably
with all men' (Rom. 12:18).

A family at war (26:34 – 28:9)

There is nothing new about family squabbles. What was unusual in Isaac's family was the cause of the trouble. Already
there existed a recipe for disaster with Isaac favouring Esau
and Rebekah favouring Jacob. Often an issue will arise that
will bring things to a head. Sometimes it is money, or the death
of a relative, that ignites the fuse. In Isaac's household it was
a 'blessing'. This was no ordinary blessing. It was more like a
will. It was a special endowment passed on from father to son.
God had made promises to Abraham which were passed on to
Isaac. Now the blessing was to be passed on to one of Isaac's
sons. Esau, the elder of the twin brothers, was the obvious
choice, but it was Jacob who was destined to receive it. This
was so because of a prophecy that had been made before they
were born (25:23).

We again see the sovereignty of God in this family situation. God's purposes came about just as he planned. However, this did not excuse the family for the terrible way in which
they behaved. It brought trouble that remained for many years.
We are held responsible for our actions and we sometimes
have to live with their consequences to the end of our lives.

The passage begins with Esau marrying two Hittite girls
when he was forty (26:34) and it ends with him marrying a
third wife, one of Ishmael's daughters (28:8-9). These references to Esau's marriages provide the frame surrounding the

sad episode within Isaac's home. The account of how Jacob, not Esau, received the coveted blessing is a marvellous example of Hebrew storytelling. It is full of interest and suspense. The best stories are always the true ones. But although the story is well told the subject matter is not pleasant, for it includes intrigue, deception, hatred and separation. There are four characters involved and six scenes.

1. Scene I — Isaac and Esau plot (27:1-5)

Isaac's part in this sorry episode is often overlooked. Though he was old and blind he had not lost his mental powers. It was normal for a father to gather his sons around him to bless them publicly before he died (see 49:1-2). Isaac, however, took Esau privately on one side and indicated his intentions to bless him before he died. Why he should think he was dying is a mystery. Isaac was to live another forty years, so why the hurry and the secrecy? There seems to have been something underhand about the way he acted.

In addition, Isaac should not have even considered giving the special blessing to Esau. Isaac would have known the prophecy that the older son would serve the younger (25:23). He would also have been aware that Esau had actually sold his birthright to Jacob. It was the birthright that entitled a son to receive the chief blessing. Then again, to make matters worse, Esau had bypassed his parents and married outside the chosen family. Both Isaac and Rebekah found these daughters-in-law **'a grief of mind'** (26:35). Esau had shown contempt for his birthright and had despised his background and the faith of the family.

Favouritism and the delights of Esau's tasty dishes clouded Isaac's mind and caused him to forget what was right. Husbands and fathers should seek to order their families according to God's Word. Be open, consult your wife and act together.

2. Scene II — Rebekah and Jacob hatch a counterplot (27:6-17)

Rebekah overheard the secret plan. Jacob was Rebekah's blue-eyed boy and she wanted the best for him. She also knew that the blessing was Jacob's by divine grace, not natural custom. In addition, she would have been aware that Jacob had bought the right to the blessing from his brother. What should she and Jacob have done? During her pregnancy she had turned to the Lord. At the very least she should have confronted her husband. Instead, she used deception. Jacob, though somewhat reluctant at first, fell in with his mother's plan.

Unlike Isaac, Rebekah had good reason for what she did, but the end did not justify the means. She did wrong and caused Jacob to sin. Mothers should be careful, in their desire to get the best for their children, not to lead them into sin.

3. Scene III — Jacob deceives Isaac (27:18-29)

This is the nail-biting scene where Jacob comes to his father pretending to be Esau. What a cad, deceiving his blind old father in that way! The law pronounces a curse on 'the one who makes the blind to wander off the road' (Deut. 27:18). Isaac was not easily fooled. He asked some searching questions and was not prepared to accept the mere word of Jacob. One lie gave birth to another and Jacob even brought God's name into his deception (27:20). No doubt Jacob was thankful that his mother had thought of everything, even the possibility that his father would want to feel the hairy Esau. Isaac was uncertain to the end: **'The voice is Jacob's voice, but the hands are the hands of Esau... Are you really my son Esau?'** (27:22,24). In the end all went according to plan and Isaac blessed Jacob. The latter part of the blessing included promises that God had made to Abraham and renewed to Isaac.

Jacob gained what he wanted, but at what a price! God used it in his eternal purposes, but he did not condone the sin. In the same way, God ordained and prophesied that Jesus would die for our sins, but he was not the instigator of the wicked act of putting Jesus on the cross.

4. Scene IV — Esau pleads for a blessing from Isaac (27:30-40)

No sooner had Isaac finished blessing Jacob than Esau arrived. What a heart-rending scene this is! When he heard the real voice of Esau, **'Isaac trembled exceedingly'** (27:33). Then, when Esau heard the words of his father, **'He cried with an exceedingly great and bitter cry'** (27:34). He was in a panic. For the first time he realized the true force of Jacob's name. Esau said, **'Is he not rightly named Jacob? For he has supplanted me these two times'** (27:36). Jacob had originally been given his name to mark the clutching of his brother's heel at birth (25:26). Now its significance was seen in this act of 'over-reaching' or 'supplanting' his brother. Esau complained, **'He took away my birthright, and now look, he has taken away my blessing!'** (27:36).[4] Esau yearned more for the blessing than the birthright. Three times he pleaded desperately: **'Bless me, even me also, O my father! ...'** (27:34,36,38). Having lost the rights of the first-born, he was actually not entitled to the birthright blessing.

Isaac knew that he could not undo what had been done. The fulfilment of the blessing was in God's hands. Esau was given a secondary blessing, which was a prophecy of the kind of life he would live, and it was made clear that he did not belong to the chosen line. God had decreed it before the children were born and Esau himself had despised his birthright until it was too late. All the tears in the world could not bring him the divine blessing. He tried marrying a woman more acceptable to his parents to gain their favour (28:8-9). The whole incident is a warning to us of the danger of apostasy. Repentance after apostasy is an impossibility. Do not be like Esau, who 'when he wanted to inherit the blessing, he was rejected, for he found no place for repentance, though he sought it diligently with tears' (see Heb. 12:15-17).

5. Scene V — Rebekah plans Jacob's escape (27:41-45)

Rebekah became aware of what Esau intended to do to Jacob when his father died. Esau consoled himself with evil thoughts: **'The days of mourning for my father are at hand; then I will kill my brother Jacob'** (27:41-42). We are reminded of Cain's unholy anger which led him to kill his brother. In order to save her son from Esau's raging fury, Rebekah made plans for Jacob to leave home and stay with her brother Laban **'a few days'**. She reckoned that time would abate Esau's anger and heal his bitter spirit (27:43-45). For her plan to be successful she needed Isaac's consent.

6. Scene VI — Rebekah talks to Isaac (27:46 – 28:5)

For the first time we find Rebekah speaking to her husband. She skilfully used the one thing they were both agreed on — Esau's marriage to the Hittite women — to persuade Isaac to seek a wife for Jacob from within Terah's chosen family. Isaac had failed Esau and he did not want Jacob marrying Canaanite women, especially as he was now the recipient of this special blessing.

With his wife's encouragement, Isaac took the lead and urged Jacob to go to Rebekah's home in Padan Aram. He then gave his son a much richer blessing than he had received earlier. It is much closer to the promises that Isaac had received from his father. Isaac's own faith was re-established as he confirmed the blessing on Jacob.

This is the last we read of Jacob's parents apart from Isaac's death. Rebekah apparently never saw her beloved son again and there is no record of her death. There was no happy reunion on earth for this family. Jacob had **'the blessing of Abraham'** (28:4), but at the high price of exile from the family home. The future 'Seed', in whom was no deceit, was exiled for us, 'that the blessing of Abraham might come upon the Gentiles in Christ Jesus' (Gal. 3:13-14). Those who belong to Christ must behave in an upright, transparent way. 'We have renounced the hidden things of shame, not walking in craftiness nor handling the word of God deceitfully, but by manifestation of the truth commending ourselves to every man's conscience in the sight of God' (2 Cor. 4:2).

29.
The origin of Bethel

Please read Genesis 28:10-22

Meeting with God

Jacob had two very unusual experiences of God. The first happened when he was fleeing from Esau, on his way out of Canaan to meet up with his uncle Laban. His second experience took place when he was fleeing from Laban and returning to Canaan to meet up with Esau. He gave names to both places (28:19; 32:30). Between these encounters with God we read of Jacob's twenty-year nightmare in Haran, where God disciplined him and moulded his character.

As far as we know from Genesis, Jacob had spent most of his life in the family home at Beersheba. He was now heading for Haran, the place where his grandfather's relatives lived, from where Abraham had journeyed to settle in Canaan and where Abraham's servant went to find a wife for Isaac. Isaac and Rebekah agreed that this was where Jacob should go to escape Esau's wrath and to find a wife.

This was Jacob's first personal experience of the Lord. We can know many things about God, but do we know God personally? Joseph Hart, the hymn-writer, once wrote:

True religion's more than notion,
Something must be known and felt.

The circumstances

It was about 500 miles north to Haran from Beersheba, a very long way to walk. Jacob would have taken at least two days to travel the fifty miles to Luz. The first night or two are passed over in silence. It is what happened at Luz that is reported in some detail because of its significance.

Jacob was alone and he came to the area where Abraham had set up camp in Canaan, between Luz and Ai, where he had first built an altar (28:19; see 12:8; 13:3-4). Normally, travellers in those days would look for someone's tent or home where they could spend the night. But Jacob found no home. He was forced to sleep in the open under the stars.

All this was new to Jacob. Unlike Esau, who loved the open spaces, Jacob had always lived at home. Esau was the adventurous one, taking risks to find good meat and to look for women. Now Jacob had been forced out of his comfortable existence to flee for his life and to fend for himself. Leaving home for the first time to go to college, or to find work, can be quite traumatic. You feel vulnerable, fearful and uncertain of what the future may hold. When Jacob determined to return to this spot many years later he expressed something of his state of mind. He speaks of 'the day of my distress' (35:3). It often happens at low points in our lives that God graciously comes to us and we are made aware of his presence. Many students have found the Saviour during their college days. My own wife was converted in this way. The God who had revealed himself to Jacob's grandfather and father now came to him as he slept in that uncomfortable and dangerous place.

The dream

We all dream from time to time. Some dreams can be so vivid that they wake us up and it takes some moments to appreciate that it was all a dream. For Jacob, on this occasion, this was no ordinary dream. God brought on this dream and it was God who spoke to Jacob in it. This was the way that God often revealed truth about himself in those times. The Bible tells us that God spoke at different times and in various ways (Heb. 1:1). Do not let anyone tell you that you are missing out on what Jacob and others received if you are not having such direct revelations of God. The Bible is not only a record of God's revelations to people in the past; it is itself revelation to us. It is God's Word to us today. What a precious gift to have God speaking to us in this way! God also uses the preaching of this Word to speak to us. Do not think that if you have never had a dream like the one Jacob received, then you have never met with God. Ask the Lord to meet you as you read his Word and hear it preached. This is the way God speaks to us, moves us, challenges us and changes our lives.

Our attention is drawn to three features of the dream, each introduced by **'behold'**. The term often introduces the contents of a dream and expresses the immediacy and excitement of what is seen: **'Behold, a ladder ... and there** [or "behold"] **the angels of God... And behold, the Lord ...'** (28:12-13). The first thing that caught Jacob's eye was a ladder, or stairway, stretching from the earth to heaven. On this ladder, **'The angels of God were ascending and descending.'** The focal point is the Lord, who **'stood above it'**. It was a very vivid and powerful way of communicating the truth of God's concern for what happens on earth. Jacob was being assured of God's interest and protection. The Lord's angels are 'ministering spirits sent forth to minister for those who will inherit salvation' (Heb. 1:14).

Jacob was not left to surmise what the dream meant. God spoke to him. This was the central and all-important feature. The Lord identified himself as the covenant God: **'I am the Lord God of Abraham your father and the God of Isaac'** (28:13). The blessings first promised to Abraham, and reaffirmed to Isaac, are now made to Jacob. Jacob no longer received the promises second-hand. Jacob heard God speaking to him, confirming the word passed down from Abraham and Isaac. There are two parts to what the Lord said.

The promises confirmed

The first part confirms those long-term promises he had received from Isaac (28:13-14; see 28:3-4). They included the following:

   1. Land. Jacob was about to leave the land of promise, yet he was assured that the land was God's gift to him and his descendants.

   2. Many descendants. To have descendants **'as the dust of the earth'** meant he would be successful in finding a wife and having children.

   3. Nations blessed through his descendants. The promised 'Seed', in whom **'all the families of the earth shall be blessed'**, would be through Jacob.

   The ladder between earth and heaven also taught Jacob to see something of the future Messiah. It was in the mind of Jesus when he said to Nathaniel, 'Hereafter you shall see heaven open, and the angels of God ascending and descending upon the Son of Man' (John 1:51). The angels are not mediators between earth and heaven. The ladder joins earth to heaven. Jesus saw himself as that ladder. As the angels moved up and down the ladder, so they do on Christ, the heavenly man. Christ, not the angels, is the mediator. The angels are the ones who do the will of Christ. However wonderful the ministry of angels is, it cannot be compared with the ministry of Christ. The book of Hebrews reminds us that Jesus is far greater than angels. He became a little lower than the angels, so that, as our representative and substitute, he might taste death as a man. But his position as the God-man is far above all principalities and powers. In order to know God in a personal way we must know Jesus Christ as the only Mediator between heaven and earth. He is the only one who can bring us to God. Jesus said, 'No one comes to the Father except through me' (John 14:6).

Jacob's needs would be met

The second part of God's message dealt with Jacob's immediate needs (28:15). He was assured of three things:

    1. *God's presence:* **'I am with you'**;
    2. *God's protection:* **'... and will keep you wherever you go'**;
    3. *God's promise:* **'... and will bring you back to this land.'**

These were very comforting and supportive words in his time of need.

One of the amazing things about God's word to Jacob is that there is not one word of rebuke. God does not kick people when they are down. That is what the devil will do. The Lord was gracious to Jacob and lifted his spirits. This is the God and Father of our Lord Jesus Christ, the God of all grace.

The response

Jacob was very moved by this experience. He was aware that God had specially met with him. Of course, God is everywhere, but his presence is particularly known and experienced in heaven. That is spoken of as his home. But God can make his presence felt on earth and in people's lives when he chooses to do so. Jacob had not experienced the felt presence of God before and he was certainly not expecting to find it that night. Yet God met him and blessed him. What was his reaction? It is the response of a godly person when confronted with the divine reality.

Fear

'He was afraid and said, "How awesome is this place! This is none other than the house of God, and this is the gate of heaven!"' (28:17). Why did he not jump and dance, especially when he had received such comfort and assurance? When faced with the presence of God, all the Lord's people in the Bible have been made acutely aware of their sin and unworthiness. 'Moses hid his face, for he was afraid to look upon God' (Exod. 3:6). Isaiah said:

> Woe is me, for I am undone!
> Because I am a man of unclean lips...
> For my eyes have seen the King,
> The LORD of hosts
>
> (Isa. 6:5).

Worship

Jacob made it a place of worship. He did not set up an altar like his grandfather and father, but took one of the large stones by his head and set it up as a memorial stone, **'and poured oil on the top of it'** to dedicate it.[1] It became for him **'God's house'** (28:22) and he called the place **'Bethel'**, which means **'the house of God'** (28:17,19). Jacob was to return to this place many years later. Worship in the Old Testament period continued to be associated with particular places. The Israelites were to worship wherever the tabernacle was placed. When the temple was built, worship was centralized in Jerusalem, although people often resorted to places associated with Abraham, Isaac and Jacob. Jesus put an end to special holy places (John 4:21-24). He said, 'Where two or three are gathered together in my name, I am there in the midst of them' (Matt. 18:20). Every place where the Lord's people gather for worship becomes a Bethel. As we get attached to the place we call home, so we can get attached to the place where the spiritual family meet. This is not wrong, but sinful nature being what it is, we must be careful not to think of the place as the all-important thing. It is the Lord himself we are to seek, not the site.

A vow

'Jacob made a vow' on the basis of what God had promised him (28:20-22). He vowed that if the Lord brought him back to his father's house in peace, **'then the LORD shall be my God'**, the stone pillar would be **'God's house'** and he would give back to God a tenth of all that he had received. Some commentators suggest that his vow was selfish and manipulative. Others see it as a right response to God's promises. True prayer and expressions of devotion are always on the basis of God's Word. Jacob's vow, as Robert Candlish indicates, 'is the response of faith to the divine promise'.[2] This spontaneous pledge to tithe his future wealth is a challenge to Christians today. In the light of God's goodness a tenth is the least we can give to the Lord's work.

30.
Jacob's exile

Please read Genesis 29:1 – 30:43

Jacob now began his long exile from the promised land. It was through the sufferings he endured in exile that he became prosperous and the father of many sons. He became an exile because of Esau's vengeful anger and in order to find a wife. Jacob's experience points us to the true 'Seed', Jesus Christ, who experienced the lonely exile of separation from God on account of human sin and for the purpose of gaining a heavenly bride. The Son of God suffered 'outside the camp' to bring 'many sons to glory' (Heb. 13:12,13; 2:10).

Jacob meets his relatives (29:1-14)

After the experience at Bethel, Jacob resumed his journey with a cheerful spirit and a new confidence. This is suggested by the opening words, **'So Jacob went on his journey'**, which translate literally as, 'Jacob picked up his feet' (29:1).[1]

Unlike Abraham's servant, Jacob had no camels and carried no gifts. He had nothing but the clothes he was wearing. After many weeks of walking, he came to an area where three flocks of sheep were gathered near a well in the middle of the day. A huge stone covered the well, which was the reason why no water had been drawn. Jacob learned that it was a local custom to wait until all who wanted water had arrived so that the stone might be removed when all were together. The shepherds who had arrived early obviously did not believe in over-exerting themselves. Jacob received from them the briefest of replies to his questions. Nevertheless, he was encouraged to learn that he was near Haran, that his mother's brother was known to them and that the girl approaching them with a flock of sheep was Laban's daughter.

Were the shepherds waiting for Laban's daughter to help them with the stone or with watering their sheep? Jethro's daughters experienced unacceptable behaviour from shepherds (Exod. 2:16-19). As Moses was to do later, Jacob did the honourable thing and came to the support of the girl. Before the shepherds had an opportunity to react, Jacob removed the stone himself and watered his cousin's sheep. He was not the wimp that some have suggested. This impressive demonstration of strength and initiative made up for Jacob's lack of costly presents.

It would have been unusual to find a man kissing a girl and weeping aloud in public, but it was an expression of immense relief and joy to Jacob that he had been directed, like Abraham's servant of old, to his parents' family. God had prepared his way and given him good success. For God's people, 'chance' happenings bear witness to a divine hand at work behind the scenes.

Rachel, like Rebekah before her, left the sheep and ran quickly to tell Laban, her father. Jacob was warmly welcomed by his uncle and assured that he was one of the family: **'Surely you are my bone and my flesh'** (29:14; see 2:23). Unlike Abraham's servant, who was in a hurry to return home after successfully completing his mission, Jacob was quite content to remain where he was and a whole month passed without incident. The ease with which this stage of the journey had progressed was symbolized by the ease with which Jacob

moved the stone from the mouth of the well. He was to find
that there were many more obstacles to move before he could
return to Canaan.[2]

Jacob marries (29:15-30)

Jacob's parents wished him to marry a woman from among
his relatives in Haran. Laban had two daughters, Leah, the
first-born, and Rachel. It did not take Laban long to appreciate that Jacob had his eye on Rachel. She was beautiful and
attractive, while Leah had **'delicate'**, or gentle, eyes that probably lacked the youthful sparkle of her sister's (29:16-17). The
Bible does not frown on physical attraction. It is not everything, but it is an important ingredient in what we call 'falling
in love'. With Jacob it seems to have been love at first sight
and he was prepared to do anything to obtain Rachel's hand.
We are about to see God working in his strange providence to
fulfil his purposes.

1. A desperate Jacob

'Jacob loved Rachel' (29:18). Isaac had not given Jacob any
presents to offer Laban for the hand of his daughter. After a
month's stay in the household, Laban proposed a deal. It
sounded good to Jacob. His uncle offered him work and asked
him to name his wages (29:15). Instead of bargaining with
him in the usual Eastern way, Jacob responded immediately,
and somewhat rashly, by declaring that he was prepared to
work seven years for Rachel (29:18). This was a far higher
price than was normally expected.[3] It showed how desperate
he was to marry Rachel.

The deal was very acceptable to Laban but his reply was
not quite the definite promise that Jacob took it to mean, as

the latter would learn later. Laban said, **'It is better that I give her to you than that I should give her to another man'** (29:19).

Those seven years were carefree, happy times. Jacob's work was purposeful. The prospect of taking Rachel to be his lawfully wedded wife helped him to do his work gladly. Unlike his time back at home when his determination to get what he wanted led him to act deceitfully, he learned to wait patiently and was prepared to work honestly for the prize. Seven years **'seemed but a few days to him because of the love he had for her'** (29:20). Rebekah, his mother, had spoken of staying with Laban 'a few days' while Esau's rage subsided (27:44). The 'few days' had now turned into seven years of devoted service for the woman he loved. We live in an age which is not prepared to wait for anything. People want to live together before marriage, or do not bother to get married at all. Jacob enjoyed the company of Rachel without violating her. It indicated 'genuine affection, respect and concern for her'.[4] All this only added to the awful disappointment he was to experience.

2. A deceitful Laban

Jacob lost no time in letting Laban know that the seven years were up and that Rachel should be his wife (29:21). Laban sent out the invitations and arranged for the wedding breakfast. Weddings in that part of the world in those times normally involved 'processions to and from the bride's house, a reading of the marriage contract, and a large meal attended by both families and neighbours. The first day's celebration ended with the groom wrapping his cloak around the bride, who was veiled throughout the ceremony (24:65), and taking her to the nuptial chamber where the marriage was consummated. However, the feasting and celebration continued for a whole week.'[5]

Jacob's immediate family were not present for the occasion and this provided Laban with his opportunity to trick Jacob. In the evening, when it was dark, Laban substituted his elder daughter Leah for Rachel. He also gave his maid Zilpah to Leah as a wedding present. Jacob, no doubt in high spirits, never thinking for a moment that anything was wrong, took his bride into the nuptial tent. Not until daylight did Jacob realize that instead of his beloved Rachel it was Leah who was lying beside him. What an anticlimax! It must have made him sick. He had worked hard and patiently for his dream girl only to find he had been tricked into marrying her elder sister. **'What is this you have done to me? ... Why then have you deceived me?'** (29:25) catches Jacob's shock and grief at what had happened. Laban's reply left Jacob speechless: **'It must not be done so in our country, to give the younger before the first-born'** (29:26). Why had he not told Jacob this at the beginning? It was a mere excuse.

After seven wonderful years with no one in his thoughts but Rachel, he was suddenly confronted with his sinful past and the hurt he had caused his own brother and father. Through trickery Jacob had done what Laban had said was not the practice, for the younger to take the place of the first-born. All unwittingly Laban's words became to Jacob the voice of justice. He had put himself in front of the first-born and he was now on the receiving end.

Laban further played on Jacob's vulnerability by suggesting that immediately after Leah's wedding week was over, he could marry Rachel and complete another seven years of service for her. Jacob had little option but to comply with his uncle's neat scheme. He completed the week of celebrations dutifully and then Laban gave him Rachel. He also gave Rachel another of his maids, Bilhah, as a marriage gift.

Jacob's plans of an idyllic future with the woman he loved and had worked for were shattered. He was forced to work a further seven years before he was free to return to Canaan. In addition, there was now another woman in his life to consider. To Laban it might have appeared a good deal. He had married off both his daughters. Jacob, on the other hand, was now a husband to two sisters who would naturally be vying with one another for his affection. This situation was later forbidden in the Mosaic law (Lev. 18:18).

3. A disciplining God

While Jacob was having his schemes for the future brought to nothing, God was quietly fulfilling the promises he had made to Jacob. He was also using the various circumstances of Jacob's life to discipline him and make him a better person. We should 'not despise the chastening of the LORD, nor detest his correction; for whom the LORD loves he corrects, just as a father the son in whom he delights' (Prov. 3:11-12). Though it is painful, it is for our eternal good.

> These inward trials I employ,
> From self and pride to set thee free,
> And break thy schemes of earthly joy,
> That thou mayest seek thy all in me.
>
> (John Newton)

The origins of the Israelite tribes (29:31 – 30:24)

Whereas the early fathers of Israel were afflicted with the problem of childlessness, Jacob was blessed with many sons. In his case childbearing became a contest between his two wives. The rest of Genesis reveals how this rivalry between mothers turned into a conflict between brothers. A situation developed which set the course for the whole history of Israel.

Through all the troubled relationships God continued to work his sovereign purposes and to keep his covenant promises. Out of this unpleasant background there eventually appeared the promised 'Seed' who has brought unity and peace to all who put their trust in him. The twelve tribes of Israel become symbolic of the whole people of God (the 144,000) who stand with Christ, the Lamb, on Mount Zion and as citizens together in the New Jerusalem (Rev. 7:1-17; 14:1-5; 21:12-14).

1. Frustrated wives (29:31 – 30:2)

When the text says that **'Leah was unloved'** (29:31; literally 'hated'; see Mal. 1:2-3) it means that Jacob loved her less than he did Rachel. The previous verse has stated that 'He ... loved Rachel more than Leah' (29:30). Jacob had never intended marrying Leah in the first place and, in addition, he would have resented the part she had played in Laban's deceit. She had pretended to be her sister when Jacob consummated the marriage that first wedding night.

But though Jacob loved Rachel, she was not able to bear him children: **'Rachel was barren'** (29:31). The same problem that afflicted Sarah and Rebekah brought added problems to the relationship between Jacob and Rachel. Reluctantly, it would seem, Jacob could not ignore Leah. He was forced to consider her also as his wife. God's overruling hand was at work in the situation.

The Lord was gracious to Leah for we read, **'When the Lord saw that Leah was unloved, he opened her womb'** (29:31). God acted in a decisive way and enabled Leah to bear children (see 6:5;11:5;18:21). It was the one who was despised whom God used to fulfil his purposes in building the future nation and sending the promised 'Seed'.

While Rachel was desperate to have children, Leah gave birth to four sons. Even so, she failed to win the affection of her husband. This is expressed in what she said as she named the first three. At the birth of Reuben she said, **'Now, therefore, my husband will love me'** (29:32). She confessed at Simeon's birth, **'I am unloved'** (literally 'hated' — 29:33). When Levi was born she said, **'Now this time my husband will become attached to me'** (29:34). The word-plays on the names also revealed her gratitude to God for his goodness. Reuben means 'See, a son!', **'for she said, "The LORD has surely looked on my affliction."'** She called the second, Simeon ('Heard'): **'Because the Lord has heard ... he has therefore given me this son also.'** When the fourth son, Judah ('Praise'), was born, she exclaimed, **'Now I will praise the LORD'** (29:35).

If you find yourself unloved and unhappy in your marriage, remember that the Lord knows your plight. Trust him and find your joy in him. Divorce was not an option for Jacob and Leah, and it is not the answer for a Christian. Those hard providences that we experience are meant to bring us closer to the Lord and we should make the most of the blessings he does give us.

Rachel was not a happy woman either. Though she was loved by her husband she could not produce him children. She was also jealous of her sister's success and in her frustration she cried out to Jacob, **'Give me children, or else I die!'** (30:1). An exasperated Jacob protested at this ungodly outburst: **'Am I in the place of God, who has withheld from you the fruit of the womb?'** (30:2). The 'fairy-tale' love affair was well and truly over. It was wrong of Rachel to have blamed her husband and Jacob was quite right to remind her that children are a gift from God (Ps. 127:3). We have already been informed that the Lord had opened Leah's womb and the implication is that he had closed Rachel's (see 29:31). Jacob now boldly expressed this view. With all the latest techniques for producing babies, we are still dependent on God for new-born life. It is not an automatic process. While God some-times allows scientists to experiment and produce so-called 'test-tube babies', there are many couples who are prevented from having children for no apparent reason.

2. Surrogate mothers (30:3-13)

The rivalry between the women in Jacob's life is expressed in the methods they employed to obtain children. Rachel gave Jacob her maid, Bilhah. Any children born through this means would still belong to Rachel, which is what the idiomatic phrase, **'She will bear ... on my knees'** (30:3), means (see 50:23; 16:1-3). Bilhah gave birth to two sons, and Rachel gave them names — Dan ('He has judged' or 'vindicated') and Naphtali ('My wrestling'). Unlike Sarah, Rachel was overjoyed and considered the first son an answer to prayer, as the word-play on his name suggests: **'God has judged my case ... heard my voice and given me a son'** (30:6). She saw the second son as a vindication of her struggles (30:8).

The phrase **'great wrestlings'** is literally, 'wrestlings of God'. Most translations assume that the word for God *(Elohim)* is here used as a Hebrew way of expressing the superlative (see another example in Jonah 3:3). It may, however, be an indication that Rachel was beginning to see this struggle with her sister as one in which God was involved. The phrase could be legitimately translated 'divine wrestlings'. She had come to see that God was the one who had shut her womb and opened that of her sister. When she says, **'I have prevailed'**, or 'over-come', her words anticipate the reference to Jacob's struggles with God in which he also prevailed (32:28).

Not to be outdone, Leah gave her maid Zilpah to Jacob as wife. This union resulted in two sons. Like Rachel, Leah was well-pleased with the outcome. Gad means 'troop' or 'fortune',[6] while Asher means 'blessed' or 'highly favoured'. She reckoned that **'the daughters'** (of men), or 'women', would consider her **'blessed'** (30:13). Leah's words remind us of Mary's expression of joy on hearing that she was to be the mother of the Messiah (Luke 1:48).

3. Sisters at war (30:14-15)

Little did the young lad Reuben think what a stir it would cause when he brought his mother some mandrakes he had found. Although they grow all over Canaan, they would have been rare in the Haran region. Mandrakes have no stalk and produce a yellow, plum-like fruit with a distinct smell (see S. of S. 7:13). They were thought to arouse sexual desire and to be a remedy for infertility. To this day they are popularly known as 'love apples'.

When Rachel saw the mandrakes she immediately asked her sister if she could have some. The request brought a bitter outburst from her sister. Leah blamed Rachel for taking Jacob from her and now she wanted to take away the fertility herb. A solution was suggested by Rachel that Leah accepted. Jacob was traded for mandrakes. Leah would have Rachel's Jacob for one night in exchange for the mandrakes belonging to Leah's son (30:14-15).

The incident shows how desperate Rachel was to have a child of her own. Bilhah's children did not ultimately satisfy her longing. It also indicates how attached Jacob and Rachel were to each other and the extent to which Jacob was ignoring Leah. We also see how desperate Leah was to gain the attention of her husband. All this only underlines the problems

caused by Jacob's bigamous relationship. Although not actually condemned in the Old Testament, every kind of polygamous marriage is seen as less than ideal. The examples in Genesis of such marriages show the disastrous results of such
unions.

4. Leah and Rachel rewarded (30:16-24)

What Jacob thought about this horse-trading we are not told.
When he came home that evening, Leah made sure she greeted
him before he set eyes on Rachel. In no uncertain terms she
informed him that she had hired him to sleep with her that
night. Jacob felt duty-bound to comply. Again, Jacob was finding his own past catching up with him. First, it was Laban who
had worked out a commercial deal for his wives. Now his
own wives had bartered for his affection. Jacob must have
remembered the way he had once exploited Esau's hunger to
obtain the coveted birthright.

The low and despicable attempts to gain affection and become pregnant were certainly not the way of faith. Although
the women made use of God's name when naming their children, they showed very little real dependence on God. On the
other hand, they did pray to God, for we are informed that
'God listened to Leah' and **'God remembered Rachel, and
God listened to her'** (30:17,22). The text also indicates that,
whatever psychological or medical benefits accrue from herbal
remedies, children remain gifts from God. Indeed, the passage
suggests that Leah conceived without the aid of mandrakes
and Rachel, despite the mandrakes, remained barren. Leah's
fifth son was called Issachar ('There is recompense' or 'hire').
In the word-play on the name, Leah first alludes to the hiring
of Jacob. She also implies that her action in giving Zilpah to
Jacob was very costly. Through it all she saw her son as a gift
from God (30:18).

Jacob went beyond the arrangement that Rachel and Leah had made. It suggests that the whole episode awakened him to his responsibilities towards Leah, for she bore Jacob a sixth son and a daughter. Leah recognized God's goodness to her in giving her more children. By calling her son Zebulun ('Dwelling') she not only nursed the hope that her husband would now live with her (or 'honour' her) but, by another play on words, acknowledged that **'God has endowed me with a good endowment'** (30:20).[7] The name of her daughter, Dinah, comes from the same word-group as Dan and means 'vindication' or 'judgement'.

The God who opened Leah's womb (29:31) now did the same for Rachel (30:22). As God had remembered Noah and Abraham, so he remembered Rachel and delivered her from the shame of childlessness. It was not the 'love apples', but the grace of God, that blessed her with a child. Not to have a child was considered a disgrace and a curse, so we can appreciate her remark: **'God has taken away my reproach'** (30:23). In calling him Joseph she showed that she did not see this birth as the end, but as a new beginning. She expected more: **'The Lord shall add to me another son'** (30:24).

Though the birth of Joseph is presented as a climax, this son of Rachel, who became Jacob's favourite, was not the one through whom the promised 'Seed' would come. Nevertheless, there is something special about Joseph. As the closing chapters of Genesis will emphasize, Joseph points us forward to the great Deliverer to come.

Jacob outwits Laban (30:25-43)

Jacob had been with Laban well over fourteen years. Despite his uncle's deceit, Jacob had not retaliated. He had served Laban well and had kept his word. Now that Rachel had at last borne him a child, Jacob asked permission to return home with his wives and children. As he was part of Laban's household, he needed his consent before leaving.

'**Send me away, that I may go to my own place**' (30:25) reminds us of a similar request that Abraham's servant made to Laban after he had found Rebekah (24:54,56). As Laban had tried to hinder the servant's departure, so he now made every effort to delay Jacob. In refusing to let Jacob go he couched his words in very polite and flattering language (30:27).

After such loyal service, a fair-minded father might well have given his son-in-law a golden handshake. Instead, Laban offered to pay Jacob wages if he continued to work for him (30:28,31). To mean-minded Laban Jacob pressed home the point that '**What you had before I came was little, and it is now increased to a great amount.**' We can understand his frustration: '**When shall I also provide for my own house?**' (30:30).

Jacob realized that he could not depend on Laban to give him anything worthwhile. In order to be free of his dependence on his father-in-law he devised a plan that Laban was bound to agree to because it seemed to favour Laban and put Jacob at a great disadvantage. Jacob requested Laban to give him the mottled sheep and goats from the flocks and any lambs born black. Normally sheep are white and goats are dark brown or black. Jacob asked for what was abnormal and unusual. Laban readily agreed to this request, for it appeared that Jacob was asking for almost nothing. To make sure there was no cheating, Laban removed from the start all the mottled animals and black lambs and gave them to his sons. This made it easier for him to check on the agreement. In order to keep the flocks apart, he put a three-days' distance between himself and Jacob.

Jacob was now left to look after pure white sheep and black or dark brown goats, which under the agreement all belonged to Laban. In order to have flocks of his own with which to return to Canaan, he would need to find a way of breeding multicoloured animals. Jacob devised two main methods of breeding, which he used simultaneously. Firstly, he peeled the bark from branches of poplar, almond and chestnut trees in such a way as to form white strips. He put these striped wooden rods near the water troughs so that when the goats came to drink and mate, they would give birth to spotted kids. Jacob also put the dark goats in front of the white sheep when they mated and found that they produced dark sheep. Jacob acted on the common belief that doing this would have an effect on the colour of the animals conceived. The results had more to do with the laws of heredity than with his clever scheme. It is reckoned that about two-thirds of the animals would have had the spotted or dark gene, which would have produced some twenty-five per cent multicoloured animals. Secondly, Jacob only used the best of Laban's animals for this type of breeding. This meant that Jacob's spotted kids and dark lambs were stronger than Laban's monochrome flocks. In all this Jacob displayed not deceit but ingenuity. He also acknowledged later the hand of God at work (31:9-12).

These verses indicate that God had kept his word and was fulfilling the promises he had made to Abraham, Isaac and Jacob himself (see 28:13-15). We notice four points.

1. Jacob's descendants

Jacob had been told that his descendants would be 'as the dust of the earth' at a time when he had no wife or family (28:14). Now he was able to say to Laban, **'Give me my wives and my children for whom I have served you'** (30:26). The promise was taking shape. He had fathered eleven sons and one daughter.

2. Jacob's blessing

God had said to Jacob that 'In you and in your seed all the families of the earth shall be blessed' (28:14; see 12:3; 22:18). Laban confessed that he had been blessed as a result of Jacob. He said, **'I have learned by experience that the Lord has blessed me for your sake'** (30:27).[8] Jacob underlines the point in his reply: **'The Lord has blessed you since my coming'** (30:30).

3. Jacob's possessions

He was blessed with material wealth: **'Thus the man became exceedingly prosperous, and had large flocks, female and male servants, and camels and donkeys'** (30:43). This summary is similar to what is said of Abraham in Egypt (12:16). Despite their sinful folly, both Abraham and Jacob had been blessed with possessions outside the land of Canaan.

4. Jacob's land

God had told Jacob that he would bring him back to the land of promise (28:15). Now that Rachel had borne a son and Jacob had fulfilled the stipulated years of service, he was eager to return: **'Send me away that I may go to my own place.'** He also added **'... and to my country'**, or 'land' (30:25). Calvin comments, 'He does not use this language concerning Canaan, only because he was born there, but because he knew that it had been divinely granted to him.'[9] Jacob never forgot, even after years in exile, the divine promise concerning the land. He did not count the ancestral home at Haran as his country. His eye was on the land which God had promised. We too are encouraged to bear patiently the trials and afflictions of the present visible world and keep before us the promised glories of the yet unseen but eternal world (2 Cor. 4:16-18).

31.
Jacob's return

Please read Genesis 31:1 – 33:20

We have all heard stories of sons who have left home with nothing and then returned years later having made a fortune. This was Jacob's experience.

The great escape (31:1-55)

What God had revealed to Abraham concerning exile and exodus (15:13-16) was experienced on a small scale by Jacob. His escape from Laban's hard labour foreshadowed the deliverance from Egyptian bondage by his descendants. The exodus from Egypt in turn became symbolic of an even greater deliverance to come. God used these events to point towards the promised Deliverer who would rescue his people from slavery to sin and Satan.

1. Reasons for escaping (31:1-3)

Jacob would have left earlier, but his hard taskmaster of an uncle had forced him to stay. What moved him to leave when he did?

Changed circumstances

Jacob's wealth made him a person to be reckoned with.[1] His new status had its effect on those whom he served in the same way as Israel would later find in Egypt.

Firstly, **'Jacob heard'** Laban's sons talking among themselves (31:1). They were jealous of his acquired wealth at their father's expense, or so they thought. Jacob had become a threat to their own position in the family. Similarly, Israel multiplied in Egypt and became a threat to the Egyptians. Divine blessing often brings its own problems in a hostile world.

Secondly, **'Jacob saw'** Laban's face, that it was no longer **'towards him as before'** (31:2). This meant Laban was angry with Jacob. Despite Laban's efforts to keep Jacob in subjection, he had prospered.

A divine call

Jacob was given direct guidance to leave (31:3). It may be that Jacob was referring to this call when he informed his wives of the dream he had (31:11-13). The way the Hebrew is worded makes the promise, **'and I will be with you'**, dependent on Jacob's response to God's command to return home (see 12:1). Wenham points to a principle in biblical theology that when divine grace is responded to in obedience this leads to more grace being given. God had already promised to be with Jacob (28:15). That promise was now reaffirmed in the context of the command to return to Canaan.[2]

2. The consent of his wives (31:4-16)

Jacob found himself in a vulnerable position. He had no other family to turn to but his own wives, who were the daughters

of the uncle who had turned against him and the sisters of the
cousins who envied him. It was necessary for Jacob to persuade Leah and Rachel to support him rather than their father
and brothers.

Jacob's appeal (31:4-13)

In order to prevent anyone overhearing, Jacob called his wives
into the open country (31:4). He began by relating how their
father's attitude towards him had changed (31:5) and reminded
them how he had given long and faithful service (31:6), despite the many attempts by Laban to make a fool of him (31:7).[3]
As he reviewed his life he acknowledged three times God's
blessing and protection (31:5,7,9). It was God who had rescued (**'taken away'**) Laban's livestock and given it to Jacob
(31:9).

Jacob also told them of a dream (either referring to God's
revelation to him in verse 3 or to an earlier event) in which he
pressed the point home to his wives that he had not cheated
their father with his clever breeding scheme. It was **'the Angel
of God'**, described also as **'the God of Bethel'**, who had
helped him (31:11-12) and who had told him to return to
Canaan. Jacob was duty bound to return in view of the vow he
had made (31:13).

In the face of such a mean and cunning person as Laban,
Jacob had shown exemplary patience and tenacity. Some em-
ployers are unprincipled and miserly and while in their employment, there is the temptation to do less than the minimum
required. Jacob is a challenge to us to put our heart and soul
into what we do, knowing that God is with us and we are
answerable finally to him. We are not to be 'men-pleasers',
but God-fearers (Col. 3:23).

The response of his wives (31:14-16)

Both Leah and Rachel were united in denouncing their father. In cheating their husband, Laban had cheated them (31:14-15). The prosperity that Jacob now enjoyed they enjoyed, and clearly saw the hand of God in it (31:16). They therefore whole-heartedly encouraged Jacob to do what God had commanded him.

It was no easy matter choosing between father and husband. These daughters of Laban had kept their thoughts to themselves up to this point out of respect for their father. Now that Jacob had raised the issue they gave vent to their feelings: **'Are we not considered strangers by him?'** (31:15). While children are to honour their parents, fathers are urged, 'Do not provoke your children, lest they should become discouraged' (Col. 3:21). Laban justly lost the respect of his married daughters, and they both submitted to their husband after he had brought them into his confidence.

3. The flight from Laban (31:17-21)

As the Israelites left Egypt in haste, so Jacob, as soon as he had the all-clear from his wives, assembled his family, his live-stock and his possessions and set out immediately **'to go to his father Isaac in the land of Canaan'** (31:18). **'So he fled with all that he had'** and crossed **'the river'** (the Euphrates) and headed south **'towards the mountains of Gilead'**, which lay east of the Jordan between Galilee and the Dead Sea (31:21).

The text emphasizes that Jacob took what belonged to him (31:18). This contrasts sharply with the action of Rachel in stealing her father's **'household idols'** or '*teraphim*' (31:19). These 'gods' (31:30,32) were probably images of the ancestors whom the living descendants were expected to honour.

They were like little dolls that could easily be hidden (31:34). Rachel probably regarded them as lucky charms for the journey, and tangible links with her ancestral home. Such idols continued to be a snare to Israel throughout the nation's history (Judg. 17:5; 2 Kings 23:24).

There is a play on the word 'steal'. While Rachel **'had stolen'** her father's idols, Jacob **'stole away, unknown to Laban'** (literally, 'stole the heart of Laban'). He purposely did not tell Laban he intended to go. In a figurative sense he stole from Laban. Jacob had acted in self-defence by deceiving him and escaping while his uncle had gone sheep-shearing. Rachel, however, using the occasion of her father's absence, committed an actual theft. Laban, the arch-deceiver and thief, had been outwitted by his son-in-law and robbed of his gods by his daughter.

While Jacob's action was justified, Rachel wronged her father and sinned against God. Instead of trusting God for the journey and her future, she continued to have a superstitious attachment to idols. Calvin observes that 'Idolatry is almost innate in the human mind.'[4] Christians are continually warned against the sin: 'Little children, keep yourselves from idols' (1 John 5:21).

4. Laban meets Jacob (31:22-55)

Laban pursues (31:22-24)

It was three days later that Laban heard what had happened. He may have taken another couple of days to stop the shearing, gather his sons and servants together and pursue Jacob. It took him a week to catch up with Jacob's more slow-moving caravan. Laban overtook them in the mountains of Gilead, some 300 miles from the Euphrates. Some of Laban's hot fury was dissipated by a dream he had the night before the confrontation. In it God warned him not to harm or contradict Jacob in any way (31:24,29: cf. 20:3-7).

Confrontation (31:25-42)

Laban began by accusing Jacob of having duped him and of carrying off his daughters **'like captives'** (31:26-30). We know, of course, that Leah and Rachel were consulted and freely chose to accompany Jacob. Laban put psychological pressure on Jacob and made himself out to be a hurt father. He also hypocritically suggested that he had been deprived of the privilege of giving his family a proper send-off and implied that it was in his power to do them harm had he not been prevented by God's intervention. For the first and only time he did give an indication that he appreciated Jacob's desire to return home (31:30). Then, at the end, came Laban's serious complaint: **'Why did you steal my gods?'** Up to this point his accusations were the result of hurt pride and it is difficult to believe he would have pursued them for that. But the household gods were missing. That was reason enough for chasing after them at top speed.

Jacob, in reply, did not deny that he had acted contrary to custom, but explained that he had left in haste because he suspected Laban would forcibly steal his wives. As for the household gods, Jacob was so convinced no one had taken them that he invited Laban to search the camp and pronounced the death penalty on anyone found guilty. A tense situation then developed as Laban searched the tents — first Jacob's, then Leah's and the maids' tents and, finally, Rachel's tent. She was a true daughter of her father. Her deceit and cunning certainly matched his. Rachel had hidden the gods in the camel's saddle and sat on the saddle in her tent. She made the excuse of not rising to greet her father because of her menstrual period. Thus Laban searched in vain for his treasured gods (31:35).

Laban's failure to discover the idols gave Jacob the opportunity to go on the offensive. He was furious at what he believed to be Laban's unjustifiable assumption about his lost
gods. Jacob reminded his uncle of the despicable way he had
been treated for the past twenty years. Under ancient Near-
Eastern law the owner, not the worker, would have been held
responsible for any sheep lost due to attacks by wild beasts or
to stealing. Laban, however, had charged all losses to Jacob.
What he said behind his back to his daughters Jacob now repeated to Laban's face (31:41). Jacob also knew that, far from
giving them a great send-off with festive music (see 31:27),
Laban would have sent him away empty-handed. Jacob confessed that God had been with him, had seen his troubles, had
acted to release him from Laban's grip and had rebuked Laban
in his dream.

God is spoken of as **'the God of Abraham and the Fear
of Isaac'** (31:42). He is the God who keeps his covenant promises to bless and to be with his people. The only other place
where the expression, 'the Fear of Isaac', appears is in verse
53. Isaac reverenced the God who had been sovereignly active
in his life and had blessed him as he had promised. Unlike the
pagan gods which can be stolen and hidden away, the God of
Abraham and Isaac is powerfully active to protect and guide
his people and to bring judgement on all who live in opposition to him. Let us serve God acceptably with reverence and
godly fear.

Agreement (31:43-55)

Laban could not make any reply to Jacob's charges, yet he still
tried to make out that his daughters and all Jacob's possessions belonged to him (31:43). He had never really treated
Jacob as his son-in-law and had treated his daughters as
strangers. It was too late to talk about **'my daughters'** and
'my children' and their welfare.

It was Laban's idea to enter into a treaty with Jacob. He had seen that God was with Jacob and decided the best policy was reconciliation. Jacob set up two witnesses to the agreement (31:51-52): first, a stone pillar (31:45); then a stone mound or cairn. Both Laban and Jacob called it 'Heap of Witness'. Laban the Syrian spoke Aramaic and named it in the Aramaic language, while Jacob called it by its Hebrew name, **'Galeed'** (31:47). It was also called **'Mizpah'** ('Watch') for Laban said, **'May the Lord watch between you and me...'** (31:49). Laban wanted the agreement because he was suspicious of what Jacob might do to his daughters and to him personally (31:50,52). It seems ironic that Laban should now be so concerned for his daughters. Maybe he had a guilty conscience and was afraid Jacob might punish Leah.

As in many standard ancient treaties, the gods of both parties were invoked by Laban, the polytheist, as witnesses to the agreement. Because he was a believer in many gods it may be that we should translate 'gods of their father' rather than **'God of their father'** (31:53). This is suggested by the plural form of the verb for 'judge'. If the true God were meant the verb would normally be in the singular. Jacob, on the other hand, swore by **'the Fear of his father Isaac'**. He knew the one true God who had revealed himself to Abraham and Isaac. Jacob **'offered sacrifice'** and took part in a communal meal, both of which were common practices at that time when ratifying agreements (see Exod. 24:5-11). Thus they parted peacefully.

This is the last we hear of Laban. He had plenty of opportunities for knowing and trusting the God of Abraham. He had himself been blessed by the presence of Jacob. Yet he lived for this world and its possessions. He enjoyed the blessings but did not care to trust the God from whom all blessings flow.

Preparing to meet Esau (32:1-21)

Having made peace with Laban, on the borders of Syria and Canaan, Jacob needed to make peace with his brother Esau. There was no way in which he could live peacefully in the promised land while there was the threat from Esau and his own feelings of guilt.

1. Jacob's protection (32:1-2)

As he continued on his way to Canaan, Jacob met **'the angels of God'**. The only other place in the Old Testament where the phrase, 'the angels of God', appears is in Jacob's dream (28:12). We are not given as much detail as the Bethel incident, but Jacob explained the experience as **'God's camp'**. He named the place where it happened, **'Mahanaim'** ('Double Camp'). It is located east of Jordan, near to the River Jabbok.

Did he see two angelic camps, or did he have in mind the angelic camp and his own camp? Either way this company of angels would have brought assurance of safety. He saw something of what Elisha's servant was enabled to see (2 Kings 6:16-17). It was one more indication of God's promise made at Bethel that Jacob would be brought back safely to the land of his fathers. David Brainerd, the famous missionary to the North American Indians, knew similar heavenly protection when hostile Indians sought to attack his home. 'The angel of the Lord encamps all around those who fear him, and delivers them' (Ps. 34:7). While some are occasionally permitted to see angels, most of the time we rely on God's Word that they are there ministering on our behalf.

2. Jacob's plans (32:3-8)

The heavenly encounter must have encouraged Jacob to make immediate contact with his brother, for we read, **'Jacob sent**

messengers before him to Esau his brother.' Griffith Thomas comments, 'He knows that there can be no peace and quiet until his relations with Esau are assured and put on a proper footing... Is not this a great principle of the spiritual life? We must put right what we know to be wrong before we can enjoy settled peace.'[5]

In the message that Jacob sent to his twin brother, he was careful to play down his position as lord over his brother which he had achieved through deceit. In seeking to gain his brother's goodwill (**'find favour in your sight'**) he calls Esau **'my lord'** and himself **'your servant Jacob'** and lists some of his possessions that he intended to give to his brother.

Bush telegraph was very effective in those days, for it would appear that Esau, now living in Seir, south of the Dead Sea, already knew that Jacob was back before the messengers arrived. Like Jacob at the time, we are kept in suspense, not knowing what Esau's reaction to Jacob's homecoming would be. No reply from Esau is given, only the report that he was on his way with 400 men. Was he coming to take revenge, or to welcome Jacob? Despite his knowledge of the angelic presence, Jacob was **'greatly afraid and distressed'** (32:7). How like us he was! He assumed the worst. But it did not paralyse him. He made contingency plans. Dividing his camp into two, he reckoned that if Esau attacked one company the other would have time to escape (32:8). It was a wise procedure in case of trouble. But he did more.

3. Jacob's prayer (32:9-12)

He poured out his heart in fervent prayer for deliverance. When in need every believer is encouraged to pray (Ps. 55:22). It is a model prayer. Many expositors never give Jacob the benefit of the doubt for anything. Even this prayer is seen by some as defective. But a man who could pray like this was clearly a man of faith, someone who knew God personally. We can learn several things from his prayer.

A proper approach (32:9)

He did not rush into God's presence with his requests. There was a reverent approach. He reminded himself of the one before whom he was praying: **'O God of my father Abraham and God of my father Isaac...'** This invocation called to mind the fact that God was a personal God who had revealed himself to his ancestors and had entered into a covenant relationship with them, giving them and Jacob himself many precious promises (see 28:15; 31:3). We are directed to pray to the same God, the God and Father of our Lord Jesus Christ, the God of the new covenant, who has given us 'exceedingly great and precious promises' (2 Cor. 1:3; 2 Peter 1:4).

Humility of spirit (32:10)

He acknowledged his own unworthiness and God's mercy and faithfulness. Jacob had left Canaan with only his staff in his hand. He had returned with such wealth that he could divide his party into two camps. God does not owe us anything. We are sinners and debtors to mercy alone. What we do have is due entirely to the Lord. David confessed, 'Both riches and honour come from you' (1 Chr. 29:12).

Presenting the petition (32:11)

He poured out his fears to the Lord both for himself and his family: **'Deliver me, I pray...'** The Psalter is full of such cries to God for help in time of need. Paul urges us to 'Be anxious for nothing, but in everything by prayer and supplication ... let your requests be made known to God' (Phil. 4:6).

The basis for the request (32:12)

Jacob reminded God of his promises not only to treat him well (see also 32:9) but to make his 'seed' as **'the sand of the sea'**. Reminding God of what he has said is a common feature of biblical prayers. We plead on the basis of God's Word.

4. Jacob's present (32:13-21)

He sent a large gift of 550 animals to pacify his brother. They were divided into separate herds, with servants in charge of each one. When each in turn met Esau they were to answer his questions with the same message: **'They are your servant Jacob's. It is a present sent to my lord Esau; and behold, he also is behind us'** (32:18).

Many commentators assume that Jacob displayed weakness and lack of trust in God by continuing with his plan to send a present to pacify Esau (32:20). But, is it necessarily a sign of weak faith to take what measures we can to put things right? God uses our plans as well as our prayers in fulfilling his great purposes.[6]

His plans, prayers and presents did not prevent Jacob from feeling uneasy and apprehensive. We know in our own experience how fear and trust can go hand in hand. May the Lord help us to be more trustful and less fearful.

Wrestling with God (32:22-32)

All are agreed that there is something very mysterious and fascinating about this unusual incident.

1. The sleepless night (32:22-23)

Jacob had thought to lodge for the night in the camp (32:21), but then he decided he would bring his family across the Jabbok. This fast-flowing stream runs through Gilead in a deep cleft. It runs rapidly from 1,900 feet above sea level to about 100 feet below into the River Jordan, some twenty-five miles north of the Dead Sea. Jacob must have been feeling quite desperate to have helped his family cross a dangerous ford in the dark. Perhaps he wanted the confrontation with Esau to take place sooner rather than later. But why he stayed behind on the north side of the stream is a mystery. We can only surmise that he wished to pray to God on his own.

2. The struggle (32:24-25)

While he was alone he was suddenly attacked by a man and forced to fight for his life. The struggle continued until day-break. When the man saw that he was not winning, he touched Jacob's thigh, the hip socket, and put it out of joint. With all the wrestling the man got nowhere, and yet with a single touch he was able immediately to disable Jacob. Here was someone superhuman; nevertheless, Jacob continued to fight on.

3. The conversation (32:26-29)

The man demanded to be let go before the day dawned. We are not told the reason for this request. Realizing that he was struggling with no ordinary person, Jacob was encouraged to seek a blessing: **'I will not let you go unless you bless me!'** The man then asked, **'What is your name?'** and the reply came back: **'Jacob'**. The question drew attention to Jacob's past. Over twenty years earlier, Isaac his father had asked who he was and through lying and deceit Jacob had obtained the covenant blessing (27:18-19). His very name expressed his nature. Jacob meant 'heel-grasper', 'deceiver', 'supplanter'. In uttering his name he was admitting he was a cheat (27:36). The prophet has this pun in mind as he mourns for the people of Judah: 'And do not trust any brother; for every brother will utterly supplant' (Jer. 9:4).

Blessing comes to Jacob through a change of name: **'Your name shall no longer be called Jacob, but Israel'** (32:28). While the old name recalled his past underhand dealings, his new name would remind him of this incident in which he had **'struggled with God and with men, and [had] prevailed'.**[7]

For the first time the man's identity was disclosed. He represented God in some way. Jacob then politely asked the name of the heavenly fighter. Instead of a straight answer, he received a counter-question: **'Why is it that you ask about my name?'** (32:29). We are reminded of the Angel of the LORD's reply to Manoah: 'Why do you ask my name, seeing it is wonderful?' (Judg. 13:18). Jacob was in the presence of one too great to be described. But the important thing as far as Jacob was concerned was that this heavenly Being **'blessed him there'** (32:29).

4. The result (32:30-32)

'Jacob called the name of the place Peniel' (spelt elsewhere, **'Penuel'**; 32:31), which means 'face of God'. He was convinced that he had **'seen God face to face'** and, what is more, his life had been **'preserved'** ('rescued').[8] Seeing God put people in mortal danger (Exod. 33:20). The realization that his life had been spared in this encounter would have encouraged Jacob to believe that he would be delivered in his encounter with Esau.

As Jacob crossed over at Penuel the sun rose on him. A new day dawned for him. It marked a new turning-point in his life. Though he had prevailed and been preserved, God left his mark upon him: **'He limped on his hip.'** He could no longer be self-sufficient. The custom of not eating the sciatic nerve is mentioned nowhere else, but it would have reminded the Israelites of Jacob's meeting with God and the promise of ultimate victory through struggle. What Jacob experienced was no dream or vision, but a physical encounter with God which left him lame. As so often in the Old Testament, physical experiences had spiritual dimensions. The physical pointed to spiritual realities. There are two interesting points to note.

God started the fight

When Jacob was alone, **'A man wrestled with him'** (32:24). The man is known as 'the Angel' in Hosea 12:4. He is the Angel who had spoken to Jacob and said, 'I am the God of Bethel' (31:11-13). Jacob became aware that God had met with him.

Why did God attack Jacob? It was, as Calvin explains, 'to teach us that our faith is tried by him... As all prosperity flows from his goodness, so adversity is either the rod with which he corrects our sins, or the test of our faith and patience... What was once exhibited under a visible form to our father Jacob, is daily fulfilled in the individual members of the Church.'[9]

God allowed Jacob to contend successfully in his own strength for a time. As he had taken 'his brother by the heel in the womb', so 'In his strength he struggled with God' (Hosea 12:3). The ease with which God touched him and dislocated his hip showed who was in control and that his fight was indeed with God. It also revealed to Jacob that though he was winning, his success was not due to his own prowess but to the grace of God, who had allowed him to prevail.

Jacob continued the fight

After the debilitating touch the struggle changed to one where Jacob hung on until he was blessed. This is interpreted for us as an example of one who was persistent in prayer with tears (Hosea 12:4). All through his early life in Canaan, Jacob had been struggling to obtain the covenant blessing and it had involved his own ingenuity and deception. In God he met more than his match, yet God condescended to engage him in a struggle. This time he won the blessing legitimately through his struggle with God. At the same time it kept him humble and reliant on account of his dislocated hip. Paul was allowed to see unspeakable glory, but he was also given a 'thorn in the flesh' to keep him humble. God did not allow Jacob to re-enter the promised land as Jacob, cunning and deceiving, but as Israel. He also learned, like Paul, that the Lord's grace is sufficient and that his strength is made perfect in our weakness (2 Cor.12:9).

Brothers united (33:1-17)

We have all known times when we have had to brace ourselves and 'face the music'. Even though we may have prayed and made what preparations we could, we are still apprehensive. The dreaded day came for Jacob: **'Esau was coming, and with him were four hundred men'** (33:1). It is a tense moment in the narrative.

1. Final preparations (33:1-2)

Jacob again took precautions by dividing his children up into groups. To save the 'seed' he divided his family into three. He put the children of the maids in front with their mothers, then **'Leah and her children behind, and Rachel and Joseph last'** (33:2). Rachel was his first love and he no doubt thought that Joseph was the one who would follow in the line of promise. Unlike the pre-Penuel Jacob, however, he was prepared to go ahead of the company and face his brother (33:3). Having had power to prevail with God, he was strengthened in spirit to confront Esau (see 32:28).

2. The meeting (33:3-7)

As he approached his brother, Jacob respectfully bowed to the ground seven times, according to ancient protocol. Esau, on the other hand, dispensed with ceremony and ran to greet him, embracing him with kisses and tears. God had done for Jacob what he can still do for his people today, 'exceedingly abundantly above all that we ask or think' (Eph. 3:20).

3. The present (33:8-11)

Having introduced his family, Jacob pressed Esau to receive the present. The gift had three functions.

Firstly, it had been sent **'to find favour'** (33:8; see 32:20: 'I will appease him'). The present was a kind of propitiatory offering to appease Esau's wrath. Esau replied that he did not need the animals (33:9).

Secondly, when Jacob saw that he did not need to be pacified, he encouraged Esau to accept **'my present'** as a kind of thank offering.[10]

Thirdly, Jacob called the gift **'my blessing'** (33:11). By using this term he brought to mind the incident when Jacob had stolen the blessing from Esau. Although he could not give back the blessing itself, he could share its fruits with his brother. He was trying to make amends. Jacob **'urged him'** to accept it and so Esau **'took it'**. By Esau's taking the gift Jacob was assured that he was truly reconciled to his brother.

There is an important principle here. If we have wronged someone, it is not only necessary to seek God's forgiveness, but to seek to be reconciled with the person we have wronged (see Matt. 5:23-24). We should make restitution where necessary (Luke 19:8) and show that we are sorry in some tangible way.

A contrast is drawn between godly Jacob and ungodly Esau. Esau said, **'I have enough,'** but he did not acknowledge that his wealth came from God (33:9), whereas Jacob, when he said, **'I have enough,'** saw his possessions as the result of God's grace (33:11; see 33:5). His twenty years' experience in exile had humbled him and made him aware that he owed everything to God's favour.

4. The peaceful separation (33:12-17)

Generous Esau invited Jacob to follow him back to Seir (later called Edom). When Jacob made the excuse that he would need to travel slowly in view of the frailty of his children and the newborn among his livestock, Esau offered him an escort. Jacob also declined this second offer (33:15).

Esau moved directly south to his home in the mountains, whereas Jacob moved only a short distance north and west of Penuel, to Succoth in the Jordan valley (33:16-17; see Joshua 13:27). He built a house there **'and made booths for his live-stock'** (33:17).[11] No doubt he felt the need to rest and recuperate after the excitement of leaving Haran and his meeting with Esau.

But Jacob was not straightforward with his brother. Though he was a changed man as a result of his encounters with God at Bethel and Penuel and his disciplining experiences with Laban, he was not a perfect man. Jacob was probably right not to trust his brother too far. He was also right not to go to live in Seir. Canaan was the land of his fathers. But why did he need to deceive his brother when Esau had been so kind to him? The human heart is 'deceitful above all things, and desperately wicked; who can know it?' (Jer. 17:9). If people like Abraham and Isaac could lie and deceive we should not be surprised to find Jacob committing similar sins. The ugliness of the old sinful nature still spoils the testimony of God's children in this world. We are urged: 'Putting away lying, let each one of you speak truth with his neighbour' (Eph. 4:25).

Settled in Canaan (33:18-20)

After resting on the borders, Jacob finally moved safely[12] over the Jordan to the city belonging to Shechem, **'which is in the land of Canaan'** (33:18). This settlement was the first place mentioned when Abraham came into Canaan and where he built an altar. It is understandable to find Jacob pitching his tent and building an altar in this same region when he re-entered Canaan from Haran.

Abraham passed on to his son one burial plot of ground he had bought from the sons of Heth. A second piece of ground was bought by Jacob from **'the children of Hamor, Shechem's father'** (33:19). On this land Jacob built an altar which he called **'El Elohe Israel'** ('God, the God of Israel'). By so naming the altar, he acknowledged that the God of Bethel who had changed his name to Israel at Penuel was his God. Thus he fulfilled part of the vow made at Bethel that 'If God will be with me ... so that I come back to my father's house in peace, then the LORD shall be my God' (see 28:20-21).

Joyce Baldwin has written, 'Two generations on from Abraham all the covenanted purposes of God were vested in one man, Jacob, and his sons. Was it possible that from so small and unpromising a beginning the whole world could be significantly changed? In terms of human understanding the proposition was highly unlikely, but there was dynamism in the word of the Lord, and it would not fail. Jesus saw his own ministry in a similar light; it was "like a grain of mustard seed..." (Mark 4:30-32).'[13]

32.
The children of Jacob

Please read Genesis 34:1 – 35:29

The incident recorded in chapter 34 again puts God's promises in jeopardy. Yet, despite human folly, the divine purposes are accomplished and Jacob settles in the family home.

Rape and massacre (34:1-31)

Jacob had camped near the Canaanite city of Shechem and he remained there for a considerable time. Isaac had never settled in the area and Abraham had moved on quickly from Shechem to the Bethel region. This, along with Jacob's own experience at Bethel, should have encouraged him to move on. But instead of making his way to Bethel, which was only about another day's journey, he settled for the quiet life. The area was a good place to do business. He would have found the lush pastures around Shechem very tempting. Like Lot, he was attracted by worldly values and pitched his tent too near the Canaanite city. Jacob forgot his calling to be a stranger and pilgrim. We can, as Christians, get so caught up with making money, setting up lovely homes and enjoying the benefits of this life that we lose sight of the fact that 'Our citizenship is in heaven.'

When Abraham came to Shechem, the text sounded a warning note: 'And the Canaanites were then in the land' (12:6). Jacob should have known better than to put himself and his family in such danger. Parents have a great responsibility to consider their children's spiritual and moral well-being when they move house. God is absent from this chapter, yet, as so often in the history of man's inhumanity to man, religion played a significant part in the sordid incident.

1. Defilement (34:1-4)

The story of Dinah is sadly that of many young people today. Dinah was a typical teenager, brought up in a religious home, but fascinated by the attractions of the world. Dinah was the 'kid' sister of Leah's six sons. By this time she must have been about fifteen years old. With so many half and full brothers older than herself around her, Dinah **'went out to see the daughters of the land'** (34:1). She wanted to be with girls of her own age, to catch up on the latest fashions and enjoy the pleasures of city life.

Dinah was no ordinary peasant girl, but the daughter of a foreign herdsman of considerable wealth. This is, no doubt, why high society became attracted to her. Finding himself alone with her, Prince Shechem, the son of the ruler of those parts, took advantage of her. He **'lay with her'**[1] and **'violated her'**.[2] We often read of young women out in the early hours of the morning, after a night of clubbing, being raped and murdered. They are asking for trouble. It does not excuse the criminal behaviour, but wise children will heed the advice of their parents not to be out late and on their own.

Having seduced her, Shechem tried to woo her (34:3). How typical this is of modern life! Sex before marriage is the order of the day. God's Word plainly teaches marriage before sex (2:24). Shechem had reversed the biblical order. Having defiled her, **'His soul was strongly attracted to Dinah'**, and **'he loved'** her and **'spoke kindly'** to her.[3] This was the one thing in his favour. Instead of despising her, as Amnon did in the case of Tamar (2 Sam. 13:14-19), or being compelled to marry her, as the Mosaic law would later require, Shechem wanted to marry her. He therefore requested his father, **'Get me this young woman as a wife'** (34:4; cf. Judg. 14:2). It was the normal practice for the parents to arrange the marriage. The difference in this case was that Shechem had committed rape and the girl was already living in his house (34:26).

2. Deception (34:5-24)

Jacob remained remarkably unruffled when he heard that his daughter had been defiled. It was **'Dinah his daughter'** who had been violated and yet he **'held his peace'** until his sons came home (34:5). On hearing of the rape of Tamar, David was very angry. Jacob's lack of action may have been diplomatic, but his lack of emotion was unnatural. When his favourite son, Joseph, was reported missing, assumed killed, he was devastated. Had Jacob given up on the daughter of his unloved wife Leah? Had he left her older brothers to be responsible for her?

When Jacob's sons heard what had happened, they **'were grieved and very angry'** (34:7). Their reaction was like that of God over the wickedness that existed in Noah's day (6:6). The sons of Jacob knew that a shameful act had been committed and that it had repercussions for the whole of Jacob's clan (**'a disgraceful thing in Israel'**). Moses emphasizes the immorality of it by adding that it was **'a crime which ought not to be done'**. The contrast between Jacob's attitude and that of his sons could not be greater.

Shechem went with Hamor his father to negotiate the marriage. Hamor intended speaking to Jacob (34:6), but in the event Hamor and his son met with Dinah's brothers as well as her father. Hamor expressed no sorrow for the wrong committed and there was not the faintest hint of censure from Jacob's lips. In fact, Jacob took a back seat in the negotiations. His sons listened to what the ruler and his son had to say in stony silence. They were forced to listen to the Canaanites because Dinah was already in Shechem's house.

The Canaanites' case (34:8-12)

In requesting on behalf of Shechem the hand of Dinah in marriage, Hamor was very diplomatic and stressed his son's genuine love for her (34:8). Then he proposed large-scale intermarrying between Jacob's household and the inhabitants of Shechem (34:9). Hamor also spelled out the economic and social benefits (34:10). He had his own agenda, as his speech to his own people makes clear, but he made out a good case to Jacob and his sons. Shechem, however, brought them back to the main issue, his marriage to Dinah. He was so desperate that he was prepared to pay any amount as a **'dowry and gift'** ('the bridal price' — 34:11-12).

The brothers' response (34:13-17)

In responding to Shechem's impassioned plea and Hamor's shrewd speech, Jacob's sons raised a fundamental religious stumbling-block to the proposed union of the two communities. To allow their sister to marry an uncircumcised man would, they said, **'be a reproach to us'** (34:14; cf. 30:23). For there to be full integration, all the Canaanite males of Shechem would need to be circumcised. In their argument, they used the covenant stipulation that 'Every male child among you shall be circumcised' (17:10). This proposal would have been seen by the Canaanites as part of an initiation ceremony into marriage rather than having any spiritual significance. If the proposal was not accepted, the brothers were prepared to take their sister **'and be gone'** (34:17). There is the suggestion of force being used if necessary to bring Dinah home. They could describe her in one breath as their **'sister'** (34:14) and in the next as **'our daughter'** (34:17), for they were negotiating both as her brothers and as her guardians.

In this reply, we are informed that the sons of Jacob **'spoke deceitfully'** (34:13). Like father, like sons! In their eyes Shechem had done a shocking thing which had affected the good name of the whole family. All their religious talk was part of an equally shocking plan of vengeance which they felt was justified.

The Canaanites accept the terms (34:18-24)

The unsuspecting Canaanites readily agreed to the proposal. Hamor gathered the representative men of the city together at the recognized public meeting-place, just inside the city gate, and explained to them all the advantages of an alliance with Jacob's clan (34:20-21). In order to encourage them to accept the deal and to agree to undergo an unpleasant operation, Hamor diplomatically said nothing of the concessions he had made. Instead, he stressed that his people would become rich at the expense of Jacob and his sons (34:22-23). Circumcision was a small price to pay for gaining so much. Little did they realize what was being planned. Far from being **'at peace'** with them (34:21), **'these men'** were about to kill them. While the men of Shechem dreamed of taking their women and possessions, Jacob's sons were preparing to plunder the city. Hamor's son, Shechem, led the way in getting circumcised. He did it because **'he delighted in Jacob's daughter'** (34:19). The people submitted to it because of Hamor's appealing word and his son's example, for they held him in high honour

(34:19,24). All the adult men capable of fighting (**'all who
went out of the gate of his city'**) were circumcised (34:24).

3. *Destruction* (34:25-31)

The painful effects of circumcision would have been particularly intense by the third day. This was when two of the oldest
brothers of Dinah made their surprise attack on the city. Acting like a couple of SAS men, Simeon and Levi (probably
with their servants), stormed the city while the fighting men
were incapacitated. They killed all the males, including Hamor
and Shechem, took Dinah from Shechem's house and escaped
(34:25-26). Other sons of Jacob then continued where the two
brothers had left off. They plundered the city and its surrounding area, taking all they could lay their hands on (34:27-29).
Instead of the Canaanites gaining from Jacob, it was Jacob
who had become rich as a result of this massacre.

No one comes out of this incident unscathed. Jacob, as
head of his household, did not deal with the affair in a decisive
way. Even at the end his response draws attention to his fears
and lack of faith in God: **'I shall be destroyed, my household and I'** (34:30). On the other hand, Simeon and Levi
overreacted and gave God a bad name among their neighbours. Their action reminds us of what happened when Israel
entered Canaan under Joshua. On that occasion the Israelites
were called to exterminate the Canaanites for their sins, according to the strict rules that God had laid down. Simeon and
Levi had gone ahead of God's purposes. The time had not yet
come for the Canaanites to be removed (15:16). What is more,
they had mowed down a people who had entered into an agreement with them. Joshua did not do that when the Gibeonites
tricked Israel into making a covenant with them. However,
the last words spoken by Simeon and Levi do make the point
that Shechem's treatment of their sister was a heinous crime.

It prepares us for the later action of the faithful Levites during the golden-calf incident (Exod. 32:26-29).

Joy and sorrow (35:1-29)

Unlike the previous chapter, God is mentioned. He appears, is worshipped and is remembered.

1. Jacob returns to Bethel (35:1-15)

It was about ten years since Jacob had returned to Canaan.

The divine call

Jacob was told to go to Bethel and live there, where God had first appeared to him. It was about thirty miles south of Shechem. Why did God instruct him to do this?

Firstly, *at Bethel he had made a vow* (28:20-22; 31:13). Since his return to Canaan no mention has been made of this vow. Had Jacob forgotten? This reminder gently disturbed his conscience.

Secondly, *Jacob had brought his family too close to the ungodly world.* 'He pitched his tent towards the city' (33:18). The last time that phrase appeared was in relation to Lot and Sodom. It did not do Lot any good and it brought trouble to Jacob and his family. The fact that an altar had been built there did not alter the situation (33:20). In fact, it made matters worse. God was now associated with a most atrocious act. Jacob was, therefore, instructed to build an altar at Bethel. This is the only occasion in Genesis where God directs someone to build an altar.

Thirdly, as a result of the treacherous action in the name of religion, *the family had become repugnant in the eyes of their*

neighbours and were in danger of being the subjects of revenge killing (34:30). God reminded Jacob of the time he had
fled from his brother. It was at Bethel he had promised to
protect him and bring him back.

Jacob's response

He moved quickly to obey. He prepared himself and his family
to worship at Bethel by urging them to do four things.

First, they were to **'Put away ... foreign gods'**. These
could have been the gods that Rachel had stolen from Laban
(31:19), other idols that his servants had brought, or they could
have been gods taken as spoil from the people of Shechem
(34:27-29). Worship of other gods is incompatible with serving the true God (Exod. 20:3; Josh. 24:14,23-24). Christians
are urged to 'Flee from idolatry' (1 Cor. 10:14).

Secondly, he told them to **'Purify yourselves'**. They were
unclean. Jacob was aware of the pollution which the previous
incident had caused. Rape and bloodshed made them outwardly
unclean. Worshipping the holy God demanded inward and
outward purity. In the law of Moses ritual washings of the
body and clothes and shaving were expressions of the need
for inner spiritual cleansing. When the Israelites arrived at Sinai
they were called to prepare themselves to meet God (Exod.
19:10-15). In coming near to God, the command is still:
'Cleanse your hands, you sinners; and purify your hearts, you
double-minded' (James 4:8).

The third instruction was to **'Change your garments'**.
Again, this was associated with washing. It represented respect for God and a new way of life (see 41:14). The New
Testament calls us to 'Put on the Lord Jesus Christ, and make
no provision for the flesh' (Rom. 13:14). Those united to Christ
are called to put off the characteristics of the old life in Adam

and to put on the characteristics that belong to life in Christ (Col. 3:8-14).

Finally, they were to **'Go up to Bethel'**. Jacob told his family what Bethel had meant to him. God had wonderfully answered the prayers he had made there. The implication is that Jacob had been slow to respond and worship at the place where God had revealed himself. God was associated with the places of revelation in these early times. Now that God has been seen in the flesh and has ascended to glory he has promised to be specially present wherever people meet in the name of Jesus.

The family's response

They put away the gods and the earrings. Possibly the earrings had idolatrous significance. Earrings were among the items used to make the golden calf (Exod. 32:2-4). They gave up everything directly or indirectly associated with idolatry. On the other hand, the earrings may have been part of the booty taken from the people of Shechem and considered inappropriate for those approaching God (see Num. 31:21-24). Why Jacob hid them under the terebinth tree, rather than destroying them, is not certain. But anything that is going to hinder our worship of God must be surrendered. Not everything can be consecrated to God. Magic books had to be burned. We are also called to put to death sinful passions. Sin must be dealt with in a ruthless way.

> The dearest idol I have known,
> Whate'er that idol be,
> Help me to tear it from thy throne,
> And worship only thee.
>
> (William Cowper)

The journey (35:5)

As they set out in obedience to God's word, they knew God's
protection. Jacob's experience in Canaan anticipated that of
his descendants when they conquered the land (Deut. 7:20-24).
When God is among his people to bless them, they are
invincible.

Worship at Bethel (35:6-8)

The importance of God's revelation at this place is conveyed
through the repetition of what has been said in chapter 28. At
Shechem Jacob had called the altar 'God the God of Israel'.
He called the place where he now sacrificed **'El Bethel'** ('God
of the house of God'). Instead of thinking of God in relation
to himself and his change of name, he thought of God alone.
The statement concerning the past suggests that he fulfilled
his vow although it does not actually say so (35:7).

While we have this link with the past renewed, another link
with the past is broken. His mother's nurse, Deborah, died.
Rebekah, Jacob's mother, had left her home in Haran with her
nurse many years earlier to become Isaac's wife (24:59). Why
Deborah's death is recorded and not Rebekah's is strange.
Evidently Rebekah had died before Jacob came back to Canaan.

Renewal of the covenant (35:9-15)

The revelation at Penuel was reconfirmed at Bethel. God appeared again to him, talked with him and blessed him. His
name Israel was a sign of God's blessing. Jacob received the
strongest statement of God's covenant promises that he ever
heard. At the end of his life, when he was blessing Joseph's
sons, he recalled this occasion (48:3-4).

God introduced himself as **'God Almighty'** (35:11; 17:1), the God who can do what seems impossible to humans. The call to be fruitful and multiply reminds us of the creation blessing and what God had said to Noah and Abraham (1:28; 9:1; 17:2,6). The promises also included becoming a nation, with many nations coming from him, a royal line and the assurance that the land promised to Abraham would be his. The statement that **'God went up from him'** recalls 17:22.

After such wonderful promises, Jacob set up a more permanent monument, pouring a drink offering and oil over it. The renewal of the covenant promises encouraged him to confirm the name of the place as Bethel.

2. Sin and sadness in Jacob's family (35:16-29)

The death and burial of Rachel (35:16-20)

As Jacob journeyed south from Bethel to Ephrath tragedy struck the family again. The woman who had cried to Jacob, 'Give me children, or else I die', died giving birth to her second son. She had named her first son Joseph expecting that God would give her another (30:24). During difficulties in the delivery, the midwife encouraged her with the news that she would have a son. As her life ebbed away, she was able to name him Ben-Oni ('Son of sorrow') but his father called him Benjamin ('Son of the right hand').[4] The right side was the specially favoured side (see Ps. 110:1) and suggests that Jacob saw this son, the only one born in the land of promise, as of special significance. Benjamin was, in fact, born in territory that would later be allocated to his descendants (1 Sam. 10:2).

Some dear missionary friends lost their twenty-eight-year-old missionary daughter from a brain tumour. Hours earlier she had given birth to a healthy little girl whom she was able to cuddle before she died. As in Jacob's case, joy came out of much sorrow.

Rachel's body was not buried in the family cemetery near Hebron but in the area where she gave birth and died. To mark the spot and as a memorial to his favourite wife, Jacob set up a pillar which was still standing centuries later. The modern tomb that tourists are told is where she is buried cannot be authentic. It is interesting that the passage associates her with Bethlehem, the birthplace of David and David's greater son. Rachel was later idealized as the mother of Israel weeping for her exiled children and is used by Matthew to show that hope comes through Jesus the Messiah (Jer. 31:15; Matt. 2:17-18).

The sons of Jacob (35:21-26)

More sorrow for Jacob is evidenced here with the brief account of Reuben's disgraceful action. His sin was not simply sexually motivated. He was probably attempting to usurp his father's position as head of the household in much the same way as Absalom attempted to do (2 Sam. 16:21-23).

This shocking act by Reuben, along with the extreme violence of Simeon and Levi, indicates why these three oldest sons lost favour with their father (see 49:3-7). As the following list shows, Judah is next in line of the sons of Leah. We are already being prepared for the final section of Genesis where, contrary to expectations, Judah takes the leading position in the line of promise.

The birth of Jacob's last son and the wicked act of Jacob's first-born son prompt a summary statement concerning the sons of Jacob, all of whom, apart from Benjamin, **'were born to him in Padan Aram'**. Their names are not listed according to order of birth but according to the one who gave birth. The list begins with the sons of his first wife Leah (35:23), then Rachel's sons (35:24) and closes with the sons of the maids, Bilhah (35:25) and Zilpah (35:26). This is the first of three listings of Jacob's sons in Genesis and indicates their importance in God's future purposes (see 46:8-27; 49:3-27).[5]

The death and burial of Isaac (35:27-29)

The account of Isaac's death is very similar to that of Abraham's death (25:7-11). It tells of Isaac's age at death, 180 years, how he **'breathed his last and died, and was gathered to his people, being old and full of days'**, and how both his sons were present to bury him.

The paragraph shows that God fulfilled his promises to Jacob in that he **'came to his father Isaac at Mamre ... where Abraham and Isaac had sojourned'**. The purchase of the burial site at this place was a sign of faith in God's promises. Neither sin nor death can frustrate God's purposes for his people. While Bethel reminds us that the 'house of God', with all the promises attached, is to be prized above all human habitations, Mamre (or Hebron) encourages us to live on earth looking in faith to the coming Deliverer and the defeat of sin, Satan and death itself. 'By faith Isaac blessed Jacob and Esau concerning things to come' (Heb. 11:20).

Part 10:
What Esau produced (36:1 – 37:1)

33.
The Edomites

Please read Genesis 36:1 – 37:1

Before continuing with the main line of descent through Jacob, we have this brief survey of Esau and what he produced. As we saw with Ishmael, the offspring of the non-elect elder son is considered before proceeding with the chosen line.

The unusual feature is the repetition of the formula: **'This is the genealogy of Esau'** (36:1,9). Two sections (36:1-8; 36:9 – 37:1) are devoted to Esau. The nearest example to this is in the case of Shem (10:1,21-31; 11:10-26). The double entries have the effect of calling our attention to their importance. Shem, as we saw, is in the line of promise but although Esau is not, we are not allowed to dismiss him. He is important in his own right and his descendants become a significant factor in relation to Israel.

Esau and his family (36:1-8)

This section is concerned with Esau's immediate family and where they settled.

1. Encouragement

The section highlights the fact that Esau was blessed with offspring and many possessions in the land of Canaan. Five sons

'were born to him in the land of Canaan' (36:5) and he had become a very wealthy man **'in the land of Canaan'** (36:6). All this was in fulfilment of his father's inspired blessing on him (27:39). As God brought promised blessings to Ishmael, so he did to Esau. What is more, Esau had found prosperity in the land promised to Abraham, Isaac and Jacob. If the non-elect line saw promised blessing in Canaan, then this was further encouragement to Israel to believe that all the blessings promised to their forefathers would be fulfilled in God's good time. Those promises are fully realized in Christ the Lord.

For us, too, who believe in Christ for salvation, the grand finale still lies in the future. We walk by faith, not by sight. Scoffers ridicule and our faith is tested, but we look forward with great anticipation to the appearing of our great God and Saviour Jesus Christ. If unbelieving Esau experienced the promised temporal blessings, how much more will believers enter into the promised heavenly inheritance guaranteed by Jesus' resurrection and the indwelling Spirit!

2. Warning

This section was a warning to Israel not to treat with contempt God's covenant into which, by God's grace, they were born and brought up. We today are urged not to despise the Christian influences on our lives. It is a great privilege to grow up in a godly home, or to be taught the Bible by Christian teachers at school or church. Even more serious warnings are given to those who turn away having experienced many of the blessings of the new covenant (Heb. 6:4-6).

Esau despised his birthright

'Esau, who is Edom' (36:1,8). Esau, who was red when he was born, was called Edom ('red') in memory of the time when he sold his birthright because of his craving for the 'red' stew (25:25,30). Whereas the bad associations of Jacob's name are superseded by his experience of God at Penuel and his change of name to Israel, Esau's link with the despising of his birthright is retained and emphasized. The future nation that arose from Jacob and the place where they lived are known, not by the name that is connected with his past behaviour as a supplanter, but by the name of Israel, which means 'wrestler with God' (32:28). On the other hand, the place and the people linked with Esau are known as Edom. Both at the beginning and end of the section our attention is drawn to this: **'Esau, who is Edom... Esau is Edom'** (36:1,8). He is for ever associated with the 'red stuff', rather than with the unseen, spiritual blessings associated with God's covenant.

Hebrews draws our attention to this as it warns against spurning the grace of God (Heb. 12:15-17). Esau sold his birthright 'for one morsel of food'. His action betrayed a settled attitude that despised God and his promises. What is more, his attitude not only affected his own actions, but it had a detrimental effect on succeeding generations. 'Esau is Edom,' is a warning to us all.

Esau despised his family roots

'Esau took his wives from the daughters of Canaan' (36:2). These words recall his ungodly way of life. He had no real interest in his family roots. The chosen family meant nothing to him. Instead of keeping himself apart from the sinful people around him, he came into the closest possible union with them, again to the detriment of his soul and his offspring. So many have become entangled in close relationships with unbelievers and this has sadly led them away from the Lord.

We were informed earlier that Esau had three wives: Judith the daughter of Beeri, Basemath the daughter of Elon (26:34)

and Mahalath the daughter of Ishmael (28:9). These are probably their birth-names. In the present passage his three wives
have been given other names, which was not an uncommon
practice, then as now. We have all met people who are known
by names quite different to the ones on their birth certificates.

Judith has become Aholibamah. She was the daughter of
the well-finder (Beeri) whose family name was Anah (see
36:20,25). Aholibamah is also said to be 'the daughter of
Zibeon the Hivite' in the sense of descendant or granddaughter
of Zibeon (not the Zibeon of 36:20,24 who was a brother of
Anah her father). These Hivites are spoken of later as Horites
(36:20) in much the same way as Welsh people are often classed
as English! Basemath, the daughter of Elon, has become known
as Adah, while Mahalath the daughter of Ishmael has become
Basemath.

Esau despised the land of promise

Esau **'went to a country away from the presence of his
brother Jacob... So Esau dwelt in Mount Seir'** (36:6-8).
Jacob and Esau had been blessed with material possessions,
for we are told that **'Their possessions were too great for
them to dwell together, and the land where they were
strangers could not support them'** (36:7). These words echo
what is said of Abraham and Lot (13:6). Prosperity brought
its problems and, as they did not own the promised land, they
found it difficult to live together. Although Esau was in Seir
when Jacob returned from Haran, he still had a stake in Canaan
up to the time of his father's death. Jacob's presence with his
large family and livestock meant that the area where they lived
was not capable of sustaining them all. Esau, therefore, decided to take his family and possessions and move out of
Canaan, 'away from the presence of his brother', and to settle
permanently in Seir. Thus was fulfilled the other part of the

blessing given him by his father. He broke his brother's yoke from his neck (27:40).

Like Lot, Esau moved east away from the land which God had promised to give to Abraham's descendants. In doing so Esau turned his back on God's gift and on the places that had become precious to his grandfather and father. Esau lived by sight rather than by faith. He looked for present gain and advantage and despised the divine promises and everything associated with God's revelation. He found his pleasure in the things of this world. Let us make sure that we are not among those like Esau 'who draw back to perdition, but of those who believe to the saving of the soul' (Heb. 10:39).

Without realizing it Esau fulfilled God's purposes by leaving Canaan free for the chosen family line to inherit. God predestinates, but human beings choose and are responsible for their actions. Jacob had returned from exile to live in the land God had promised him, but God by his providence gave 'Mount Seir to Esau as a possession' (Deut. 2:5).

3. Reminder

The fact that Esau and his descendants were not of the chosen line did not give Israel grounds for hating them, or treating them with disdain. This section devoted to Esau, 'who is Edom', reminded Israel that they were brothers (36:6). They were the twin sons of Isaac and Rebekah. They were in a much closer relationship than that which existed between Isaac and Ishmael or Abraham and Lot. Israel was again reminded of this in the law dealing with those who were to be excluded from full membership of the covenant community. Though 'Esau is Edom', who later refused the Israelites access through Edomite territory, Israel was commanded: 'You shall not abhor an Edomite, for he is your brother.' The grandchildren of Edomites who took up residence within Israel could become full members of the worshipping community (Deut. 23:7-8).

Close relatives of Christians can be very cruel. Jesus warns that 'Brother will deliver up brother to death, and a father his child' (Matt. 10:21-22). Though we can expect to be hated by all for Jesus' sake, we are still called to love our enemies (Matt. 5:44-45). When such enemies become Christians they are to be welcomed into the fellowship. When the apostle Paul was converted the Jewish believers in Jerusalem were reticent to receive him because 'They were all afraid of him, and did not believe that he was a disciple.' But we read that Barnabas, the encourager, 'took him and brought him to the apostles' (Acts 9:26-27).

The Edomite nation in Seir (36:9-43)

This additional section falls into three parts. The first concerns the sons of Esau and their children who became chiefs of Edom (36:10-19); the second consists of a family tree of Seir's sons, called chiefs, who inhabited the area when Esau conquered them (36:20-30); the final part lists the kings of Edom and **'the chiefs of Esau'** (36:31-43).

1. Esau had many descendants

Five sons and ten grandsons are mentioned (36:10-14). God was clearly fulfilling the promise made to Abraham and Isaac even along branches that did not belong to the main trunk.

Teman, one of the grandsons of Esau, gave his name to a district and a tribe of that name in Edom. The inhabitants of Teman were renowned for their wisdom (Jer. 49:7). Eliphaz, one of Job's friends, was called a Temanite (Job 2:11). He was a wise man who had a great respect for God. Job was instructed by God to offer sacrifice and intercede for him (Job 42:7-10). This is one example of people who did not belong to the line of promise but who nevertheless participated in the spiritual blessings of the promise. They remind us that our background is no barrier to divine grace.

2. The origin of the Amalekites

One of Esau's sons, Eliphaz, had a **'concubine'**, or secondary wife, called Timna. She was the sister of one of the leaders of the Horites in Seir (36:22) and **'She bore Amalek to Eliphaz'** (36:12). Because Amalek did not have the same mother as the other sons of Eliphaz it may be that he was ostracized by his brothers and that it was this that led him to live in a separate area.[1] The Amalekites were called 'the first of the nations' (Num. 24:20), probably because they were the first to wage war on Israel after they left Egypt (Exod. 17:8-13). As they 'did not fear God', but attacked a weary, defenceless people, Israel was directed to 'blot out the remembrance of Amalek from under heaven' (Deut. 25:17-19).

3. Edomite chiefs

Esau increased in power and influence and his descendants soon organized themselves into political and administrative units. His ten grandsons and the three sons of his wife Aholibamah became **'chiefs'** (36:15-19). The term 'chief' is associated with the word for 'a thousand' and seems to have been an Edomite name for a leader of a tribe.[2]

The words, **'These were the sons of Esau, who is Edom, and these were their chiefs'** (36:19), indicate that these sons and grandsons had become heads of tribes which formed the Edomite nation. By contrast Jacob's descendants lagged behind. At the time of the Exodus they still had no land and could not call themselves a nation. But, as Matthew Henry comments, 'God's promise to Jacob began to work late, but the effect of it remained longer, and it had its complete accomplishment in the spiritual Israel.'

4. *The sons of Seir*

'Edom' and 'Seir' are often used synonymously in the Old Testament. This passage helps us to see why, especially the paragraph concerning the sons of Seir (36:20-30). **'The land of Edom'** (36:21) is also spoken of as **'the land of Seir'** (36:30). The original inhabitants of the area conquered by Esau were Horites. These Horites are not to be identified with the well-known Hurrians who occupied parts of Syria and Canaan in the time of Moses. We find the Horites 'in their mountain of Seir' when the kings of the East attacked them in the days of Abraham (14:6). The name 'Hore' means 'hole', suggesting that these Horites were cave-dwellers and, certainly, the towering red sandstone rocks of Edom are full of ornately carved caves. The area occupied by these Horites is called Seir, which is the name of the father of the Horites. Seir probably gave his name to the region. Concerning these Horites, we are later informed that 'The descendants of Esau dispossessed them and destroyed them from before them, and dwelt in their place' (Deut. 2:12). Prior to this, Esau had married the daughter of Anah, one of the descendants of Seir (36:2,20,25) and his son Eliphaz married the sister of one of the clan's leaders (36:12,22). With this intermarrying between Esau's family and Seir's descendants, we can understand why the genealogy of Esau contains these **'sons of Seir'** and **'chiefs of the Horites'**. Not all the Horites were destroyed; some of Seir's descendants were absorbed into the Edomite community and their leaders are identified (36:20-30).

The interesting little comment concerning **'the Anah who found the water in the wilderness as he pastured the donkeys of his father Zibeon'** (36:24) is given to distinguish him from his uncle who had the same name (36:20,25). Such incidental information also reminds us that we are dealing with real, not imaginary, people.

This conquering and subduing of the original inhabitants of Edom by Esau's family anticipated the conquering of Canaan by the Israelites nearly five hundred years later. Those who stood in the line of promise had to wait for the working out of God's promises and all God's people are called to wait patiently for him. Let us remember that God's time is always the right time.

5. Edomite kings

The Edomites had kings as well as chiefs. **'Now these were the kings that reigned in the land of Edom'** (36:31) heads a paragraph naming eight kings (36:32-39). What is interesting in this list is that there is no father-son succession and the capital city changes with each king. Some of the place-names, such as Bozrah (36:33) and Teman (36:34), are known but the others remain uncertain. The two Hadads named are distinguished in that the first is said to have **'attacked Midian in the field of Moab'** (36:35), while the second (called Hadar in the NKJV) is known as having a wife of some importance, in that her mother and grandmother are named (36:39). The death of each king is noted apart from the last, which may indicate that Hadad was alive in the time of Moses. We read later how Moses sent messengers to the King of Edom to ask permission to pass through his territory (Num. 20:14-17).

One of the main reasons for mentioning these Edomite rulers is to show that there were kings in Edom **'before any**

king reigned over the children of Israel' (36:31). It is often assumed that this allusion to monarchy in Israel must mean that this section was inserted into Genesis in the time of King David. But kings had been prophesied among the descendants of Abraham and Sarah (17:6,16) and Jacob had been told by God that 'Kings shall come from your body' (35:11). Moses was also directed to give instruction to Israel on the subject of kingship (Deut. 17:14-20). Though Esau, who is Edom, was first in achieving nationhood and kingly rule, Jacob, who is Israel, had to wait many centuries for these promised items to find some fulfilment. Their complete realization comes with the promised 'Seed' who defeated the ruler of this world and set up a kingdom which is everlasting. As in the days of Cain, worldly people seem to advance rapidly. The kingdoms of this world seem to flourish at the expense of the kingdom of God. But though it delay, wait for it. Be assured, the final announcement will be: 'The kingdoms of this world have become the kingdoms of our Lord and of his Christ, and he shall reign for ever and ever!' (Rev. 11:15). It is interesting that the judgement pronounced on Edom by Obadiah ends on this note: 'And the kingdom shall be the LORD's' (Obad. 21).

6. The Edomites possessed the land

The list of chiefs in the final paragraph is given **'according to their families and their places'** (36:40). It seems that the names have more to do with administrative districts. The heads of clans had given their names to the districts over which the chiefs governed under the king. Like Israel, when they came into the land of promise, the land was parcelled out and each clan was given a specific area in which to live: **'These were the chiefs of Edom, according to their dwelling-places in the land of their possession'** (36:43). They not only took the land; they possessed every part of it. Great emphasis is put on these chiefs. The second half of each of the three parts of this section concerns the chiefs: **'the chiefs of the sons of Esau'** (36:15-19); **'the chiefs of the Horites'** (36:29-30); and **'the names of the chiefs of Esau'** (36:40-43). They administered the whole land in a most effective way. We find later in the case of Israel that when they did conquer Canaan, 'There [remained] very much land yet to be possessed' (Josh. 13:1). Unlike Esau, Israel was slow in possessing and administering the land. The prophet whose book is devoted to prophesying judgement on Edom is the one who also proclaims that 'The house of Jacob shall possess their possessions' (Obad. 17). God's people will finally and fully possess the land. The prophecy looks to the end-time state when the meek shall inherit the earth.

Calvin comments, 'There is, therefore, no reason why the faithful, who slowly pursue their way, should envy the quick children of this world their rapid succession of delights; since the felicity which the Lord promises them is far more stable, as it is expressed in the psalm, "The children's children shall dwell there, and their inheritance shall be perpetual" (Ps. 102:28).'[3]

7. Edom is a picture of a world destined for destruction

Most of this section (36:9-43) reappears at the end of the Old Testament era in 1 Chronicles 1:35-54. During the intervening period from Moses to the times of Ezra and Nehemiah, the relations between Israel and Edom deteriorated. Though Israel treated Edom as a brother, Moses found them hard and unbrotherly. Under King David the Edomites were defeated and came under his empire. Hadad, the Edomite prince who escaped to Egypt, later became a source of trouble to Solomon. There were various battles between Edom and Judah from the time of Jehoshaphat to Ahaz. The Edomites were a very proud people and assumed that their natural defences made them impregnable. Their unbrotherly attitude towards Judah was particularly shocking when Jerusalem was captured by the Babylonians. They rejoiced in the people's misery, helped themselves to the loot and even killed those who fled from the enemy (see Ps. 137:7; Lam. 4:21-22; Ezek. 25:12; 35:5,12). Both Obadiah and Jeremiah (Jer. 49:7-22) prophesy Edom's destruction. It lost its independence in the fifth century B.C. and was later controlled by the Nabateans.

The prophecies against Edom are seen as part of a bigger picture. Edom typifies the proud nations of the world who set themselves up against God and his people. Their pride is an affront to God. They act like the prince of darkness whom they serve. Edom becomes symbolic of the serpent's brood, those ungodly forces arrayed against the people of God. The judgement on Edom is an example of what lies ahead for a world in rebellion against God. The 'Seed' of the woman will bring an end to all opposition. 'For he must reign till he has put all enemies under his feet' (1 Cor. 15:25).

Esau's brother in Canaan (37:1)

1. Jacob and Esau contrasted

The final verse of this section contrasts sharply with the end of the previous section (36:8). Whereas 'Esau dwelt in Mount Seir', **'Jacob dwelt in the land where his father was a stranger, in the land of Canaan.'** While Esau moved away from his roots and the place promised by God, Jacob remained in the land of promise.

This verse concerning Jacob is also particularly appropriate following the summary statement concerning the Edomites (36:43). While Esau possessed the land he had conquered and settled in it as his permanent home, Jacob did not possess the land of Canaan. Like his fathers he was a stranger and a pilgrim on the earth. Esau had kings, land and tribal districts. Jacob had none of these earthly blessings that had been promised him. But he did have the blessing of knowing God and he was prepared to wait patiently for the rest.

Matthew Henry comments crisply, 'The children of this world have their all in hand, and nothing in hope (Luke 16:25); while the children of God have their all in hope, and next to nothing in hand. But, all things considered, it is better to have Canaan in promise than Mount Seir in possession.' The Christian lives by faith, not by sight, and we are not to envy the prosperity of the wicked, but to remember that their end is destruction (Ps. 73:1-28).

> 'The LORD is my portion,' says my soul,
> 'Therefore I hope in him!'
> The LORD is good to those who wait for him,
> To the soul who seeks him.
> It is good that one should hope and wait quietly
> For the salvation of the LORD
>
> (Lam. 3:22-26).

2. Chosen for salvation

Jacob and Esau are used in the Bible to illustrate the principle of God's sovereignty in salvation. Malachi states the truth in a startling way: 'Jacob have I loved; but Esau I have hated' (Mal. 1:2-3). It would be wrong to conclude from this that every Edomite is damned and every Israelite saved. The passage is referring to God's choice of Jacob to be in the family line that would lead to the Messiah. The prophet's words are taken up by the apostle Paul to show that being a child of God is not dependent on birth, or what a person does, but on God's choice and calling (Rom. 9:6-29). Not all who belong to Israel are the Israel of God. 'Jacob have I loved,' stands for all who have been chosen and called by God, however deprived their background and rebellious their past, but who by God's grace trust the promise of God in Christ. 'Esau have I hated' stands for all those who are excluded from salvation in Jesus Christ, however privileged their background and religious their lives, and who in the end remain stubbornly opposed to God and his Christ.

No one will be able to accuse God of being unfair or make the excuse that they did not believe because they were not chosen. We are all responsible for our actions as moral beings and if we are found guilty and condemned to hell on the Day of Judgement it will be because of our rebellion against God and our refusal to humble ourselves and receive God's salvation in Jesus Christ. Esau had every advantage to believe the promises but he deliberately went his own sinful way. Be like Jacob and let nothing hinder you from finding the blessing of sins forgiven and peace with God through our Lord Jesus Christ. 'Whoever calls upon the name of the LORD shall be saved' (Joel 2:32; see Rom. 9:30 – 10:13).

Part 11:
What Jacob produced (37:2 – 50:26)

34.
Jewish origins

Please read Genesis 37:2 – 38:30

The story of Joseph has held generations of children spell-bound. Adults too have continued to find it a fascinating account. This section, however, is not only about Joseph. The heading itself makes that clear (37:2). It concerns what Jacob produced, namely, his twelve sons and their activities.

Prominent themes in this final section

1. Promises

By the close of Genesis, there is a partial fulfilment of the promises made to Abraham. His descendants are protected by God, are associated with blessing and become a blessing to others. But complete realization still lay in the future. Possession of Canaan seemed further away than ever, yet the assurance is given that God would bring Israel back to the promised land.

2. Preparation

This final section prepares us for the events recorded in the book of Exodus. Abraham had been told that his 'descendants' (literally, his 'seed') would be 'strangers in a land that is not theirs' and that they would eventually return (15:13-16). The movement from Canaan to Egypt recalls this prophecy and we are prepared for the troubles ahead.

3. Providence

God is seen to be in control of all events. While Exodus opens with God intervening directly, Genesis closes with God hidden behind his providential activity through the twists and turns of good and evil circumstances.

4. Pattern

Derek Kidner notes that this section exhibits 'a human pattern that runs through the Old Testament to culminate at Calvary'.[1] Stephen reminded the Jewish council of how God's chosen ones were rejected and persecuted through the envy and unbelief of their own people. He began with the brothers' treatment of Joseph and ended with their opposition to Jesus (Acts 7:9,52). That pattern has continued from the time of Stephen to the present day.

5. Preview

It indicates the way the future history of Israel will look. While reference is made to all the sons of Jacob, the two who stand out are Joseph and Judah. The tribes of Joseph and Judah become the dominant ones in Israel. It also reveals that Judah is the chosen tribe who will produce the promised 'royal seed'. But it is Joseph's life that is presented as a preview of the kind of royal seed we are to expect. From within the Genesis account we can rightly consider Joseph to be a type of Christ.

Joseph and his brothers (37:2-36)

This is a story that could be repeated across the world, where favouritism, tale-bearing, holding grudges and murderous hatred bring division and grief to many a household.

1. Joseph (37:2-4)

The section opens by noting that Joseph was **'seventeen years old'** (37:2). There are a number of age references in this final part of Genesis. They enable us to appreciate the period in Jacob's life when Joseph was sold into Egypt and the length of time he spent there before he was elevated by Pharaoh at the age of thirty (41:46). Joseph was thirty-nine when he revealed his identity to his brothers (see 41:47; 45:6). He could not have been much older when he introduced his father, aged 130, to Pharaoh (47:9). This means that Jacob was about ninety when Joseph was born, and aged 107 when Joseph was seventeen. Genesis 25:26 informs us that Isaac was sixty when Jacob was born. Isaac died when he was aged 180 (35:28-29) which means that Isaac was still alive, aged about 167, when Joseph was seventeen years old.

Loved by his father

Jacob **'loved Joseph more than all his children'**. Joseph was the **'son of his old age'** (37:3), the first-born of his favourite wife, who had later died giving birth to Benjamin. For a parent to feel drawn to one particular child in the family is understandable. Trouble looms when that child is spoilt. Jacob seems to have learned nothing from his own experience as a child when his brother Esau was his father's favourite.

To express his love for Joseph, Jacob made him a very valuable garment. This **'tunic'**, traditionally known as the 'coat of

many colours', was probably a long colourful robe.² There
could not have been a more visible indication of Jacob's special
love for Joseph. Here was a garment fit for a king! When he
wore this distinctive robe it would have set him apart from the
rest of the family. Perhaps Jacob already had it in mind to give
Joseph the rights of the first-born son in place of Reuben (see
48:5-6; 1 Chr. 5:1-2).

Hated by his brothers

While the sons of Leah had good cause to be jealous of Joseph,
the sons of Bilhah and Zilpah had other reasons for despising
him. They would have hated him for bringing **'a bad report
of them'** to their father' (37:2).³ Joseph sided with his father
over against his brothers and we can understand their reaction.
No one likes a talebearer, even if the stories are true.

Joseph's special treatment caused resentment. **'When his
brothers saw that their father loved him more than all his
brothers, they hated him'** (37:4). The rich royal robe was an
ever-present reminder to them of who the favourite was. Their
hatred of him became so great that they **'could not speak
peaceably to him'**. They did not have a civil word to say to
him.⁴ We can partly sympathize with them, but they were developing a spirit that was first found in Cain and we can see
the danger signals (see 4:5-8).

2. Joseph's dreams (37:5-11)

Things went from bad to worse when Joseph told them his
dreams, for we read that **'They hated him even more'** (37:5)
and **'envied him'** (37:11). He was somewhat naïve and insensitive as he related these dreams to men who could not tolerate being in his presence.

Joseph had two special dreams. The double dream made it
important and certain of fulfilment, as Joseph explained when

he interpreted Pharaoh's dreams (41:32). That is why he shared his dreams with his brothers. Although God did not directly speak to Joseph, these dreams were revelation from God.

The first dream involved sheaves belonging to his brothers bowing down to Joseph's sheaf, while in the second, the sun, moon and eleven stars bowed down to Joseph. Even his father rebuked him for drawing attention to himself and making himself more important than his father and mother. However, like Mary, who 'kept all these things and pondered them in her heart', Jacob too **'kept the matter in mind'** (37:11; see Luke 2:19,51).

These dreams were prophetic and both carried the same message. They foretold a time when Joseph would rule over his family. His brothers got the message: **'Shall you indeed reign over us?'** (37:8). Already Joseph is being portrayed as a type of Judah, of whom it is prophesied, 'Your father's children shall bow down before you' (49:8). While the New Testament nowhere speaks of Joseph as a type of Christ, by foreshadowing what is later said of Judah, Joseph's future royal status does become a very special picture of Messiah's rule.

These dreams would have helped Joseph when he was passing through his severe trials. It is said of our Lord that he 'endured the cross, despising the shame' because of the 'joy that was set before him' (Heb. 12:2). Christians too are called to suffer in this world, but they are encouraged by the expectation of the 'glory which shall be revealed' (Rom. 8:18). Calvin adds that God 'revealed in dreams what he would do, that afterwards it might be known that nothing had happened fortuitously'.[5]

3. *The brothers' revenge* (37:12-36)

This passage takes Joseph from the love and protection of his father's home in Hebron, via the hostility of his brothers in Dothan, to the completely alien world of Egypt.

Joseph's pursuit of the brothers (37:12-17)

Shechem was fifty miles north of Hebron. Jacob and his sons
were still interested in this area even after the Dinah affair (see
Gen. 34). They had plundered the city and taken captive the
little ones and the wives, so there was good reason to return
there and the pasture-land around the city was excellent. But
their father was concerned enough to send Joseph on this
mission, as he put it, to **'see if it is well with your brothers
and well with the flocks'** (37:14). He sent the son whom he
could trust to bring him a faithful report, whether good or ill.
Despite the distance and attitude of the brothers towards him,
Joseph was quick to obey his father (37:13). Amazingly, Jacob
seems to have been in the dark concerning his sons' hatred of
Joseph. While Jacob was interested in the well-being (or
'peace') of his sons and the flock, neither he nor his son Joseph
seemed worried about the lack of peace that existed between
Joseph and his half-brothers (see 37:4).

From what we know of the brothers' attitude to Joseph,
we begin to fear for his safety. It comes as a relief to be told
that Joseph could not find his brothers. He is depicted as a lost
sheep found wandering in the field by a certain man. The unnamed man was very helpful, but in his directing Joseph to
Dothan, which lay another fifteen miles north of Shechem, we
again have cause for concern. They were in an area where no
one knew them. It says much for Joseph's devotion to duty
that he did not give up, but plodded doggedly on until he found
his brothers.

The brothers' plot (37:18-20)

It revealed how strong their resentment of Joseph was, particularly over the dreams, that no sooner had they caught sight
of him (how could they miss him in that distinctive robe?) than

they called out, **'Look, this dreamer is coming!'**[6] Then **'They conspired against him to kill him,'** and said, **'We shall see what will become of his dreams!'** The idea was to kill him, throw his body in some pit and then lie about the crime by saying that **'Some wild beast has devoured him.'** The explanation would have sounded very plausible (see 1 Sam. 17:36). While they try to hide their crime from men, says Calvin, 'It never enters into their mind that what is hidden from men cannot escape the eyes of God.'[7]

Reuben's plan (37:21-25)

While the initial plot was to kill Joseph, Reuben, when he heard of it, planned to deliver him: **'Shed no blood, but cast him into this pit.'** His idea was to **'deliver him out of their hands, and bring him back to his father'**. Did he feel some responsibility as the first-born? But why did he not have the courage to tell the brothers, there and then, to abandon their scheme and allow Joseph to return home unharmed? Was he trying to make amends for his disgraceful behaviour with Bilhah by personally rescuing Joseph from the pit and returning him to his father? In the purposes of God Reuben's plan was not allowed to succeed.

But the brothers accepted the plan. No sooner had Joseph arrived than they seized him and threw him into a dry cistern. Reuben did not want him to drown in a well of water, but the others did not mind his dying of thirst. They no doubt took great delight in stripping him of his tunic. The narrative stresses that this was **'the tunic of many colours'**. It was the symbol of all that they had come to hate about him. They stripped him of the robe that spoke not only of his father's love for him, but of his dreams of dominion.

How cruel and callous they were! They turned a deaf ear to their brother's appeals for mercy (42:21) and **'sat down to**

eat a meal' (37:25). Calvin warns against allowing our consciences to become insensitive.[8]

Judah's proposal (37:25-30)

The brothers spotted a caravan of camels. It was **'a company of Ishmaelites'**. These traders were on their way from Gilead via Canaan to Egypt to sell their perfumes and ointments. They are also called 'Midianites' (37:28,36). The names were interchangeable, as we see from Judges 8:24. 'Ishmaelite' is used in this chapter as a general term for a nomadic trader, while 'Midianite' relates specifically to the tribal grouping.

Judah hit on the bright idea of selling Joseph to these traders. It would bring them some money and they would cease to be guilty of murder through allowing their brother to die in the pit. To round off his argument he reminded the others, **'He is our brother and our flesh'** (37:27). So they agreed. They pulled Joseph out of the pit and sold him **'for twenty shekels of silver'** (37:28). Their action was no less a crime. To sell a brother into slavery was a capital offence.[9]

Ironically it was Judah, not Reuben, who saved Joseph from death. All unwittingly, he also helped towards the realization of the prophetic dreams. Reuben had evidently not been present for some time. He was naturally taken aback when he returned to find the pit empty. His reaction showed a genuine concern for the lad and his father's feelings (37:29-30).

Jacob's pain (37:31-35)

Instead of telling Jacob that Joseph had been taken to Egypt, they continued with their original plan of fooling their father into thinking he had been killed by a wild animal. The irony was that Jacob was deceived by his sons, using similar means to those with which he had deceived Isaac his father. They used their brother's garment and **'a kid of the goats'** (37:31; see 27:9-17). Emphasis again falls on the **'tunic'**. The blood-stained royal robe, the symbol of the brothers' hatred, was now the means by which his father recognized what he assumed had happened to his beloved son (37:32). The conclusion Jacob came to was the one the brothers had planned: **'A wild beast has devoured him'** (37:33).

Jacob was devastated. He **'tore his clothes, put sackcloth on his waist, and mourned for his son many days'** (37:34). These were the customary expressions of mourning. Reuben had already shown sorrow by tearing his clothes over what had really happened to Joseph. The whole family gathered to comfort their father, but he would not be consoled. If the brothers thought that Jacob would soon get over his loss they were mistaken. He intended to carry on grieving till his dying day. This meant that his sons' consciences would not be easily pacified. They would be constantly confronted with their father's grief and would be forced to keep up the pretence.

We cannot help but feel sorry for Jacob. This is now the lowest point in the whole of his life. Through deception he had been denied an exclusive married relationship with Rachel. Now, through deception, he had been deprived of the first-born son of his favourite wife. Yet out of this trial God was to bring him blessing before his days were ended.

Joseph's plight (37:36)

Meanwhile, the Midianite nomadic traders had sold Joseph in Egypt **'to Potiphar, an officer of Pharaoh and captain of the guard'**. We are left wondering how those dreams will come true. One thing is clear: he had come through this major crisis and was still alive.

Joseph's brothers conspired to destroy the very person ordained by God to preserve them. In a similar way, Jesus' own people plotted to destroy the one ordained to save them. These events in the life of Joseph, like the earlier ones concerning the birth and sacrifice of Isaac, turned out, in God's purposes, to be symbolic of what happened to Jesus the Messiah.

Judah and his family (38:1-30)

The scandal that often fills our newspapers is nothing compared with the outrageous activity reported here concerning Judah and his family. Instead of continuing with the story of Joseph, we have what Kidner calls this 'rude interruption'.[10] There have been similar digressions before, but they all contributed to the purpose of Genesis. Why has the family history of Judah been included at this point?

Firstly, it holds us in suspense as we wonder what will happen to Joseph.

Secondly, it allows us to sense the passing of time. It was **'at that time'** (38:1) when Joseph was taken to Egypt that the events of chapter 38 began to unfold. During the twenty years that followed, Judah married and had sons who grew up and married.[11]

Thirdly, in the light of Judah's sinful actions, Joseph's moral and spiritual integrity (see chapter 39) is something of a rare commodity.

Fourthly, it draws our attention to Judah and prepares us for what will be said later when Jacob comes to bless his sons (49:8-12).

Fifthly, it focuses on Tamar and her connection with the 'seed' of the woman. Unlike Judah and his sons, Tamar identified herself with the promises made to Abraham and showed her concern to see them fulfilled. She is like Ruth and became the ancestor of Ruth's husband, of David and of Jesus the Messiah.

Finally, it captures themes that keep reappearing in the history of the fathers of Israel. These include: the deceiver being deceived; the choice of the younger over the elder; the vindication of those denied justice while the guilty are forced to acknowledge their sin; and lives changed for the better through severe trials.

1. Judah (38:1-2)

At the time when Joseph was sold into Egypt, **'Judah departed from his brothers.'** He 'departed' (literally, 'went down') from his father's home in Hebron (37:14), which is one of the highest points in the south of Canaan (3,040 ft, or 926 m., above sea level), to the foothills north-west of Hebron, to Adullam (see 1 Sam. 22:1). Judah 'went down' in more ways than one. He withdrew from the covenant community and became great friends with an **'Adullamite whose name was Hirah'** (38:1,12,20). It is quite possible that Judah tried to salve his conscience by getting away from those involved with him in deception and a father who would not stop grieving over Joseph.

The downward spiritual spiral continued when Judah **'saw there a daughter of a certain Canaanite'** and **'married her'** ('took her'). No mention is made of the woman's name; only her father's name is given — Shua. The combination of 'saw' and 'took' in Genesis (see 3:6; 6:2; 34:2) suggests that in this relationship there was more lust than love. Judah's action reminds us of David, who 'saw a woman bathing ... and took her' (2 Sam. 11:2-4). There was also no excuse for Judah's marrying a Canaanite. He knew of God's covenant, as is clear from the incident over his sister Dinah (see 34:13-14).

These verses challenge us over the company we keep. To stop attending the place where you will hear God's Word and meet God's people is a step on the downward path. While we are to be civil and friendly to all, we must be careful about making close friendships with people who will draw us away from the Lord. Worldly people can often have very attractive personalities and may seem more pleasant and affable than the Christians we know. Do not be taken in by this. Judah's friendship with Hirah led him to marry a Canaanite and later encouraged him in immoral practices. 'Do not be deceived: "Evil company corrupts good habits"' (1 Cor. 15:33).

Parents should also see to it that they make time for their children. Jacob was so caught up in grieving for his favourite son that he showed no concern for the needs of his other sons. His own father Isaac had been no better. He adored his son Esau because of the good stews he made, and this made him forget his responsibilities towards both his sons' future marriage partners. Rebekah had to prompt him into action to help Jacob find a wife.

2. The sons of Judah (38:3-11)

From his marriage to the Canaanite woman, Judah had three sons in quick succession. The first was named Er by his father. As for the other two, Onan and Shelah, they were named by their mother. Her third son was born while Judah **'was at Chezib'** (38:5).[12] It lay three miles west of Adullam. This piece of information explains why descendants of Shelah settled there (1 Chr. 4:21-22).

Er

While Judah had felt free to choose a wife for himself he saw the importance of helping his own family to find wives. **'Judah took a wife for Er his first-born, and her name was Tamar'** (38:6). We are not given any indication of her background or family connections, but it is clear from the rest of the chapter that Tamar, despite the glaring sins, was a young woman with courage and determination.

Judah's first-born turned out to be a very evil person. The Hebrew word for 'wicked' ('evil') is Er's name spelled backwards. **'Er ... was wicked in the sight of the LORD, and the LORD killed him'** (38:7). Judging from what is said of his brother Onan and what happened to him, Er's evil may well have been of a sexual nature. Untimely deaths are often reserved for very serious sins. God acted very decisively in the time of Noah on account of 'the wickedness of man' (6:5). The cities of the plain were destroyed because they were 'wicked and sinful against the LORD' (13:13; 18:20).

We should not be startled that 'The LORD killed him.' The Creator and Judge of all has the right to terminate life, for he is the one who gives life and keeps life going. The phrase refers to a premature, but not necessarily to a direct, divine intervention to end life. What it does emphasize is that the death was a punishment from God. In the case of King Saul, even though he died by suicide we are told that the Lord killed him (1 Chr. 10:4,14). In Er's case it may be that God allowed him to reap the fruits of his immoral lifestyle in a rapid, untimely death without offspring.

Onan

No sooner was the young Tamar married than she was left a widow with no children. Judah therefore instructed his next son, Onan, to marry her, and produce children for his brother. According to this ancient and widely practised custom of 'levirate' marriages, it was the duty of the next oldest brother to marry the widow who had died childless. The term comes from the Latin *levir*, meaning 'brother-in-law'. A first-born son of such a marriage was regarded as belonging to the dead brother and thus carried on his name and inherited his property (see Deut. 25:5-10).

Onan, out of respect for his father and local custom, married Tamar, but he had no respect for his new wife or his dead brother. He coveted for himself the first-born rights of his brother, which he would never have if he produced a son through Tamar. When he realized that any son and heir born through this union **'would not be his'** but his dead brother's, he made sure that Tamar would never become pregnant. The force of the Hebrew means that not just once, but every time Onan had intercourse with Tamar, he wasted his sperm. Onan also used his wife to satisfy his sexual desires with no thought for her feelings and desires.[13]

'The thing which he did displeased the Lord; therefore he killed him also' (38:10). Onan was not punished with an untimely death because he was the first person to practise birth control, or because he engaged in a form of masturbation. Obviously, if these were persisted in as a regular habit for self-gratification and particularly if they were engaged in to avoid the responsibilities of the marriage bond, then they would run counter to God's creation blessing to 'be fruitful and multiply' (1:28; 9:1) and would incur God's displeasure. Such actions would come close to being in the same category as homosexual practices. A hedonistic world where pornography is one of the fastest-growing 'industries' on the internet is one which is already experiencing the judgement of divine abandonment and is ripe for disintegration.

Onan, as a son of Judah, and a descendant of Abraham, Isaac and Jacob, should have known better, but he showed no respect for God. God had promised to make them fruitful and that through their 'seed' all nations would be blessed. Onan was deliberately acting against these good purposes of God.

For this reason his life, like that of his brother, came to an abrupt end.

Shelah

Judah's two oldest sons had now died while still in their teens after marrying Tamar. He was therefore reluctant to allow his third son, Shelah, to suffer a similar fate: **'For he said, "Lest he also die as his brothers did"'** (38:11). Under the pretext that Shelah was too young to marry, Judah told Tamar, **'Remain a widow in your father's house till my son Shelah is grown.'** He no doubt hoped that she would forget his promise to give his remaining son to her.

3. Tamar's plan (38:12-23)

Time passed and Judah's wife also died. After the period of mourning was over, he **'went up to his sheep-shearers at Timnah'**, taking with him **'his friend Hirah the Adullamite'** (38:12). The time of sheep-shearing was like harvest, a time for feasting and drinking (see 1 Sam. 25:2-8; 2 Sam. 13:23-24).

Tamar had by this time realized that her father-in-law had no intention of giving his son Shelah to her in marriage. If Judah had forgotten his responsibilities, Tamar certainly had not. When Tamar was told that Judah was going to shear sheep at Timnah, she devised a plan whereby she could become pregnant by her father-in-law. She removed her widow's clothing, **'wrapped herself'** to look like a prostitute but veiled her face to conceal her identity. Then she sat **'in an open place'** (or more literally, 'at the opening of Enaim'; see Josh. 15:34) **'which was on the way to Timnah'** (38:14) and waited for Judah to pass by. She took advantage of Judah's sexual vulnerability now that he had no wife.

When Judah saw Tamar by the roadside he naturally took her for a common prostitute. In order to satisfy his animal lusts he immediately asked for her services. Naturally Tamar agreed but she asked Judah what he would give her in payment. He offered to send her a young goat from the flock. Because he did not have the goat with him, she demanded a pledge. Judah allowed her to choose and she said, **'Your signet and cord, and your staff that is in your hand'** (38:18). Only rich men owned their own seal, which was worn on a cord round the neck. With these items in her possession, proof of her father-in-law's identity, Judah was allowed to use her for his sinful pleasure. Tamar, however, became pregnant by him, as she had hoped she would. Having accomplished her purpose, she returned to her father's house, **'laid aside her veil and put on the garments of her widowhood'** (38:19).

As soon as it was convenient, Judah sent his best friend with the goat to redeem the pledge, but he could not find the woman. Hirah asked the men of that place if they had seen her. Instead of using the more coarse term, 'common prostitute', he referred to her using the more polite term, 'cult prostitute'. The practice in Canaanite religion was for young women to pose as temple prostitutes. To speak in terms of a 'holy woman' prostitute would therefore have sounded more respectable. The men of that place knew of no such woman. Hirah reported back to Judah, who decided to leave the matter well alone. He did not want it broadcast that a woman had tricked him (38:23).

4. The descendants of Judah (38:24-30)

Three months later Judah was told that Tamar had played the prostitute and had become pregnant. Self-righteous Judah immediately called for her to receive the maximum penalty: **'Let her be burned!'** (38:24; see Lev. 21:9). As Tamar was being brought out to receive her punishment, she played her trump card. **'She sent to her father-in-law, saying, "By the man to whom these belong, I am with child,"'** and she held out the signet and cord, and staff (38:25). Judah was mortified and acknowledged the articles as his. In owning up to his guilt he declared Tamar to be more in the right than he (38:26). Judah had not fulfilled his responsibilities whereas Tamar, though she had used desperate and sinful means, had her heart in the right direction. She was far more concerned to preserve the promised line than Judah. He did not marry Tamar (**'He never knew her again'**) but he obviously cared for her and the family.

This part of the story reminds us of David's affair with Bathsheba (2 Sam. 11-12). Both men expressed righteous indignation when informed of another person's misconduct and both were trapped into admitting their own guilt. How hypocritical and self-righteous we can all be! In condemning others we so often condemn ourselves. Jesus said, 'Judge not, that you be not judged' (Matt. 7:1).

When the time came for her to give birth, Tamar was found to have twins. As in the birth of Jacob and Esau, there was a struggle to be first from the womb. As one child put out his hand the midwife tied a scarlet cord around it to identify him as the first-born.[14] But then the second baby managed to come out unexpectedly and the midwife said, ' **" How did you break through? This breach be upon you!" Therefore his name was called Perez'**, which means 'breach' or 'break through' (38:29). Afterwards the baby with the red cord came out and they called him Zerah. The meaning of Zerah is not given and is therefore not important to the story. These twins made up for the two sons that Judah lost.

God is not mentioned in this account, but through this sordid story he was working to fulfil his promises. It reminds us that God can use the most unlikely people to further his purposes. This does not excuse sinful action, but it does bring consolation to repentant sinners.

This is what Judah produced! The Jews have nothing of which to boast when it comes to origins. Yet 'Salvation is of the Jews' (John 4:22). These are the ancestors of King David. Tamar, along with Rahab the prostitute, is among the women mentioned in the genealogy of Jesus the Messiah, the Saviour of the world (Matt. 1:3,5). There is also a biblical principle here. God takes 'the base things of this world and the things which are despised God has chosen ... that no flesh should glory in his presence'. If anyone wants to boast, 'Let him glory in the Lord' (1 Cor. 1:28-29,31).

35.
God's strange providences

Please read Genesis 39:1 – 40:23

The contrast between Judah and Joseph could not be greater. Though Judah and his descendants belong to the chosen royal line, they are examples, or types, not of the future promised 'seed', but of Israel's future disloyalty and rejection of God's promises. It is Joseph who is presented as the type of the true people of God and of the royal 'seed'.

Have you ever felt that you have been treated unfairly? Do you wonder sometimes whether living an upright life is really worth the effort? Joseph's experience and the way he remained faithful to God under severe pressure should be an inspiration to us all.

Success in adversity (39:1-23)

This whole chapter must be viewed in the light of what we are told at the beginning and end of the chapter: **'The LORD was with Joseph'** (39:2,3,21,23). God was with Joseph in trouble and he was the one who gave Joseph good success in adverse circumstances. The Lord did not take him out of the trouble, but enabled him to triumph in adversity. This is a hard lesson to learn. God has not promised his people an easy ride, but he has said, 'When you pass through the waters, I will be with you; and through the rivers, they shall not overflow you' (Isa. 43:2). We all know examples of ordinary Christians whose experiences have, in some way, mirrored those of Joseph.

1. Trusted and successful in Potiphar's house (39:1-6)

The opening words, **'Now Joseph had been taken down to Egypt'** (39:1), pick up the story from 37:36 and prepare us for what follows. Abraham went down to Egypt but ended up by being expelled (12:10-20). Joseph was forced into Egypt, where he was to stay for the rest of his life. This is where Jacob's descendants settled for over 400 years, so fulfilling the prophecy made to Abraham (15:13).

Egypt was already a well-organized and highly civilized place when Joseph arrived there, with a history stretching back hundreds of years. About a thousand years before Joseph, there occurred the first great flowering of Egyptian culture, the Great Pyramid of Kheops being the most obvious monument to it. There are differences of opinion as to the exact time when Joseph was taken to Egypt. The majority of scholars would place the event during the Second Intermediate Period, which included the time when foreign Semitic pharaohs, called Hyksos, ruled the land (c. 1786–1570). Other respected scholars disagree, suggesting that Joseph came to Egypt much earlier, around 1900 B.C., during the Middle Kingdom period, when the second great age of Egyptian culture took place (c. 2134–1786 B.C.). The biblical data would seem to favour an early date.[1]

Joseph was purchased by Potiphar, a 'eunuch' in the more general sense of **'an officer'** of Pharaoh. His particular position was **'captain of the guard'**. From what we learn in the following chapters, it would appear that he was in charge of the prison for royal officers (40:3-4; 41:10,12).

Though Joseph had been separated from his family and sold as a slave in a foreign country, he did not sulk or complain. He worked in the way that Paul encouraged Christian slaves to act in the Roman Empire: 'not with eye-service, as men-pleasers, but as bondservants of Christ' (see Eph. 6:5-8). Joseph might have chosen to reject his past and the dreams he had experienced, but all through his ordeals and disappointments he lived by faith in God's promises.

Joseph was **'a successful man'** because **'The LORD was with him.'** Potiphar, whose name means 'He whom Re [the sun god] has given', became aware that Joseph's God was with him and had made him to prosper (39:3). In the end, Joseph was raised to chief manager of Potiphar's whole estate, a position of great trust and responsibility.

Joseph, in his situation as a slave, experienced the truth of God's promise to Abraham: 'I will bless you... I will bless those who bless you' (12:2-3). From the time that Joseph was promoted to this high position in the household, **'The LORD blessed the Egyptian's house for Joseph's sake; and the blessing of the LORD was on all that he had in the house and in the field'** (39:5). This is how God prepared Joseph for high office in Egypt at a crucial moment in the history of God's people. What he saw happening in Potiphar's home as a result of God's blessing, he was to see on a large scale when he became prime minister of Egypt. He was entrusted with much as a result of being found faithful in a little (see Matt. 25:21,23).

Potiphar came to trust Joseph so completely that **'He left all that he had in Joseph's hand'** (39:6). It meant that Potiphar 'didn't have a worry in the world, except to decide what he wanted to eat!'[2] To this very favourable view of Joseph is added a note about his physical appearance. He was like his mother, who is also described as **'handsome [beautiful] in form and appearance'** (39:6; 29:17). With this information we are prepared for the next episode in the narrative.

2. Tempted and imprisoned (39:7-20)

Joseph had come through the initial testing experience with flying colours. He was in favour both with God and with his earthly master. It was when all was going so well for Joseph that he was suddenly confronted with an altogether different type of test.

With this fine figure of a man constantly around the house, Potiphar's wife **'cast longing eyes'** at him and determined to seduce him. Choosing the right moment, she boldly accosted him and said, **'Lie with me'** (39:7). Joseph was living in a society much like our own where all restraint was thrown to the wind. People wanted immediate gratification of their lustful passions and worried about any consequences later. It was a severe temptation, for it was not a slave-girl who made the proposal, but **'his master's wife'**.

His reply displayed courage, self-control and a consciousness of God. He gave three reasons for rejecting her advances. To yield to this temptation would mean:

1. to betray trust (39:8-9a);
2. to damage a marriage. He reminded her that his master had kept nothing from him **'but you, because you are his wife'** (39:9b);
3. to **'sin against God'** (39:9c).

It was a great temptation for a young, virile, single man to have sex with the boss's wife. The temptation occurred day after day. He not only refused to go to bed with her, but wisely tried to avoid being **'with her'** (39:10). The first refusal helped him to say no on subsequent occasions.

Yield not to temptation, for yielding is sin;
Each victory will help you some other to win.

(H. R. Palmer)

Potiphar's wife was a determined woman who was obviously used to having her own way. The opportunity that she had been waiting for came when Joseph was in the house by himself (39:11). She grabbed him, no doubt hoping that the feel of her body would overcome his resistance to her advances. Aware of the danger, he broke free of her grasp and ran outside, leaving behind some of his clothing in her hands. Temptation of this kind needs to be dealt with in a radical way. 'Flee sexual immorality' (1 Cor. 6:18).

Humiliated by Joseph's refusal to lie with her, this frustrated woman got her revenge. She took the initiative by calling the servants and appealing to their jealousy of Joseph, a foreigner, and their resentment against Potiphar who had elevated him to such a high position only to insult them: **'See, he has brought in to us a Hebrew to mock us'** (39:14). She accused Joseph of attempting to rape her and claimed that she had only escaped because she had had the presence of mind to shout at the top of her voice so that he had run off leaving his clothes behind. Joseph's clothing was used to falsely accuse him of doing the very thing he had been so careful to avoid.

The story was repeated to her husband when he came home. She also made a point of reminding him that he was the one who had brought the foreign slave into the house who had ended up insulting her by seeking to be intimate with her. Potiphar was naturally angry at what had happened and put Joseph in prison (literally, 'the round house'), **'where the king's prisoners were confined'** (39:20). It is surprising that Joseph was not immediately executed for such a crime. This has led some scholars to think that Potiphar was not entirely convinced of his wife's accusations but felt obliged to believe her and to put Joseph in the fortress prison over which he was responsible. Whatever the truth, Potiphar was restrained from carrying out the death sentence.

History seemed to be repeating itself for Joseph. For the second time he had been taken prisoner for being faithful and his clothing had been used to present a false report. How would we have felt? Why had God allowed him to be treated unjustly yet again when he had sought to do what was right?

We know that through such persecutions God moulds our characters so that the genuineness of our faith 'may be found to praise, honour and glory at the revelation of Jesus Christ' (1 Peter 1:6-7). Joseph considered it more important to please God and retain his integrity whatever the cost than to indulge in the momentary pleasures of sin. Christians must learn to live in the light of the Day of Judgement. It is one of the lessons of this chapter that sometimes 'God chooses to bless us and make us people of integrity in the midst of abominable circumstances, rather than change our circumstances.'[3] Joseph may have drawn some comfort from his former experience. If God could change his situation for the better when he was first taken as a slave, he could do it again.

3. Trusted and successful in Potiphar's prison (39:21-23)

Joseph had again been humbled and found himself at rock bottom. As people looked upon this Hebrew slave now thrown into prison, they might have thought that his God had forsaken him. Yet, despite outward appearances, **'The Lord was with Joseph.'** Whatever the circumstances, the Lord has promised to be with his people: 'I will never leave you nor forsake you' (Heb. 13:5-6).

God also **'showed him mercy'** (or 'covenant love'). The evidence is seen in the fact that God **'gave him favour'** in the sight of the prison governor. It was not long before Joseph was being given responsibility and authority in the prison. The keeper **'committed to Joseph's hand all the prisoners who were in the prison'**. Because the Lord was with Joseph he was again successful. These last verses of the chapter echo those at the beginning and remind us that God was preparing him for the fulfilment of his dreams. As he prepared him for high office he strengthened his character and humbled his spirit.

The picture we have of Joseph is an example of what it means to be wise. The wise 'find favour and high esteem in the sight of God and man' (Prov. 3:4). They fear God and keep away from evil (Prov. 1:7; 4:14-15). Potiphar's wife, on the other hand, is an example of what it means to be foolish. Proverbs contrasts Madam Wisdom and Madam Folly in terms of a virtuous woman and an adulterous woman respectively (see Prov. 8:32-36; 5:1-6; 9:1-6,13-18).

Joseph also foreshadowed the experience of his descendants who became slaves of the Egyptians. God was with them, as he was with Joseph, and eventually led them out in fulfilment of his promises. In addition, he points us to Christ, the wisdom of God, and to God's Suffering Servant who was treated as the worst of criminals. Yet, 'It pleased the Lord to bruise him,' for through it the Lord's plan for the salvation of his people prospered (Isa. 53:10).

The forgotten friend (40:1-23)

The way Joseph conducted himself in prison and correctly interpreted the dreams of the royal prisoners contributed towards his spectacular rise to power.

1. Joseph serves the royal prisoners (40:1-4)

We are introduced to two of Pharaoh's officials. The **'chief butler'**, or cup-bearer, like Nehemiah in the Persian court (Neh. 1:11), did more than literally hold the king's wine cup. It was a responsible political position. The same may well have been true of the **'chief baker'**. He would have been another close adviser to the king. Pharaoh was angry with them because for some reason they had **'offended their lord'** (literally, 'sinned against their master'). While Joseph had ended up in prison for refusing 'to sin against God' (39:9), the butler and the baker were imprisoned for sinning against the Egyptian king.

They were put in custody in the place where the king's prisoners were confined. This was where Joseph was a prisoner and where the keeper of the prison had given him considerable responsibility. It is not surprising to learn that the captain of the guard, who was probably still Potiphar (see 39:1), assigned Joseph to take care of them. Joseph would never have had the opportunity of getting so close to these men if he had not behaved himself with such dignity and patience. He proved to be a model prisoner who could be trusted to look after these high-ranking officials.

2. Joseph's concern for the royal prisoners (40:5-8)

This is a remarkable paragraph, for it shows that Joseph was far more concerned about how others felt from one day to the next than to bemoan his own sorry situation. How many of us in similar circumstances would have cared how others were feeling? Certainly we would hardly have noticed any changes in a fellow prisoner's facial expressions. Not so Joseph. When the two royal officials had special dreams during the same night, Joseph immediately detected something was wrong. **'Why do you look so sad today?'**, he asked. He took his responsibilities seriously and was a friend as well as a servant to them.

Our own frustrating experiences should make us more sympathetic to the needs of others. It was because Joseph was kind and showed such concern that these officers of Pharaoh opened their hearts to him. Thus began a series of events which was eventually to lead Joseph to be the means of saving thousands of people. It should be an encouragement to us to be more interested in the sad lives of others and to win their confidence. It may lead to their eternal salvation.

The two men were dejected because, having had unusual dreams, they had no one to interpret them. They sensed that the dreams had something to do with their own futures. They were not free to visit the experts. Interpreting dreams was a special science involving superstitious beliefs and occult practices.

Joseph immediately bore testimony to his faith in God: **'Do not interpretations belong to God?'** When he referred to God he was not thinking about any of the gods of Egypt, but the God who had revealed himself to his father. This is the God who does control the future. He had made promises and had been working out his purposes in the lives of Joseph's ancestors. Joseph himself had experienced unusual dreams which he believed were God-given. He did not say so, but Joseph implied that God would give the interpretation through him. Joseph therefore invited the men to tell him their dreams. The important thing to notice is that Joseph did not boast of his qualifications and skills in interpreting dreams. His own experiences had humbled him. He witnessed to God's ability to interpret God-given dreams concerning future events. Daniel made this same point clear to Nebuchadnezzar (Dan. 2:30).

3. The cup-bearer's dream and its interpretation (40:9-13)

The dream was appropriate to the traditional work of the chief butler. He had seen a vine with three branches, which budded and blossomed and produced grapes. With Pharaoh's cup in his hand, he had seen himself squeezing the grape juice into the cup and giving it to the king. Joseph was immediately given the ability to interpret the dream. In three days the cup-bearer would be released and restored to his former position.

Matthew Henry observes that, although Joseph was able to foretell the chief butler's deliverance, he did not foresee his own. He had to support himself with the remembrance of those youthful dreams concerning the distant future without any new or fresh discoveries. Christians have in God's Word visions concerning the glory to come but, like Joseph, we are called to trust what God has revealed.

4. Joseph's request (40:14-15)

This is the centre point of the narrative. Joseph used the occasion to make a plea on his own behalf. He asked the royal cup-bearer to **'remember'** him and **'show kindness'** to him when he was restored to his position with the king. In support of his appeal, Joseph informed the cup-bearer of his own wrongful imprisonment. Probably for the first time, the officer of the king realized that he had been helped by a foreigner, who had been **'stolen away from the land of the Hebrews'**. Joseph protested his innocence and described the present place of his confinement as **'the dungeon'** (literally, 'the pit'). This is the same word that is used to describe the well into which his brothers had first put him (37:20,22,24).

Joseph was not wrong to use this occasion to seek redress. All the time Joseph had not complained but trusted God and waited patiently for him (see Ps. 37:3,7). It is not a denial of this trust to use the opportunities that God gives to change our situation for the better. Paul used his civil rights when he thought it necessary (Acts 22:25-29; 23:17-22; 25:11-12). We must not confuse providence with fatalism. We are encouraged, as Don Carson puts it, 'to trust the goodness of the sovereign, providential God, while confronting and opposing the evil that takes place in this fallen world.'[4]

5. The baker's dream and interpretation (40:16-19)

The baker was naturally encouraged by the cup-bearer's dream and its interpretation, so he related his own dream. This dream was also appropriate to his profession. He saw himself carrying three baskets of bread on his head. In the top basket were all kinds of baked foods for Pharaoh which the birds ate before they could be delivered. Joseph was again able to interpret the dream. He was courageous and faithful in reporting an unpleasant message. In three days the baker would be executed and his body would be left hanging for the birds of prey to eat.

Again, the words of Matthew Henry are apposite: 'Ministers are but interpreters; they cannot make the thing otherwise than it is; if therefore they deal faithfully, and their message prove unpleasing, it is not their fault.' The true prophets of the Lord were faithful in preaching judgement as well as salvation. Preachers today must not be afraid of proclaiming the bad news that 'The wages of sin is death,' as well as the good news that 'The gift of God is eternal life in Christ Jesus our Lord' (Rom. 6:23).

6. The dreams fulfilled (40:20-22)

Everything happened three days later as Joseph had predicted. The occasion was Pharaoh's birthday. Egyptian texts mention that amnesties were granted on the birthday of a pharaoh, or on the anniversary of his accession to the throne. The chief cup-bearer was restored and the chief baker was executed. It clearly indicated that God had sent the dreams and had enabled Joseph to interpret them correctly. What an encouragement to Joseph to believe that his own dreams would also come true in God's good time!

7. The interpreter forgotten (40:23)

Joseph's elation at seeing the cup-bearer reinstated was soon turned to disappointment. As the days turned into weeks and months with no hint of a change in his situation, it was obvious the royal official had forgotten him. The text emphasizes the cup-bearer's ingratitude: he **'did not remember Joseph, but forgot him'**. This was another test of faith for Joseph. He had received a further setback when he thought for certain things were moving to a favourable conclusion. It would have taught him yet again not to rely on human help. He was thrown wholly on the Lord.

> Do not put your trust in princes,
> ... in whom there is no help...
> Happy is he ...
> Whose hope is in the Lord his God
>
> (Ps. 146:3,5).

Joseph's experience is typical of that of many of God's people. The cry of the psalmist and the prophet, 'How long, O Lord?', witnesses to the same frustration when situations seem hopeless and there appears to be no divine movement to change things for the better. This was to be the experience of Israel in Egypt when they cried to the Lord for help in their bondage and when at first things got worse before they got better (Exod. 2:24-25). The Lord does not forget his people, but at the right moment acts to save them.

36.
From the pit to the palace

Please read Genesis 41:1-57

There are fascinating stories the world over of people who have made it to the top from humble beginnings. Egyptian sources give numerous examples of people of Semitic origin being given positions of authority in Egypt during the Middle Kingdom period (*c.* 2134–1786 B.C.) as well as in the time of the Semitic pharaohs, the Hyksos (*c.* 1786–1570 B.C.). Joseph's meteoric rise is the most interesting of them all.

As part of God's Word to us, this true story reminds us that what we call 'chance happenings' are all in God's plan. We can become very discouraged when we look at life's trials from a purely human angle. The life of Joseph encourages us to look higher. On the human level Joseph had been languishing in prison on account of injustice and ingratitude and he could have become bitter and cynical. Instead, he viewed his situation from a divine perspective. He did not understand at the time what God was doing. But he continued to trust God and to believe that the promises made to him would be fulfilled in due course. God was never far from his thoughts, as was evident when he spoke to the royal prisoners and, as we shall see, from his first encounter with Pharaoh. Through the severe trials in his life God had been training him and preparing him for the high position which his own, now distant, dreams had suggested.

The dreams (41:1-13)

1. Pharaoh's dreams recounted (41:1-7)

Joseph's own special dreams had been the reason for the beginning of his troubles. His brothers had mockingly called him
'this dreamer' (37:19). Many years later, the dreams of Pharaoh's officers, and particularly of Pharaoh himself, were the
occasion for the fulfilment of Joseph's dreams.

The time-reference reminds us of Joseph's predicament. To
a young man of twenty-eight (see 41:46) another **'two full
years'** in prison must have seemed like a lifetime. God does
not make mistakes. He works all things according to his eternal plan. The seemingly bad experiences of life, as well as those
we like, work together for good to those who love God and
who are called according to his purpose (Rom. 8:28).

Pharaoh's dreams occurred at the time of his birthday,
exactly two years after his cup-bearer had been released from
prison. In the first dream Pharaoh found himself standing by
the **'river'**.[1] Seven well-fed cows came out of the water and
grazed in the **'meadow'**.[2] Such cows can be seen in ancient
Egyptian artwork. They symbolized Egypt and its fertility.
These cows were closely followed by seven thin and ugly-
looking cows. The dream then turned into what we would call
a nightmare because the ugly cows ate up the seven fat cows.
With that Pharaoh suddenly awoke. But he soon fell back to
sleep and dreamed again. This time he saw seven plump heads
of grain on one stalk suddenly appear. After them sprang up
seven thin heads, all blighted and withered by the east wind
from the desert. Again, Pharaoh saw the thin devouring the
fat and it was so vivid he thought that it was real until he
awoke.

2. The experts fail (41:8)

These were not the sort of dreams that people laugh at in the cool light of day. When morning came Pharaoh did not laugh. **'His spirit was troubled.'** He knew he had experienced something important, so he called the men skilled in interpreting omens and signs.

The Hebrew for **'magicians'** is a word of Egyptian origin and describes a class of priests who taught wisdom and delved into mysteries. Centuries later this same priestly group were called upon to copy the miraculous signs that Moses did before Pharaoh (see Exod. 7:11,22). Though they succeeded at first, they were forced to bow before the superior power of God (Exod. 8:7,18-19). As a kind of preview of that later encounter, we have these magicians at a loss to understand the symbolism of Pharaoh's dreams. Similarly, the Babylonian magicians could not interpret Nebuchadnezzar's dreams (Dan. 2:2,10; 4:7).

God used dreams on this occasion rather than direct verbal communication in order to show Pharaoh and his people that God was in supreme control. The gods of Egypt and their priestly representatives, with all their magical powers, were no match for the King of heaven. God says, 'For the wisdom of their wise men shall perish, and the understanding of their prudent men shall be hidden' (Isa. 29:14).

3. The cup-bearer remembers (41:9-13)

When the cup-bearer heard of Pharaoh's dreams and the failure of the magicians to explain their meaning, he recalled his past faults which had resulted in Pharaoh's putting him in prison.[3] He explained how **'a young Hebrew man'** had correctly interpreted what he and the chief baker had dreamed. Joseph 'the dreamer' was now seen as the interpreter of dreams, which is what Pharaoh desperately wanted.

God's timing is always right. Though human faults and failures are never excused, God uses even our imperfections and sins to further his purposes. If the cup-bearer had remembered to mention Joseph's plight to the king earlier, Pharaoh might have released Joseph and sent him back to Canaan, from where he had been kidnapped (see 40:15). Joseph's dreams would then never have been fulfilled and he would have failed to be a blessing to Israel and others.

The interpretation (41:14-46)

This section provides us with the climax of the story. One minute Joseph was a forgotten slave; the next he was the second most important person in Egypt. The term used to describe the place where Joseph was languishing, **'the dungeon'** (literally, 'the pit' — 41:14), emphasizes the contrast between his state of humiliation and the exalted position to which he was about to rise. Our Lord Jesus Christ literally rose from the lowest position of all, death on a cross, but was highly exalted and given the name which is above every name, so that 'At the name of Jesus every knee should bow' (see Phil. 2:8-11).

1. Joseph meets Pharaoh (41:14-16)

Pharaoh had no option but to call for Joseph. His own experts had let him down badly. He was desperate to find the correct interpretation to his dreams. God often has to bring people to the end of themselves by cutting off all the well-known aids and comforts so that they will turn in humility to the Lord.

With all speed Joseph was summoned to stand before Pharaoh. In accordance with Egyptian culture and to make himself respectable to meet the king, Joseph was required to shave and to change his prison clothes. Egyptians were clean-shaven, whereas the Hebrews allowed their hair and beards to grow.

Pharaoh explained the reason why Joseph had suddenly been called to the palace (41:15). Joseph might well have felt flattered by Pharaoh's words and taken the opportunity to bargain with the king for his release. Instead, utterly forgetful of himself, he promptly corrected the king and gave all the glory to God: **'It is not in me; God will give Pharaoh an answer of peace'** (that is, a favourable answer). Wisdom to interpret divine communications is not a science that humans can master.

We constantly need to remember that whatever gifts we have are from God and we should be as quick as Joseph to give God the credit. 'Every good gift and every perfect gift is from above' (James 1:17). Paul challenged the proud, boastful believers, at Corinth: 'What do you have that you did not receive? Now if you did indeed receive it, why do you glory as if you had not received it?' (1 Cor. 4:7).

Before Pharaoh, whom the Egyptians considered to be a god, Joseph was not afraid to testify to the living God. He conducted himself like a prophet, fearlessly proclaiming to the world of his day that God rules in the affairs of human beings. Joseph prepares us for Moses and Daniel, who dared to confront proud monarchs with this same message. All God's faithful servants down the centuries have let it be known that God is the ruler of the universe. Above all the so-called gods is the one true and living God.

2. Pharaoh relates his dreams (41:17-24)

Pharaoh proceeded to tell Joseph his dreams. The details are repeated, which indicates that Moses considered them important in the history of God's saving purposes. As Pharaoh related the dreams in his own words, additional pieces of information are supplied. He highlighted the fact that the thin cows were **'very ugly'** (41:19). Also, he observed that even after they had eaten the fat cows, **'No one would have known that they had eaten them for they were just as ugly as at the beginning'** (41:21). The plump, full heads of grain are described as **'good'**, but the **'good heads'** were devoured by the thin.

These extra details show Pharaoh's concern over what he considered to be the threatening nature of the dreams. Adding to his anxiety was the failure of the magicians to explain what it all meant. He admitted to Joseph that the representatives of the gods who were skilled in the magic arts were helpless to unravel the meaning.

3. Joseph interprets the dreams (41:25-32)

As Joseph interpreted the symbolic nature of the vivid dreams, he again testified to the true God. Twice he told the King of Egypt, **'God has shown Pharaoh what he is about to do'** (41:25,28). He also brought the interpretation to a close by a double reference to God (41:32). There is no place for pluralism when it comes to religion and morality. The living God is active in the affairs of this world, working out his purposes and making known his will through his servants. He does so in such a way that the so-called gods are left impotent and are made to acknowledge that God is the absolute ruler. There are times when evil seems to take all before it, as Joseph must have thought when he was thrown into the pit by his brothers and later imprisoned in Potiphar's pit. But then God suddenly intervenes to revive his work and to show his stunning importance. The history of spiritual awakening in the church is a thrilling story.

Joseph made clear to Pharaoh that:

　　1. The two dreams had one and the same message (41:25).

2. Both the seven cows and heads of grain represented seven years (41:26-27).

3. Seven years of plenty, symbolized by the healthy
cows and heads of grain, would be followed by seven
years of famine. The famine would be so severe that the
years of plenty would be forgotten (41:29-31).

4. The duplicate dreams were God's way of indicating that the message was certain of fulfilment and would
happen soon (41:32).

The terms 'good' and 'evil' are prominent both in the account of Pharaoh's dreams and in Joseph's interpretation. There
has not been such a concentrated use of these terms since we
read of the tree of the knowledge of good and evil. The text
speaks of **'the seven good cows'** and **'the seven good heads'**
of grain, while 'evil' (translated **'ugly'**) is the regular adjec-
tive used to describe the thin cows. Joseph is depicted as the
wise man who fears God and is given divine discernment to
unravel the meaning of Pharaoh's dreams. He is able to distinguish between the good and the evil, the years of plenty (the
'good years', 41:35) and the years of famine. The good is
associated with life, while evil is associated with death (see
41:35-36). Moses returns to this theme in Deuteronomy 30:15:
'See, I have set before you today life and good, death and
evil.' The good is associated with God's Word. To love God
and to do his revealed will is life, but to turn to other gods and
serve them is death.

4. Joseph advises Pharaoh (41:33-36)

Joseph was no fortune-teller but, like the prophets who came
later, he was a spokesman for God. He realized that God had
made these things known for a purpose. God did not reveal
his future plans for Pharaoh to wag his head and say, 'What
will be will be.' There is no encouragement here, or anywhere

else in the Bible, for a fatalistic or deterministic attitude to life.
Though God has planned everything in eternity past and has
revealed to us important parts of his plan, human beings are
responsible for their actions. They are encouraged to oppose
evil, to alleviate suffering and to pray and work for the advance-
ment of God's kingdom.

Thus Joseph advised the king what action he should take.
He suggested that a qualified person should be appointed to
be in overall control of the food supply of Egypt. The two
qualities mentioned, **'discerning** [or "understanding"] **and
wise'**, are those most desired in a good leader (see Deut. 1:13;
1 Kings 3:12). Joseph also recommended that Pharaoh should
appoint other officers to oversee the food conservation pro-
gramme. A fifth of the produce from the **'good years'** should
be stored in order to carry them through the years of famine.
Joseph is again depicted as a wise man offering sound advice.

Joseph becomes prime minister (41:37-46)

Pharaoh and all his courtiers were very impressed. They recognized in Joseph a man of ability and integrity. This is what
Pharaoh meant when he asked, **'Can we find such a one as
this, a man in whom is the Spirit of God?'** (41:38). Wisdom is a gift of God's Spirit which can range from everyday
skills and wise rule to grappling with the deep problems of
life. Pharaoh also took to heart Joseph's testimony when he
said, **'God has shown you all this'** (41:39). It meant that the
King of Egypt, who was himself considered a divine figure,
recognized the supremacy of Joseph's God.

Without further ado and no doubt to Joseph's amazement,
Pharaoh immediately appointed him to take charge of the whole
fourteen-year plan. In order to fulfil such an important task,
Pharaoh raised him to a position second only to that of the
king himself: **'Only in regard to the throne will I be greater**

than you' (41:40). From a place of pre-eminence in Potiphar's home, and then to a position of influence in Potiphar's prison, Joseph now found himself in charge of Pharaoh's people (41:40-41).

Joseph was then installed into the office of prime minister, or vizier, of Egypt. He received the royal signet ring and fine linen clothes, and had a gold chain placed round his neck. To indicate to the people his high position, Pharaoh made him ride **'in the second chariot which he had'** and ordered his servants to shout before him, **'Bow the knee'** (41:43). Such was Joseph's authority that no one could move a hand or foot without his consent (41:44).

To complete his new status, Pharaoh gave Joseph an Egyptian name and an Egyptian wife. There is no agreement among scholars as to the meaning of his new name, **'Zaphnath-Paaneah'**. His wife, **'Asenath'**, was a daughter of one of the leading families. Her father was Poti-Pherah (similar in meaning to Potiphar, 'given by Ra'), priest of On. This city is better known as Heliopolis, 'the sun city' (see Jer. 43:13). It lay by the River Nile, seven miles north-east of Cairo. Although his wife was of pagan background, the fact that Joseph gave his sons Hebrew names suggests that she did not lead him astray to worship Ra, the sun god, whom her father served.

This rise to fame and power reminds us again of Daniel, who, after correctly relating and interpreting the king's dream, was promoted to high office. Under Belshazzar's regime, when Daniel had explained the writing on the wall, he was acclaimed third ruler in the kingdom (Dan. 2:48; 5:29).

'Joseph was thirty years old when he stood before Pharaoh' (41:46; cf. Num. 4:3). Joseph, the mature man of thirty, is presented to us as the ideal man and a type of the royal 'Seed' who did not allow evil to devour him. He overcame evil in his own experience and through his victory was able to bring benefits to the world, especially to God's chosen people.

We have here a picture of what Adam was called to be. He was given authority to rule as God's representative, to trust God and live dependent on God for the knowledge of good and evil. Where Adam failed, we see Joseph fulfilling that role to some degree. He was faithful to God, dependent on God for wisdom and given authority **'over all the land'** (41:41,43-46). We also have in Joseph a glimpse at the ideal ruler, who will conquer the evil serpent. It points us to the coming ruler from Judah's family line (see 49:10). David, a descendant of Judah, is presented as the ideal ruler, who began his reign at the age of thirty. In Jesus the Messiah, 'the Son of David', we have the reality. As the Second Man, who fulfils all the types, he began his public ministry at about the age of thirty (Luke 3:23). He is the one who has bruised the serpent's head and brought eternal benefits for God's people. Jesus Christ 'is the Saviour of all men, especially of those who believe' (1 Tim. 4:10).

The fulfilment (41:47-57)

The following verses report the fulfilment of Pharaoh's dreams and how Joseph prepared for the years of famine.

1. Years of plenty (41:47-52)

As Joseph had predicted, there were seven very fruitful years in which he was able to put into action his plan of storing the surplus grain. There was so much grain that it was **'as the sand of the sea ... it was without number'** (41:49).

There was fruitfulness in Joseph's domestic life also. Two sons were born to Joseph and Asenath during these years of plenty. **'Manasseh'** ('causing to forget') was the first-born. Joseph gave him this name, **'For God has made me forget**

all my toil and all my father's house' (41:51). In giving his son a Hebrew name and mentioning his 'father's house', Joseph demonstrated that he had not forgotten his roots. The name revealed that instead of going over the past with a bitter spirit and wallowing in self-pity, Joseph had drawn a line under it all. He recognized that God had been good to him and had changed his situation for the better. His early rejection had worked out for his own good and the benefit of others. May Joseph's example encourage us not to nurse grudges or to keep past wounds forever open. Healing of painful memories comes by looking at life from God's vantage-point and a determination to move forward trusting the God who has our best interests at heart.

Joseph's second son was called **'Ephraim'** ('fruitfulness'), **'For God has caused me to be fruitful in the land of my affliction'** (41:52). There is a prophetic note in the name, for Ephraim was to become one of the largest tribes in Israel. It is also interesting that the word 'affliction' is used of Israel's bondage in the land of Egypt (15:13; Exod. 3:7; 4:31). Joseph's experience in Egypt was a foretaste of Israel's fruitfulness and affliction in Egypt.

2. Famine begins (41:53-57)

During 'never-had-it-so-good' years there is the danger of thinking that prosperity is a right that we can take for granted. But pleasure and prosperity in this world are like bubbles that quickly burst. Natural disasters can completely ruin economic forecasts. Let us thank God if we live in a time of plenty and make sure we do not squander the benefits but use them wisely. Furthermore, do not put your trust in the fleeting gains of this life, but let the Lord be your treasure. When disaster strikes, we shall then be able to say, 'I have learned in whatever state I am, to be content' (Phil. 4:11).

Joseph was again vindicated when the years of fruitfulness gave way to years of famine. The rains failed not only in East Africa but in the Middle East. Due to Joseph's wise policy there was ample grain, not only to sell to the Egyptians, but to people from neighbouring countries (41:54). The final verse shows the seriousness of the situation and prepares us for the next stage in the story (41:57).

It does more, for it highlights the importance of Joseph: **'All countries came to Joseph.'** The Egyptians themselves, when they looked to Pharaoh for bread, were told, **'Go to Joseph; whatever he says to you, do it'** (41:55). Again we are directed to Christ.

> For he will deliver the needy when he cries,
> The poor also, and him who has no helper...
> There will be an abundance of grain in the earth...
> His name shall endure for ever...
> And men shall be blessed in him;
> All nations shall call him blessed
>
> (Ps. 72:12-17).

Mary, the mother of Jesus, said to the servants, 'Whatever he says to you, do.' They obeyed and there was plenty of good wine. Jesus' first miracle displayed his glory and indicated that the time of fulfilment had arrived (John 2:1-11). We are directed to Christ. He is the bread of life (John 6:51).

37.
Joseph's dreams come true

Please read Genesis 42:1 – 45:28

Joseph had correctly interpreted the dreams of Pharaoh and his courtiers, but what about his own dreams? Suddenly, we are taken back to Joseph's home in Canaan. Jacob was still alive and the head of the extended family of eleven sons, their wives and children. Life had settled down to the usual routine. Nevertheless, Jacob never stopped grieving over Joseph, and the ten older brothers could never completely forget their dark secret.

These chapters, which give a detailed account of Joseph's contact with his brothers, reach a climax when he reveals who he is. It is at this point that the main reason for the narrative is made clear (45:7).

Consciences awakened (42:1-38)

1. Jacob and his sons (42:1-5)

Abraham, Isaac and now Jacob all felt the effects of famine in the land of Canaan. Although Canaan is later described in terms which remind us of the Garden of Eden, it was not a perfect place. It was only a type of the paradise of God. The famines taught them to look beyond Canaan to a better country (Heb.

11:14-16). God also used this particular famine to bring Jacob's family together again and to prepare for the great Exodus event.

On hearing there was grain in Egypt, instead of moving his family and belongings there as Abraham had done, Jacob decided his sons should go to Egypt to buy grain. His comment, **'Why do you look at one another?'** (42:1), suggests that the sons were uncertain what to do. Jacob, as head of the extended family, took the initiative and directed them.

All **'ten'** of Joseph's half-brothers obeyed their father and joined with others in making the trek to Egypt. Only Benjamin, the youngest and dearest to Jacob, was kept at home, being the sole remaining son of Jacob's beloved Rachel. Their father's reason for not sending Benjamin, **'lest some calamity befall him'** (42:4), calls to mind the lie with which the family were still living.

2. The brothers in Egypt before Joseph (42:6-28)

It so happened that the brothers found themselves, not before an Egyptian civil servant appointed to deal with selling grain, but in the presence of the prime minister himself. Following the custom of the day, they **'bowed down before him with their faces to the earth'** (42:6). When Joseph saw them he recognized them and **'remembered the dreams which he had dreamed about them'** (42:9). The brothers did not recognize him, dressed as an Egyptian, clean-shaven and speaking through an interpreter (42:23). At that moment Joseph was the last person they expected to see.

Joseph decided to act **'as a stranger to them and spoke roughly to them'** (42:7). It is clear that the way he treated his brothers was not born out of malice or revenge. We know how difficult it was for him to hold back his emotions (see 42:24). But as God's man in this powerful position, he was used to awaken their consciences, humble their proud, hard hearts and bring about the complete fulfilment of the prophetic dreams. Before his brothers could live peaceably together in the safety of Egypt they needed to be brought to the end of themselves. Joseph therefore needed to elicit from them the truth concerning his father and his young brother, and to make them say something about himself as one of the family: '... **and one is no more**' (42:13).

By accusing them of being spies, Joseph may well have been reminding them of what they had no doubt accused him of doing, for he used to bring back evil reports of their activities. Indeed, the last time they had been together was because Jacob had sent Joseph to see if it was well with them. The brothers protested their innocence: **'We are honest men; your servants are not spies'** (42:10-11).

Putting them in prison for three days and then showing them leniency because he feared God was meant to awaken their consciences concerning their own lack of leniency in their treatment of Joseph. They had thrown him into a pit and sold him as a slave.

By suggesting that only one of them should remain in prison and the rest return home with the grain, Joseph showed his concern for his father and the whole family. His holding Simeon hostage would have encouraged his brothers to return with their youngest brother. Would they leave Simeon to the mercy of the Egyptians as they had left Joseph to the Ishmaelite traders? At the same time it would have continued to prick their consciences. It meant that they would again be in the position of appearing before their father without one of their brothers. Simeon, Leah's second son, was the one chosen to remain a prisoner, to remind them that Benjamin was Rachel's second son. No doubt Joseph was also impressed by the speech of his father's first-born son, the natural person for him to have taken captive. Reuben's words revealed to Joseph that he had no part in the plot.

Joseph's action had its desired effect. In agreeing to his proposal that one should remain until they appeared with Benjamin the brothers recalled their heartless treatment of Joseph (42:20-21). They confessed their guilt to one another: **'We are truly guilty concerning our brother,'** and they understood their present predicament as a punishment from God (42:21). Reuben rubbed salt into the wound and emphasized that they were experiencing divine judgement: **'His blood is now required of us'** (42:22; see 9:5). His words suggest that kidnapping was considered to be as great a crime as murder (see Exod. 21:16). The brothers began to see that their past was catching up with them.

Before they left, Joseph commanded that the money his brothers had brought to purchase the grain should be planted in their sacks without their knowledge. On the way home, their consciences were again disturbed when one of them opened his sack to feed his donkey and found the payment money. Their hearts sank and they wondered what God was doing to them (42:28). 'Guilty consciences', says Matthew Henry, 'are apt to take good providences in a bad sense.'

God uses circumstances to awaken both the consciences of people dead in sin and believers who have not owned up to past sins. A guilty conscience can lead to great torment of soul. If we come with a repentant spirit, asking the Lord to forgive us, we can know with assurance that we are in a right legal standing before God through faith in the blood of Jesus (Rom. 5:1-11). Do you know what it is like to have your innermost being 'sprinkled from an evil conscience'? (Heb. 10:22). Until David was challenged, he continued to live with unconfessed sin (2 Sam. 12; Ps. 51).

3. The brothers in Canaan before Jacob (42:29-38)

Back home the brothers reported what had happened to them. This time they told no lies, but they omitted to mention that they had been held prisoners for three days or that if they did not take Benjamin with them on their next visit they would all die (see 42:20). They tactfully stated that the **'lord of the land'** had asked them to leave one brother behind and that if their youngest brother was brought to him the one detained would be freed and they would be allowed to trade in the land (42:33-34). No mention was made of the returned money, but when they came to empty their sacks of grain they discovered **'each man's bundle of money'** (42:35). Their sense of guilt was expressed in their fear. It was yet another indication that God was pursuing them for what they had done to Joseph.

Jacob's outburst revealed his continued grief over Joseph. It seemed to him to be a rerun of what had happened before: **'You have bereaved me: Joseph is no more, Simeon is no more, and you want to take Benjamin away'** (42:36). Jacob seemed to be blaming the brothers for the loss of his sons. Reuben showed his own sincerity with an oath that suggested he was prepared to think of Benjamin as equivalent to his own two sons: **'Kill my two sons if I do not bring him back to you'** (42:37). Jacob was determined that Benjamin would not go with them to Egypt. Since Joseph was presumed dead, Benjamin was Jacob's delight. The other sons had had to learn to live with this and to understand how much grief they had caused their father.

Although Jacob had known God's presence during previous difficult experiences, in this crisis he considered that **'All these things are against me'** (42:36). Little did he realize that all these things were working together for the good of all his family.

Testing experiences (43:1-34)

Joseph said he needed to test the brothers' words in case they were spies (42:15-16). The 'real test', as we observe in this chapter and the next is, as Kline observes, 'whether they had a change of heart'.[1]

1. Jacob and his sons (43:1-14)

Necessity moved Jacob to direct his sons to return to Egypt to buy food. Probably no one expected the famine to continue for so long. It was Judah who spoke on behalf of the others to remind their father that unless they took Benjamin with them they would have no audience with **'the man'**, they would receive no food, Simeon would remain in prison and they would be treated as spies (43:3-5).

Jacob was annoyed with his sons for having revealed so much to **'the man'**. But, as they pointed out, **'Could we possibly have known that he would say, "Bring your brother down"?'** (43:7). This was as much a test for Jacob as for his sons. Would he let go his dear son for the sake of Simeon and the rest of the family? Judah reminded his father of the harsh realities. Benjamin either went with them, or they all remained home and starved to death (43:8). Judah urged his father to send Benjamin with him and not to waste any more precious time, vowing to take the blame if anything happened to him (43:9).

Jacob saw the logic of the argument and allowed his beloved son to go with Judah so that the extended family, including the **'little ones'**, might be kept alive. He prepared a present of items he had in stock which would have been in great demand because of the famine. On a previous occasion he had done something similar in order to appease his own brother Esau (32:20). He also gave them money for more grain and returned the money that had been found in their sacks. Finally, Jacob entrusted them to the care of **'God Almighty'** (*El Shaddai* — 43:14).

It was a great sacrifice that Jacob was making. Would Simeon be released and would Benjamin be returned to him in safety? For the sake of a new generation growing up he reconciled himself to the possibility that he might not see Benjamin again. When he said, **'If I am bereaved, I am bereaved!'** (43:14), he was not resigning himself to fate. Esther uttered similar words after she had instructed her uncle and maids to fast: 'If I perish, I perish!' (Esth. 4:16). Jacob had done what he could to show they were honest people and he had committed them to the God who he knew could do what seemed impossible to humans. This was no leap into the dark. He was trusting the God of Abraham, the 'Fear of Isaac' and the God of Bethel and Penuel. It may be because of his expression of trust in God, despite the circumstances, that Jacob's new name, Israel, is used in these verses.

2. The brothers in Egypt before Joseph's steward (43:15-25)

After a brief appearance before Joseph, who immediately spotted Benjamin, the brothers were escorted to his home by the steward. This new development brought further fears and guilt in the men. They could not believe that they were receiving pure kindness. Their imaginations worked overtime and they suspected that they were walking into a trap on account of the money they had found in their sacks (43:18). The brothers therefore took the opportunity to set the record straight before they went into the house (43:19-22). Distrust and suspicion often arise because of unconfessed sin.

The steward must have been instructed by Joseph how to respond, for he reassured them and encouraged them to regard the treasure in their sacks as a gift from God (43:23). This encouraging statement prepared them for Joseph's own confession when he revealed to them who he was (45:4). God was indeed at work fulfilling his purposes through all the events of their lives.

The steward's word was followed by action. He brought Simeon to them, gave them water to wash their sandy feet and gave their animals feed (43:23-24). This made them feel more at ease and they prepared the present to give to the prime minister (43:25).

3. *The banquet* (43:26-34)

When Joseph came home all eleven brothers bowed before him and offered their present. His friendly enquiries after their well-being and that of their father further encouraged them and they again prostrated themselves before him. Joseph's eyes turned to Benjamin, **'his mother's son'**, and asked whether he was the young brother of whom they had spoken. He spoke kindly to him and pronounced a blessing upon him: **'God be gracious to you, my son'** (43:29; see Num. 6:25). Speaking to him in this way made it impossible for Joseph to contain his feelings any longer. He was forced to go out of the room in order to weep in private. After composing himself, he returned and gave orders for the meal to be served (43:30-31).

Attention is drawn to the seating arrangements. Joseph, in view of his high position, sat on his own, the brothers were at another table and Joseph's Egyptian officials sat at a third table. It was regarded as a detestable thing for Egyptians to eat with the Hebrews. What the brothers found remarkable was that they had been seated in order of their ages, from the first-born to the youngest. The odds against that happening by coincidence would be in the order of forty million to one. No wonder they **'looked in astonishment at one another'** (43:33).

They were very honoured in having food served to them from the top table. Benjamin, however, was specially honoured in being given a portion that was five times larger than those

of the other brothers. Joseph deliberately favoured Benjamin
to test them for jealousy. Jealousy had been the prime reason
for the brothers' hatred of Joseph.

It was a great meal and they were all in good spirits (43:34).
Despite the uncanny nature of the seating arrangements and
the favoured portion, they enjoyed the evening.

As Joseph tested his brothers he was displaying the qualities of a wise ruler who feared God and who was acting to
promote righteousness, peace and unity among his people. He
is a pointer to the one whose rule is characterized by truth,
humility and righteousness (Ps. 45:4).

Guilt confessed (44:1-34)

1. Joseph's plan (44:1-13)

Joseph put his brothers through one last testing experience
before he revealed who he was. He commanded his steward
to fill their sacks with as much grain as they could carry and
again returned their money. In addition, Joseph's silver cup
was placed in Benjamin's sack. When morning came the brothers were sent on their way. They must have felt very pleased
with themselves for having completed their mission so successfully. Their feelings of elation were suddenly destroyed
when Joseph's steward overtook them and accused them of
repaying **'evil for good'** (44:4) by stealing the prime minister's cup, the one with which he **'practises divination'** (44:5)
This last comment did not necessarily mean that Joseph actually practised divination. It was probably one of the instruments associated with his royal office and the reference to its
function stressed the gravity of the offence.

The brothers solemnly protested their innocence, arguing
that if they were dishonest people they would not have returned

the money they had found in their sacks after their first trip to Egypt. So confident were they of their innocence that they made a solemn declaration similar to the one Jacob made when Laban accused him of stealing (31:32). If any of them was the thief, then he should die and the rest of them would become slaves of the prime minister. But the steward indicated that that would be unnecessary. Only the guilty one would be taken as a slave; the rest would be blameless. Little did they realize that they were offering to suffer the kind of punishment they had meted out to the innocent Joseph when they left him to die and then sold him into slavery.

Moments of tension followed as each man's sack was opened and searched, beginning with the oldest down to the youngest. To their horror the cup was found in Benjamin's sack. They all expressed their grief by tearing their clothes. Instead of allowing Benjamin to be carried off to bear the consequences of his crime, they all accompanied him to the city.

2. Benjamin's punishment (44:14-17)

The opening words of this section, **'So Judah and his brothers came to Joseph's house,'** introduce us to Judah's leading role as spokesman for the rest. It had been Judah who had argued that Joseph should be sold into slavery rather than left to die (37:26-27). He was next seen as a man of double standards who had mistreated his daughter-in-law (38:24-26). It is a much more subdued and honourable person that we meet with in these verses. He had offered to become surety for Benjamin and it was therefore natural that he should take the lead in speaking on behalf of the others.

When the brothers prostrated themselves once more before him, Joseph continued to put pressure on them by suggesting that it had been through divination that he had found out who was responsible. He spoke as an Egyptian official would speak and it was all part of the scheme to humble his brothers. There is no reason to suppose that Joseph had really used magical arts and the reader knows that the brothers were innocent of this particular crime. But there was no way they could prove their innocence. Everything was stacked against them. Joseph's claim to have supernatural powers made them realize, perhaps for the first time, that they could not hide anything from God. Judah, therefore, could do nothing but admit that God had found them out, not only about the cup but about their dark secret.

We begin to see more clearly that Joseph's aim all along had not been to obtain personal revenge but to bring his brothers to acknowledge their guilt. Reuben had earlier concluded that they were being treated harshly because of what they had done to their brother Joseph. Now Judah confessed unwittingly before Joseph himself, **'God has found out the iniquity of your servants.'** He considered it right that they should all suffer the punishment of slavery (44:16). But Joseph would not hear of it. They were all allowed to depart in peace apart from Benjamin, **'in whose hand the cup was found'** (44:17).

What would be the reaction of the brothers to this? Would they abandon Benjamin as they had abandoned Joseph?

3. Judah's plea (44:18-34)

It is generally agreed that this paragraph is one of the most powerful pleas in all literature. This uncaring, heartless man had been subdued through all the experiences of the last few years. What is more, Judah was speaking for all the brothers, for they too had been broken by recent events.

As he interceded for Benjamin, Judah began very respectfully and reminded Joseph of the great interest he had shown in the family and how he had specifically requested to see Benjamin. Judah showed a concern both for his father and for his brother Benjamin. He recounted how his father had given his consent for Benjamin to accompany them and how he had reminded them all that he had two sons by his favourite wife. One he assumed had been torn to pieces by wild animals and if harm were to come to Benjamin, the other son, then he said, **'You shall bring down my grey hair with sorrow to the grave'** (44:29). Judah then pleaded that if he were to return home without Benjamin the shock would kill his father. He explained how close the bond was between father and son: **'His life is bound up in the lad's life'** (44:30).

Judah's emotional appeal closed with an offer to take Benjamin's place, seeing that he had vowed to his father to stand surety for his brother. He could not bear to go home and witness **'the evil that would come upon my father'** (44:34).

There was clearly no longer any jealousy or bad spirit in the brothers. The experience had brought them to confess the guilt of their past action and to show a repentant attitude by this real concern for their father and brother. They had at last come to terms with the special affection that their father had for his wife Rachel and her two sons. Judah, the one who had callously suggested the idea of selling Joseph into Egypt as a slave, was now prepared to receive the punishment of slavery in the place of Rachel's son rather than to see his poor father die of a broken heart. For the first time we see Judah directing us to the truth concerning the promised 'seed'. He offered himself as a substitute for his brother. Jesus Christ, who is from the family line of Judah, offered himself as the perfect substitute in order to release his brothers from slavery to sin and Satan (Heb. 2:10-15; John 8:33-36).

All this convinced Joseph that there existed in the family a new bond of love. For unity to be maintained among God's people it is important that envy and hatred be confessed and dealt with, otherwise God may use very unpleasant disciplining experiences. We are urged to put away lying and 'Let each one ... speak truth with his neighbour, for we are members of one another... Let all bitterness, wrath, anger, clamour, and evil speaking be put away from you, with all malice. And be kind to one another...' (Eph. 4:25,31-32). Spiritual revivals often begin with the pain of confessing sins that have hindered blessing in local congregations.

Brothers reconciled (45:1-28)

1. Joseph's identity revealed (45:1-4)

Joseph had had difficulty controlling his emotions in the presence of his brothers on previous occasions (42:24; 43:30). Judah's moving words were the last straw and after ordering his Egyptian attendants out of the room, Joseph **'wept aloud'** in front of his brothers. When he told them who he was they were dumbfounded. They were too terrified to speak when he tried to ask after his father. Joseph realized how necessary it was to reassure them that he loved them and wished them no harm. When he said, **'I am Joseph your brother, whom you sold into Egypt'** (45:4), it confirmed that it really was their brother, but would also have caused them renewed distress.

2. Divine sovereignty (45:5-15)

Joseph calmed their fears by indicating that God had planned what had happened. Their wicked actions, for which they were now truly sorry, had been used by God **'to preserve life'**.

Four times Joseph emphasized God's overruling hand: **'God sent me before you to preserve life'** (45:5); **'God sent me before you to preserve a posterity** ["remnant"] **for you in the earth'** (45:7); **'So now it was not you who sent me here, but God'** (45:8); **'God has made me lord of all Egypt'** (45:9).

The fact that God overruled their sin to bring about blessing did not lessen the guilt of the brothers. Peter made the same point when he preached on the Day of Pentecost. It was part of God's plan that Jesus should die, but lawless hands took him and crucified him (Acts 2:23). As God used the sins of Joseph's brothers for good, so he used the betrayal of Judas, the hatred of the Jewish leaders and the cruelty of Roman crucifixion to bring salvation to the nations. Those sins are never excused. Guilt must be acknowledged and repented of in order that God's salvation might be experienced.

God's sovereignty helped Joseph to forgive his brothers. He could look beyond his own little life to see God's good hand working for the benefit of others. 'No one who believes in the sovereignty of God in the affairs of life can bear a grudge or take revenge.'[2] Joseph was able to calm the fears which his brothers had with this comfortable teaching. It is one thing to give assent to this doctrine in an intellectual way; it is quite another to act in the light of it in the everyday affairs of life. May God give us the grace and spirit of Joseph.

God's sovereignty works with his grace to bring about **'a great deliverance'**, or a better translation would be 'a great number of survivors'. In this God was acting to fulfil promises first made to Abraham that he would have many descendants and that all nations would be blessed through him. God so acted that Joseph was a means of blessing to all the nations who came to Egypt for grain. It points to the ultimate fulfilment when the 'Seed' of Abraham, the Lord Jesus Christ, would bring spiritual food to all the nations. Speaking of his sacrificial death he said, 'The bread that I shall give is my flesh, which I shall give for the life of the world' (John 6:51).

The words used to express the divine purpose suggest that Joseph was like a new Noah, used by God **'to preserve life'** (45:5) and **'to save your lives'** (45:7; see 6:19-20; 7:3). Verse

7 also brings to our attention the idea of a saved 'remnant' (**'posterity'**) and 'survivors' (**'deliverance'**). The two words come together again in 2 Kings 19:31, where Isaiah speaks of the remnant who survive the Assyrian siege (cf. Isa. 10:20). These descendants of Abraham are important in God's plans concerning victory over the serpent. Jacob and his offspring are like a remnant who have escaped destruction and become a sign of future hope. It is a theme taken up by the prophets. The escaped remnant becomes the means through which the future promises of God are fulfilled.

3. *The invitation to Jacob to live in Egypt* (45:16-28)

In his final word to them Joseph encouraged his brothers to return to their father and tell him the good news of how God had made him such an important person (**'all my glory'**) in Egypt (45:13). They were to urge Jacob to come down quickly to live in Egypt so that Joseph could provide for them all. He was able to tell them what they could not find out for them-selves — that the famine would last another five years. The kisses and embraces followed. Only then did the brothers find words to speak to Joseph (45:14-15).

Pharaoh soon heard about the reunion of Joseph with his brothers and he was happy for the whole family to live in Egypt. He encouraged them to occupy **'the best of the land'** and to **'eat the fat of the land'**. At Pharaoh's command Joseph ar-ranged for carts to be sent to carry the wives and children. Joseph was also able to send his brothers back, each with a new robe and accompanied by donkeys laden with gifts for their father and food for the journey back to Egypt. Benjamin was given extra gifts.

Before they left, Joseph also counselled them, **'See that you do not become troubled along the way'** (45:24). He knew the human heart and how his brothers had reacted earlier (see 42:21-23). Even at this point things could have gone sadly wrong, so he warned them, 'Let there be no recriminations.'[3]

When **'the sons of Israel'** (45:21) arrived home they broke the news to their father: **'Joseph is still alive, and he is governor over all the land of Egypt'** (45:26). Jacob was stunned, for he could not believe what he was hearing. It was only when they showed him the carts which Joseph had provided that his spirit revived and he accepted the news as genuine. **'Then Israel said, "It is enough. Joseph my son is still alive. I will go and see him before I die"'** (45:28). He already expected to 'go down' to Joseph in death *(Sheol)*, mourning (37:35) and was fearful that if some calamity happened to Benjamin the same would happen (42:38). Instead, he was to go down to Egypt to see Joseph alive and well and the agent of God's salvation for his own family and those of other nations.

It is fitting that Jacob is described as 'Israel' in the closing verse, for it speaks of a new beginning. We too have a message of hope concerning the 'Seed' of Israel. Jesus Christ, who descended so low and suffered the pangs of hell for our sakes, is alive never more to die and has been exalted to the highest place in the universe. He is exalted to be a Prince and a Saviour. We are called to go to him. For with him there is fulness of life and eternal security.

38.
Israel in Egypt

Please read Genesis 46:1 – 47:31

Moving house can be one of the most stressful and emotional experiences in life. I am sure we can identify with Jacob as he moved from his familiar surroundings to another country and an alien culture.

We are coming towards the end of another stage in the history of redemption. The God who had brought Abraham from the east to live in the land of promise now encouraged his grandson to move his whole household out of Canaan and settle in Egypt. What was God doing? Why was this necessary? Could not God make them into a great nation and cause them to be a blessing to all nations by keeping them in the land of Canaan? Of course he could! But God did it this way to teach Israel, and us, important truths concerning the gospel.

If they had not gone into Egypt Israel would never have experienced God's redeeming grace, rescuing them from the power of the enemy and forming them into a nation with God as their King. They were also taught that they were to be a worshipping community and a pilgrim people, marching like an army at God's direction. The promised land was seen as a goal, a place of rest and plenty, an end point after years of trial and suffering. They were taught that they would be preserved alive by living by God's Word, which they were to acknowledge as more important than physical bread (Deut. 6:24; 8:2-5).

All these experiences, and more, are instructive and direct us to God's redeeming love in Christ and to the trials of faith as God's pilgrim people journey towards the inheritance reserved in heaven.

Israel moves to Beersheba and meets God (46:1-4)

Joseph had told his brothers that God had sent him to Egypt ahead of them in order to preserve life (45:5; Ps. 105:17). This, along with the prospect of seeing the son whom he supposed was dead, encouraged Jacob to make the journey. But it was not an easy decision to make. He would have recalled the prophecy that his descendants would become slaves in a foreign country for 400 years (15:13). Quitting the land was something that Abraham did not want his son Isaac to do (24:8). In a time of famine, Isaac was commanded by God not to go to Egypt (26:2). Earlier in his life, Jacob had been forced to leave the land but had been encouraged by God to return to it. He needed confirmation that what providence was suggesting was correct. We can read providences wrongly. To go against God's revealed will in the Bible simply because we consider the circumstances are favourable is sin.

Before going to Egypt, Jacob decided to stop at Beersheba **'and offered sacrifices'** (46:1). Beersheba was for all practical purposes the southernmost point in the land of Canaan (2 Sam. 24:2). It was desert from there to Egypt. Abraham had made a treaty with the Philistine ruler and had worshipped the Everlasting God at this place (21:32-33). It was here that God had appeared to Isaac (26:23-25). Not unnaturally, therefore, Jacob worshipped at this spot before leaving the land of promise. He offered sacrifices on the altar his father had built. Sacrifice was an important part of worship in Old Testament times. Animals and incense are no longer required, for we have boldness to come to God through the blood of Jesus, but prayer is likened to incense and animal offerings (Ps. 141:2).

Jacob worshipped the same God as his father (46:1). Abraham, Isaac and Jacob all trusted the same God. Abraham had gone to Egypt and his concerns at going led him into sin. As Jacob worshipped, God graciously came to him, as he was to come to prophets like Daniel, in **'a vision of the night'** (see 15:12; see Dan. 2:19). God called him by his old name: **'Jacob, Jacob!'** (46:2). The repetition of his name recalls a critical moment in Abraham's life when God called out to him by name (22:11). At this last crucial point in Jacob's life God encouraged him as he had done years earlier at Bethel when he was about to leave Canaan for Haran (28:10-22; see also Exod. 3:4; 1 Sam. 3:4,10).

The divine message (46:3-4) gave Jacob the following assurances.

Firstly, **'I am God, the God of your father.'** The supreme God *(El)* was the God whom Jacob had come to revere as 'the God of my father' (see 31:5,29,42,53;32:9). God introduced himself to Moses by saying, 'I am the God of your father...' (Exod. 3:6). This same God is known to us as 'the God and Father of our Lord Jesus Christ' (2 Cor. 1:3; Eph. 1:3).

Secondly, God said, **'Do not fear to go down to Egypt.'** Jacob was not afraid in the way that Abraham had feared on entering Egypt (see 12:11-13). His fears arose out of his concern not to go against the divine purposes concerning the land of promise. He had been encouraged by God to believe that Canaan was his country (32:9). God's people are not of the world, but are to live in the world (John 17:14-18).

Thirdly, God made four promises.

'I will make of you a great nation there' (see 12:2; 28:14). Jacob was informed that Egypt, not Canaan, would be the place where this great nation would arise (see Ps. 105:23-24). This implied that they would be in Egypt for a considerable time (15:16). Hundreds of years later God said, 'When Israel was a child, I loved him, and out of Egypt I called my son' (Hosea 11:1). Israel's representative and ours went through the same experience (Matt. 2:15). God sent his Son to live in a hostile world so that a great nation might be formed there from every ethnic group.

'I will go down with you to Egypt.' God had given Jacob a similar reassurance when he was leaving Canaan for Haran (28:15). We can go anywhere if we are assured that the Lord is with us. 'Yea, though I walk through the valley of the shadow of death, I will fear no evil; for you are with me...' (Ps. 23:4). This same Lord who commands his people to go and make disciples of all the nations promises to be with us always, 'even to the end of the age' (Matt. 28:18-20).

'And I will also surely bring you up again.' This is a very emphatic promise. It is not merely saying that God would make sure that Jacob would be buried in Canaan, but that his descendants would be brought out of Egypt. 'You' here means the future nation that will be formed in Egypt. It looks forward to the Exodus. It also points us on to the final exodus, the redemption of the body and the inheritance that has been reserved for God's people. We can be assured that the Lord who is with us through the trials of this life will bring us up again and preserve us 'for his heavenly kingdom' (Rom. 8:18-23; 2 Tim. 4:18).

'And Joseph will put his hand on your eyes.' This means that Joseph would be with him when he died. God was most kind to Jacob and assured him that he would die contented, with his favourite son at his side to perform the final loving act of making sure his eyelids were closed and his body buried.

The sons of Israel move to Egypt (46:5-27)

Special attention is given to this move of Jacob and his sons to Egypt. It is comparable to Abraham's leaving his home to journey to Canaan. Weak and frail though he was and needing to be carried by his sons, Jacob was strong in faith and, like Abraham, obeyed God's will. He was placed, along with the wives and small children, **'in the carts which Pharaoh had sent to carry him'**.

Far from being ruled by his sons, Jacob was still in charge. He was the leader who **'brought with him to Egypt'** all his sons and their dependants (46:7). The repetition of **'all his descendants'** ('all his seed') emphasizes that no one was left behind (46:6-7). Despite the major differences between the sons, they were all leaving Canaan together for Egypt to join their remaining brother who was already there. Unlike Abraham and Isaac, Jacob possessed no Ishmael or Esau who went their separate ways and were outside the covenant promises. All Jacob's sons belonged to the promised 'seed'. Not one of them was excluded from God's covenant blessing first made to Abraham. This is the family unit that would become a great nation.

To mark the importance of this momentous move in the history of redemption and to stress again that all Israel's descendants went down into Egypt, a new family list is given (46:8-27; see 35:23-26). It is appropriate that Jacob's sons are described as **'the sons of Israel'** (46:5) and again as **'children** [literally "sons"] **of Israel'** (46:8). It prepares us for the use of this term when the tribes were formed into a holy nation at the time of the Exodus. The book of Exodus begins by listing the sons of Israel who came to Egypt (Exod. 1:1-5).

The family list is divided according to the mothers of Jacob's sons.

1. The sons of Leah (46:8-15)

'These were the sons of Leah, whom she bore to Jacob in
Padan Aram, with his daughter Dinah' (46:15). Leah's six
sons, Reuben, Simeon, Levi, Judah, Issachar and Zebulun, are
mentioned, along with their sons. We are reminded that Reuben
was 'Jacob's first-born' (46:8) and that Judah's sons, Er and
Onan, 'died in the land of Canaan' (46:12). One of Simeon's
sons, Shaul, was 'the son of a Canaanite woman' (46:10).
Judah obviously was not alone in going to the Canaanites for
a wife (38:2). His grandsons through Perez, Hezron and Hamul,
are included even though they were not born till later (see
38:14,29). They are probably mentioned to show that God
made up for the loss of Er and Onan. The total number listed
as belonging to Jacob through Leah (including Er and Onan)
is 'thirty-three' (six sons, twenty-five grandsons and two
great-grandsons). Dinah is added because of what we know
of her in chapter 34 and to indicate that daughters were also
born to this family. The thirty-three named boys plus Dinah
represent this family line of 'his sons and his daughters'.

2. The sons of Zilpah (46:16-18)

'These were the sons of Zilpah...' (46:18). She was Leah's
maid 'whom Laban gave to Leah' and whom Leah gave to
Jacob to produce children. We are not allowed to forget Laban,
Leah's father. Her two sons, Gad and Asher, are mentioned
and their sons, along with two grandsons of Asher through
Beriah. Asher's daughter 'Serah' is also included (46:17; see
Num. 26:46; 1 Chr. 7:30). All the persons named, including
the daughter, added up to 'sixteen' (two sons, eleven grandsons, one granddaughter and two great-grandsons).

3. The sons of Rachel (46:19-22)

'These were the sons of Rachel...' (46:22). This part is distinguished from the other three in several ways. First, the section refers to the **'sons of Rachel'** at the beginning as well as at the end. Secondly, only Rachel is described as **'Jacob's wife'** in this list. Thirdly, special attention is paid to Joseph when his two sons, Manasseh and Ephraim, are named. Fourthly, Joseph is the only son whose wife, Asenath, is mentioned in the list. Finally, Benjamin is Jacob's most fruitful son, with ten sons named. Through Rachel, **'fourteen'** persons are named (two sons and twelve grandsons).

4. The sons of Bilhah (46:23-25)

'These were the sons of Bilhah...' (46:25). She was Rachel's maid and again Laban is mentioned as the one who gave Bilhah to Rachel. Her sons were Dan and Naphtali. Dan is the least fruitful of Jacob's children, having only one son. Those named belonging to Jacob through Bilhah are **'seven'** (two sons and five grandsons).

5. The figure of seventy persons

The grand total of **'all the persons of the house of Jacob who went to Egypt'** is given as **'seventy'**, which is the sum of the four family sub-totals (33+16+14+7 = 70). The text itself suggests that this number must not be taken literally:

1. The sub-totals include people not yet born, such as Judah's two grandsons and Benjamin's ten sons (46:12,21).
2. Joseph came to Egypt but not with Jacob.

3. Joseph's sons, Manasseh and Ephraim, **'were born to him in Egypt'** (46:20,27).

4. Er and Onan died in Canaan (46:12).

5. Dinah is mentioned but not counted in the sub-total of thirty-three, even though the figure is said to include **'sons and daughters'** (46:15).

6. Verse 26 gives a different number. There were **'sixty-six persons in all'** who **'went with Jacob to Egypt'**. It is emphasized that this number is limited to those who came from **'his body'** (literally 'his loins'; Exod. 1:5), which, as we have seen, includes grandchildren and great-grandchildren. An example of those not from his body is given: **'besides Jacob's sons' wives'** (46:26). The sons of Joseph are also mentioned again as an example of those who were from Jacob's loins but were actually born in Egypt. Other examples would have included Benjamin's sons and Judah's grandsons. They came into Egypt in the same kind of way that it is later said of Levi that he paid tithes to Melchizedek while 'still in the loins of' Abraham (Heb. 7:10). Taking Joseph's two sons (46:27) plus Er and Onan (46:12) away from seventy gives the reduced total of sixty-six. Dinah is still not included in the figure but she is a reminder that there were other unnamed daughters and granddaughters, represented by their brothers, who came to Egypt (see 46:7,15).

The question then arises, why has Moses added the names of people who did not actually come down to Egypt with Jacob? Why has he chosen the number seventy? (Exod. 1:5; Deut. 10:22).[1] As we have seen in other parts of Genesis, numbers are used symbolically to express truth. Seventy is a round number and is used here to represent **'the children of Israel'**

(46:8), all the descendants of Abraham's chosen line who went into Egypt. Just as all the names descended from the sons of Noah added up to seventy in the table of nations (10:1-32) so all the names descended from Jacob add up to seventy (see Deut. 32:8-11). The seventy nations represented the entire world of human beings under the curse. Jacob's family of seventy persons is a miniature world. It is about to become the great nation promised to Abraham, a representative and substitute nation, through which all the nations of the world will find blessing. Seventy persons is still considered a small number, and yet in Egypt they will become exceedingly numerous and fill the land (Exod. 1:7; Deut. 10:22). As Genesis draws to a conclusion, we are encouraged to look forward to the fulfilment of God's promises, when the chosen 'Seed', Jesus Christ, will appear to undo the works of the Evil One and bring about salvation for people from every nation.

Israel meets Joseph (46:28-34)

1. Judah

Judah is given the job of leading the party into Egypt and preparing for the meeting with Joseph. This is remarkable, for it was Judah who had been instrumental in cutting off Joseph's contact with his father. Since then, however, he had grown in influence, particularly after pleading with his father (43:3-10) and with Joseph (44:14-34).[2] It is Judah who points out the way to the good land of Goshen (46:28). All this prepares us for God's plan to use the 'Seed' of Judah to bring about the greater deliverance and to lead his people 'to living fountains of waters' (Rev. 7:17).

2. Joseph

What an emotional time it must have been for Jacob and Joseph! They had not seen one another for twenty-two years. The first thought on Joseph's mind when he made himself known to his brothers in Egypt was to ask after his father (45:3). Now he saw him face to face. Though Joseph was such an influential man in Egypt he did not wait for his father to appear before him. Instead, he humbled himself and respected his old father by going to Goshen in his chariot to meet him. Then we have the dramatic moment when Joseph embraced his father **'and wept on his neck a good while'** (46:29).[3]

Jacob never thought he would see his son alive again. He had told his other sons that he would go to the realm of the dead *(Sheol)* in mourning (37:35). When he heard that Joseph was still alive he said, 'I will go and see him before I die' (45:28). Having set eyes on Joseph he could say, **'Now let me die, since I have seen your face, because you are still alive'** (46:30). Jacob's words remind us of what Simeon said when he saw Jesus: 'Lord, now let your servant depart in peace … for my eyes have seen your salvation' (Luke 2:29-30). To Jacob, Joseph's appearance was like a resurrection from the dead. Jacob could die peacefully because Joseph was alive. We too can face death with confidence because a greater than Joseph actually did die and rise triumphant from the dead. Praise God, who 'has begotten us again to a living hope through the resurrection of Jesus Christ from the dead' (1 Peter 1:3).

3. Goshen

Joseph took the necessary diplomatic steps to ensure that his family would be safe and well provided for in Egypt. Pharaoh needed to be told that they had arrived and that Joseph intended them to live in an area by themselves. As the Egyptians hated shepherds, Joseph reckoned that Pharaoh would have no objections to his family living apart in the land of Goshen. We do not know why it was that **'Every shepherd is an abomination to the Egyptians'** (46:34). It may be that the sophisticated Egyptian city-dwellers despised the foreign no-madic shepherds in much the same way as people today detest gypsies. Joseph used this aversion to good advantage before Pharaoh to secure the land of Goshen for his family.

In this way, the people of God would be kept apart from the Egyptian culture, and would remain a distinct group with their own traditions, a fact which would help preserve the memories of the covenant that God had made with the fathers of Israel. Although the people of God were in Egypt they did not belong to Egypt. Though God's people in Christ are to live in the world they are not part of the world system ruled by the Evil One. When Jesus prayed for his people 'in the world', he did not pray that they should be taken out of the world, but that they might be kept from evil, because 'They are not of the world' (John 17:9-16). It is part of true religion to keep our-selves 'unspotted from the world' (James 1:27).

Goshen does not appear in Egyptian records. It is also called 'the land of Rameses' (47:11) which suggests that it lay on the eastern side of the Nile delta in an area well suited to pasture sheep, away from the centre of population. Pharaoh describes Goshen as 'the best of the land' (47:6). While Judah led his brothers to the land of Goshen, it was Joseph who actually secured the place for them. Both Joseph and Judah point us to Jesus Christ and his relationship with his people. In Christ we already enjoy blessings and privileges in this world in antici-pation of the heavenly inheritance. Jesus said, 'There is no one who has left house … or lands, for my sake and the gospel's, who shall not receive a hundredfold now … with persecutions — and in the age to come, eternal life' (Mark 10:29-30).

The family meet Pharaoh (47:1-10)

1. Pharaoh meets Joseph's brothers (47:1-6)

Pharaoh was informed of the arrival of Joseph's family in Goshen. This helped to prepare the way for the request for them to remain there. Five brothers were selected to have an audience with Pharaoh and when the king asked the leading question, they dutifully responded by informing him that they were shepherds and had come as immigrants because of the famine. They had not come to be a burden on the state for they had livestock of their own. Their one request was to be allowed to live as temporary residents in the land of Goshen. Pharaoh responded with generous words. He not only granted them their wish, but encouraged Joseph to appoint some of them to take charge of the royal cattle. Here was another example of divine providence working for the good of God's people. As God had caused Joseph to prosper in the land of the pharaohs, so God caused the brothers to prosper through their association with Joseph.

2. Pharaoh meets Joseph's father (47:7-10)

This frail old man, so dependent on others and on Pharaoh himself, took the initiative on entering and leaving the royal presence. In earthly terms Pharaoh was superior, but in spiritual terms Jacob was the greater. **'Jacob blessed Pharaoh'** (47:7,10). He prayed for the king's well-being. Jacob knew the promise to Abraham that God would bless those who blessed the descendants of Abraham and that they would be a blessing to others. We are also called to pray for those in authority over us that the blessings of the gospel might reach more people (1 Tim. 2:1-7).

Pharaoh acknowledged Jacob's blessing by asking about his age. Jacob's reply seems surprising. **'Few and evil have been the days of the years of my life,'** does not seem to accord with the fact that he was 130 years old and would live another seventeen years. Yet his years were few compared with those of his father and grandfather. Abraham was 175 when he died and Isaac was 180. Life had also been 'evil', or 'hard'. More than his father and grandfather, he had experienced severe troubles, including escaping from his brother, an unhappy married life, the death of his favourite wife in childbirth, and mourning the loss of a son he assumed had been killed. Jacob's words were not a complaint. He was merely stating the truth. They teach us three things about life.

Life is a pilgrimage

Jacob confessed that he and his ancestors had been pilgrims all their lives. God's people are travellers through this world. 'Here we have no continuing city, but we seek the one to come' (see Heb. 11:13; 13:14).

It is a short pilgrimage

Compared with eternity our days on earth are few. Because of this we need to number our days and gain a heart of wisdom (Ps. 90:12).

It is a difficult pilgrimage

It is through much tribulation that we enter the glory of God's kingdom (Acts 14:22). Nevertheless, 'The sufferings of this present time are not worthy to be compared with the glory which shall be revealed in us' (Rom. 8:18).

Joseph manages his family and Egypt (47:11-26)

1. Providing for his family (47:11-12)

After the official sanction by Pharaoh, Joseph settled his family in Egypt. He actually gave them a permanent stake **'in the best of the land … as Pharaoh had commanded'**. Moses uses the contemporary name, **'the land of Rameses'**, for what in Jacob's day was called the land of Goshen (see 46:28,34; Exod. 12:37). Israelite slaves later helped build the city of Rameses in that same area (Exod. 1:11). Joseph also provided food for his father's extended family, making sure that each family's allocation was in proportion to the number of children in the household. His management skills were such that Joseph did not forget the needs of the smallest child. The Hebrew for **'according to the number in their families'** is, 'according to the little children'. A greater than Joseph did not forget the little children. Jesus is the bread of life for children as well as grown-ups: 'Let the little children come to me' (Mark 10:13-16).

2. Providing for the nation (47:13-26)

A considerable amount of space is given over to recounting Joseph's skill in governing Egypt during the famine crisis. First, he accepted money from the Egyptians as payment for grain (47:14). When their money ran out Joseph gave them food in exchange for their livestock (47:15-17). Finally, at the end of the years of famine, in exchange for themselves and their lands Joseph gave them seed to plant. He made it a law which still survived in the days of Moses (47:26) that one-fifth of the produce should thereafter be given to the crown. As the Egyptian priests already received their lands from Pharaoh they did not need to give them up and they were exempt from the harvest tax (47:18-26).

Joseph was operating a humane policy within the system of the times and we should not judge him by our own modern Western ideas of government. The Egyptologist Kenneth Kitchen notes that 'Joseph's economic policy ... simply made Egypt in fact what it always was in theory: the land became Pharaoh's property and its inhabitants his tenants.'[4] Joseph treated the people fairly and no one was left without food. He did not line his own pockets but **'brought the money into Pharaoh's house'** (47:14). Far from there being any social unrest because of the austere measures, the people were grateful to Joseph and actually suggested that they should become Pharaoh's servants (47:19,25). The rendering, **'And as for the people, he moved them into the cities'** (47:21), suggests that Joseph engaged in a mass displacement of people from the rural districts to the urban areas. His policy has been likened to that of Communist dictators. A more literal translation would be: 'He caused the people to pass over to the cities.' All the verse indicates is that the people were brought to the cities to receive the grain that was stored in the granaries (41:48).[5]

Why are so many details given of his policy to alleviate the plight of the Egyptians?

Firstly, it highlights *Joseph's wise management of Egypt.* After Joseph had announced his plan to deal with the famine, the king had said, 'There is no one as discerning and wise as you' (41:39). The passage illustrates Joseph's wisdom in governing a nation like Egypt. Wisdom says, 'By me kings reign, and rulers decree justice. By me princes rule' (Prov. 8:15-16). It is prophesied of the Messiah that 'the Spirit of wisdom and understanding' would be given to him and that he would bring justice to the Gentiles, 'and the coastlands shall wait for his law' (Isa. 11:2; 42:1-4).

Secondly, *Joseph is depicted as the saviour of Egypt* as well as of his own people (42:1 – 47:12; see 42:2; 43:8; 45:5). The Egyptians came before Joseph on two occasions and said, **'Why should we die…?'** (47:15,19). They afterwards confessed, **'You have saved our lives'** (47:25). The living God is the 'Saviour of all men, especially of those who believe' (1 Tim. 4:10). There is here a partial fulfilment of the promise to Abraham that 'In you all families of the earth shall be blessed' (12:3). It was said of our Lord Jesus by the Samaritans, 'This is indeed the Christ, the Saviour of the world' (John 4:42). God our Saviour desires all 'to be saved and to come to a knowledge of the truth. For there is one God and one mediator between God and men, the man Christ Jesus' (1 Tim. 2:4-5).

Thirdly, the situation under Joseph's rule invites *comparison with the situation when Moses lived*. Because the pharaoh in the time of Joseph treated Israel well, Egypt prospered despite the famine. When a new dynasty of pharaohs arose which did not know Joseph, Egypt began to enslave Israel and in the end they experienced the great plagues. God had said to Abraham, 'I will bless those who bless you, and I will curse him who curses you' (12:3).

Fourthly, another comparison can be drawn between *the legislation introduced by Joseph and the laws given by Moses*. As with Joseph's policy, those in Israel who became destitute could sell their land and even themselves. Also, land belonging to the Levites, the tribe associated with the tabernacle and its worship, could not be sold. Joseph worked under the authority of Pharaoh, where the land and the people belonged to the ruler. In Israel, where God was the recognized King and owner of the land, all Israelites were to be released in the seventh year and in the year of Jubilee (Deut. 15:1-18; Lev. 25:25-54). The Israelites were to show compassion by remembering that they were once slaves of the Egyptians before God released them.

Israel's main concern (47:27-31)

1. Blessing in Egypt

Through the wisdom of Joseph, Abraham's descendants lived safely and prospered in the land of Egypt. God blessed them and they became fruitful and **'multiplied exceedingly'** (47:27; see 46:3). Though they were aliens in a foreign land, they were greatly blessed. This anticipates the situation described in the first chapter of Exodus (1:7,12,20). Nothing can hinder God's commitment to his people, even though situations may seem to run contrary to God's purposes. 'If God is for us, who can be against us? ... Who shall separate us from the love of Christ? Shall tribulation, or distress, or persecution, or famine...?' (Rom. 8:31,35).

For seventeen years in Canaan Jacob had taken good care of his son Joseph and provided him with the best before he was so cruelly taken away. Now the tables are turned and Joseph provided for his father with the best of the land in Egypt during the final seventeen years of his life (47:28). The time reference also moves the narrative on to the last days of Jacob's life with the famine at an end and the family well established in Egypt.

2. Jacob's request

Jacob had one big request before he died. He made his favourite son, the one who had the authority to carry out his will, swear that he would bury him, not in Egypt but in Canaan, with his father and grandfather. This special favour mattered as much to him as Abraham's concern over finding the right bride for his son Isaac. In both cases the same symbolic gesture was used in swearing the oath (47:29; see 24:2). It stressed the seriousness of the request and guaranteed that the oath would be carried out. When Joseph had solemnly sworn that he would carry his father out of Egypt and bury him with his ancestors, **'Israel bowed himself on the head of the bed'** (47:31).[6] His bowed head probably denoted an attitude of prayer or praise to God (see 1 Kings 1:47-48).

There are ancient as well as modern examples of people wanting to be buried in the place of their birth, or in the same burial spot as their ancestors. Many do so for sentimental or superstitious reasons. This was not the case with Jacob. It was because of his faith in God that he wanted to be buried in Canaan. Although life had turned out very favourably for him in the end, Jacob's one great concern was not with present advantage but future hope. He believed the word that God had given him before he set out for Egypt: 'I will also surely bring you up again' (46:4). Canaan, not Egypt, was the land of promise. This was another important element in God's covenant with Abraham: 'To your descendants I have given this land, from the river of Egypt to the great river, the River Euphrates' (15:18). To be buried in the land **'with my fathers'** revealed Jacob's trust in the faithfulness of God to keep his word. In the face of death, 'His ultimate hope is the promise of God.'[7]

Canaan is a type and pledge of the heavenly inheritance that belongs to the people of God. Often we can become too attached to this present earthly scene. May Jacob encourage us to look to the promises of God concerning the future. 'Nevertheless, we, according to his promise, look for new heavens and a new earth in which righteousness dwells' (2 Peter 3:13). It makes no difference where our bodies are buried. The important thing is that we set our minds 'on things above, not on things on the earth... When Christ who is our life appears, then you also will appear with him in glory' (Col. 3:1-4).

39.
Blessings and prophecies

Please read Genesis 48:1 – 49:28

Dr Martin Lloyd-Jones, arguably the most powerful preacher of the twentieth century, spent the last months of his life preparing for heaven. He said, 'We do not give enough time to death and to our going on. It is a very strange thing this: the *one* certainty, yet we do not think about it… People say about sudden death, "It is a wonderful way to go." I have come to the conclusion that is quite wrong… The hope of a sudden death is based upon the fear of death. But death is not something to slip past, it should be victorious.'[1]

As Jacob neared the end of his life, his thoughts were on the future promises of God. He did not die a dejected old man hanging on to past memories. How sad it is to see elderly people who can only look back on certain highlights of their earlier years and have nothing to look forward to! Jacob's death was victorious because his faith was in God and he saw the future hope with the eye of faith.

Jacob blesses Joseph's sons (48:1-22)

Out of all the incidents in Jacob's eventful life this is the one which the writer to the Hebrews selects as an example of his faith. 'By faith Jacob, when he was dying, blessed each of the sons of Joseph, and worshipped, leaning on the top of his staff'

(Heb. 11:21). As a sign of how important this blessing was, it is recounted here in great detail.

1. Jacob acknowledges the source of all blessing (48:1-4)

On hearing that his father was ill, Joseph went to visit him with his two sons. The sons are listed in the order of their birth: **'Manasseh and Ephraim'** (48:1). When Jacob was informed of their arrival, he rallied what strength he had to speak to them from his sickbed. He recalled the time when God Almighty *(El Shaddai)* appeared to him at Luz (the old name for Bethel; see 28:19) and blessed him. Jacob was referring to the second occasion on which he visited Bethel (35:9-15).

The particular blessings mentioned are important items in God's covenant with Abraham. They included the promise of **'a multitude of people'** and Canaan **'as an everlasting possession'** for his descendants (48:4). Similar words are found on the lips of his father Isaac when he blessed Jacob (28:3-4). Though Jacob and his family had been given land in Egypt by Pharaoh (47:11), God had promised him Canaan as a permanent possession (17:8). These themes run through Genesis and are emphasized again in these closing chapters. They echo the original creation blessing to be **'fruitful and multiply'** (1:28) and encourage us to look at Canaan as a prototype of what was lost in Eden. Jacob urged Joseph not to look to possessions in Egypt and the promises made by the princes of this world, but to set his sights on the divine promises and the heavenly inheritance. 'We do not look at the things which are seen, but at the things which are not seen' (2 Cor. 4:18).

2. Jacob adopts Joseph's sons (48:5-12)

Jacob declared his intention to treat Joseph's two sons as his own offspring. In order to make it abundantly clear, he compared his grandchildren to his two oldest sons, Reuben and Simeon. Ephraim and Manasseh suddenly became joint-heirs along with all their uncles of the promises made to Abraham and were treated as Jacob's first-born sons (see 1 Chr. 5:1-2). They became tribes in their own right alongside the other eleven. In this way, Joseph was honoured by Jacob. Through his sons, whom Jacob had adopted as his own, Joseph received a double share in the land of promise and a place of prominence, as the future history of Israel would reveal. Any additional sons of Joseph (no other sons are mentioned) were to be reckoned among the tribes of Ephraim and Manasseh (48:6).

The special privileged position enjoyed by Joseph and his sons caused Jacob to recall the death of his beloved Rachel. She was his legitimate wife and if he had not been tricked by Laban and Leah, Joseph would have been his first-born son and worthy of a double inheritance. Her early death, giving birth to Benjamin, also meant that Jacob was unable to have further children by her. Adopting Joseph's children made up for this loss.

As in the account of her death (35:16-19), so here, stress is laid on the burial site. In both passages, Ephrath is identified as Bethlehem. Although she was not buried in the ancestral cemetery at Hebron, Rachel certainly died **'in the land of Canaan'**, in an area later to become famous as the birthplace of Israel's great monarch. By emphasizing Rachel's burial spot, Jacob pressed home the point that he wished to be buried in Canaan and directed his son and adopted sons to remember that their inheritance lay in Canaan, not Egypt.

Before Jacob officially adopted and blessed Ephraim and Manasseh, he made sure that they really were Joseph's sons (48:8-10). Jacob's eyes were dim with age, so his question, **'Who are these?'**, was not a superfluous one. We are reminded of the time when his own father's eyes were dim and of how Jacob had tricked him into thinking he was his brother Esau

(27:1,18). Joseph brought his sons near to his father for him to kiss and embrace them. The old man felt very privileged to be alive to know Joseph's sons, especially as he had not expected to see Joseph ever again.

Any idea we might have of little boys being kissed while sitting on their grandfather's knee is out of the question. Ephraim and Manasseh must have been in their late teens at least at this time, for they were born before Jacob came to Egypt seventeen years earlier. Frail old Jacob had raised himself up into a sitting position on his bed so that they were **'beside his knees'** (48:12) in the sense of between his knees when he embraced them. This action was probably a symbolic gesture ratifying their adoption as his own sons (see 30:3). Joseph, the second most powerful man in Egypt, responded gratefully and respectfully by prostrating himself before his father.

3. Jacob blesses Ephraim before Manasseh (48:13-20)

Joseph then positioned his sons to receive the blessing. As Manasseh was the older, he guided him towards his father's right hand and Ephraim towards his left hand (48:13). But Jacob, **'guiding his hands knowingly'**, laid his right hand on Ephraim's head, **'who was the younger'**, and his left hand on Manasseh, **'the first-born'** (48:14). In the Bible the right hand often symbolizes the position of blessing and importance (Ps. 110:1; Matt. 25:33). Whereas blind Isaac was tricked into giving the main blessing to the younger son, blind Jacob deliberately chose the younger.

The actual word of blessing is in two parts and applies to both sons: the first is addressed to Joseph about the boys (48:15-16) and the second part is addressed to the grandsons (48:20). Separating the two parts is Joseph's protest of displeasure and Jacob's refusal to give way (48:17-19).

The first part of the blessing

The threefold invocation, **'God … God … The Angel …'**, reminds us of the later priestly blessing in Numbers 6:24-26: 'The LORD bless… The LORD make… The LORD lift up…' It prepares us for the threefold blessing of the New Testament associated with the three persons of the Trinity (2 Cor. 13:14). 'The Angel' is a reference, not to a heavenly messenger sent by God, but to God himself seen in human form. In special moments of crisis, God the Father revealed himself through these pre-incarnate appearances of his Son (see 16:13-14). Most notably Jacob had experienced God's visible presence at Penuel (32:30).

Jacob recounted how Abraham and Isaac knew what it was to live in the presence of God. Like Enoch and Noah, they walked with God (5:22-24; 6:9). Those believers before the Flood were one with those after the Flood in knowing personal fellowship with God. Jacob then testified that this same God had **'fed'** (literally 'shepherded') him all his life. This is the first reference in the Bible to God as a shepherd of his people (see 49:24; Ps. 23:1; 80:1). Jacob also described God as **'the Angel who has redeemed me from all evil'**. It was God, not an earthly relative, who had delivered him from all his fears and rescued him from his uncle and brother. Again, this is the first occurrence of redemption terminology in the Bible. The kinsman-redeemer was a near relative who had the responsibility of coming to the rescue of someone in grave trouble (Lev. 25:23-49). It is used of God's action in rescuing the Israelites from Egyptian bondage (Exod. 15:13). We praise God for 'the Angel of the covenant', our Lord Jesus Christ, for, 'In him we have redemption through his blood,' from slavery to sin and Satan, the curse of the law and the fear of death.

It is this God whom Jacob called on to **'bless the boys'**. He prayed that the names of Abraham, Isaac and Jacob might live on in them. It was a prayer that they would know the blessings of the covenant that God had made with this family. One item in that covenant was the promise of many descendants. Jacob expressed this by an unusual phrase. The phrase translated, **'Let them grow into a multitude,'** literally says, 'May they become a fishlike multitude in the land' (48:16).

Joseph's protest and Jacob's persistence

Joseph, like those before him and so many since, had to learn that covenant blessings are not obtained through natural birth and background, but are gifts from a sovereign God. What is more, those gifts when given cannot be reversed, however desperate the attempts, for 'The gifts and calling of God are irrevocable' (Rom. 11:29). Esau found that out (27:34-36) and Joseph similarly, when his father refused to remove his right hand from Ephraim's head (48:17-19). Jacob knew what he was doing: **'I know, my son, I know.'** Jacob did not seek to frustrate God's purposes as his father had done when he attempted to bless the wrong son. He also dealt honestly and exhibited complete confidence in the good purposes of God.

The second part of the blessing

As Esau's protests were followed by a further reaffirmation of the blessing previously announced, so Jacob stressed in the presence of Joseph that Ephraim, the younger son, would be greater than Manasseh and his descendants would become **'a multitude of nations'**. The final part of the blessing again did not differentiate between the brothers. Both would be so blessed by God with many descendants that the nation of Israel would use their names in future blessings. A similar blessing is found on the lips of the people who witnessed the agreement that Boaz made in order to marry Ruth: 'The LORD make the woman who is coming to your house like Rachel and Leah, the two who built the house of Israel' (Ruth 4:11). Jacob's words echo the promise to Abraham that he would be a blessing (12:2).

We may well wonder why so much space is given to Ephraim's position over Manasseh. It is primarily to stress what we have seen many times in Genesis — that God's blessings come to those who do not deserve it, who have no natural rights to them. God ordains to bless the underdog. We are saved not because we belong to a special race, family or nation, but on account of God's free grace. In addition, this passage prepares us for the future history of the nation. Ephraim did become the dominant tribe from the days of the judges and when the division occurred after the death of Solomon, the name Ephraim was often used to describe the whole of the northern kingdom of Israel which broke away from the southern kingdom of Judah (see Hosea 5:1 – 6:11). David of the tribe of Judah had been able to unite the tribes and hold together the fragile union between north and south which remained good under Solomon's reign. The David-Solomon era is presented as a picture of the future ruler from David's line, the Messiah, who will bring together those belonging to Ephraim and Judah (Ezek. 37:15-28).

4. Jacob looks to the land of promise (48:21-22)

Jacob still had his eye on Canaan and encouraged Joseph and his descendants that, though he must die, God would not leave them. As God had been with Jacob, so he assured them he would be with them and bring them back to **'the land of your fathers'**. The same God has promised to be with his people to the end of the age and to bring them safely through to that 'land of pure delight where saints immortal reign'.

Mentioning the land of promise again prompted Jacob to emphasize the double portion of land that would fall to the tribe of Joseph as a result of his adopting Ephraim and

Manasseh. There is a play on the word translated **'portion'** (the Hebrew word is *shechem*, 'shoulder') for it can also be used for the name 'Shechem'. The area known as Shechem later fell within the borders of Manasseh's territory just to the north of Ephraim's portion. When Israel conquered Canaan, they brought Joseph's remains and buried them at Shechem.

The reference to Jacob obtaining this land from the Amorite **'with my sword and my bow'** is difficult. There is no record of Jacob fighting to obtain the land. He had bought it from the sons of Hamor for one hundred pieces of silver (33:19; Josh. 24:32). Maybe after the incident over Dinah, Jacob found it necessary at a later date to retake the land by force from Amorites who had occupied it in his absence. It was in this area that the Samaritan community was situated. They represented people of many races who had their own sectarian allegiance to the law of Moses. It was near this spot, at Sychar, that Jesus met the woman of Samaria and many of the Samaritans in the area trusted the Lord (John 4:5,39-42). The prophecy of Jacob began to be fulfilled most wonderfully when these people of mixed race and associated with the northern kingdom of Ephraim became Christians (Acts 8:4-25).

Jacob's last words to all his sons (49:1-28)

We come now to the greatest of the deathbed pronouncements in the book of Genesis. As Jacob lay dying he called all his sons to his bedside. Today it is often left to the hospital authorities to call in the near relatives when they see a patient take a turn for the worse. In the sophisticated world of modern medical practice and as a result of Western distaste over scenes involving death there is little or no place for the dying to express their inner thoughts, or for those at their bedside to witness their last words. Gordon Keddie has written, 'The virtual disappearance from Christian literature of deathbed accounts and recorded last words is a sad and significant loss.'[2]

The memory is still vivid of my father and myself standing by my mother's bed and witnessing her last words as she lay dying of cancer. I was only thirteen at the time. She urged my father to take good care of me and then she committed herself into the hands of her Saviour. More recently, I was at the bedside of an elderly saint in a hospice for terminally ill patients. Among her final words, which she was only able to whisper in my ear, were these: 'The Lord is good.'

There is general agreement, even from liberal scholars, that these poetic words of Jacob are among the oldest in the Bible. They are not unlike Noah's verses concerning his sons (9:25-27). The words contain curses as well as blessings, prediction as well as information. As Noah's oracle comes near the close of the primeval period and looks to future events in the light of his sons' actions, so Jacob's prophetic poem performs the same function at the close of the patriarchal era.

1. The sons of Jacob (49:1-2)

Yet again we are given a list of the twelve sons of Jacob. In addition to the account of the birth of each son, this is the third time their names appear together (35:23-26; 46:8-25). The significance of these twelve sons in the purposes of God is thus underlined. At the close of Jacob's oracle, Moses makes the connection between them and 'the twelve tribes of Israel' (49:28). These twelve sons are the founding fathers of the future nation that will be formed at the time of the redemption from Egypt.

Jacob speaks of what will befall his sons **'in the last days'** (49:1). This phrase, associated with the later prophetic books (see Isa. 2:2, etc.), is used of the Balaam prophecies (Num. 24:14) and the song of Moses (Deut. 31:29). In general, Jacob prophesied of events surrounding the settlement of the tribes in the land of Canaan. He also pointed to the coming of a King to whom all would submit and to the glory of his rule.

The order in which the sons are named roughly follows the order of their birth (29:32 – 30:24; 35:18). Special consideration is paid to five sons — Reuben, Simeon and Levi, Judah and Joseph. The latter two are marked out for even further attention. While Joseph's descendants receive extensive blessing, the promised royal 'Seed' is associated with the tribe of Judah.

2. The sons of Leah (49:3-15)

Reuben (49:3-4)

Reuben was Jacob's first-born and was entitled to be the leader and to obtain a special inheritance. The build-up of phrases in praise of Reuben (49:3) followed by words of blame (49:4) reflects the shattering of Jacob's high hopes for his son. The word-play emphasizes the point. Though Reuben excelled (**'excellency'**) in dignity and power, Jacob prophesies, **'You shall not excel.'** His sinful behaviour (35:22) did not accord with his calling and his descendants would not prosper. He forfeited his first-born status (see 48:5; 1 Chr. 5:1-2) and the tribe produced no prophet, judge or king.

Simeon and Levi (49:5-7)

Simeon and Levi were collaborators (**'brothers'**) in the treacherous and ruthless attack on the inhabitants of Shechem (34:25-30). A distinction is thus made between God's right to exterminate a people and cruel human vindictiveness. As a result of their actions their descendants would not have their own portion in the promised land. The tribe of Simeon was later absorbed by the tribe of Judah with some finding their way to the north (2 Chr. 34:6). The Levites were never given territory of their own, but as a result of their loyalty at a time of national apostasy they were raised to an honourable position in Israel (Exod. 32:26-29; Num. 18:1-6; 35:1-8).

Judah (49:8-12)

The future of Judah stands in stark contrast to what is said about the previous three. There is a pun on his name, which means 'Praise' — **'... whom your brothers shall praise'**. Though he did not receive the rights of the first-born, Judah is given a place of pre-eminence among his brothers — **'Your father's children shall bow down before you'** — and will be victorious over his enemies (49:8). There is a deliberate allusion here to Joseph's dream. What actually took place when Joseph's brothers bowed before him is picked up here and transferred to Judah. He will be like a young lion resting after devouring its prey (49:9). What is already hinted at in the kingly figure of the lion is made clear with the references to **'the sceptre'** and the **'law-giver'** or 'ruler's staff' (49:10).[3]

Those who reign in Judah will do so **'until Shiloh comes'**, or 'until he comes to whom it belongs' (see Ezek. 21:26-27).[4] To this future ruler all the nations will gather in obedience. The word **'people'** is plural in the original Hebrew, suggesting that this kingship will extend beyond the boundaries of Israel (49:10; see Ps. 72:8-11; Isa. 11:10). His reign will be marked by great prosperity. This is conveyed poetically through the imagery of the young donkey tied to a choice vine tree and clothing washed in wine. It is a picture of plenty and a return to paradise (49:11). Using the imagery of wine and milk (49:12), this royal figure is portrayed, as in the Song of Songs, as 'altogether lovely', or 'desirable' (S. of S. 5:16).

This prophecy began to be fulfilled when David and Solomon of the tribe of Judah ruled over the whole of Israel and other countries brought their tribute to them. But this was merely a foretaste and prototype of the reign of King Jesus, who is the Lion of the tribe of Judah and the Root of David. He has triumphed over the enemy and redeemed people to God by his blood 'out of every tribe and tongue and people and nation' (Rev. 5:5,9). Before the coming of Jesus, Jacob's prophecy was interpreted as referring to the days of Messiah (Micah 5:2; Amos 9:11-12). Jesus himself drew attention to this passage prior to his death, when he called for a young donkey that had been tied and rode into Jerusalem as a king, with the people shouting, 'Blessed is he who comes in the name of the LORD! Blessed is the kingdom of our father David...' (Mark 11:1-10).

The emphasis on a special family line and royal 'seed' that we have seen running through Genesis finds its fulfilment in this coming King. God's promise in the Garden of Eden concerning the 'seed' of the woman is traced, not to Joseph, as we might have thought, but to Judah. Through this King the enemy of God and humans is defeated and his evil works undone, and in fulfilment of the promise to Abraham, all families of the earth will be blessed through him. The prophecy concerning Judah is anticipated, graphically, in Joseph's rise to a position of importance in Egypt. But God indicates again, through the choice of Judah, that the future ruler is not determined by human choice and favouritism but by the sovereign will of God (Ps. 78:67-68).

Zebulun (49:13)

'Zebulun shall dwell' is a pun on his name, which means 'Dwelling'. Though his tribal boundary did not reach the sea (Josh. 19:10-16), nevertheless the tribe would be enriched by its associations with Sidon, which lay on the coast. This may well be pointing to the time of prosperity suggested in the days of the victorious king (49:11).

Issachar (49:14-15)

Issachar was before Zebulun in order of birth (30:17-20), but he deserved to be in second place to Zebulun. Instead of using his strength to good effect he relaxed and became a slave to others. He rested in the good land too soon. The final rest lies beyond this present world order (Ps. 95:11; Heb. 4:9-10).

3. *The sons of the servant girls* (49:16-21)

The four sons of his wives' maids are considered together. They are in no way inferior to the other sons and are to play a full part in the make-up of the future nation. The order is interesting in that the two sons of Zilpah, Leah's maid, are named in between the two sons of Bilhah, Rachel's maid. The first-born sons of each are mentioned first.

Dan (49:16-18)

'Dan shall judge' is a pun on his name, which means 'Judge'. This tribe was to be the smallest in Israel, yet it would be capable of striking panic into those much stronger than itself. The exploits of Samson the Danite come to mind, who overcame the might of the Philistines on more than one occasion. Jacob's unexpected prayer at this point, **'I have waited for your salvation, O Lord!'** (49:18), suggests that he saw in these victories a foretaste of the hope of salvation that is centred on the royal 'seed' of Judah. The coming King would heal all the effects of the fatal bite inflicted by that old serpent the devil.

Gad (49:19)

Gad provides Jacob with a stream of puns, using the letters of his name. More literally it reads, 'Gad, raiders [a troop] will raid him, but he will raid them at their heel.' The Gadites were famous for their military might and joined David (1 Chr. 12:8). Again, the prophecy expresses the hope of final defeat for the enemy in connection with the Lion of Judah.

Asher (49:20)

Asher, as his name suggests, would be blessed with plenty of food and royal delicacies. This reminds us of the prosperity that will be enjoyed under the rule of Messiah.

Naphtali (49:21)

'**Naphtali**' was given territory next to Asher and under Barak broke loose from the oppression of the Canaanites (Judg. 4:1-7). The verse speaks of a time of freedom.[5]

4. The sons of Rachel (49:22-27)

Joseph (49:22-26)

Joseph receives even more attention than Judah, despite the blessings already heaped upon him and his sons. Five times in this passage the word '**blessings**' is used (49:25-26) and it prepares us for the final statement by Moses at the close (49:28). Jacob begins by describing Joseph as a blessed man flourishing like a well-watered tree.[6] Despite the ill-treatment he received at the hand of his brothers (49:23), Jacob's God had made him strong (49:24). This same God would help him and bless him in the future, far surpassing anything known before (49:25-26). Again, we must see this as finally fulfilled in Jesus the Messiah.

God is described, literally, as '**the Mighty One of Jacob**' (49:24; see Ps. 132:2); '**the Shepherd**' (see 48:15); '**the Stone**

of Israel', a unique expression but similar to 'Rock of Israel' (see 2 Sam. 23:3); **'the God of your father'**, a reminder of the covenantal relationship; and **'the Almighty'** *(Shaddai)*, which is one of the main names for God during this period (17:1). This is the God whom Jacob knew face to face and who is well able to perform the blessings pronounced. This is 'the God and Father of our Lord Jesus Christ, who has blessed us with every spiritual blessing in the heavenly places in Christ' (Eph. 1:3).

Benjamin (49:27)

Benjamin is described as **'a ravenous wolf'**, so different from what we presume him to be from the Genesis accounts. The military strength and exploits of this tribe were seen in the period of the judges (Judg. 3:15-30; 5:14; 19:1 – 20:48).

5. *Summary* (49:28)

For the first time in the Bible we read of the twelve **'tribes'**. It is made clear that what has been said about Jacob's sons concerns **'the twelve tribes of Israel'**, and not just the founding fathers of the nation. Though Reuben, Simeon and Levi were cursed for their crimes, they were also blessed through belonging to the covenant nation of Israel. The blessings given to the sons are associated with victory over the enemy, peace and prosperity. They find their fulfilment through the Ruler who will come from the tribe of Judah. This is the one who, though he will be injured in the process, will triumph over the tempter and bring about a return to the paradise that was lost. Only those who trust this Ruler and come under his authority will enjoy the blessings.

In his preaching the apostle Peter proclaimed, 'The God of Abraham, Isaac, and Jacob, the God of our fathers, glorified

his servant Jesus.' This suffering Messiah, the Prince of life,
God raised from the dead. Peter saw in Jesus Christ the fulfil-
ment of God's promise to Abraham that 'In your seed all the
families of the earth shall be blessed.' This is why he urged
Jew and Gentile to repent and receive the forgiveness of sins
(Acts 3:13-26; 10:34-43).

40.
Dying in hope

Please read Genesis 49:29 – 50:26

In these closing chapters of Genesis our attention is drawn to the sad spectacle of death. It seems we have moved no further than chapter 5, with its melancholy refrain, '… and he died'. Paul draws our attention to this when he writes, 'Death reigned from Adam to Moses' (Rom. 5:14). Yet promises are given in Genesis to indicate that death will not have the last word. A 'Seed' is promised who will triumph over the tempter and undo the evil effects of his regime. People from all nations who identify themselves with God's promises to Abraham will be blessed with life. The statement concerning Enoch (5:22-24) encourages us to believe that there is a life which death cannot touch, a life lived in fellowship with God. Abraham knew this life and received many long-term promises that were handed down from father to son along the chosen family line. They believed God and looked forward to the day when God's promises would be consummated.

Euthanasia means, literally, 'good death'. The word is used for what is popularly known as 'mercy-killing'. People who suggest such ideas express their opposition to God and fail to appreciate the awful suffering that awaits unbelievers after death. It is those who die trusting God who die well. Death is the last enemy and should not be underestimated. Jacob and Joseph had good deaths, for they died 'in faith', resting in the promises of God.

Death and burial of Jacob (49:29 – 50:14)

More space is given over to recounting the death and burial of Jacob than any other person in the Bible apart from Jesus Christ.

1. Jacob died believing (49:29-33)

Having blessed his sons, Jacob again drew attention to his wish to be buried in Canaan. This time he spoke to all his sons and gave very explicit instructions concerning the place of burial. He wanted to be buried with his fathers in the cave which was in the field that Abraham had purchased from Ephron the Hittite (23:17-20). This was where Abraham and Sarah were buried (25:9-10). Jacob also informs us that Isaac, Rebekah and Leah were buried there. His sons carried out his wishes and the exact spot is detailed (50:13).

This was the one plot which Abraham owned in the land that God had promised him and his descendants. It was a small guarantee and sign that the whole land would be theirs one day. The request showed that Jacob's faith did not waver. To the very end of his life he believed the promises that God had made. With these last words of faith, he resumed a sleeping posture **'and breathed his last'**. For the people of God in new covenant times, the Holy Spirit's presence in our lives 'is the guarantee of our inheritance until the redemption of the purchased possession' (Eph. 1:13-14).

While he wished his bodily remains to rest with his relatives in the family tomb, Jacob the person **'was gathered to his people'** (see 25:17; 35:29). However dim the picture might be at this time for the people of God, Jacob, like his father and grandfather, envisaged a personal existence beyond the grave. Jesus spoke of the poor man Lazarus being taken to 'Abraham's bosom' (Luke 16:22). In the light of Christ's death, resurrection and ascension, Christians 'sleep in Jesus' (1 Thess. 4:14) and the apostle Paul can state with assurance, 'Absent from the body … present with the Lord' (2 Cor. 5:8).

2. *A family and nation mourns* (50:1-3)

While the other sons would also have expressed their sorrow at the death of their father, attention is drawn to Joseph. There was a close bond between Jacob and Joseph, as the previous narratives have shown. Joseph's affection for his father was deep and his grief was genuine: **'Joseph fell on his father's face, and wept over him, and kissed him.'** Expressing grief over the loss of loved ones is not unspiritual, or a sign of weakness. Our Lord himself wept at the grave of Lazarus. It is a kind of safety valve to help us deal with emotional crises in our lives.

This very dramatic scene, without parallel in the remainder of the Old Testament, also meant that God's word to Jacob had been realized. God had assured Jacob before entering Egypt that his son Joseph would 'put his hand on your eyes' (46:4). If God could look after a detail like that, then all the other promises made would find their fulfilment in God's good time.

A further reason for focusing on Joseph concerned his position in the Egyptian court and his responsibility for looking after the whole of Jacob's family. He was the one who could implement his father's dying instructions. According to Egyptian custom Joseph arranged for his father's body to be embalmed. Mummification was a long and expensive process. It could take anything from twenty-eight to seventy days. Joseph did not use the professional embalmers, with their pagan religious rites, but **'physicians'** 'who were more than competent to perform the task'.[1] They took forty days. As it happened this was a wonderful provision for preserving the body from decomposing during the time it took for the funeral to be arranged and for them to make the slow journey to the burial site in Canaan.

There was also national mourning, for **'The Egyptians mourned for him seventy days,'** just two days short of the period appointed for a Pharaoh. The seventy days probably included the forty days it took to embalm the body. Thirty days was the time of mourning for important leaders in Israel like Moses and Aaron (Num. 20:29; Deut. 34:8). This was to be a state funeral. Queen Elizabeth ordered a state funeral for Winston Churchill even though he was not a member of the royal family. His body lay in state in Westminster Hall, London, for three days, when over 300,000 people filed past to pay their last respects to Britain's great wartime leader. Pharaoh showed similar respect for the father of the one who had saved Egypt from the ravages of famine. A world superpower paused and mourned over the father of the Israelite nation. Something of the worldwide significance of what God was doing in choosing this family is conveyed to us by this scene. Through Israel a second Joseph would arise to bring salvation to the peoples of the world.

3. An acted prophecy (50:4-14)

It might have been expected that such an important person's mummified body would be buried in one of the tombs of Egypt. There was therefore need to gain special permission from Pharaoh himself, who had ordered the state funeral in the first place, to allow the burial to take place in Canaan. Because Joseph was still in mourning he sent messengers to Pharaoh, pointing out respectfully that it was his father's wish to be buried in Canaan, at the site which had already been prepared.

Great stress is placed on the state funeral procession from Egypt to Canaan. The people who **'went up'** to bury Joseph's father included the royal officers of Pharaoh and the elders of the land of Egypt, Joseph's family, his brothers and other members of Jacob's household. Only the young children and the flocks and herds were left in Goshen. Pharaoh's chariots and horses also went up. It was **'a very great gathering'**. The funeral cortège stopped at **'the threshing floor of Atad'**, a place in Canaanite territory in the region of the Jordan. There Joseph appointed a further seven days of mourning for his father. It must have been a very unusual sight to see what appeared to the Canaanite inhabitants as an Egyptian funeral procession having stopped in their area to mourn **'with a great and very solemn lamentation'**. Such was the impression made upon them that the locals renamed the place 'Abel Mizraim' ('Mourning of Egypt'). It may be that the Egyptians remained there while Jacob's sons did the honours of carrying their father's body to the cemetery and **'buried him in the cave of the field of Machpelah'**. Then they all made their way back to Egypt in accordance with Joseph's word to Pharaoh (50:5).

The time was not right for the whole family to return to the land of promise, but Jacob's burial was an impressive indication to the family that Canaan was where the future lay. We can well imagine Jacob's sons recounting the incident to their children and grandchildren, and so on, until the time of Moses. In this way God's promise concerning Canaan was kept alive in the minds of the Israelites and the burial site was remembered.

This pilgrimage to Canaan was an acted prophecy of what would happen when they would eventually leave Egypt. The route they took was a long and cumbersome one. They did not enter from the south into Canaan but went round the Dead Sea area and crossed over the Jordan near to Jericho. We are not told why they did this. In the providence of God it anticipated the Exodus route. There is an ultimate homecoming, when God's people from all nations will come to the mountain of the Lord (Isa. 2:2-4; 66:18-20; Ezek. 39:25; Rev. 21:24).

Joseph reassured his brothers (50:15-21)

After the account of Jacob's death and burial, there is no new section, as in previous cases, entitled 'These are the generations of Jacob's sons'. The final two paragraphs must, therefore, be seen in the light of what has gone before.

1. Fear (50: 15-18)

When the head of the family dies changes are inevitable. Jacob was dead and Joseph's brothers were afraid that Joseph, who was such a powerful person in Egypt, would now get his revenge on them for their treatment of him. They felt vulnerable and uneasy. Following strict protocol they sent a message to him. Jacob had once thought it necessary to send a message to Esau when he felt apprehensive over meeting a brother he had wronged years before. They made up a fictitious story of how their father had, before he died, left instructions that Joseph was to forgive the crime they had committed. With this emotional introduction, they pleaded for forgiveness, reminding Joseph that they were **'the servants of the God of your father'**. It was well thought up. How could Joseph possibly go against his father's will? How could he take revenge on fellow believers who worshipped the God of his father? Then, when they actually came into his presence, they prostrated themselves before him and were ready to do anything to appease him, even willing to make restitution by offering themselves as slaves.

2. Forgiveness and faith (50:19-21)

Their pleas reduced Joseph to tears. He was no doubt moved that they should still harbour such feelings after so many years. How could they misinterpret his actions and generosity! Yet we know how people who have unresolved guilty fears can think bad thoughts and mistrust even those nearest and dearest to them. As they bowed down before him Joseph must have again been reminded of his dreams and their fulfilment. But these things did not make him proud and hard.

Joseph's response showed that he had already forgiven them and that their unfounded suspicions towards him did not alter his attitude to them. It only remained for him to calm their fears and comfort them by speaking kindly to them. This he did in three ways.

He reminded them of the divine Judge

Though he was a high official in Egypt, he was not God, to take it upon himself to punish their sin against him. God says later, 'Vengeance is mine, and recompense' (Deut. 32:35; Rom. 12:19). We are to leave the righting of personal wrongs to God.

He taught them about divine providence

When Joseph first revealed who he was he had sought to allay their fears by telling his brothers that though they had sold him into Egypt it was God who had sent him to preserve life (45:5,7). Here he in no way minimized the wrong they had done, but bluntly told them, **'But as for you, you meant evil against me.'** Nevertheless, he was also convinced that **'God meant it for good.'** Joseph could see with the eye of faith the unseen hand of God at work in this turn of events. The good that had come from the brothers' evil intentions is spelled out in the words: **'to bring it about as it is this day, to save many people alive'**. His own brothers and their families, among many others, were alive because of what had happened to Joseph.

He promised to do them good

'I will provide for you and your little ones' (50:21). We are called to repay evil with good. Jesus said, 'Love your enemies, bless those who curse you, do good to those who hate you' (Matt. 5:44). Paul adds, 'Repay no one evil for evil... Do not be overcome by evil, but overcome evil with good' (Rom. 12:17,21).

Joseph's words express complete trust in God's sovereignty and goodness. In this he is like the Lord Jesus Christ, who committed himself into the hands of the God who judges righteously and who brought everlasting provision and comfort to those who through envy and hatred despised and rejected him (Isa. 53:3-5; 1 Peter 2:21-24).

This famous wisdom saying from the lips of Joseph (50:20) emphasizes one of the key messages of this part of Genesis. God brings about his purposes despite human sinfulness. Divine sovereignty and human responsibility are affirmed and both must be taken into account. The amazing truth is that, although God hates every sin, because he is God, he is able to bring good out of the evil actions of human beings and the devil. Calvin writes, 'Whatever poison Satan produces, God turns it into medicine for his elect.'[2] While the brothers were plotting the end of their brother, God was acting to preserve their very lives. At the same time, human beings and the devil remain responsible, blameworthy and deserving of punishment for all their sinful actions. This verse should be an encouragement to all God's people. Christians are to see God's good hand, not only in those circumstances that are clearly favourable, but also in difficult and painful experiences.

The verse also teaches us that through the sufferings of a righteous individual blessing comes to many. Righteous Joseph suffered at the hands of his brothers, but through him many, including his brothers, were saved from starvation. God's righteous Servant 'shall justify many, for he shall bear their iniquities'

(Isa. 53:11). Jesus Christ the righteous one suffered for the sins of the unrighteous that he might bring us to God (1 Peter 3:18).

Death of Joseph (50:22-26)

The previous section of Genesis had concluded with the words: 'Now Jacob dwelt in the land where his father was a stranger, in the land of Canaan' (37:1). The conclusion to this section opens with the statement: **'So Joseph dwelt in Egypt, he and his father's household.'** While Jacob's remains had been taken to the promised land for burial, Joseph and his brothers continued to live in an alien land. In Egypt the family remained together. All their earlier experiences had knit them into a close family grouping and this is how they continued, as they awaited God's next move.

1. A full life (50:22-23)

Joseph lived a further fifty-four years after the death of his father, reaching the age of 110 years. This was Joshua's age when he died (Josh. 24:29). There are many references in Egyptian texts to people living this long. It seems to have been regarded by them as the ideal lifespan. Joseph did not live as long as his forefathers but it was nevertheless a full and complete life. The symbolic nature of the ages of Abraham, Isaac, Jacob and Joseph have been noted by a number of recent scholars. While Joseph literally lived for this length of time, the figure indicates that he was both the spiritual successor to his fathers and the one who completes this part of the nation's history.[3]

It was an indication of God's favour for a father to live to see his grandchildren and great-grandchildren. 'Children's children are the crown of old men' (Prov. 17:6). Joseph saw the great-grandchildren of his son Ephraim and the grandchildren of his son Manasseh. Machir's children were actually adopted by Joseph — **'on Joseph's knees'** (see 30:3). They did not become separate tribes like Ephraim and Manasseh, but they did become an important clan (Judg. 5:14).

2. Full of faith (50:24-25)

Joseph remained true to the faith to his dying day. Though he had made it to the top surrounded by the wealth and glory of Egypt, his thoughts were on the promises of God. As with Daniel in the pagan atmosphere of the Babylonian and Persian court, so with Joseph in pagan Egypt, 'We can see how possible it is for a man to serve God humbly and faithfully in the highest walks of life. God was first, and everything else was dominated by that simple but all-embracing principle.'[4]

Of all the interesting and varied events that happened in Joseph's life, the writer to the Hebrews chose his dying words as an example of his faith: 'By faith Joseph, when he was dying, made mention of the departure of the children of Israel, and gave instructions concerning his bones' (Heb. 11:22).

The last will and testament of Joseph fastens on the covenant that God had made with Abraham. Joseph's family may well have been concerned as to what would happen to them in Egypt when their influential relative was gone. He assured them that, though he was dying, **'God will surely visit you and bring you out of this land to the land of which he swore to Abraham, to Isaac, and to Jacob.'** Jacob had comforted Joseph with similar words when he was dying (48:21). Matthew Henry reminds us, with echoes from the apostle Paul, that we must comfort others with the same comforts with which we ourselves have been comforted by God, 'and encourage them to rest on those promises which have been our support' (see 2 Cor. 1:3-4). Our trust must not ultimately rest on earthly supports, but on the God of all comfort, who does not change or pass away.

Like Jacob before him, Joseph saw to it that **'the children of Israel'** swore to return his bones to the land of promise. Joseph did not want to be buried in the tombs of the great men of Egypt, many of whose mummified bodies have been discovered over the past two centuries and transported to museums. He showed his faith by wanting to be associated with the people of God and their future in God's purposes, and not with the pagan Egyptian ideas of an afterlife. As he did so he repeated a second time his faith in God's promise: **'God will surely visit you, and you shall carry up my bones from here.'**

3. *Future hope* (50:26)

With Joseph we reach a peak in the history of the fathers of Israel. Even more so than Abraham, he had become great in the eyes of the world and the means of preserving the lives of many. Yet even **'Joseph died'**. He too was a sinner. Sin and death are present to the end of the book. The question is, has that old serpent, the tempter, triumphed in his evil desire to bring to ruin the whole of humanity? Where is the promise concerning 'the seed' of the woman? There have been indications of God's activity to change the situation. Seth, Noah, Abraham and Isaac have been shown as pointers to the coming Saviour. With Joseph God's promises to Abraham find their fullest implementation, but he was not *the* Saviour. He too was overcome by death and in his last will to his family he looked forward to something greater.

The book that began with God, the author of life, creating, ordering and filling the world with life ends with death, disorder and de-creation. The one who had been raised up to preserve life in Egypt himself 'died' and his body was preserved

— 'embalmed' — 'in a coffin in Egypt'. Genesis opens with human beings in a garden in Eden enjoying the fulness of life that God provided. It ends with a human corpse in a coffin in Egypt preserved from disintegration through human ingenuity. But the coffin which was such a powerful symbol of death also spoke of life and hope. All the time that it was held by the Israelites in Egypt it reminded them of Joseph's faith in God's promises associated with the land of Canaan.

Jacob's body had been carried to Canaan in anticipation of the exodus from Egypt. Joseph's bones were to remain in Egypt to await God's time when the great Exodus would take place under God's new leader, Moses (Exod. 13:19). Joshua, Moses' successor, would be the one responsible for seeing those bones buried at Shechem (Josh. 24:32). It was a sign that Israel had taken the land of Canaan and had found a measure of rest.

The word translated 'coffin' is the same as the word for the 'ark' of the covenant. Israel journeyed to Canaan carrying two 'arks', or 'chests'. The one held a copy of the Ten Commandments, and the other the bones of Joseph. The former was a sign of God's covenant with his people at Sinai; the latter was a sign of his covenant with Abraham concerning the land. Canaan represented God's future purposes for his people. But Israel was never allowed to be completely settled in that land, for the earthly Canaan is only a type of the heavenly country, associated with the new creation. The exodus from Egypt was itself a type of Christ's exodus via the cross to obtain eternal redemption for his people. The bones of Joseph, which were preserved to await the Exodus, point us beyond the Old Testament to the Christ who 'died for our sins according to the Scriptures and … was buried, and … rose again the third day according to the Scriptures, and … was seen… Thanks be to God, who gives us the victory through our Lord Jesus Christ' (1 Cor. 15:3-5,57).

Notes

The three most helpful commentaries have been:

> John Calvin, *A Commentary on Genesis,* translated and edited by
>   John King, Banner of Truth edition, 1965;
> Derek Kidner, *Genesis,* Tyndale Old Testament Commentaries,
>   IVP (Tyndale Press), 1967;
> G. J. Wenham, *Word Bible Commentary,* Genesis 1-15 (vol. 1),
>   Word, 1987 and Genesis 16-50 (vol. 2), Word, 1994.

Unless otherwise stated all references to Calvin, Kidner and Wenham
are from these volumes.

For literature concerning Genesis and science the reader is directed
to Douglas F. Kelly, *Creation and Change,* Mentor, 1997.

Introduction
1. John Calvin, *Institutes of the Christian Religion,* Book I, ch. 6, para. 2
(The Library of Christian Classics edition, translated by F. L. Battles,
The Westminster Press, 1960, vol. 1, p.74).
2. E. J. Young, *Studies in Genesis One,* Presbyterian and Reformed Pub-
lishing Co., 1964, p.102.

Chapter 1
1. See Psalm 104:5-9 or Job 38:8-11 for poetic descriptions of creation.
Genesis 1 does not use poetic parallelism, simile or metaphor.
2. It is a similar construction to 3:1, 'Now the serpent...' and 4:1, 'Now
Adam...'
3. See 'mighty prince', 23:6; 'great city', Jonah 3:3, where the original
for 'mighty' and 'great' is *elohim*.
4. Wenham, vol. 1, p.16.

5. See D. F Kelly, *Creation and Change,* pp.112-35, for a refutation of 'The Framework Hypothesis' popularized by M. Kline and developed by H. Blocher.
6. The discussion concerning the 'days' of creation is not a recent dispute with the advent of Darwin. It existed in the Early Church period. See ' " In the Space of Six Days": The Days of Creation from Origen to the Westminster Assembly,' by Robert Letham (*Westminster Theological Journal,* 61, 1999, pp.149-74).
7. Wenham, vol. 1, p.21.
8. Kidner, p.48.

Chapter 2
1. Calvin, p.92.
2. V. P. Hamilton, *The Book of Genesis, Chapters 1-17,* The New International Commentary on the Old Testament, Eerdmans, 1990, p.137.
3. H. Blocher, *In the Beginning,* IVP, 1984, p.93.

Chapter 3
1. For similar reasons sun and moon are not mentioned (see 1:16).
2. In the whole of the Old Testament there is only one other reference to a holy day (Neh. 8:9-11).
3. B. H. Edwards, *The Ten Commandments for today,* Day One, 1996, p.133.

Chapter 4
1. See the section on 'Structure' in the introduction (pp.17-18).
2. The Greek version of the Old Testament, called the Septuagint *(LXX)* translates 'the Garden of Eden' in Genesis 3:23 as 'the Paradise of Delight'.
3. The verb 'to do' is this same word, 'to serve', in the original.
4. The verbs are translated 'to attend' and 'to do' in the NKJV.
5. Compare also the bronze serpent put on a 'tree' in the Septuagint version of Numbers 21:8-9.

Chapter 5
1. J. Murray, *Collected Writings,* vol. 2, *Systematic Theology,* Banner of Truth, 1977, p.9.
2. Calvin, pp.132-3.

Chapter 6
1. There is a word for divination which uses the same Hebrew letters as that for snake (Gen. 30:27; 44:15; Num. 23:23; etc.).
2. The construction is similar to that in 1:2, but in place of 'Now the earth was...', we have 'Now the serpent was...'

Chapter 7

1. Many in the past did oppose anaesthesia for mothers in labour on the grounds that it would be interfering with God's curse on the woman.
2. Deuteronomy 18 uses 'prophet' to mean both the prophetic movement as a whole and the future Messiah.
3. It is interesting that the ancient Greek translation, the Septuagint, took it in an individual sense. A number of Jewish Aramaic paraphrases also saw this verse as a reference to victory over Satan through Messiah.
4. 'In Eden — sad indeed that day,' by William Williams, translated by Bobi Jones.
5. E. J. Young, *Genesis 3,* Banner of Truth, 1966, p.149.
6. M. Dods, *The Book of Genesis,* The Expositor's Bible, Hodder & Stoughton, p.25.

Chapter 8

1. This is one possible translation of the unusual Hebrew. The phrase could also be rendered, 'I have acquired a man, the LORD', suggesting that Eve took the promise of 3:15 seriously and thought that she had given birth to the Messiah. This has early Jewish support and was the way Luther read it, but it has not been generally accepted.
2. 'Days' can refer to an indefinite period of time (Gen. 40:4), or specifically to a year (Lev. 25:29; 1 Sam. 1:21).
3. It is in the law of Moses that regulations are given concerning the 'fat' of animal sacrifices. There is no mention of an altar in the text, but bringing an offering to the Lord suggests an altar to which the sacrifices were brought. Later, we read that Noah knew of clean and unclean animals, but the details are only given in Leviticus.
4. Kidner, p.76 (see Luke 16:24,27,28; 23:41; cf. Rev. 16:11).
5. R. Dawkins, *Climbing Mount Improbable,* Penguin, 1996, p.75.
6. It points to continuous action in the past.
7. Notice particularly how the first line parallels the second line:

> Adah and Zillah, hear my voice,
> O wives of Lamech, listen to my speech!

The third line parallels the fourth:

> For I have killed a man for wounding me,
> Even a young man for hurting me.

The fifth line parallels the sixth (4:24).

Chapter 9

1. Kidner, p.80.

2. H. M. Morris, *The Genesis Record,* Baker, 1976, p.154. Jude's reference to Enoch as 'the seventh from Adam' (Jude 14) is sometimes used to teach that 'Genesis 5 cannot have gaps' (see Andy McIntosh, *Genesis for today,* Day One, 1997). But this argument backfires because at face value Matthew's fourteen generations allow for no gaps and yet we know from the Old Testament that there are gaps. See chapter 17 (commentary on Gen. 11:10-26) for a further treatment of this subject.

Chapter 10
1. For example, S. R. Driver, *The Book of Genesis,* Methuen & Co., 1904, p.83.
2. M. G. Kline, 'Divine Kingship and Genesis 6:1-4', *Westminster Theological Journal,* vol. 24, 1963, pp.187-204.
3. W. J. Dumbrell, *Covenant and Creation,* Paternoster Press, 1984, p.12.
4. Lamech had hopes that his son, Noah ('Comfort'), would bring relief from the curse. Here there is another play on Noah's name. The Hebrew word for 'grace' is made up of the letters of Noah *(nh)* written backwards *(hn)*.

Chapter 11
1. J. A. Motyer, *Look to the Rock,* IVP, 1996, p.44.
2. It is not the same verb that is translated 'destroy' in verse 7.
3. Because it says in 9:8-17 that God established his special arrangement not only with Noah but the whole earth, some have argued, wrongly in my opinion, that this covenant goes all the way back to creation itself. God's act of creation 'established an enduring relationship between God and the world' (W. J. Dumbrell, *The Faith of Israel,* Apollos, 1989, p.22. See commentary on 9:8-17).
4. Motyer, *Look to the Rock,* p.44.
5. Kidner, p.88.
6. Whereas the outer court of the tabernacle was 100 cubits long and fifty cubits wide, the ark was three times as long (300 cubits) but the same width. The height of the ark was thirty cubits. This would have divided into three decks of ten cubits each. Similarly, the tabernacle was ten cubits high and divided into three sections — the outer court, the Holy Place and the Holy of Holies. The tabernacle was constructed so that sinful Israel could continue to have God's presence among them and yet remain alive.

Chapter 12
1. Wenham, p.177.
2. There is probably a pun on Noah's name. It found no Noah ('resting-place') outside and returned to the Noah it knew inside the ark.

Chapter 13

1. F. A. Schaeffer, *Genesis in time and space,* Hodder & Stoughton, 1973, p.145.
2. Wenham, p.193.
3. This principle is emphasized by the way in which the memorable lines of verse 6a are presented in Hebrew:

1	2	3
Whoever sheds	the blood	of man
3a	2a	1a
by man	shall his blood	be shed.

A strict correspondence exists between the punishment and the crime.
4. Schaeffer, *Genesis in time and space,* p.148.

Chapter 14

1. Moses has already prepared us for this curse on Canaan by referring to him earlier as 'Ham, the father of Canaan' (9:18,22).

Chapter 15

1. Wenham, p.214.
2. Wenham, p.214.

Chapter 16

1. D. Atkinson, *The Message of Genesis 1-11,* The Bible Speaks Today, IVP, p.182.
2. Libby Purves' article in *The Times,* 6 April 1999, p.18.

Chapter 17

1. Henry Morris, in his commentary, *The Genesis Record,* pp.27-8, is entirely wrong in translating it 'origins' or 'record of origins' and making the phrase into a postscript.

Chapter 18

1. The Genesis text suggests that Abram left Terah in Haran and moved to Canaan without him. Terah was seventy years old when he fathered Abram (11:26) and Abram was aged seventy-five when he left Haran (12:4). This means that Terah must have been 145 years old when Abram moved from Haran to Canaan. Terah had another sixty years to live before he died aged 205 (11:32). The Jewish tradition that Abram moved to Canaan after his father's death is built on the assumption that 12:1 is chronologically after 11:32.
2. Dating the patriarchs is problematic, but the Middle Bronze I period (*c.* 2000-1800 B.C.) seems to fit the biblical evidence quite well. See J. J.

Bimson, 'Archaeological data and the dating of the patriarchs,' in *Essays on the Patriarchal Narratives,* eds., A. R. Millard and D. J. Wiseman, IVP, 1980.

3. Haran or 'Charran' is not to be confused with Abram's brother, whose name is spelt differently in Hebrew.

4. For example, James Boice writes, 'From God's point of view the years in Haran were wasted. Abraham learned no new lessons there.'

5. Wenham, p.275.

6. Either the passive 'shall be blessed', or the true Hebrew middle 'shall find blessing', is appropriate, but not the reflexive, 'shall bless themselves'.

Chapter 19

1. W. A. Griffith Thomas, *Genesis I-XXV, A Devotional Commentary,* Religious Tract Society, 1909, p.155.

2. *The Merchant of Venice,* Act II, Scene 7.

3. Calvin, p.373.

Chapter 20

1. It may be, as is often done in other parts of the Old Testament, that the names of the kings of Sodom and Gomorrah have been deliberately altered. See Ishbosheth ('Man of shame') in 2 Samuel 2:8, etc. for Eshbaal ('Man of Baal') in 1 Chronicles 8:33 and 9:39.

2. In saying the two kings 'fell there', it cannot mean that they died, for the King of Sodom is mentioned later. The Hebrew word for 'to fall' is used for jumping or sliding down, as Rebekah did from her camel (24:64). The kings may well have jumped into old bitumen pits to hide from the enemy.

3. Abram is called 'the Hebrew', a term used later by the Egyptians to describe Joseph and the Israelites (see 39:14,17; 41:12; also 10:21). As it is used in the Old Testament it seems to be an ethnic term, frequently used by non-Israelites when speaking of Israelites (see Exod. 1:16; 1 Sam. 4:6), or to distinguish the Israelites from people of other races (40:15; Exod. 1:15; 1 Sam. 13:3; Jonah 1:9). The word 'Hebrew' is associated with the name Eber, as we have noted in the commentary on 10:24-25; see also 11:14. Whether the word is also associated with the *'Habiru'* found in ancient Near-Eastern texts is hotly debated. This was a derogatory term used to describe a migrant, something like the word 'gypsy' today. Certainly, Abram was an outsider and a stranger in the land, but the biblical evidence would suggest that the word is not so much a social label as an ethnic term.

4. *'Shaveh'* is probably an old Hebrew word for ruler, hence the editorial comment.

5. In the time of the conquest of Canaan under Joshua, we read of an 'Adonizedek' ('My lord is righteous'), who was King of Jerusalem (Josh. 10:1). 'Zedek' may have been an ancient name for God, so that Melchizedek and Adonizedek could be translated, 'My king is Zedek,' and 'My lord is Zedek,' respectively.

6. Wenham, vol. 1, p.317.

7. For a discussion of the various views see H. R. Jones, *Only One Way,* Day One, 1996.

Chapter 21

1. The word for 'shield' is associated in Hebrew with the word 'delivered'.

2. In the light of the Greek translation it could be rendered 'Sovereign Lord'.

3. Kidner, p.123.

4. The Hebrew in the latter part of verse 2 is difficult. It reads, '... and the son of Mesheq is my house; he is Damascus, Eliezer.' 'Mesheq' may be a shortened version of 'Dammeseq', which is the Hebrew for Damascus. However we translate the latter part of verse 2, verse 3 makes clear what is meant. As the first phrase, 'Look, you have given me no offspring' (15:3) parallels 'What will you give me...?' (15:2), so the second, 'Indeed, one born in my house is my heir!' parallels '... and the heir of my house is Eliezer of Damascus.'

5. Legal texts concerning marriage and adoption have been unearthed at the site of the ancient city of Nuzi, east of the Tigris.

6. We have already experienced a similar ambiguity in 9:27, where the object of the first half becomes the subject of the second half of the sentence ('May God enlarge Japheth and may he [Japheth, not God] dwell in Shem's tent').

7. Wenham, vol. 1, p.330.

8. See further, P. H. Eveson, *The Great Exchange,* Day One, 1996.

Chapter 22

1. In 16:6 'dealt harshly' is from the same Hebrew word-group as 'affliction'. So also is 'submit yourself' in verse 9.

Chapter 23

1. Wenham, vol. 2, p.22.

2. J. A. Motyer, 'Old Testament Covenant Theology,' Lecture 1, Theological Students Fellowship, 1973, p.8; see also chapter 3 of *Look to the Rock.*

3. Kidner, p.130.

Chapter 24

1. For the timescale compare 17:21 and 18:10.

2. The singular ('LORD') in 18:1, the plural in verse 2 ('three men'), the singular 'your' in verse 3, the plural 'your' in verses 4-9 and the singular in verses 10-15. The shift between singular and plural is seen in chapter 19 (compare verses 1-18 with verses 21-22).
3. Griffith Thomas, *Genesis I-XXV,* p.211.
4. Literally, 'There ceased to be for Sarah the way of women' (see 31:35).
5. Some think that God was talking to himself when he asked, 'Shall I hide from Abraham what I am doing…?' Others argue that he was talking to the angels who accompanied him.
6. Wenham, vol. 2, p.50.
7. Calvin, p.481.
8. Perhaps Abraham began with fifty because it represented half the able-bodied men of the city. A hundred is used as a number for completeness (see 26:12). If a small city could produce 100 fighting men, then fifty would represent half the city (see Amos 5:3). Would God destroy the whole city if half of its inhabitants were righteous? Abraham then reduced the number each time until he reached another complete number.
9. His 'sons-in-law' may have been the husbands of other daughters of his in addition to the two who were at home. On the other hand, the text could read 'who were to marry his daughters', suggesting that they were future sons-in-law.

Chapter 25
1. The same verbal form was used of Lot's attempt to warn his 'sons-in-law'. They did not take him seriously (19:14; see also 26:8). Ishmael's 'laughing' was not what it seemed.
2. The text indicates Sarah's low opinion of Hagar and her son. Instead of calling her 'my maid' (16:2,5), she refers to her as 'this bondwoman'. She could not bring herself to use the name Ishmael, but called him 'the son of this bondwoman' (21:10).
3. Although human sacrifice was practised in the ancient world of the Near East, it would have been seen as something exceptional.
4. This parallel between Abraham's action and the Passover event did not go unnoticed by the Jews during the period between the end of the Old Testament and the beginning of the New Testament. About 100 B.C. in the book of *Jubilees* a connection is made between the Passover and the sacrifice of Isaac.
5. V. P. Hamilton, *The Book of Genesis Chapters 18-50,* The New International Commentary on the Old Testament, Eerdmans, 1995, p.114.
6. R. S. Candlish, *Studies in Genesis,* A. & C. Black, 1868, pp.380-81.
7. Compare the descendants of Isaac and Jacob who lagged behind Ishmael and Esau.

Chapter 26

1. From 'My God I thank thee, who hast made', Hymn 94 in *Christian Hymns*.
2. There is a subtle play on words in that the Hebrew for 'ten thousand' *(rebabah')* is similar in sound to Rebekah.
3. Sheba and Dedan are mentioned in 10:7, suggesting there were other tribal groups in these areas of Hamite descent.

Chapter 27

1. The NIV translates: 'They lived in hostility towards all their brothers.'

Chapter 28

1. Literally, 'I thus why am I this?'
2. Normally when this phrase, 'enquire of the LORD', is used in the Old Testament it means to consult a prophet of the Lord. There is no suggestion of this in the present passage. God often spoke directly to people at this time either in dreams or through the Angel of the LORD.
3. Satan, 'adversary', comes from the same word-group.
4. There is also a play on 'my blessing' *(brkthi)* and 'my birthright' *(bkrthi)*, which sound similar in Hebrew.

Chapter 29

1. Such practices were later forbidden in the law of Moses because of their pagan, Canaanite associations.
2. R. S. Candlish, *Studies in Genesis*, A. & C. Black, 1868, p.484.

Chapter 30

1. The phrase is found only here in the Bible.
2. Wenham, vol. 2, p.232.
3. The maximum marriage dowry which the groom's family was expected to give the bride's family was set at fifty shekels in the law of Moses (Deut. 22:29). In practice, the gifts would generally be much lower than that. It is believed that a casual worker received half to one shekel a month in those days. Jacob, therefore, was prepared to give Laban the equivalent of about eighty-four shekels.
4. J. G. Baldwin *The Message of Genesis 12-50,* The Bible Speaks Today, IVP, 1986, pp.122-3.
5. Wenham, vol. 2, p.236.
6. The name 'Gad' is much debated. Some associate it with a pagan god of that name (see Isa. 65:11 and Matthew Poole). It can also mean 'Troop', which is how it is used in Genesis 49:19. Most commentators prefer 'Good luck, Fortune' (see the early Greek translation, the Septuagint) and compare it with the name of the second son, Asher, which means, 'Happy, Fortunate'.

7. There is a play on two Hebrew verbs, *zabad* ('endow') and *zabal* ('dwell' or 'honour').

8. Literally, 'I have divined' (see 44:5,15). The word is probably used here in a figurative sense — 'I have observed' or 'learned by experience' — although we cannot rule out the use of omens.

9. Calvin, p.149.

Chapter 31

1. The word 'wealth' is often translated 'glory' in other contexts. It carries the idea of weightiness, which suggests that Jacob had become an important person on account of his possessions.

2. G. J. Wenham, 'Grace and Law in the Old Testament' in *Law, Morality and the Bible,* eds., B. N. Kaye and G. J. Wenham, IVP, 1978, pp.5-7.

3. The verb translated 'deceived' has the idea of 'to make a fool of' (see Judg. 16:10,13,15).

4. Calvin, p.170.

5. W. A. Griffith Thomas *Genesis XXV.11–XXXVI.8, A Devotional Commentary,* Religious Tract Society, 1909, p.97 (see Isa. 32:17).

6. Calvin suggests that Jacob did not act distrustfully in seeking to appease his brother with presents. He continues, 'For though by prayer we cast our cares upon God, that we may have peaceful and tranquil minds; yet this security ought not to render us indolent. For the Lord will have all the aids which he affords us applied to use.' We can properly use lawful means in our power while at the same time 'leaving success in the hands of God' (p.193).

7. There is a play on the name 'Israel', which is made up of two Hebrew words. The verb for 'to struggle, to fight' *(sarah)* is coupled with the word for God *(el)* to give the meaning, 'God struggles' or 'Struggler with God'. In the Septuagint the name is related to the verb 'to rule' *(sarar)*, hence 'God rules', or 'Ruler with God'. The AV tries to collect both ideas with its translation: 'For as a prince hast thou power with God and with men.'

8. The word for 'preserved' is the same word translated earlier as 'deliver' (see 32:11).

9. Calvin, pp.195-6.

10. The Hebrew word for 'present' is used by Moses particularly for the grain (or cereal) offering (see Lev. 2:1-14). Jacob saw his brother's forgiveness as a mirror of God's forgiveness. God had graciously dealt with Jacob at Penuel ('face of God') and Esau's favourable acceptance had been like seeing 'the face of God' (33:10). At Penuel Jacob had seen the face of God and his life had been spared ('preserved' — see 32:30). Here, he had seen the face of his brother and his life had been spared ('You were pleased with me,' or 'You have accepted me' — 33:10). Jacob

therefore wanted Esau to receive the present as God would have accepted the grain offering. It was an expression of gratitude and thankfulness.
11. Succoth means 'Booths'.
12. The word translated 'safely' or 'in peace' could be a place name, 'Salem', near Shechem. This is how the ancient versions took it. On the other hand, as Wenham points out, there could be a play on the name, especially in the light of the bitter conflict that occurs in the next scene.
13. Baldwin, *The Message of Genesis 12-50,* p.142.

Chapter 32
1. The Hebrew has 'laid her', suggesting illicit sexual relationships. A similar phrase is used in Numbers 5:13.
2. The word implies that Dinah had been humiliated. It is used of Israel's 'affliction' at the hands of the Egyptians (Exod. 1:11).
3. The Hebrew for 'strongly attracted' is 'His soul cleaved to Dinah.' The same word, 'cleave', is used as in 2:24. The Hebrew for 'spoke kindly' is 'spoke upon the heart' (see Isa. 40:2).
4. 'Son of the right' could mean 'Son of the south'.
5. The order is different in each but this list is the same as the one given in Exodus 1:1-4.

Chapter 33
1. There has already been a reference to the Amalekites in the days of Abraham (14:7). This does not mean that there were Amalekites around at that time. It is an editorial comment by Moses to indicate that the kings of the East made their attack in the area later occupied by the Amalekites.
2. Some scholars think it stands for the tribe itself. We find Moses using the term again in his song (Exod. 15:15). Note that there are two Korahs (36:16,18). It may be that some of Korah's people became attached to the Eliphaz clan. (See Hamilton, *Genesis Chapters 18-50,* pp.395-6).
3. Calvin, p.254.

Chapter 34
1. Kidner, p.179.
2. There is evidence for a multicoloured patchwork-quilt-type robe in the Mari tablets, excavated between 1933-1960 in south-east Syria. The Hebrew could also suggest a long robe with sleeves to the wrists. The same phrase is used of Princess Tamar's royal robe (2 Sam. 13:18-19).
3. Some scholars think that Joseph maligned his brothers (understanding 'bad' in the sense of 'false' — see Num. 13:32), while others suggest that he reported their evil deeds. This latter view seems more in keeping with what we know of the brothers. As for Joseph, he may have been

immature and pretentious, but there is no suggestion that he was insincere and untruthful.

4. They 'were not able to speak civilly to him' (Wenham, vol. 2, p.351).

5. Calvin, p.260.

6. **'Dreamer'** in Hebrew is 'lord of dreams' and some scholars wish to translate it 'master dreamer'. But the Hebrew is a recognized idiom. See 'lord of hair' for 'hairy' (2 Kings 1:8) and 'lord of wing' for 'bird' (Prov. 1:17).

7. Calvin, p.266.

8. Calvin, pp.268-9.

9. See King Hammurabi's law-code (*c.* 1750 B.C.) as well as the Mosaic law (Exod. 21:16).

10. Kidner, p.187.

11. Joseph was probably still in his teens when Judah persuaded his other brothers to sell him to the Ishmaelites (see 37:2). When Joseph later revealed who he was to his brothers he was aged thirty-nine (see 41:46-47; 45:6).

12. Chezib is probably the same as Achzib (Josh. 15:44) and Chozeba (1 Chr. 4:22).

13. From the name Onan has come the term 'onanism' which is a euphemism for masturbation. What he did would be more accurately described as *coitus interruptus*, or withdrawal before ejaculation, a very unsatisfactory form of contraception.

14. Rahab the prostitute is the only other person in the Bible who tied a scarlet thread for the purpose of identification (see Josh. 2:18,21).

Chapter 35

1. See especially 1 Kings 6:1. This verse tells us that Solomon constructed the temple 480 years after the exodus from Egypt. On this reckoning the date of the Exodus would be around 1446 B.C. As Israel's period in Egypt is put at 430 years (Exod. 12:40), this would give a date for Joseph's entry into Egypt in about 1896 B.C. (see 37:2 and 41:46-47 which indicate that we should add on a further twenty years before Jacob and his sons came to live in Egypt. See Chapter 18, note 1 for the date of the patriarchs).

2. The New Living Translation.

3. D. A. Carson, *For the Love of God,* IVP, 1998, insight for February 6.

4. As above, insight for February 7.

Chapter 36

1. The Hebrew word is of Egyptian origin and used for the Nile.

2. Another Hebrew word of Egyptian origin is used. It describes the papyrus grass that once grew extensively along the river bank.

3. Was the pharaoh's cup-bearer recalling 'the cause of his imprison-ment' (Calvin), or the fact that he had forgotten Joseph (Matthew Henry), or both faults (Wenham, vol. 2, p.391)?

Chapter 37

1. M. G. Kline, 'Genesis', in *The New Bible Commentary Revised*, eds., Guthrie, Motyer, Stibbs, Wiseman, IVP, 1970, p.109.
2. A. P. Ross, *Creation and Blessing*, Baker, 1988, p.674.
3. E. A. Speiser, *Genesis: Introduction, Translation and Notes*, Anchor Bible, Doubleday, 1964, p.339.

Chapter 38

1. Stephen's seventy-five persons (Acts 7:14) is due to his using the Greek translation of Genesis. It omits Jacob and Joseph and reckons nine sons to Joseph (66+9=75).
2. The Hebrew text actually emphasizes Judah's importance by placing his name at the beginning of the sentence.
3. The subject is ambiguous, although the context suggests Joseph.
4. See *The New Bible Dictionary*, ed. J. D. Douglas, IVP, 1962, p.659.
5. Many follow the Greek (Septuagint) and Samaritan versions which read, 'He made them into servants,' which certainly fits the context better.
6. The Septuagint has 'staff' in place of 'bed'. It may be that the Greek translators read the Hebrew letters *m-t-h* as *mattah* ('staff') because it is a more common word than *mittah* ('bed'). Hebrews 11:21 may have the Septuagint reading in mind, although Hebrews is referring to Jacob's blessing Joseph's sons in Genesis 48.
7. Wenham, vol. 2, p.452.

Chapter 39

1. I. H. Murray, *D. Martyn Lloyd-Jones*, vol. 2, Banner of Truth, 1990, pp.730-31.
2. G. J. Keddie, *Triumph of the King, The Message of 2 Samuel*, Evangelical Press, 1990, p.231.
3. Though the word is 'legislator', many modern versions translate 'staff' (belonging to the legislator), in order to preserve the parallelism with the first line.
4. The Jewish Aramaic paraphrase, *Targum Onkelos*, took it in a Messianic sense: 'until the Messiah comes, whose is the kingdom, and him shall the nations obey'. One of the Dead Sea Scrolls takes the verse Messianically. There is much debate over the meaning of 'Shiloh'. The following are some of the suggestions which have been made.

1. *A personal name for the Messiah.* The problem is that nowhere else in the Old Testament is it found as a person's name and none of the ancient witnesses suggests it.

2. *A place name* for the city near Bethel (Josh. 18:1; Judg. 21:19). However, it is difficult to see what 'until he comes to Shiloh' means. This has few advocates.

3. The Hebrew letters are taken to mean *'tribute'.* This is accepted by Wenham, and see the NIV alternative reading, 'until he comes to whom tribute belongs' (see Ps. 72:10-11).

4. A Hebrew compound word for *'whose it is'.* It is thought that this is the reading which lies behind the Septuagint and Syriac *(Peshitta)* versions. This suggestion is accepted by the NIV text ('until he comes to whom it belongs'). It is this reading which seems to be alluded to in Ezekiel 21:27 ('until he comes whose right it is').

5. 'He uses beautiful words' may be a reference to the good news brought by Barak to Deborah. While 'words' could also mean 'lambs', this is hardly satisfactory and scholars change it to 'fawns' to parallel 'deer' in the previous line (see NIV, 'that bears beautiful fawns'). The traditional reading is better.

6. Though the vine metaphor is not without its problems, this is the traditional view and has wide support. Because animal metaphors abound in Jacob's blessing it is suggested that instead of 'fruitful vine' the Hebrew words should be translated 'wild ass' (see NIV alternative reading, 'Joseph is a wild colt, a wild colt near a spring, a wild donkey on a terraced hill…').

Chapter 40
1. Kidner, p.222.
2. Calvin, p.488.
3. The symbolic nature of Joseph's age can be seen from the following amazing pattern of ages:

Abraham: $175 = 7 \times 5^2$;
Isaac: $180 = 5 \times 6^2$;
Jacob: $147 = 3 \times 7^2$;
Joseph: $110 = 1 \times 5^2 + 6^2 + 7^2$.

Thus Joseph is seen to be the end of a line (7-5-3-1). He also sums up in himself the promises made during their lives ($5^2 + 6^2 + 7^2$).

4. W. A. Griffith Thomas, *Genesis XXXVII-L, A Devotional Commentary,* Religious Tract Society 1909, p.195.